LAND OF THE
FALLEN
STAR GODS

The Celestial Origins of
Ancient Egypt

J. S. GORDON

Bear & Company
Rochester, Vermont • Toronto, Canada

Bear & Company
One Park Street
Rochester, Vermont 05767
www.BearandCompanyBooks.com

Bear & Company is a division of Inner Traditions International

Originally published in the United Kingdom in 1997 by Orpheus Publishing House
Published in 2004 by Bear & Company under the title *Egypt, Child of Atlantis: A Radical Interpretation of the Origins of Civilization*

Library of Congress Cataloging-in-Publication Data

Gordon, J. S. (John S.), 1946–2013.

  Land of the fallen star gods : the celestial origins of ancient Egypt / J.S. Gordon.

    p. cm.

  "Originally published in the United Kingdom in 1997 by Orpheus Publishing House. Published in 2004 by Bear & Company under the title Egypt, Child of Atlantis: A Radical Interpretation of the Origins of Civilization."

  Summary: "A radical reinterpretation of Egypt's ancient origins and its esoteric philosophy"—Provided by publisher.

  Includes bibliographical references and index.

  ISBN 978-1-59143-164-0 (pbk.) — ISBN 978-1-59143-838-0 (e-book)

 1. Astronomy, Egyptian. 2. Mythology, Egyptian. 3. Pyramids. I. Gordon, J. S. (John S.), 1946–2013. Land of the fallen star gods. II. Title.

  QB20.G67 2013

  932—dc23

                                                                      2013014947

Printed and bound in the United States by P. A. Hutchison

10 9 8 7 6 5 4 3 2 1

Text design and layout by Priscilla Baker
This book was typeset in Caslon, with Minion and Avant Garde used as display typefaces

LAND OF THE
FALLEN
STAR GODS

"That an advanced lost civilization is part of our human heritage should now be self-evident to all those capable of rational thought. John Gordon's book takes the currently neglected 'long' view of the lost civilization hypothesis (derived mainly from theosophy and Hindu/Vedic accounts) and defends it with solid scholarship, reasoned argument, and a deep understanding of esoteric philosophy. At once gutsy and erudite, this is a really interesting book."

JOHN ANTHONY WEST, AUTHOR OF *SERPENT IN THE SKY*
AND *THE TRAVELER'S KEY TO ANCIENT EGYPT*

"Painstakingly researched and eloquently written, J. S. Gordon's *Land of the Fallen Star Gods* paints a broad, detailed picture of what must be an ancient language of science embedded in an ancient civilization's expression. The Egyptian's use of symbol and metaphor in art, architecture, and civil planning was no mere function of primitive religiosity. Rather, it was the philosophical foundation of civilization expressing deep insights into human existence and the significance of the human experience. *Land of the Fallen Star Gods* is not only fascinating but also an important work of scholarship. It should be required reading for anyone interested in civilization's origins and the birth of the Western religious and esoteric traditions."

EDWARD F. MALKOWSKI, AUTHOR OF *BEFORE THE PHARAOHS*,
THE SPIRITUAL TECHNOLOGY OF ANCIENT EGYPT, AND *ANCIENT EGYPT 39,000 BC*

"Brilliant, erudite, and controversial, John Gordon has used Madame Blavatsky's insights to throw a new light on the problems of ancient Egyptian civilization."

COLIN WILSON, AUTHOR OF THE BESTSELLING *THE OUTSIDER*, *THE OCCULT:
A HISTORY*, AND *ATLANTIS AND THE KINGDOM OF THE NEANDERTHALS*

Contents

PART THREE

KNOWLEDGE

ACKNOWLEDGMENTS

For some of the research carried out preparatory to writing this book (this being its third edition), I am indebted to the library of the School of Oriental and African Studies and the Theosophical Society, both in London. I am similarly indebted to the Peabody Museum of Archaeology and Ethnology of Harvard University for their courtesy in permitting me to use photographic reproductions of ethnic types as shown on page 53. Others formally approached for similar permissions for use have regrettably failed to reply, possibly because of being unable to identify records now nearly half a century old. It is hoped that any missing acknowledgments may be incorporated into subsequent editions.

I am particularly grateful to Fred Hapgood, son of Professor Charles Hapgood and trustee of his works, for permitting me to use his father's cartographically modernized version of the Piri Re'is map, shown in figure 2.1. If anybody has provided future generations with a scientific challenge as regards ancient climatic and geographical change in the Atlantic, Charles Hapgood must surely stand among the forerunners. Still in relation to geographical issues, Marie Tharp has kindly permitted me to use two of her wonderful reproduction drawings of the topography of the Atlantic and northwest Indian Ocean seabeds. For a really graphic indication of the effects of cataclysmic movement in the earth's crust, these are hard to equal, and I am very pleased to be able to use them. The Woods Hole Oceanographic Institute were also most helpful in providing me with backup information and references related to the Strataform Initiative (on undersea slope failure), which is being sponsored by the U.S. Office of Naval Research, Washington, D.C.

Bruce Cathie was good enough to write to me all the way from New Zealand, once I had managed to track him down. His article on the levitation of stone will be of considerable interest to many in several fields of research. Unfortunately, I was unable to obtain any photographs of the rock levitation in Shivapur, which is also mentioned in appendix Q. Perhaps a later edition will enable me to do so.

I feel that I should, in passing, voice a considerable vote of thanks to Sir Wallis Budge, who—although himself deceased for more than half a century—has himself provided me in absentia with a vast range of Egyptological "hors d'oeuvres" from which to select useful references in substantiation of my various suggestions concerning ancient Egyptian mysticism, occultism, and architecture. Without his voluminous works before me for easy reference, my task would have been considerably longer and far more laborious.

In a more contemporary context, I cannot conclude without adding a particular mention here of Robert Bauval, who became a friend and compatriot subsequent to the publication of the first edition of this book, although not originally consulted concerning any specific material in it. Robert has by his own efforts succeeded in opening up a completely new field of archaeoastronomical research through his work at Giza. His pioneering efforts will, I am sure, be gratefully remembered by many generations yet to come (including the many future generations of Egyptologists!). He, Graham Hancock, and John West—another compatriot in this field who has since become a friend—have surely done us all a great service by so effectively reawakening worldwide public interest and debate on the underlying background to ancient Egyptian culture, notwithstanding the resistance they have met from academic orthodoxy.

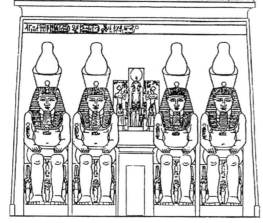

FIGURE 0.1. THE DOUBLE TEMPLE OF RA AND HATHOR AT ABU SIMBEL

Top, the temples as seen from the Nile in this early 20th century photograph, with the desert sands still encroaching; *middle,* artist's rendering of the original façade of the King's temple; *bottom,* plans of the two temples.

1. Raised court
2. Seated colossi
3. Hall of the 8 "Kabiri"
4. Ancillary chambers
5. Outer antechamber
6. Innermost sanctuary
7. Hittite marriage stele
8. Southern rock-cut chapel
9. Northern rock-cut chapel
10. Perimeter of modern concrete dome wall

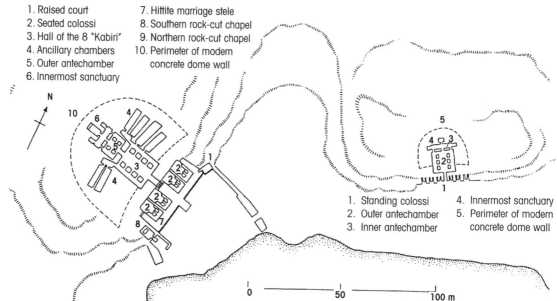

1. Standing colossi
2. Outer antechamber
3. Inner antechamber
4. Innermost sanctuary
5. Perimeter of modern concrete dome wall

0   50   100 m

INTRODUCTION

A FRESH APPROACH

The original writing of this book first came about as a result of a discussion at a dinner party, just before the turn of the millennium. Over the hors d'oeuvres I had complained with some vexation about the fact that few if any of those writing about ancient Egypt actually paid any real attention to understanding, or even mentioning in due context, the true nature of its sacred Mystery tradition. The academic community pay the subject mere lip service, regarding it as a mere cultural hodgepodge accrued over the millennia. Most of the "New Age" fraternity, however, wax mystically lyrical about it without even beginning to understand the basic and essentially practical principles around which these same Mysteries functioned. The other guests at the dinner party laughed, but one of them then suggested with a twinkle in her eye that, instead of complaining about others not having done it, I should perhaps write the book myself, thereby ensuring that such a work would be more generally available. This suggestion was met with such unanimity from the others present that I could hardly decline and thus the work started the following morning, long before dawn had broken. Little was I to realize then, however, the full extent of what I had embarked upon. That is because, not altogether surprisingly, the one book has proved altogether inadequate to deal with the subject in adequate breadth and detail. Consequently, a followup providing that even greater breadth and depth has already been written and will be published by Inner Traditions in 2014. It is called *Esoteric Egypt.*

In the meantime, however, it is hoped that this book about ancient Egypt's "fallen star gods" (the *akhu*) will set the scene with a number of foundational suggestions which have either not been touched on before at all by others or have otherwise not been considered in anything like adequate detail from an esoteric viewpoint. Not least of these include the highly important association of Egyptian sacred culture (as also the ancient Indian culture) with the astronomical cycle known to us as the precession of the equinoxes (although originally known in ancient times as The Great Year of the Pleiades). Associated with this is the strangely archaeoastronomical shape of the river Nile itself and the rationale of why its most important temples are located very precisely where they are. It otherwise focuses on explanation of the sacred metaphor and allegory to be found in temple carvings and paintings, plus the sacred geometry of the Giza pyramids, thereby showing precisely why the Great Pyramid never actually possessed a capstone. When such foundational issues are better understood, the whole rationale of ancient Egyptian sacred culture should become much more self-evident.

The subject of ancient Egypt, its chronology and civilizations, has perhaps excited more speculation than any other culture in any other part of the world. To some extent that must be due to the sense of mystery and magic that has always surrounded that uniquely formed country, even in the rational minds of the Greek tourists and historians of some 2,500 years ago. In those days, as much as in our own, Egypt's ancient associations with the legendary Atlantis were already widely known and discussed. To some extent also, Egypt's striking atmosphere must be due to the fact that the joint endeavors of the sinuously tropical river Nile and the country's otherwise desert landscape and climate provide all its temples with a visual contrast that no other land in recorded history appears ever quite to have matched. Allied to the richly colored and massive, symmetrical grandeur of its architecture and colossi, the overall effect upon the personal psyche inevitably has to be one of pure awe.

As far as other issues are concerned, the fact that contemporary archaeological science sets out to limit Egypt's many civilizations and cultures to the last 5,000 to 7,000 years, despite the many and highly curious inconsistencies that such a willfully myopic hypothesis throws up, adds but a further spice of mystery on which the imagination can run riot. There is nothing that human beings love more than a mystery to be solved or, at the very least, picked at. Consequently, because Egypt's "lost" background and its empty temples present such an enigmatic façade—like the wreck of the *Marie Celeste*—the appetite of a fascinated human curiosity is merely sharpened.

So many books have been written and documentary films produced on the subject of Egypt's ancient past that one is forced to wonder sometimes whether anything new and original could, by now, possibly be put forward. Yet there are so many large and unsatisfactory gaps in the historical record, and mainstream Egyptology seems to be so keen to concentrate on mere cataloging of minutiae at the expense of all sorts of wider possibilities, that intelligently speculative amateurs with an indefatigable sense of wider horizons to be discovered are drawn to the subject like bees to nectar-laden flowers.

R. A. Schwaller de Lubicz, in the 1940s and 1950s, initiated the modern trend of intelligent disbelief in the literalistic interpretations of the Egyptological Establishment. He conclusively demonstrated that the ancient Egyptians not only understood astronomical science so well that they recognized the 25,920-year period of the precession of the equinoxes but that they also founded every aspect of their civilization upon a star-oriented, religio-mystical culture derived from such knowledge. Robert Temple's *The Sirius Mystery*, published in 1976, added fuel to his fire by showing that the Dogon people of Mali in West Africa indisputably knew that Sirius—a central focus of Egyptian religious myth—was a binary star and that they had derived such knowledge from the Egyptians in ancient times. Hard on the heels of the Dogon revelation came the work of buccaneering scholar and self-taught Egyptologist John Anthony West. His 1979 book, *Serpent in the Sky*, followed in de Lubicz's tracks by expanding upon his ideas and subsequently confirming (through the use of "hard" geological proof) that the height of Egyptian culture and civilization must have long preceded the eleventh millennium B.C.

More recent books such as Robert Bauval and Adrian Gilbert's *The Orion Mystery* and Graham Hancock's *Fingerprints of the Gods,* which are based on careful research with a wider perspective than orthodox Egyptology will allow itself, have undoubtedly been very helpful in widening the scope of potential inquiry. They have done so by seeking to demonstrate that ancient Egyptian civilization goes back at least 15,000 years—perhaps even 40,000 years—and may have some sort of divinely inspired origin.[1] Unfortunately, however, through sometimes missing the central point of the esoteric traditions that they themselves mention, the authors of even these well-researched books have occasionally managed to confuse some of the mystical allegories found in the hieroglyphic texts and elsewhere in the folklore that they describe. Consequently, their historical chronologies (particularly relating to the period prior to 10,000 B.C.) sometimes appear to lack confidence and thereby allow occasional areas of confusion to persist.

Bauval has clearly confirmed that Egyptian astronomical knowledge was sufficiently sophisticated by at least the eleventh millennium B.C. to conceive of the Pyramids at Giza being built as an exact replication of the three stars of Orion's belt.[2] Hancock has taken matters a stage further by forcefully reminding us that the ancients associated world cataclysms with astronomical cycles. In addition, he has very originally pointed out the probable association of ice ages with the precession of the equinoxes.[3] Unfortunately, however, inadequate distinction has been drawn in his book between purely allegorical cataclysms (associated with the cosmic creation myth) and scientifically recorded upheavals in Nature. His approach has nevertheless managed in the main to distance itself from the kind of arbitrary disasters suggested in modern catastrophe theories, such as that proposed by Immanuel Velikhovsky,[4] which, although often highly original in their misguided attempts to give validity to the Old Testament as a supposed history, are extremely misleading.

Understanding Ancient Worldviews

This minor criticism of the pioneering work of Bauval, Gilbert, and Hancock is not meant unkindly. Nor does it seek to deny the concept of periodically recurring cataclysms that succeed not only in destroying human and animal life in the mass but also in greatly changing the geographical appearance of the lands on which they existed. It is, nevertheless, intended to highlight the fact that much greater attention needs to be paid to the background philosophies and beliefs of ancient peoples, rather than to the (often degenerate) form and appearance of their cultural rites.

The latter, on their own, without some guidance as to an original esoteric key, actually tell us very little about their essential raison d'être. That, in particular, is something that this book intends to highlight in some detail. It proposes to do so by showing how and where overliteral interpretations can lead to completely false trails of thought; also how in other cases, where literal descriptions are intended, they are treated as impossible by modern thought, due to a willfully ignorant, knee-jerk disbelief in the feasibility of their rationales.

Several problems arise out of paying insufficient attention to the detailed esotericism behind ancient metaphors and supposedly historical allegories[5]—especially those concerning the origins and subsequent geographical and evolutionary mutations of our world. One is that allegorical deluges and cataclysms very easily become thoroughly mixed up and confused with real ones resulting from the natural cycles of our planetary and solar systems. Where that occurs, any associated hope of establishing an accurate chronology of human existence and civilization on this planet is also doomed to failure.

A further effect is to leave in midair the theory of a possibly far more ancient *Homo sapiens* than is currently thought possible, because of being denied an adequately solid foundation on which its case might be reasonably argued. Much of the blame for this situation lies historically with allowing the Old Testament to be regarded (up until the 20th century, at least, and even by some today) as a merely slightly faulty record of actual events. The idea that biblical recorders and later interpreters may just have got their chronological sequences wrong, although the stories themselves are true, is but the latest in a line of *apologia theologica* trying to provide additional shoring to several desiccated and by now rather creaky religious belief systems. Supported as these are on one side by blind faith in an increasingly myopic and superficial theology (hence the growth of fundamentalism) and on the other by a taste for the materialistic rationales of modern science, inward collapse upon their own foundations can hardly be long delayed, for reasons that will become obvious later in the book.

The modern archaeological background to ancient Egypt, on the other hand, is only some two hundred years old, although the seventeenth and eighteenth centuries certainly saw some European travelers bringing back stories that initiated foundational research into the classical literature of not only Rome and Greece, but also the Middle and Far East. It was this that provided the footings of Victorian and Edwardian antiquarianism and amateur archaeology, the predecessor of our modern, technologically oriented "science." But to understand why the latter has taken root in its present myopically entrenched attitudes, we need to examine, in general terms at least, the historical development of modern archaeological practice itself. That should provide us with the necessary perspective to underwrite some of our more obvious later criticisms of its limitations and failings in arriving at a correct interpretation of available evidence.

The Methodology of Modern Archaeology

First of all, it would perhaps be fair to suggest that modern archaeology has two quite distinct strands. The first, based upon history and classicism, is empirical and expansive in nature; the other, based upon scientific interpretation and technological measurement, is centripetal and reductive. The first is often untidily catholic in its approach, while the second tends very quickly to throw out that which cannot be made to fit a tidily operating paradigm based upon other scientific theories that it assumes to be correct.

The expansive, empirical approach constantly seeks to open up the field to new material and fresher ideas with an ever-broadening perspective. The reductive, technological method seeks to subject the ideas and evidence to critical examination, analytical segregation, and physical organization. When these two approaches work together in complementary fashion, common sense and insight reign hand in hand. However, when the technological approach dominates—as it tends to do today—the inevitable result is an introspectively incontinent fascination with finding out more and more about less and less.

Left to itself, the "orthodox" archaeological method (at least as currently practiced) quickly becomes both sterile and actively hostile toward any suggested change. For that reason, it is absolutely vital that intelligent amateurs such as West, Hancock, and Bauval, skilled in their own professional fields, continue to blast their way indefatigably into the sanctum sanctorum of Egyptological expertise. Nor should they allow themselves to worry overmuch about criticisms as to the unashamedly skeptical modern knight Sir Apis crashing around among the ancient ceramics. If even the Kingdom of Heaven may be taken by storm by the seeker after hallowed Truth, the stronghold of Egyptological and archaeological orthodoxy must surely prove rather more vulnerable to straight and independent scrutiny. There has been no truly forward thinking in the field of Egyptology during the last (twentieth) century. So the wind of change is long overdue.

Current inertia on the part of the orthodox regime in broadening its scope is due, partially at least, to the fact that it is restricted by current theories and chronology in the field of paleontology. That is, in turn, constrained by general anthropological theory based upon Darwinian concepts of natural selection and the evolution of species—neither of which has yet been categorically and indisputably proved, at least in relation to man. The whole is a "house of cards" with many large and unexplained holes in it, some of which we intend to examine.

Man's Divine Origins

The Ancients started off with the basic philosophy that man was essentially the projection or emanation of an ethereal, divine parentage and had on no account been evolved from the animal state in the somewhat louche manner proposed by Darwinian theory. In response to this, our modern savants have decided that ancient humanity can only have derived such "unscientific" ideas from wishful thinking arising out of ignorant worship of the Sun, Moon, and stars, thereby proving man's evolution from a savage state in line with their existing prejudices.[6] This attitude has not changed much in the last three hundred years, although it may have "softened" within the last thirty years to allow the Ancients their use of such religious techniques as an expedient method of maintaining social, cultural, economic, and political dominance over an ignorant peasantry. Such is the modern jargon. Is it then so strange that the two approaches are mutually incompatible?

Our modern genius for "scientific research" also suffers extensively from its own tendencies toward "dead letter" interpretations of ancient glyphs and symbols, apparently unable to perceive the fact that allegory and metaphor were the main methods used in both the thinking process and its outward expression in ancient days. The fundamental effect of the latter was that one form of linguistic expression could be interpreted in a variety of ways, according to the context, in a manner that could be commonly understood by peoples of varying tongues and intelligence. Such is the case today, for example, with the ideograms of the Chinese, which can be understood by the Japanese even though their languages are different.

Consequently, whereas alphabetical and grammatical/syntactical presentation are regarded as fundamental to our modern way of thinking and to expressing ourselves with unambiguous clarity, why should we fondly imagine that this form of sophistication is the single most important criterion in determining the question of cultural superiority—and thus of relative intelligence? Surely it was as true then as it is now that the essence of an idea (that is, its "spirit") is more important than the "letter." Anyway, one of the other areas we shall touch upon involves linguistic distortions often concealing the same ideas and even names in cultures thousands of miles and even oceans apart.

As to the often voiced suggestion that it would not be possible today to run and coordinate a scientifically organized culture based upon glyphs and ideograms, our modern traffic signs and computer programs immediately give it the lie. "But," counter our modern technocrats, "the Ancients did not have either computers or even a very sophisticated technology, as we can prove by archaeological data spanning the last ten thousand years at least."[7] Here, however, we run into one of the most basic of all our misconceptions—of mistaking modern intellectual sophistication (whether "scientific" or not) for proof of intelligence. The two are by no means always related. This chapter is not intended as a philosophical dissertation on the issue, but the point is nevertheless fundamental to understanding the culture of the Ancients.

FIGURE 0.2. THE "ANTIKYTHERA"
(now kept in the National Museum in Athens)

Briefly, therefore, we might suggest that, while real intelligence has to do with conscious perception of things as they are (or were originally intended), intellectually based knowledge has to do solely with organization and presentation of what appears to be available, or potentially available, in the way of information purely to explain or support current scientific/academic theories. That is why our contemporary science is based upon the latter, although still (sometimes) relying upon a mixture of common sense and intuitive perception to provide originality and a sense of direction.

The Search for Scientific Truth

"Orthodox science works," so it has been said, "because approximations are allowed." But real intelligence has no truck with approximations. It concerns itself only with Truth. Whereas contemporary science (and scholarship) says that its whole existence is based upon the search for Truth, it would be more realistic to suggest that it is perpetually straining to increase the universal viability of its own favorite theories. That is why science is forever throwing away its theories to make way for supposedly "better" ones, this being—self-confessedly—the approved "scientific method."

One also sometimes gains the impression from the touchiness of many archaeologists and anthropologists that they must themselves be aware of the all too evident inconsistencies of their fragile structure of theories. Perhaps that is why they dare not look at the alternatives too closely—is it for fear that they will highlight their own inadequacy? Thus, so it seems, they perforce keep their eyes ever closer to the ground (psychologically as well as literally) and the gently brushed bones and artifacts, hoping against hope that it will fall to someone else from another discipline (or perhaps better still, a complete amateur) to fatally undermine any shaky theories, the ruins of which they can then professionally demolish with absolute equanimity.

Egyptologists can hardly move their historical chronology at all in its present "box." That is because the currently accepted wisdom is that nothing in the way of urban civilization could possibly have existed during the Ice Age that finally (so we are told) ended some 10,000 to 12,000 years ago.[8] From such an assumption (and a few assorted graves) evolved their idea that the human type of that prehistoric era could only have been "hunter-gatherers" and that the fabrication of metal tools could also only have commenced some 9,000 years ago (5,000 to 6,000 years ago in Europe) because the current paleontological record (painfully sketchy though it is) appears to suggest this.[9] No heed seems to have been paid to the fact, however, that alongside our own technologically driven modern civilization, we still have literally tens of millions of people scattered around the world, eking out the most meager rural and even urban existences, many only marginally above the level of the equivalent Stone Age culture. Nor has much been made of the fact that as civilizations and cultures decline and fall, so the technological knowledge associated with them always seems to wither and die temporarily, only to surface again later. Some of the Anglo-Saxon settlements in England within two hundred years of the final fall of Rome are a certain testament to this fact. In addition, metal tools rust and eventually crumble to dust wherever there is dampness of any sort, so their life span is also highly limited.

Quite apart from all this, few archaeologists have cared to query too loudly the curious but self-evident fact that ancient Egyptian and Mesopotamian cultures and civilizations—according to the current wisdom—seem suddenly to have appeared, some 5,000 to 6,000 years ago, fully fledged and possessing highly sophisticated social, scientific, and technological knowledge (plus a complex linguistic system) with no prior cultural "learning curve" or support from any then current technological equipment or instrumentation. How could this possibly occur—except as a legacy?

The Frequent Uncertainty of Scientific and Scholarly Opinion

If we look back over the period of the Victorian era, we shall find certain "scientific" preconceptions that have taken root in the Occidental mind and hardly been questioned at all since, despite their clearly defective nature. The assumption or interpretation of ancient texts with their mystical allegory and metaphor as the mere workings of a colorful, superstitious, and otherwise still semibarbaric mind is arrogance of the worst sort at the very root of much of our modern scholarship. How, in the face of such arrogance, could we reasonably expect any true degree of accuracy in interpreting essential meanings? As we intend to demonstrate in this book, many of the treasured interpretations of scholars are themselves partially or completely defective for this very reason.

Just as an example, the very latest Paleolithic finds in Africa and Spain have already set the cat among the academic and scientific pigeons. Fifteen to twenty years ago, paleontologists were fairly certain that *Homo erectus*—the supposedly immediate human predecessor of *Homo sapiens*—first appeared in Africa around 1.5 million years ago. So it was said, Europe itself remained unoccupied until about 500,000 years ago, while *Homo sapiens sapiens* was deemed to have first appeared there only about 35,000 years ago.[10] A mere fifteen years later, the thinking is almost unrecognizably different, for *Homo sapiens sapiens* is now believed to have appeared at least 120,000 years ago, while southern England and Spain are known to have been occupied by human beings 1.5 to 1.8 million years ago.[11]

In addition to this, it is now admitted that the human brain has remained roughly the same size for at least 1.7 million years. And when we look closely, we otherwise find that different paleontologists have different sets of criteria as to what supposedly confirms a skeleton as being that of *Homo sapiens* in the first place.[12] So, if the most up-to-date scientific information is so clearly based on shifting sands, do we not have every right to wonder if what ancient historians tell us might, after all, have some foundation in fact?

In his book *Black Athena: The Afroasiatic Roots of Classical Civilization* (itself a weighty tome of pure scholarship in two large volumes), Martin Bernal, professor of government at Cornell University, criticizes "the tenacity of an academic convention in the face of massive contrary evidence from outside scholars using independent sources, who have no particular interest in causing trouble and often a strong reluctance to upset the status quo. The extraordinary slowness to accept the new evidence demonstrates the way in which scholars tend to rally to the structures they have been taught and upon which they have spun their hypotheses; they demand absolute proof from challengers without pausing to reconsider the bases of their own beliefs."[13]

The Involvement of New Age Thought and Research

As we shall see in later chapters, what Bernal describes is very much a current problem in the field of Egyptology, as "outsiders" like John Anthony West have found out. But if modern scientists and scholars do not clearly understand something, they should unashamedly admit the fact together with the shortcomings and limitations of their current stock of knowledge, rather than fudging the issue with technical and technological hocus-pocus while gratuitously deriding the considered thoughts of others outside or on the fringes of their own discipline. As things are, their peremptory and often unconsidered ululations about supposedly unsubstantiated New Age theories—many of which are themselves founded upon serious and careful research into ancient traditions and philosophies—often leave the informed public increasingly skeptical as to their own general reliability. If a fair point is raised by someone from another discipline or field of research, can these scholars not be big enough to admit the fact graciously rather than commit the age-old arrogance of the academic in attempting to subvert its recognition by ridicule? Scientists and academics are often the least objective of people if someone else conceives or opens up a better and more informative perspective on their subject than they themselves have been able to.

Having raised these criticisms of the often blinkered and pedestrian approach to modern archaeology caused by both prejudice and overreliance on technology to lead interpretation, rather than as a corroborative backup to common sense and intuitive intelligence, there is no avoiding the necessity for accurate data and clearly argued foundations to suggested alternatives. Keeping that principle firmly in mind, the approach in this book has been to increase the usual number of perspectives adopted in interpreting data associated with ancient Egypt. It remains a fond (if as yet faint) hope that this—in conjunction with what West, Bauval, and Hancock have already done—might perhaps, given time, encourage an eventually corresponding broadening of attitudes by professional archaeologists themselves, as well as attracting interest on the part of others.

This book itself involves an attempt to look afresh at certain of the fundamental and thus highly significant issues that are known or believed to have been associated with both Atlantis and ancient Egyptian culture and civilization, some of them being entirely outside the normally recognized sphere of archaeology. Some of the ideas put forward will undoubtedly prove familiar, even though perhaps occasionally unorthodox in their angle of presentation and interpretation; others may throw a completely different light on existing (even unorthodox) perspectives. In some cases, what might appear to be wholly and radically new suggestions are presented. However, none is really new; each is merely borrowed from a dusty and unconsidered cupboard of esoteric lore with which the reader may be unfamiliar.

The intention here is not merely to argue a set of alternative theories, but rather to point out the reasons behind inconsistencies and misrepresentations in existing concepts in a manner making for more rational sense. Whether this aim actually succeeds will of course be for individual readers to decide for themselves. But even if some of the preliminary ideas here appear at first too extraordinary or rather too difficult for the reader to assimilate or digest all at once, it is hoped that they will be put to one side for later reconsideration (in the light of what is suggested toward the end of the book) instead of being summarily rejected. Initial perceptions are not always entirely accurate, and if one is but patient, time has a habit of showing how a drawerful of "widgets" can be gradually adapted and assimilated.

The Structure of This Book

The book is arranged in three parts. The first part deals with a variety of scientific and semi-scientific issues related to what we believe we currently know about Egyptian culture and civilization. It covers astronomical, astrophysical, and geophysical factors first of all—as a prelude to the very appearance of northeast Africa and its colonization in ancient times. It also deals with the question of Atlantis, its supposed location and the distinctions between Plato's island and a vastly larger continent of which it once formed a part. Associated with this, various cosmological issues are discussed in relation to both the progressive disappearance of Atlantis and its populations and also the common sidereal religion of the time.

The second part deals specifically with the belief systems of the ancient Egyptians, how these were derived (in a way often clearly misunderstood by Egyptologists) and how their art, architecture, and religion were all built around them—for, as we shall see, the so-called multitude of Egyptian gods were actually all part of one single, internally coherent and self-consistent pantheon. Additionally, in order to put many of the associated concepts into a modern context, direct comparisons are occasionally drawn with so-called

New Age thought. Some of the latter is thereby shown to be clearly identifiable in ancient times, although in another guise as allegory or metaphor, while some is shown to have arisen through overly simplistic interpretation of the ancient concepts.

The third part of the book deals more specifically with the cosmological and astronomical derivations of ancient Egyptian thought, plus their architectural associations. Certain of the associated figures and maps should make understanding of these issues very much simpler than readers might otherwise expect in a book on such a subject, and they should also serve to show how the coherence of Egyptian mystical thought was clearly expressed in their built environment. In addition, it is believed that these same maps and figures will provide graphic evidence of the fact that only an immensely ancient and sophisticated culture and civilization could possibly have arrived at such a high degree of scientific knowledge while also combining it so precisely with the most sublimely universal spiritual philosophy.

That this was able (simultaneously) to incorporate within itself a detailed allegorical depiction of the "celestial mechanics and dynamics" of our planetary, solar, and galactic existence, plus a thorough rationale of the psycho-spiritual states of being (both of which we shall describe in some detail), also shows beyond any lingering shadow of a doubt that the ancient Egyptians possessed certain areas of knowledge equivalent to—and probably even in advance of—our own. Not least of all the issues associated with this latter fact is the background to the way in which the Egyptian Mystery School itself originally came into existence and why it subsequently fell into degeneration at a time when most Egyptologists regard Egyptian civilization as having been at its height.

Finally, certain associations clearly evident (but not hitherto remarked upon) are outlined in relation to the temples and occult rites of initiation of the time. These are described with particular reference to the Sphinx and the Pyramids at Giza, and from them the origins of both Masonic ritual and various aspects of the Jewish and Christian mystery traditions are shown as being traceable.

Because the subjects treated involve a number of areas of complexity that may be unfamiliar to some readers, various explanatory appendices are provided at the back of the book.

PART 1

ORIGINS

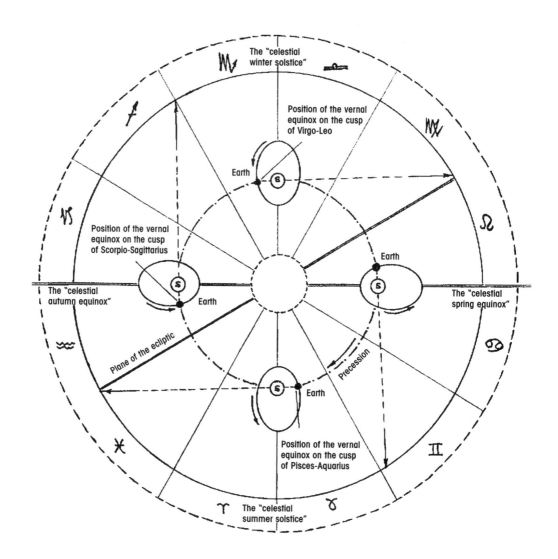

FIGURE 1.1. THE CELESTIAL PASSAGE OF THE SOLAR SYSTEM DURING THE 25,920-YEAR ANNUS MAGNUS (GREAT YEAR)

In order to follow the sequence of precession, one should remember that when the Sun at the vernal equinox appears to be "in" a particular sign, the solar system (and thus Earth) actually lies at an angle to that sign consistent with its position on the path of the ecliptic. Thus, for example, as the solar system precesses through the plane of its own parent star at the celestial autumnal equinox, the Sun at the vernal equinox (as seen from Earth) appears to be on the cusp of Scorpio-Sagittarius. Hence it is that the path of the ecliptic appears to pass through the celestial equator at that point. As shown in the figure, the angle of the ecliptic is not quite accurate, as will become obvious in discussions below. It is shown this way purely to simplify the explanation of the principles of precession.

ONE

Cosmic Seasons and Astronomical Cycles

Whether the origin of the Zodiac is Aryan or Egyptian, it is still of immense antiquity. Simplicius (sixth century A.D.) writes that he had always heard that the Egyptians had kept astronomical observations and records for the last 630,000 years. . . . Diogenes Laertius carried back the astronomical calculations of the Egyptians to 48,863 years before Alexander the Great. Martianus Capella corroborates the same by telling posterity that the Egyptians had secretly studied astronomy for over 40,000 years before they imparted their knowledge to the world.

—J. Lewis, *Astronomy of the Ancients*

As has already been established or otherwise clearly suggested in books such as R. A. Schwaller de Lubicz's *Sacred Science* and Jane B. Sellers's *The Death of Gods in Ancient Egypt,* the ancient Egyptians were fully aware of the 25,920-year cycle of the precession of the equinoxes.[1] The idea, however, that a nomadic group of hunter-gatherers about 5,000 to 6,000 years ago should suddenly within the space of a few hundred years (or even a millennium), from merely watching the night sky but without using any instrumentation, be able to quickly develop the requisite mathematical and scientific knowledge to verify such a hypothesis is patently ludicrous. That Egyptologists in general should show themselves (by their very silence on the issue) willing to support such an obvious fiction tends to confirm that they have lost interest in the radical pursuit of truth, tailoring theories instead to suit their "lowest common denominator" version of probability. Why else would they remain so willfully ignorant of astronomical issues in the study of ancient Egypt?

The recent books of John Anthony West, Robert Bauval, and Graham Hancock have all indicated the clear certainty of ancient Egyptian civilization (if not others also) having been far more ancient than archaeologists would have us believe.[2] Despite treating the subject of Egypt's antiquity at some length, however, Hancock's books have tended to concentrate more specifically on the issue of Atlantis and its whereabouts, and on sporadic worldwide cataclysms that might have led to its disappearance[3] and which he feels might occur again within the next fifteen years or so. Bauval, on the other hand, concentrating his attention upon Egypt alone, has taken the slightly curious view that, although extraordinarily sophisticated scientific knowledge evidently existed in Egypt 12,500 years ago,

Egyptologists may be more or less correct in some of their ideas of pyramid and temple construction having taken place only rather more recently (that is, progressively over thousands of years since then),[4] even though the cosmic alignments shown in the orientation of the Giza pyramids had already been noted in 10,450 B.C. For reasons to be explained in later chapters, however, we cannot accept these conclusions.

In his *Fingerprints of the Gods* Hancock arrived at the interesting concept of aligning periodic ice ages and cataclysms with the precessional cycle.[5] In other words, he highlighted the fact that, far from such phenomena occurring capriciously, they almost certainly do so cyclically and as a matter of course. However, he unfortunately failed to carry that very important observation to its natural conclusion. This chapter is dedicated to describing that conclusion and also showing that the Ancients were themselves aware of a vast range of scientific knowledge associated with such regular cycles of cosmic activity and their predictable effects upon the Earth.

We should perhaps bear in mind from the outset that the Egyptians' great god Ra—the Logos—was regarded by them (as Amen-Ra) as the unseen although immediate overall deity of our local universe (that is, of the Milky Way) in its entirety, the latter existing within his enfolding, omnipresent aura.[6] Our own sun was thus thought of as but a very partial expression of Ra's Being,[7] even the solar system as a whole representing merely a small part of his objective physical form. Consequently, our planet Earth has to be viewed here (from the Egyptian viewpoint) in the context of a (perhaps holographic?) microcosm of Ra's macrocosm, fulfilling a partial role in the life of his vast organic life cycle, and being therefore also directly subject to the effects felt within it of his feelings, emotions, and

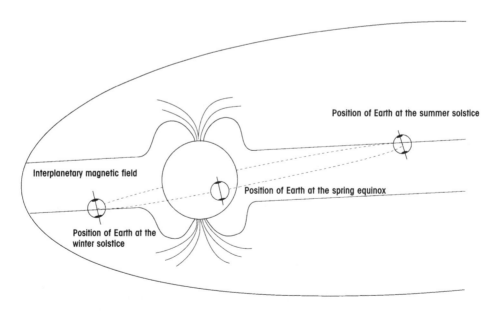

FIGURE 1.2. THE ANNUAL ORBIT OF THE EARTH AROUND THE SUN

(showing the neutrally polarized "Interplanetary Magnetic Field")

It is known by astrophysicists that one of the Earth's "wobbles" involves a short cycle of 183 days. Now, bearing in mind that 2 x 183 = 366, there is reasonable cause to suppose that the wobble might, in fact, be directly related to the intersolstitial periods. In other words, it is almost certainly caused by electromagnetic deflection resulting from the Earth passing through, or close to, the upper and/or lower edges of the interplanetary magnetic field.

mental and spiritual reflexes—however one might regard these. It would seem that, from an understandably personal viewpoint, the organism of the Earth and its attendant atmosphere were where the Ancients believed those same reflexes would be felt and seen by them. However, even this attitude was dictated by the fact that Mankind—the progeny of Ra and product of his Divine Thought—populated the Earth.

Planet Earth as a Living Organism with Its Own Cycles

We should also bear in mind that the Ancients regarded our Earth in its entirety as an integrated and living organism. While the concept of Gaea (or Gaia) has become familiar to us over the last thirty years in line with our modern interest in planetary ecology, the Ancients took their understanding a great deal further. Whereas our understanding of the concept is focused primarily on the body of the planet and its flora and fauna, they regarded its multiple atmospheric sheaths (in a manner which might surprise us) as no less a vital part of the living, breathing organism. That is something to which we shall be paying very particular attention, as it is absolutely crucial to any understanding of ancient Egyptian thought, which clearly saw all phenomenal effects in Nature as the bodily functions of Ra. From our own modern viewpoint, perhaps the most basic of these effects in the solar system derives from the "breathing of Ra," which appears to result in the regularly fluctuating cycles of expansion and contraction of the system as a whole. This would, in practical terms, seem to correlate with the phenomena of the solar wind and the eleven-year sunspot cycle, and thus also with volcanic, earthquake, and climatic activity on our planet, the "body" of which itself expands and contracts in response to solar stimulus. Some of these things were noted by the ancient Egyptians and their contemporaries in India and Asia Minor, even though the techniques used to know them may not yet be apparent to us. However, we shall expand on this in a later chapter.

It is by now generally accepted that the Earth not only undergoes periodic ice ages—the actual cause of which is still unknown to science[8]—but also that the two polar areas have, on several occasions in their history, lost most if not all their glacial coverings and then subsequently experienced temperate and even subtropical climates.[9] In confirmation of this fact, fossil remains of coral reefs and palm trees have been found in Spitzbergen and coal deposits in Antarctica. Yet, right at this moment, scientists are at sixes and sevens discussing reasons for global warming and the widening "hole" in the ozone layer. But why should all these things not be interconnected as part of the Earth's natural cycle?

As every reasonably educated child knows, Earth in its 365-day orbital passage around the Sun experiences four roughly regular seasons. In late March and September, as Earth diagonally crosses the plane of the solar horizon (its path being at an angle to it), we, as did the Egyptians in ancient times, experience the phenomenon of the equinox—equal hours of daylight and darkness. What is not so commonly remarked upon is that between March and September, the larger portion of Earth is above the solar horizon, whereas from September to March (during the autumn and winter periods) it is below it (see fig. 1.2). When it is below the solar horizon, the Northern Hemisphere experiences winter; when above it, the Southern Hemisphere has its winter.

Another significant characteristic of Earth's elliptical orbit is that it reaches what is

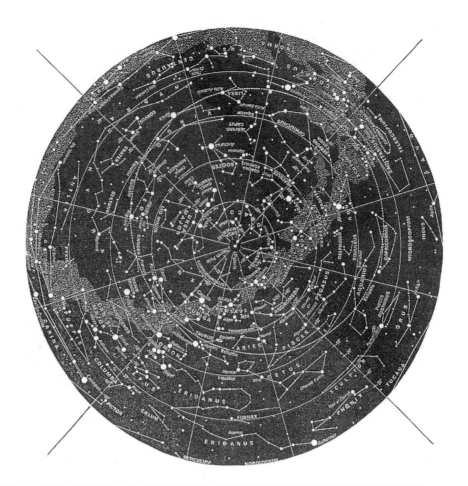

FIGURE 1.3. THE CELESTIAL PLANISPHERE SHOWING THE NORTHERN HEAVENS

called its aphelion, or furthermost point away from the Sun, in late June, while in December is to be found its perihelion, or closest point to the Sun, these two months thus containing the orbital solstices. Notwithstanding this difference, the Southern Hemisphere experiences a summer in December that is every bit as warm as our Northern Hemisphere in June. One might reasonably infer from this that distance from the Sun has little to do with climate and that warmth has perhaps more to do with atmospheric response to the electrical energies circulating in the plane of the Sun's equator and the "interplanetary magnetic field." But, as we shall see in due course, this fact has its cosmic counterpart that also significantly affects us.

The Movements of Our Solar System within the Galaxy

It is accepted by scientists that our solar system as a whole is moving in orbit within the plane of our nebuloid galaxy—the Milky Way—as the latter turns on its own axis once (from where we stand) roughly every 230 million years. However, different star groups within the Galaxy move at different speeds and consequently appear to describe different motions according to how far from the center of the Galaxy they are and also relative to our own constantly shifting viewing platform in space. As shown in figure 1.4, our solar

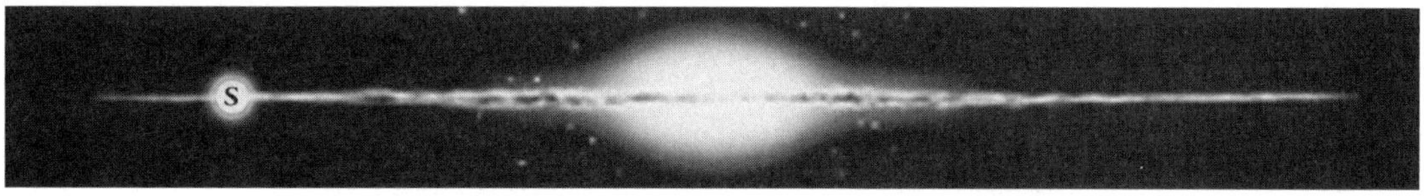

FIGURE 1.4. LOCATION OF OUR SOLAR SYSTEM IN THE MILKY WAY GALAXY

system is located nearly three quarters of the way to the periphery of the Galaxy, and so it is moving very fast indeed (over 60,000 miles per hour). It also follows a secondary series of localized orbits within its own sector of the Galaxy, and it is this movement that we refer to when we speak of the Sun traveling around the Zodiac. This circuitous path that the Sun follows, relative to adjacent star groups, is called the ecliptic[10] (see fig. 1.5).

During the period of a single year, the Sun in its own orbital path in space appears from Earth to pass once around the Zodiac, returning to its point of origin at the vernal equinox. However, in every year that it does so, it arrives "very slightly late" and, as a result, is seen to cross the celestial equator marginally behind the exact location in the Zodiac that it crossed exactly a year before. The time/distance deficit resulting from this amounts to precisely one degree of arc every seventy-two years. Rather interestingly, the "very slightly late" amounts to just over five days, or $1/72$ part of one degree. Hence, we might suggest, the true orbital cycle of 360 degrees (in what would otherwise take 360 days) is extended by this short extra period as a direct result of the forward orbital movement in space of our solar system and its centrifugal effect upon the Earth's own orbit. The Egyptians seem to have recognized this fact and consequently allocated twelve equal months (of thirty days each) to their year, with the five extra ("epagomenal") days as festive days separately dedicated to the gods Osiris, Isis, Nephthys, Set, and Horus the Elder[11]—a much more logical approach than that adopted by our own irritatingly haphazard calendar.

As a consequence of this annual loss, the Sun appears to regress through the entire Zodiac in approximately 25,920 years, thus passing through one zodiacal sign every 2,160 years. This overall retrograde motion is called the precession of the equinoxes. Its 25,920-year cycle has been referred to variously as the "Annus Magnus," or "Platonic Year," or "Great Sidereal Year," and it will be found to play a very major part in our considerations throughout this book. Of additional interest in connection with this same matter is the fact that 360 years is exactly $1/72$ part of a complete Annus Magnus of 25,920 years while the "epagomenal" period is $1/72$ part of a complete Earth year. These and other mathematical synchronicities between the Great Year and our Earth year are, to say the least, arresting.

The Existence of "Celestial Seasons"

But what if our particular sidereal system, rather than moving exactly within the horizontal plane of the Galaxy, itself follows an orbital path at an angle to it in the same way that our planet does in relation to its sun? And what if our sun and solar system themselves revolve around a greater and more powerful sun that is itself responsible for that motion in space? Could it not be that that orbit takes 25,920 years to run its course and is itself the reason for not only the precession of the equinoxes, but also the designated circumpolar stars, as per

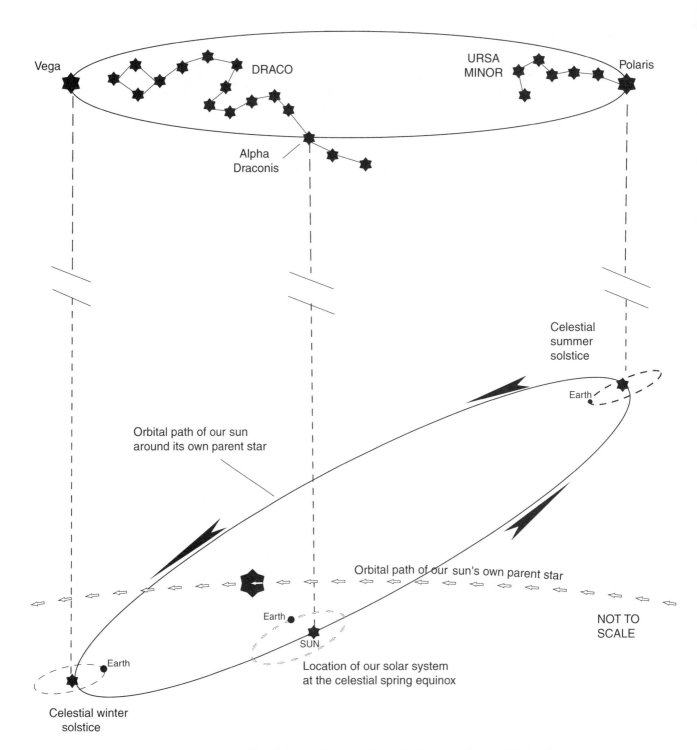

FIGURE 1.5. ASSOCIATION OF THE CIRCUMPOLAR STARS WITH EARTH'S LOCATION DURING THE ANNUS MAGNUS

As we shall see in later chapters, the location of the Pole Star played a crucial role in ancient Egyptian mythology. However, it is suggested that the ring of circumpolar stars (as seen from Earth) is clearly defined by the position of our solar system (and Earth's position within it) during the Great Year, as generally depicted in this figure. Astronomical science currently regards this phenomenon as being due to an eccentric wobble in Earth's axis. But why invent such a difficult explanation when there is a much more obvious and logical answer?

figure 1.5?[12] And could it not be that, following a similar pattern, that 25,920-year cycle also produces its own "seasons"—of about 6,480 years—macrocosmically comparable with our Earth seasons of about ninety days? Yet here again the ratio between the two is 1:72.

It surely follows that, if the solar system were itself subject to celestial "seasons" on such a massive scale, the influences of growth and decay affecting all the planets within it would also be of commensurate power and duration. But what would be the scale of the effects caused by those influences on the various kingdoms of Nature on Earth? Would they perhaps not tend to be greatly magnified by comparison with what we see and experience today during our annual cycle of four seasons? This is a fascinating question that we shall examine further in chapter 4.

Astrophysicists are already aware of the fact that the gravitational field of our solar system extends about halfway to the nearest star. That is perhaps not altogether surprising if—as the cutting edge of astrophysical theory now seems to think—space is full of "fields" that, it hypothesizes (even though it does not yet understand what these are), even preceded the contemporary theory of a "big bang"[13]—if such a phenomenon ever occurred in quite the fashion currently described. Thus, on such a basis, space would be full of spherically shaped fields (of infinitely varied size) in exactly the same way that an agglomerate mass of water is said to be full of hydrogen and oxygen atoms in a characteristic molecular blend that permits waves of energy to pass through it.

If we look carefully at the planisphere (fig. 1.3), we shall see that the angular path of the ecliptic appears to pass through the Milky Way at two points: between Taurus and Gemini on one side and between Scorpio and Sagittarius on the other. If we then hypothesize that these points represent the sidereal equivalent of our own planetary equinoxes, the equivalent sidereal solstices should be found on, or fairly close to, the zodiacal cusps of Leo/Virgo and Aquarius/Pisces, where the ecliptic is at its furthest from the celestial equator. This, as we shall see later, is of immense importance from several angles of both a mundane and an esoteric nature. Biblical enthusiasts will already have noted that four of the mutually facing astrological symbols found in these pairs are also the heavenly creatures of Ezekiel's vision—the Bull, Lion, Eagle, and Man.[14]

If this proposition concerning "celestial seasons" is correct (and further evidence to support it will be suggested in later chapters), it would appear that we are currently approaching the sidereal equivalent of the summer solstice. The early part of the Age of Leo (represented by the Egyptian Sphinx, as we shall see) would then represent the celestial winter solstice, at which our solar system returns to its own parent sun for its "annual" revitalization. But while that in itself is an interesting suggestion, it becomes even more so when we consider the probability of associated effects in relation to Earth's polar ice caps—and also of changes in the ozone layer "holes."

Cyclical Global Warming

High summer is traditionally the warmest time of the year, when least rain falls and the crops ripen and burgeon. Might it not then be that during the equivalent period in the greater, 25,920-year sidereal cycle the polar ice caps could be expected to melt (perhaps completely after a sequence of such cycles) as a matter of course? They might then be expected to re-form subsequent to the celestial winter solstice—that is, during the Ages of Leo and Cancer—as the evaporated water in the atmosphere recondensed. Interestingly, the last such "solstice" occurred around 12,500 years ago, during the eleventh millennium B.C. Then, climatologists tell us, the equatorial and subtropical zones experienced a prolonged era of particularly heavy rainfall (a "pluvial period"), lasting perhaps several thousand years, accompanied by huge rises in sea levels.[15] At that time the valley of the Nile also saw a sudden concentrated erosion of its stone escarpments and temple buildings. In addition, much of the Sahara area is now recognized by archaeologists as having become at that time naturally irrigated pastureland or savannah, widely occupied by human communities as well as many species of wild animals drifting north from central Africa.[16]

Now, so geologists tell us, the last prolonged ice age started about 100,000 years ago and concluded about 10,000 years ago.[17] Does this not rather undermine what has just been suggested in relation to the 25,920-year sidereal cycle? Not really. What also has to be taken into consideration is that as our spiral galaxy itself turns once in a complete orbit on its own axis very roughly every 230 million years, within that period our solar system would complete nearly one hundred Great Year cycles. That leaves a great deal of margin for gradual cyclical change to take place, some of it in response to other (both smaller and larger) cycles discovered by geophysicists over the last thirty years or so. Two of the latter, for example, fall at intervals of around 41,000 and 100,000 years.[18] But what they are related to is, as yet, unknown.

Sunspots and Cosmic Electricity

One of the other fascinating features of our sun that affects our weather patterns on Earth is the regular cycle of sunspot activity that reaches its zenith every eleventh to twelfth year, although scientists have not yet been able to establish any really sound reason for the phenomenon. If, however, there were a comparable relationship to the sunspot cycle on a sidereal scale—that is, in relation to our solar system's orbit of the Galaxy—could it not be that this might provide a reason for our solar system cyclically running into periods of unimaginably intense electrical phenomena, of a magnitude that could cause incalculable changes in the patterns of weather and volcanic/earthquake movement on Earth? Thus, during certain 25,920-year cycles more than others, ice ages and cataclysms might well prove far more intense and prolonged.

There is also the question (already accepted by astrophysicists) of there being parts of the cosmos through which our solar system passes where the incidence of cosmic dust is much greater than elsewhere. If at such times larger amounts than usual of such dust became drawn into our atmosphere, the latter—reacting to the inevitably greater electrical activity (and heat) resulting from its ionization—would necessarily expand. That in turn would inevitably lead to "global warming" during the associated cycle, and consequent deglaciation of the polar ice caps. It is known that each year some thirty-five to forty million tons of cosmic dust already find their way into our atmosphere via the North Pole.[19] What would be the result of a material increase or decrease in this? Surely it could not avoid significantly affecting the world's weather patterns.

There is a peculiar variable geometry in all of this, strangely suggestive of astrological influences. Major and minor sidereal cycles only infrequently coalesce, but when they do, it undoubtedly puts enormous electromagnetic tensions into the whole sidereal mechanism of our solar system. These would undoubtedly be felt by our sun, which would in turn pass them on to the planets via the solar wind and its own magnetic lines of force. That in turn would cause major tensions in our planetary ionosphere as the latter absorbs increasing amounts of energy that somehow need to be discharged. How else could this be done except by producing both creative and destructive effects, not only within the Earth's crust but also in its lower atmosphere via its weather patterns? Vastly increased ionospheric energy would also result in the organic structure of the Earth itself and its biosphere (see fig. 1.6) being put under an equivalent degree of tension through a complementary expansion of energy from the Earth's core. The latter, as already suggested, must result in increases in the normal pattern of earthquake and volcanic activity as the Earth's crust flexes in response, through radial expansion and contraction. The ionospheric tension in the Earth's upper atmosphere otherwise produces high-voltage electrical storms

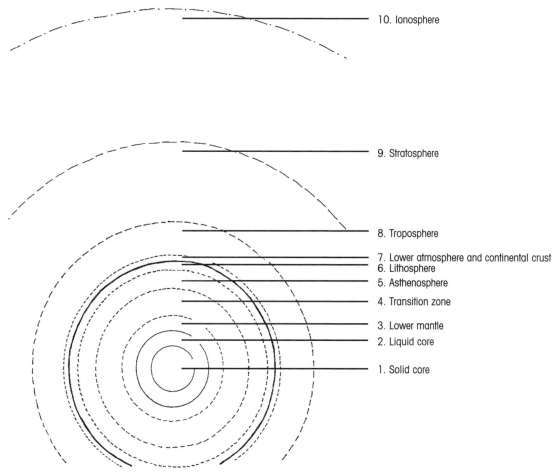

FIGURE 1.6. THE CONSTITUTION OF EARTH AND ITS ATMOSPHERE
(as regarded by contemporary science; not to scale)

that may or may not produce increased rainfall.[20] What it can certainly do, however, is increase atmospheric wind speeds with consequent (and often quite dramatically sudden) effects upon both climate and ocean currents.

Various people over the last half century—Velikhovsky in particular, but he is by no means alone even today, some fifty years later—have put forward the suggestion of other planets swinging unusually close by our own, or asteroids falling to Earth, thereby causing major cataclysms and wiping out vast numbers (or even whole species) of animal and plant life by tidal waves and earthquakes.[21] The fact is, however, that unusual asteroids and suddenly eccentric planetary motions are not necessary to satisfy the fundamental requirements of major land, sea, and air movement on our planet. It is well within the Earth's own organic capacities to produce the necessary phenomena on its own merely by responding within certain parameters to the fluctuating energies and magnetisms emanating from the Sun and other planets according to the cycle of each in the greater cosmic round, comprising several Great Years.

Curious Egyptian Views Concerning the Sun

Now we come to another apparent but highly significant curiosity. The ancient Egyptians seem to have held the uncompromising view that the Sun's disk provided none of the light[22] and very little of the heat enjoyed by our planet. At first glance such an idea seems totally and utterly absurd—until one gets out into space beyond the Earth's troposphere and finds the sky becoming increasingly dark. Light and heat are of course known to be the result of energy of a given wavelength within the electromagnetic spectrum impinging upon the resistance of a body—which includes an electromagnetic field such as that of our planet's own multilayered atmosphere. Thus, we suggest, it is the "organic" oscillation of the matter of our atmosphere that may be said to generate light out of its own mass when stimulated by the photoelectric energies projected from the Sun.[23]

Quite apart from this, the solar system itself, in its orbital passage around the heavens, undoubtedly experiences major tensions owing to its being "squeezed" by the fields of other heavenly bodies (those of the Titans, or cosmic gods), thereby generating an energetic response in the Sun at its center.[24] From our own scientific viewpoint, this might be regarded as occurring through what is called a piezoelectric effect, itself perhaps leading to the solar-wind phenomenon (depicted as the "breath of Ra," for reasons to be described in later chapters). One might otherwise speculate that the cyclical "sunspots" are also derived from the same source. This is obviously a highly significant issue because, so the Ancients had it, the Earth itself responded to external influences in the same way as does a human aura. In other words, as its own ionospheric tension increases, so the level of gravitational energy—the planet's own organic force—increases in due proportion until an electrical discharge (such as lightning) takes place. Before this can happen, however, the Earth's crust must itself flex; and that, as we know, can result in earthquake "ripple" and volcanic activity as well as unusual ocean current movements. On the same basis, extreme radial change in response to altered ionospheric tension could cause whole continents to rise—or fall. Yet current geological orthodoxy tells us that the idea of ancient continents in the Atlantic, Indian, and Pacific Oceans is not possible given the accepted concept of plate tectonics and also the present geophysical configurations of the ocean floors.[25] This is notwithstanding the fact that new mid-ocean beds are constantly being produced and new landmasses (like Hawaii) visibly created by volcanic action at the rate of dozens of acres per year. But can the theory of plate tectonics really be relied upon in its present guise when it is already accepted by the same orthodox establishment that it does not really know how the Earth's crust was originally formed? It seems rather doubtful, and in chapter 2 we shall explain why. Suffice it for the moment to suggest that the ancient traditions of Hyperborean, Lemurian, and Atlantean landmasses may well one day be proved accurate after all.

Returning, however, to the question of the orbital paths of our planet and solar system within the Milky Way, we have so far accounted for the electrical activity within the scheme, but not as yet the magnetic or gravitational forces. While this issue might seem tangential to the subject of ancient Egypt, it is important because of its association with the Egyptians' hierarchy of gods and also the disposition of the oldest temples along the Nile.

Differing Views Concerning the Earth's Structure

We have already suggested that the gravitational field of the Earth is generated at its core in response to the fluctuating tension in the planet's ionosphere. The Earth's core—it is further suggested—is not iron as mainstream geological science hypothesizes. It is, rather, more likely to be pure massed energy in the same fundamental state that physicists believe to exist in (or as) the nucleus of the atom. Professor Stephen Hawking's latest theory of the universe being full of tiny "black holes" actually (although quite unconsciously) tends to support this in a somewhat Pythagorean sense. As a consequence, the various "fields" surrounding this densely organized core state might be expected to give rise to a progressive and volatile series of condensations and crystallizations of localized energy, resulting in phenomena such as superheated gases and molten rock. On the surface of this, just like a surface patina, the thin terrestrial crust then continuously regenerates itself, in a manner similar to the dermis (skin) covering the underlying layers of human flesh.

The energies emanating inward from the ionosphere similarly give rise to concentrically organized fields—those of the various atmospheric "belts" (see fig. 1.6). But where the terrestrial and ionospheric energies actually meet, an intermediate electromagnetic substate (effectively, the dual plane known to us as the crust and lower atmosphere) forms as a result of the inherent resistance generated between these two energetic fields as each seeks, apparently, to dominate the other. The net effect of this is that both of these emanating influences—symbolized by the Egyptians as the complementary activities of Horus and the adversarial Set, with the female gods Isis and Nephthys acting as the intermediate "zones of transformation"—are forced to turn back on themselves. But in so doing, they leave behind en route a small, precipitated proportion of their energy load as localized, inertial force. In the case of the terrestrial energies, dense igneous matter and intense heat are generated. In the case of the ionospheric energies, atmospheric light is produced. The "surplus" or unexpended energy in each case then recycles itself, we suggest, by returning to its point of origin as negative force—in other words, gravity as far as the terrestrial proportion is concerned and the aerial buoyancy of the atmosphere[26] where the ionospheric is concerned.

Such a scenario will almost certainly cause the orthodox scientific mind to do more than just blink in surprise. However, this description—although undoubtedly lacking in strict scientific literacy—is not the result of an arbitrary theory, for it is based upon careful study of how the Ancients saw the genesis of the planet (as Gaea) deriving from Nature having a definite, organizing, and guiding intelligence to it. Our concern here, therefore, is not to ridicule science's present standpoints, but rather to explain how and why the Ancients structured their civilizations and cultures as they did. It is for contemporary science to examine such ideas and either accept or reject them on the basis of their own experimental findings.

Despite all this, it follows that if the plastic, igneous rock underlying the Earth's outer crust were formed in the manner described, the present theory of continental drift could not hold water—notwithstanding apparently constant movement of the crustal tectonic plates.[27] This notion is to some extent confirmed by the fact that the continental crust recycles itself constantly, progressively, and organically, rising within the mid-ocean volcanic ridges to produce the expanding seabed and then descending in a self-destructive dive into the deep oceanic trenches, ultimately remerging with the magma of the lithosphere, underlying the crust. That process itself suggests that the activity is of a rotational nature, conforming with the universal pattern of movement throughout the cosmos.

The Biggest Cataclysms Require Energy beyond Earth's Normal Capacity

Coming back to the question of precessional cycles, however, it should by now be evident that our theory implies that major re-formation or deformation of the Earth's crust to form both continents and oceans must itself be cyclical by virtue of the abnormally huge amounts of energy needed to cause such change. That is not to say that geographical and geological alterations do not take place in between the periods of major tension. They quite obviously do so; but the effects are relatively localized and can be seen quite clearly as such, even in our own time—as, for example, in the case of the volcanic cataclysm at Mount Saint Helens.

The issue of how and when cataclysms occur (and also that of their relative magnitude) is of concern to us here because it could be expected to have a fundamental bearing upon the chronology of ancient Egyptian culture and civilization. By that we mean prior to 5000 B.C.—long prior, by literally tens or even hundreds of thousands of years. For example, axial changes in our planet's position, leading to complete geomagnetic reversals, are of a major nature and appear (thankfully) relatively infrequently, apparently occurring only once every million years or so. Volcanoes and earthquakes, however, are ever active. Quite clearly, however, if cataclysms are local, only local cultures and civilizations will be affected, while adjacent ones continue in existence and often benefit from their demise. Thus many could be expected to pass from historical sight altogether without the faintest trace of their existence being left to the scrutiny of posterity. Over a very prolonged period of time—again, tens or even hundreds of thousands of years—owing to the processes of atmospheric dissolution and geological renewal, hundreds of even great cultures could pass away totally unremarked by posterity—that is, unless specific and scientifically organized steps were taken to ensure that a record of their existence continued, notwithstanding Nature's instinctive depredations. Might this, then, be what happened in prehistoric Egypt—and Atlantis?

Alternating Cataclysms of Fire and Water

In his *Timaeus* and *Critias,* Plato tells us through the memory of his ancestor Solon that the Egyptians believed the world to be subject to cyclically recurring cataclysms produced by water and fire[28]—which has been generally assumed to mean alternating volcanic activity and associated (submarine) earthquake action, plus intense rainfall. (However, what about ultraviolet radiation resulting from the perhaps natural—that is, cyclical—enlargement of the polar ozone hole?[29]) At least some of these alternating cataclysms were directly associated with the roughly 26,000-year Annus Magnus that we have already described. These same traditions are to be found scattered throughout the world.

Like many other nations, the Egyptians founded their ideas upon the gradual debasement of man from an original state of innocence (which also appears as a cyclical phenomenon) until the gods are no longer willing to put up with humanity's continuing degeneracy and so cyclically bring each such race to an end through the means of either a fiery or a watery cataclysm. Yet the latter idea is perhaps more than just mere myth. The gods themselves, being part of the universal process (as Pythagoras later confirmed in his teachings), were just as liable to face equivalent disruptions in their own greater cycle. In addition, the appearance of a new human race on Earth is (according to ancient mystical tradition) always traditionally heralded by major cataclysms—an issue to which we shall return in later chapters.

H. P. Blavatsky, in *The Secret Doctrine,*[30] relates the Greek mythic tradition in which Astraea (the goddess of justice and, as a daughter of Atlas, also one of the Pleiades) is depicted as the last deity to forsake the Earth. However, as soon as Zeus has taken the perfected man, Ganymede, off to the heavens (where he becomes the zodiacal constellation Aquarius), Astraea is forcibly thrown back down to Earth again and, in her landing, is described in the myth as "falling on her head."

Now, there is a deep, multifaceted allegory in this story and it is worthwhile pursuing because it helps us to understand the climatic exigencies associated with the Sidereal Year. That is because the time at which the gods were said to cyclically forsake the Earth and return to the heavens supposedly coincided with the moment when the ecliptic had become parallel with the meridian. As a direct result, part of the Zodiac then appeared to descend from the North Pole to the north horizon, this involving Aldebaran (the "Eye of the Bull" of Taurus—representing Zeus) following or "chasing" the Pleiades, while accompanied by the Hyades (known as the rain or deluge constellation). Apparently, according to Blavatsky, Aldebaran was, 40,000 years ago, in conjunction with the Sun, since when, she says, there has been a retrograde motion of the equator.[31] However, when Aldebaran crossed the ecliptic, the cyclical deluge of the Sidereal Year was said to be imminent. Aldebaran, according to the same source, appears to have been in conjunction with the vernal equinoctial point some 31,000 years ago.

How Could Ancient Mankind Possess Such Knowledge?

In the face of prehistoric mankind achieving such "scientific" recognitions as the 26,000-year sidereal cycle and knowledge of the associated climatic effects generated at specific points within it (even if described in symbolic language), can we really avoid the conclusion that the Ancients must have had a highly developed science and well-documented history far antedating anything we might currently imagine on the basis of our own civilization's limited perceptions and experience? To recognize such events as cyclical phenomena necessitates a continuous historical record or memory going back over several such cycles. That in turn seems to lend additional support to our theory that intelligent mankind has to be far, far older than is currently believed possible. However, as we progress through our investigations, it will become clear that cyclical cataclysms were not the primary focus of ancient Egyptian fascination with the cosmos.

Finally, we come to the question of Man himself and his relationship in evolutionary terms to these great cycles of 26,000 and 230 million years. While this topic is dealt with in more detail in chapters 3 and 4, it might be useful to make the following introductory remarks here by way of preview.

All the ancient religions and philosophical cultures regarded the individual, in his inner nature, as a divine being—literally, the son of a god, or, rather, of the One God—as we have already noted. Hence, seeing the universe in terms of a hierarchy of expression and therefore of unfoldment from a primordially divine state, they took a very different view concerning his subsequent evolution to that of our modern scientist. Starting with the (not unreasonable) hypothesis that greater sidereal systems give birth to smaller ones—rather than the other way around—the Ancients saw the various kingdoms of Nature on our planet as being expressions of different sidereal parentage, notwithstanding some obviously shared biological characteristics that have encouraged our modern science of anthropology toward the mistaken conception of man being merely a more intelligent animal than the other mammals.

The very fact of something greater wishing or needing instinctively to express itself through the medium of something lesser than itself inevitably meant that Thought, or Mind, had to be fundamentally involved in the process, along with Desire. Therefore, they took the view, because the principle of Intelligence must preexist the phenomenon of an ordered form (that is, the manifest universe), that Divine Desire had to be what actually brought about objectivity itself. Hence the modus operandi of "creation ex nihilo," a concept with which our modern philosophers and theologians, even now, cannot come to terms. From this perception, however, it is but a short step to realizing that, in the eyes of the Ancients, there could be only One Life in the totality of the universe, with everything objectively manifesting within it as a partial expression of a Universal Intelligence imbued with a sense of Divine Order. This the Egyptians called Ma'at, the same as the Mahat of the ancient Hindus, both, however, regarding it as the principle of Cosmic Mind and its associated range of universal knowledge. Following on from this, then, everything manifest—whether as a god or a man or an insect—had to be part and parcel of a hierarchically organized expression of Intelligence, projected into objectivity by Divine Thought and thus evolving within the Divine Body. Hence, it also was that Universal Law became manifest.

Ancient Egyptian Views as to an Intelligent Order in the Universe

This brings us to the question of the relationship of the cosmic macrocosm and the terrestrial microcosm in the eyes of the ancient Egyptians. As we have already indicated, and as we shall amplify in later chapters, they saw everything in the universe following a single, repetitive pattern based upon numerical (and numerological) order. It was this, inherently, that underlay the principle of hierarchy and the need for it in maintaining perfect harmony throughout the cosmos. Thus it was that man could identify his own higher (spiritual) nature with the gods Osiris and Isis and, through them proportionately, with his divine nature as a literal child of Ra himself. However, mankind as a whole was regarded in a parallel manner, as a microcosm of its own cosmic Osiris, and, in the Pyramid Texts, we find that the cosmic Osiris refers to his "bones" being made of "celestial metal."[32] This is somewhat simplistically translated by Egyptologists as "meteoric iron," given that the gigantic "metal plate" separating Heaven and the Underworld is described as being of the same substance.[33] It is in fact a metaphor, the key to the understanding of which is to be found in the description (in the Indian tradition) of the human etheric "double" (the Indian *linga sarira* being the same as the Egyptian *ka*—see appendix G) that comprised a spider's web of what were called *nadis*. These—as is now commonly understood among New Age practitioners of the healing arts—involve a network of "etheric" energies operating like

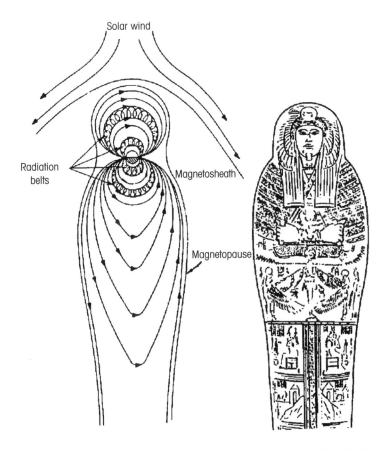

To some, this association might seem so very extraordinary as to be literally beyond belief. However, there is no doubting either the closely matching shapes or the fact that both the mummy and the magnetopause represent the *ka* of their respective inertial "energy-bodies." In addition, the ovoid "magneto-sheath" (the "crystal sphere") that encapsulates the planetary magnetosphere readily corresponds with the "astral soul" sheath that surrounds and is also parent to the human *ka*, the latter otherwise being commonly referred to as the (etheric) "double." These issues will be expanded upon in later chapters; but they are mentioned at this point in order to highlight the similitude of macrocosmic-microcosmic parallels that the Egyptians saw as part and parcel of their philosophy of life.

FIGURE 1.7. THE EARTH'S MAGNETOSPHERE AND THE MUMMY COFFIN

light filaments connecting the many major and minor chakras, or psychophysical force centers. However, the "cosmic chakras" were seen as literal stars.[34]

According to the occult philosophy of the Indians, however, this "double" comes into existence before the dense physical body—which is itself merely the accretion of denser matter around the (apparently electromagnetic) web.[35] The way in which the web itself "grows" from a single, original chakra is of interest to us here because it implies the idea of an intelligent structure emanating from a single source—and that is precisely the way in which all the ancient creation "myths" describe their genesis. It is also comparable in some ways to the modern concept of planetary genesis within our own solar system.

The Starry Heavens as Homes of the Gods

As we shall see later on, the Egyptians were very familiar with the system of chakras and various psycho-spiritual "bodies," which they incorporated into their system of thought on a large scale.[36] They also regarded these same principles and organic functions as being found in the nature of their gods in precisely the same sequence as in that of man. Thus the universe—and the Milky Way in particular—was regarded by them as the location of the "drowned body" of the cosmic Osiris. Consequently, those associations between particular constellations that we find in the hieroglyphic texts were believed to involve actual (cyclic) movement of psycho-spiritual light energy in the form of hierarchies of "gods"—the massed archangelic ranks of the creative Demiurge.

The inevitable effect of this perception was that the stars themselves—seen as expressions of Intelligence as Light—came to be regarded as the homes of literal "gods"—the Kabiri of the Babylonians and the Elohim of the Old Testament. Their subsequent attention (post Creation) could, however, be invoked only by ensuring, first of all, that whatever humanity created or built in its culture perfectly reflected the principle of Divine Order. Accuracy and symmetry in ancient Egyptian culture were thus absolutely *de rigueur* in every aspect imaginable.

Man as a God in the Making

The very capacity to design and create like the gods, using the same principle of Intelligence, allied to the highest possible sense of administrative organization, enabled a man to see that he was himself—at least, in his highest inner nature—literally the son of a god and therefore also a god in the making. He, being as yet but the imperfect expression of his own Divine Self, had to create and follow a cultural system that would so imbue him with the sense of Divine Order and Purpose that he would ultimately become, in full self-consciousness, that which he already innately knew himself to be. In this manner, the "hidden" god within would become objectively manifest—an idea incorporated (although rather distortedly) into the Christian religion in the form of the "Kingdom of Heaven on Earth." As we shall see later on, this ideal forms the very basis of the Osirian Mystery Tradition. So, it is well worth reiterating here the fact that objective humanity was regarded by the Ancients as "created by thought" and was thus only a very small and partial expression of the Divine Nature. As the human being was, in their view, but a projection of his own Divine Self, so our solar system of planets—individually and collectively—had to be seen as the partial expression of hugely more advanced intelligences (hierarchies of gods) within whose consciousness they existed.

This original basis of the true pantheism is something that has been little recognized by modern scholars—particularly those involved with the study of ancient Egypt, notwithstanding the many lucid explanations provided by the Egyptian high priest Abammon in Iamblichus.[37] Thus it was that, by recognizing (through astronomy and astrology) the natural order of divine cycles, the ancient Egyptians clearly regarded themselves as being able to predict the future and interpret scientifically what they foresaw. In the same way, they were able to work historically backward in time, aligning the periods of the celestial equinoxes and solstices to periods when they believed highly evolved intelligences (gods, or Kabiri[38]) actually appeared on Earth—as we shall further outline in chapter 8—provided that the correct invocative rites were followed. Such rites were, of course, solely the prerogative of the priesthood until the time of the later (and by then spiritually corrupted) pharaonic dynasties.

It was because of their understanding of the divine origin of everything on the Earth and of its hierarchically organized place in the scheme of things that science and art—the very foundations of all objective culture—originally came to exist and be practiced in Egypt, always with prior dedication to a particular divinity. This fact has been progressively overlooked for thousands of years by subsequent civilizations and priesthoods (succeeded by our modern generations of scholars and scientists) willing to pay tribute to the form of ritual and appearance rather than to the spirit behind the action.

For such reasons, the wise and prophetic words of Hermes-Thoth to his disciple Asclepius, describing the raison d'être of Egypt and telling of its future downfall (and long distant redemption by the gods), have often been erroneously treated by scholars as a mere narrative myth:

> Did you not know, O Asclepius, that Egypt is an image of Heaven, or, to speak more exactly, [that] in Egypt all the operations of the powers which rule and work in Heaven have been transferred to [this] Earth below? Nay, it should rather be said that the whole kosmos dwells in this our land as in its sanctuary. . . . This land, which once was holy, a land which loved the gods and wherein alone, in reward for her devotion, the gods deigned to sojourn upon Earth; a land which was the teacher of mankind in holiness and piety . . . O Egypt, Egypt, of thy religion nothing will remain but an empty tale which thine own children in times to come will not believe; nothing will be left but graven words and only the stones will tell of thy piety.[39]

However, we shall pick up such issues individually as our story unfolds, once we have dealt (in the next three chapters) with certain other fundamental issues.

So, having thus set the cosmic scene, as it were, in chapter 2 we shall come right down to earth and look at the way in which the land of Egypt itself came into existence and how cyclical cataclysms shaped it and encouraged its subsequent occupation in ancient times.

TWO

GEOLOGICAL, GEOGRAPHICAL, AND CLIMATOLOGICAL ISSUES

The famous Atlantis exists no longer, but we can hardly doubt that it did once, for Marcellus, who wrote a history of Ethiopian affairs, says that such and so great an island once existed and this is evidenced by those who compose histories relative to the external sea. For they relate that in this time there were seven islands in the Atlantic Sea, sacred to Proserpine; and beside these, three of immense magnitude sacred to Pluto, Jupiter and Neptune. And besides this, the inhabitants of the last island (Poseidonis) preserved the memory of the prodigious magnitude of the Atlantic island as related by their ancestors and of its governing for many periods all the islands in the Atlantic Sea. From this isle one may pass to other large islands beyond, which are not far from the firm land near which is the true sea.

—PROCLUS (FIFTH CENTURY B.C.)

Because of his anxiety that no Atlantean continent of the size needed to produce a highly evolved civilization (of the sort suggested by Plato and others) could possibly have existed in the area of the mid-Atlantic Ocean during the last one million years, Graham Hancock opts for the idea that the only possible alternative must be the still existing continent of Antarctica.[1] In his book, *Fingerprints of the Gods,* he then develops the idea—through the concept of "earth crust displacement"—that Antarctica had actually shifted its location some 2,000 miles south of an original position nearer the Tropics, to where it now sits, over the South Pole.[2]

However, as we shall outline in this chapter, various seriously erroneous assumptions have been made by scholars and scientists alike concerning Plato's island, which, as the quote from the *Timaeus* clearly indicates, was merely the last (and probably one of the smallest, being about the size of Ireland) of a much larger group of Atlantic islands. That fact was obviously well known to the Ancients on a broad geographical scale because even the Puranas (epic histories) of the Indian subcontinent mention it (referring to it as Atala in a derogatory sense—meaning "place of sin") and locate it "on the seventh zone"[3]—which, since each "zone" in their system comprised four degrees of latitude from the equator, is found between 24 degrees and 28 degrees north latitude—that is, on the Tropic of Cancer.

That not only the last island of Atlantis, spoken of by Plato, but a large continent, first divided and then broken later on into seven peninsulas and islands (called dwipas) preceded Europe is sure. . . . The claim is corroborated by the Indian Puranas, Greek writers and Asiatic, Persian and Mahommedan traditions; (Colonel) Wilford shows this clearly (see Vol. VIII, X and XI of "Asiatic Researches"). And his facts and quotations from the Puranas give direct and conclusive evidence that the Aryan Hindus and other nations were earlier navigators than the Phoenicians, who are now credited with having been the first seamen that appeared in post-diluvian times.[4]

This comment was made by H. P. Blavatsky in her book *The Secret Doctrine*, in which she also describes how, by the time of the last really major world cataclysms (which she put at 850,000 years ago), the original part of the Atlantic continent—mentioned as stretching from South America (Bolivia/Peru) to West Africa in the south and from Newfoundland almost to France in the north—had already been reduced by progressive cataclysms to two large main islands. These were Ruta, in the south (in the area of the Tropics), and Daitya in the north (generally reckoned to be the origin of the Azores). Apart from these, there were several other much smaller islands and island chains.[5]

Of the two larger islands, however—so she relates—Ruta was completely (albeit progressively) destroyed by the geomagnetic shift that commenced around 850,000 years ago. Daitya, on the other hand, seems to have survived until about 270,000 years ago, when it was also destroyed by some series of unspecified cataclysms that left only the desiccated island chain of the Azores as a testament to its previous existence.[6] After this, so it would appear from Blavatsky's descriptions, the only remaining bastion of truly Atlantean civilization was to be found on the island of Poseidonis (Plato's Atlantis), clearly somewhere in the area of Madeira or the Canary Islands, just off the northwest African coast.

Cartographic Evidence of the Ancient World

Now, while this chapter is specifically concerned with the geographical appearance of Egypt, we shall endeavor to show simultaneously where various wholesale flaws exist in the theory that a giant, mid-Atlantic continent could not possibly have existed. Not least of these lies in the far too brief time scales used by geologists and others in considering the whole question. However, before we move on to such issues, we should mention the fact that Hancock has based part of his theory on some very ancient maps that, in themselves, are of great interest, notwithstanding our disagreement with some of his theories concerning cataclysms and crustal displacement. These maps were produced during the fourteenth to the eighteenth centuries, but it seems that they were merely copies of much earlier maps drawn up by ancient civilizations, long preceding even the Greeks and Romans. Among the medieval maps drawn from such sources are those attributed to Piri Re'is (1513), Oronteus Finaeus (1531), Mercator (1569) and Philippe Buache (1737). All these (and others) are described in fascinating detail in *Maps of the Ancient Sea Kings*, by Charles Hapgood, who suggested, with compelling reasoning, that such maps were themselves derived from far older source maps, originally produced (through the use of spherical trigonometry) by an obviously highly advanced civilization well over 6,000 years ago.[7] He also goes so far as to state that, from evidence of such facts as the maps showing Antarctica and the North Polar regions having been surveyed at a time when little or no glaciation existed there, one must also draw the inevitable conclusion that at some immensely remote period of ancient history, far beyond the time of our earliest recorded civilizations, there existed a worldwide sea-trading civilization or culture of some sort.

The fact that these maps show the polar regions as having (at least temporarily) experienced nonglacial conditions and climate otherwise also tends, we suggest, to support our view that such phenomena are entirely cyclical in nature. However, despite the proven prehistoric existence of a benevolent climate and many subtropical animal species in the area of Alaska and northern Siberia, Professor Hapgood tends to dismiss the claims of the Indian Brahman tradition that mankind's ancestors came from a great continent far to the north of the Himalayas.[8]

He (strangely without indicating why) also takes the view that the Brahmans most probably misinterpreted their own history, which, he thought, must have been referring to Antarctica, as this is the only remaining polar continent. However, the ancient records of the Brahmans speak of a horseshoe-shaped northern continent (Sveta Dwipa), originally inhabited by giants, which clearly incorporated northern Siberia, Spitzbergen, and Norway at a time when much of central and southern Russia from the Urals to the Gobi Desert was under water.

In his very detailed analysis of the Piri Re'is and other maps, Professor Hapgood takes the view that the cartographers responsible for drawing them up—through inaccurate transposition of cartographic information from even more ancient source maps—left out certain areas of the western Atlantic coastline and also otherwise managed to distort the north–south orientation of certain landmasses (see fig. 2.1). Whether or not this is so— and he argues a very reasoned case—it is quite clear that there were once far more island landmasses in the Atlantic Ocean than there are today.

As Professor Hapgood otherwise also confirmed from his researches in connection with the mid-Atlantic Ridge that island chains along it (such as the Azores) have experienced considerable subsidence (some even disappearing below sea level as a result), it is not unreasonable to speculate that all the island chains could originally have belonged to much larger landmasses—perhaps even a single continent that subsequently broke up, as many ancient traditions actually suggest.[9]

Ill-Founded Arguments against a Mid-Atlantic Continent

Clearly, the whole oceanic area has been subject to widespread geological and geographical changes as a result of often violent movement of the earth's crust. The fact that Lake Titicaca in Bolivia is now some 12,500 feet above sea level, where once the sea flowed into it, is alone sufficient proof of that.[10] But it is by no means an isolated piece of evidence. In addition, the hugely powerful ocean currents sweeping back and forth, up and down, and across the Atlantic over a period of tens of thousands of years would cause immense natural erosion of any earthquake- or volcano-fragmented island coastlines, thereby adding to the reductive effect of sea floor shift and subsidence. Quite apart from these influences, it has

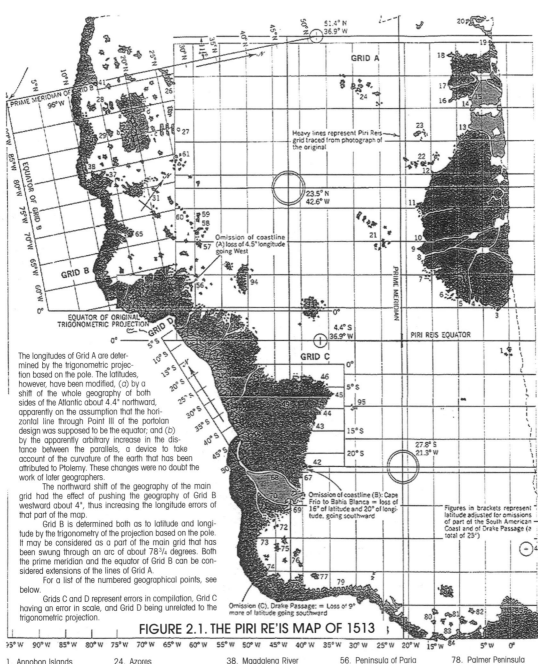

51.4° N
36.9° W

GRID A

Heavy lines represent Piri Reis grid traced from photograph of the original

PRIME MERIDIAN OF GRID B
95° W

23.5° N
42.6° W

Omission of coastline (A) loss of 4.5° longitude going West

GRID B

EQUATOR OF GRID B

PRIME MERIDIAN

EQUATOR OF ORIGINAL TRIGONOMETRIC PROJECTION

GRID D

0°

4.4° S
36.9° W

PIRI REIS EQUATOR

GRID C

The longitudes of Grid A are determined by the trigonometric projection based on the pole. The latitudes, however, have been modified, (*a*) by a shift of the whole geography of both sides of the Atlantic about 4.4" northward, apparently on the assumption that the horizontal line through Point III of the portolan design was supposed to be the equator; and (*b*) by the apparently arbitrary increase in the distance between the parallels, a device to take account of the curvature of the earth that has been attributed to Ptolemy. These changes were no doubt the work of later geographers.

The northward shift of the geography of the main grid had the effect of pushing the geography of Grid B westward about 4", thus increasing the longitude errors of that part of the map.

Grid B is determined both as to latitude and longitude by the trigonometry of the projection based on the pole. It may be considered as a part of the main grid that has been swung through an arc of about 78¾ degrees. Both the prime meridian and the equator of Grid B can be considered extensions of the lines of Grid A.

For a list of the numbered geographical points, see below.

Grids C and D represent errors in compilation, Grid C having an error in scale, and Grid D being unrelated to the trigonometric projection.

27.8° S
21.3° W

Omission of coastline (B): Cape Frio to Bahia Blanca = loss of 16° of latitude and 20° of longitude, going southward

Figures in brackets represent latitude adjusted for omissions of part of the South American Coast and of Drake Passage (a total of 25°)

Omission (C), Drake Passage: = Loss of 9° more of latitude going southward

FIGURE 2.1. THE PIRI RE'IS MAP OF 1513

95° W 90° W 85° W 80° W 75° W 70° W 65° W 60° W 55° W 50° W 45° W 40° W 35° W 30° W 25° W 20° W 15° W 10° W 5° W 0°

1. Annobon Islands
2. Cavally River
3. Cape Palmas
4. St. Paul River
5. Mano River
6. Freetown
7. Bilagos Islands
8. Gambia River
9. Dakar
10. Senegal River
11. Cape Blanc
12. Cape Juby
13. Sebu river
14. Gibraltar
15. Guadalquivir River
16. Cape St. Vincent
17. Tagus River
18. Cape Finisterre
19. Gironde River
20. Brest
21. Cape Verde Islands
22. Canary Islands
23. Madeira Islands

24. Azores
25. Cuba
   (a) Gulf of Guacanayabo
   (b) Guantanamo Bay
   (c) Bahia de Nipe
   (d) Bahia de la Gloria
   (e) Camaguay Mountains
   (f) Sierra Maestra Mountains
26. Andros Island
27. San Salvador (Watling)
28. Isle of Pines
29. Jamaica
30. Hispaniola (Santo Domingo, Haiti)
31. Puerto Rico
32. Rio Moroni
33. Corantijn River
34. Essequibo River
35. Orinoco River
36. Gulf of Venezuela
37. Pt. Galinas

38. Magdalena River
39. Gulf of Uraba
40. Honduras (Cape Fracias a Dios)
41. Yucatan
42. Cape Frio
43. Salvador
44. San Francisco River
45. Recife (Pernambuco)
46. Cape Sao Rocque
47. Rio Parahyba
48. Bahia Sao Marcos
49. Serras de Gurupi, de Desordam, de Negro
50. The Amazon (No. 1)
51. The Amazon (No. 2) Para River
52. The Amazon (No. 2) western mouth
53. Island of Marajo
54. Essequibo (Demarara) River
55. Mouths of the Orinoco

56. Peninsula of Paria
57. Martinique
58. Guadaloupe
59. Antigua
60. Leeward Islands
61. Virgin Islands
62. Gulf of Venezuela
63. Magdalena River
64. Atrato River
65. Honduras (Cape Gracias a Dios))
66. Yucatan
67. Bahia Blanca
68. Rio Colorado
69. Gulf of San Mathias
70. Rio Negro (Argentina)
71. Rio Chubua
72. Gulf of San Gorge
73. Bahia Grande
74. Cape San Diego
75. Falkland Islands
76. South Shetlands
77. South Georgia

78. Palmer Peninsula
79. Weddell Sea
80. Mt. Ropke, Queen Maud
81. Regula Range
82. Muhlig-Hofmann Mountains
83. Penck Trough
84. Neumeyer Escarpment
85. Drygalski Mountains
86. Vorposten Peak
87. Boreas, Passat Numat
90a, b. Andes Mountains
91. Peninsula of Paracas
92. Valparaiso
93. Equatorial Island
94. "Antillia" according to Piri Re'is
95. Fernando da Naronha

only recently been proved (from marine surveys of the seabed carried out by the United States Navy) that the floors of the oceans are literally covered with debris from massive submarine landslides, often several miles in length.[11] Thus, the assertion by some geologists that the present configuration of the Atlantic seabed "conclusively" shows that no such continent as Atlantis could ever have existed can hardly be regarded as sound. We would have to ask these geologists, "What period of time have you assumed in your calculations?" If it's merely some 11,000 years based upon Plato's comments as to the last remaining Atlantean island of Poseidonis, rather than the many tens of thousands of years implied by Hancock's (and others') theories, some considerable rethinking will be necessary. In addition to these general issues, a number of other highly significant points need to be mentioned in relation to the various maps cited. Some of these are most important in relation to both the history of the Middle East and the question of the location of fabled Atlantis itself.

First of all, we propose to concentrate on the Piri Re'is map because it appears so self-evidently based upon far more ancient data, and it also provides far greater detail in relation to the mid-Atlantic area than any other. Before we get down to details, however, a few overall comments may be in order with regard to the question of general proportion and coastline shown on the Piri Re'is map.

The Piri Re'is Map's Coastal Outlines

The initial reaction to the map must be that the relative locations (in terms of longitude and latitude) and the distances apart of Africa and South America—as also those of Brittany and the Iberian Peninsula—look to be astonishingly accurate, bearing in mind that neither longitude, per se, nor the necessary modern measuring technology was extant until some two hundred years later (that is, after A.D. 1513). The location or shape of various island groups—such as the Azores, Madeira, Canaries, Cape Verde Islands, the Leeward and Windward Islands—plus many of the larger rivers on each continent also indicate that the original cartographers had a very clear idea of both direction and distance.

While the northeastern coast of South America and the western coast of Africa are clearly recognizable by their contemporary shapes, the eastern coastlines of ancient Central America and the southern United States appear very different from the way they do today. A great many islands and island groups are shown located in today's Gulf of Mexico and the Atlantic itself either where none currently exists or where many of those that do exist possess distinctly different shapes (through natural erosion of coastline). In addition, the central landmass of what is now the Gulf of Mexico at some prehistoric time evidently formed or was attached to a much larger, single continental landmass. Thus, as Professor Hapgood has shown, there can be little dispute that much of the detailed cartography shows that the area of the Atlantic Ocean in general had been extensively surveyed in very ancient times, long before either Columbus or the Vikings "discovered" the Americas. However, the issue of what was happening on the western side of the Atlantic is purely incidental to the subject matter of this book, which concerns itself with ancient Egypt and Plato's Atlantis, which he quite categorically locates at no great distance somewhere west of the Pillars of Hercules (the modern Strait of Gibraltar).

The Geography of the Western Mediterranean and Atlas Area

From that point of view, the Piri Re'is map shows something else of dramatic importance in relation to the shape of the Mediterranean Sea with which, logically speaking, the Middle Eastern cartographers should have been extremely familiar. On that map (see fig. 2.1), the western Mediterranean is shown as being of tiny size compared to what exists today. We are therefore forced to the conclusion—given the apparent accuracy of other areas of the map—that it does indeed represent the correct coastal outline for the area at the time that the original source map was drawn up. Clearly, therefore, the changes that we see evident in today's map confirm that areas of both coastlines have subsequently disappeared through cataclysm—probably earthquake. In addition, the arcs of the Madeira and Canary Island chains suggest that they once formed the northern and southern perimeters of a single, roughly circular or oval landmass, approximately the size of Ireland.[12] Might this then be the probable location of Poseidonis? But if it is, then the Piri Re'is source map must have been drawn up after 9560 B.C. However, that in turn suggests that some of the other maps mentioned by us must have been based upon source maps of even greater age, because of their details in relation to nonglacial polar areas.

Now, we might also ask, What of today's eastern Mediterranean in those ancient days? Was it then an inland sea or were there continuous areas of landmass within it, above sea level? The answers to such questions have huge repercussions both on the question of the various Mediterranean civilizations known to modern archaeologists and anthropologists and also on the whole issue of mankind's evolutionary development (as seen by contemporary science) throughout the area from a supposedly primitive "hunter-gatherer" state, a mere 5,000 to 7,000 years ago.

FIGURE 2.2. RELIEF MAP OF THE ATLANTIC SEABED SHOWING, *CIRCLED*, THE POSSIBLE LOCATION OF POSEIDONIS

When we look at a relief map of the eastern Mediterranean, showing the geological contours as they are today, both above and below sea level (see fig. 2.2), it becomes clear that the Mediterranean has two main basins. The eastern one extends from Sicily to Turkey, Lebanon, and Israel, while the western one extends from Sicily to the Strait of Gibraltar. We also know that the two areas were once physically separated by the Italian Apennine range extending all the way down from the Alps, through Sicily, and connecting up with the Atlas Mountains in what is today Tunisia.[13] At that time, the western Mediterranean was occupied by a large landmass of crystalline rock called Tyrrhenia by geologists. This is believed by them to have progressively sunk below sea level from the beginning of the Quaternary Epoch, commencing some 1.6 million years ago.[14] That, in turn, was probably how the eastern and western Mediterranean first became united, and it seems not unlikely that the originating cause of the associated and much prolonged cataclysm was yet another major shift in the earth's geomagnetic polarity, similar to the later one already mentioned as commencing about 850,000 years ago.[15]

Prior to these events, most of present western Europe north of the Alps and Pyrenees was covered by open sea. Similarly, the whole of the Sahara Desert area appears at least once (prior to 1.6 million years ago) to have been covered by an eastern extension of the Atlantic. However, the Sahara has also changed its appearance very markedly over the last 1.6 million years, for, following the commencement of the Quaternary, the Ahaggar and Tibesti Mountain plateaus were raised in the central Sahara. The East African Rift Valley began to form at around the same time (reaching its present shape about 10,000 to 15,000 years ago) and later emanated the Nile Valley fault as a spur.[16] The raising of the Ahaggar and Tibesti undoubtedly isolated the eastern portion of the Saharan sea (then already united with the eastern Mediterranean) to form the Tethys Sea, the African continental part of which eventually evaporated, leaving the united Mediterranean to its own devices. The western Sahara must itself also have risen progressively above sea level (or have been sufficiently shallow to evaporate away as well) only subsequent to the beginning of the Quaternary, thereby connecting western and northwestern Africa by dry land.

If all this is reasonably accurate, it explains why the calmer eastern reaches of the northeastern Saharan sea area—which subsequently became the Western Desert of Egypt, extending into modern Libya—comprises (above the underlying rock strata) a thick, stratified limestone sheet, derived from the fossilized bodies of an imponderable number of sea creatures. This also is an important feature associated with Egyptian culture, as we shall see.

Now, the Piri Re'is map seems to indicate that the then current Mediterranean basin was contained at the eastern end either by the Apennines running down through Italy and Sicily and across to Tunisia or by a north–south mountain range running through Corsica and Sardinia—again connecting the Alps and the Atlas Mountains. Either alternative seems possible, although the latter looks more probable given the coastlines described by Piri Re'is. Whichever of these two alternatives applies, there can be no doubt that only subsequent and very substantial geological movement in the area could have caused such major changes—and that extensive climatic variations would have inevitably resulted. But the questions arising out of all this remain, When did it all happen? And second, How old is the data on which the Piri Re'is map itself is based?

Reassessing the Nature of Cataclysms

In fact, notwithstanding the vast power of earthquakes and volcanic activity, no really extensive structural changes seem to occur in Nature at any great speed. They seem rather to evolve progressively, cyclically reaching points of great critical tension that, once released into the local environment, allow a general equilibrium to be fairly quickly and naturally restored. This we can verify from scientific data related to cataclysms over the last two hundred to three hundred years. Consequently, the source map on which Piri Re'is based his map has to be many thousands of years old. Why it should then be taken for granted that the major structural changes to which our world is prone must supposedly happen as a result of single great cataclysms (by, for example, asteroids falling from space, or comets passing by and disturbing the earth's atmosphere) is a matter of conjecture. Perhaps it is that urban disasters resulting from volcanic or earthquake action—such as those at Pompeii, Thera, San Francisco, and Kobe—involving the death of large concentrations of human population induce psychological exaggeration. When such natural phenomena occur away from human habitation—even though of comparable or even greater magnitude—we pay very little attention.

As we have already suggested that certain extended periods in history possibly saw considerable increases in geothermal energy, leading to the sort of cataclysms (in progressive series) as just described, we perhaps need to look back at the local geological record itself to speculate about the question of changes in the shape and extent of the Mediterranean Sea. This is something we can certainly do with the assistance of modern science in the fields of paleomagnetism, archaeology, and geology itself.

For a start, the last major change in the earth's magnetic field is now generally accepted by science as having occurred some 780,000 to 800,000 years ago.[17] Archaeologists meanwhile tell us that Paleolithic mankind suddenly started to appear in increasing numbers in southern Europe (France, Spain, and Portugal) around 700,000 to 800,000 years ago.[18] The Alps appear finally to have ceased rising to their present height during the early Quaternary,[19] although the Rock of Gibraltar seems to have risen and fallen several hundred feet on a number of subsequent occasions. Geologists, meanwhile, say that the Ice Age began to withdraw about one million years ago, although there have been many interim advances and withdrawals of glaciers since then.[20] During these latter periods, however, it seems as though there have been no major paleomagnetic changes of quite comparable magnitude, although local cataclysms have undoubtedly continued to recur throughout the whole area. We are therefore drawn to the conclusion that the far-reaching topographical changes that seem to have occurred in the western and the central Mediterranean between, say, 750,000 and 1.6 million years ago created a major incentive toward northward migration of humans hitherto living in northwest Africa or islands off its coasts. Now, the only three possible incentives for such disruption might be defined as follows:

1. That existing southern lands became less habitable or otherwise less attractive—probably due to either flooding or drought;
2. That the climate began to improve progressively northward, thereby extending the food crop availability;
3. That new lands began to appear in the north, and/or that a land bridge formed between northwest Africa and central west Africa where none existed before.

The Advent of Human Civilization

This, however, brings us to the question of the development of civilization. Could it have existed in some or other form before the northward migration of these early "Paleolithic" humans, and, if so, where—and why have no clearly obvious traces of such a civilization been found, even though archaeologists now confirm Paleolithic mankind as having already occupied parts of southwestern Europe well over 1.25 million years ago?[21] The answers to such questions—as adduced by modern science—are (by its own admission) of a largely deductive and speculative nature, based upon a very limited amount of archaeological and paleontological evidence, strung together with large gaps in it and often very tentatively secured. Science obviously cannot conclusively tell us whether any ancient civilizations once existed in the central Mediterranean area, where the sea has plied its rolling motion for tens of thousands of years, effectively drowning and simultaneously eroding any possible trace of all associated evidence.

It does seem from what we have suggested that the central and western areas of the Mediterranean basin could well have been even quite widely populated at some ancient time when the Atlantic was still being held back by the then connected Italian Apennines and Atlas Mountains, as well as at Gibraltar. Whether it then filled up gradually as a result of seepage from the eastern Mediterranean, or adjacent rivers draining or glaciers melting into it from the north, or whether submersion happened directly through cataclysms is, however, largely irrelevant to our own immediate considerations. What is suggested by the various geomagnetic phenomena of between 1.6 million and 800,000 years ago is that the basin of the eastern Mediterranean, until then connected with the Atlantic (which still covered the Sahara Desert), gradually became landlocked from the south while being enlarged from the west. As primary civilizations always tend to be sited on seacoasts, or close to them on a major river, any such civilizations could well have been wiped out by the flooding of the western Mediterranean caused through a breach in the Italian Apennine–Atlas Mountain barrier, or by the Mediterranean seabed itself sinking, or by a combination of these.

When we look closely at the present land configuration of the eastern Mediterranean, it is clear that the Peloponnesian peninsula of southern Greece was once connected to Crete and Crete to modern Turkey. In addition, the intervening northern mass of modern Greek islands in the Aegean (the Cyclades), being at the time also part of one single landmass, meant that Greece and Asia Minor were then entirely united as part of one continent which had the Black Sea—then part of a giant inland freshwater sea—on its northern perimeter. The Aegean seabed—currently only around one hundred meters deep—has itself been progressively sinking for thousands of years (perhaps as occurred with Tyrrhenia?). Thus, more and more Greek coastline is submerged every year. Farther south, at some time or another, the landmass of Egypt's western desert seems either to have risen above the former sea level or, as the polar ice caps began to re-form, to have become visible through evaporation of its previous water covering. Once again, one is forced to ask, But when did this occur?—realizing that it too must have been a reasonably progressive phenomenon, even if originally triggered by cataclysms occurring in adjacent global areas.

Now, if the last major structural changes in the general Mediterranean area (and elsewhere) began some 850,000 years ago, the last great ice age having already started to decline somewhat prior to that, it is quite clear that civilization as we know it could not possibly have continued throughout the area affected in an uninterrupted state. Major geological change always brings climatological change in its wake, the latter taking some time to settle down to a stable equilibrium in which a continuity of human culture and civilization can establish itself and flourish. It is thus not at all surprising that the urban civilizations of Mesopotamia and Egypt—believed by archaeologists to be the earliest possible—appear to be of quite recent origin, but we hope to show that even they are far older than is currently believed.

The Cataclysm Affecting Poseidonis

At this point we should perhaps mention that the sinking of Poseidonis (Plato's Atlantis) some 11,500 years ago is unlikely to have been in itself the original cause of the Mediterranean becoming flooded. On the basis that Poseidonis was located in the area of the Canary Islands and Madeira (the likeliest continuing candidate), the tidal force generated could not have contained enough power to cause such damage on its own, although it may well have caused a widening breach of an existing channel at Gibraltar. However, a major geological fault line running east–west through the Strait of Gibraltar (see again fig. 2.2) could well have produced the necessary earthquake activity to achieve such damage. The Mediterranean Atlas area is still, today, very prone to such activity.

Certainly, there are many historic traditions of the Gibraltar channel having apparently become so clogged with huge deposits of mud and other sedimentary debris just below the surface as to make the passage unnavigable for some considerable time afterward.[22] That in itself must have caused immense economic and probably sociopolitical ramifications throughout the western Mediterranean at the very least, as a result of the disruption to existing trading relations with the Atlantic seaboard. Even today it is recognized that the seabed in this area is again rising and that, if it continues, the Mediterranean–Atlantic passage will once more become unnavigable, failing man's technological intervention. Why the island of Poseidonis itself should have sunk remains a matter for conjecture, although—if proved to be located where Madeira and the Canary Islands now lie—progressive earthquake and volcanic activity seem the most likely main causes. These islands were (only a short time ago, geologically speaking) originally connected as a single mass to that part of the northwest African mainland (the Mahgreb) which extends from the Spanish Sahara to the boundary of modern Tunisia and Libya. This whole area is a perpetually active geological fault zone, and it is known that the last major bout of volcanic disturbance affecting the islands took place between 10,000 and 12,000 years ago. It broke up large areas of the then existing landmass, leaving it under the sterile coat of lava and volcanic ash that can still be seen today.

If Plato's story and chronology were correct in suggesting that his Atlantis sank some 9,000 years before his own time (that is, about 11,500 years ago), the geological record would seem to support his case as to both location and period. That such major geological activity took place almost immediately in the wake of the celestial winter solstice, however, inevitably leaves one wondering to what extent the two are closely related.

Irrespective of this, the cataclysms must have had a very marked effect upon the geographical outlines of the western Mediterranean area as well as irrevocably altering the course of any local civilization and its culture—an issue that we shall take up in chapter 3.

Ice Ages and Pluvial Periods

We turn next to the question of cyclical ice ages and the phenomenon of glacier encroachment that results from them. That is because this too would have had a major effect upon the location and disposition of cultures and civilizations in northern Africa and southern Europe during the last several hundred thousand years in which we are particularly interested. Without going into a great deal of technical detail, it might first be useful to know something about the extent of glaciation generally, for reasons that should quickly become apparent.

First of all, the glaciation of the Northern Hemisphere at the height of the Ice Age is regarded as having moved almost as far south as the Mediterranean itself.[23] Curiously, however, although one might logically expect the North Polar ice sheet to have covered everything on its way south, there are many areas far to the north of the Mediterranean (for example, northern Siberia and the western mountains of China) that have never experienced such a glacial covering. Curiously also, in the Ruwenzori range of East Africa, we find major glaciers still expanding up to twenty years ago (right on the equator) even though the Ice Age finished declining, so we are told, 10,000 years ago. Why? Now, whether there is any connection between this and the fact that the polar glaciers are currently melting and receding is not yet clear. However, it is certain that it takes a long time for a landmass cleared of glaciation to gather a soil covering thick enough for vegetation to support any size and extent of human civilization. The same is not quite true in respect to many desert areas, for widespread parts of even the central Sahara region are known to have been occupied by agriculturally based communities between 14,000 and 6,000 years ago, when the climate was damp and an extensive river network existed.[24]

Africa Affected by Millennia of Heavy Rainfall

It is also known by geologists that eastern and northeastern Africa experienced a particularly intense period of prolonged rainy weather roughly between the tenth and fifth millennia B.C., when the level of Lake Victoria is known to have risen some three hundred feet.[25] The pattern of rainwater-led erosion to the Osireion at Abydos, the quarried enclosure of the Sphinx, and cliff edges around the Valley of the Kings at Thebes has recently been confirmed by the Egyptologist John Anthony West (in conjunction with the geologist Dr. Robert Schoch) as dating from this period,[26] and it may well be that there is a further correlation between the major floods and rising sea levels of the tenth millennium B.C. and Plato's Atlantean cataclysm of around 9500 B.C. Bearing in mind that—as we suggested at the end of the last chapter—this epoch seems to have coincided with the 26,000-year cyclical Deluge, it would perhaps not be surprising to find major climatic changes occurring in this area and affecting both river and sea levels.

It appears highly probable that the later civilizations of the Nile Valley thinned out quite dramatically as a result of this cyclically prolonged rainy period, which would have caused constant flooding and disruption.[27] It would seem, however, that if the adjacent deserts "bloomed" for some time during and even afterward, while lakes and streams continued in existence, there may well have been a considerable (although only temporary) expansion of Egyptian agricultural activity increasingly further away from the Nile Valley itself, with consequent effects upon the economy of the country. By around 6000 B.C., however, the effects may well have worn off as the wet weather ceased altogether. The areas to either side of the Nile Valley would then have gradually returned to their original desert state. The effect of that would have been to leave many communities in the peripheral areas increasingly destitute and eventually forced to abandon their villages.

The First Appearance of Egyptian Culture

The reason for making this point is that archaeologists regard 5,000 to 5,500 years ago as providing the start date for Egyptian civilization,[28] supposedly commencing with the dynasty of Menes-Narmer. The problem is that they seem to have taken the archaeological remains of abandoned villages from just before this time as indicating a commencement of the main culture, whereas these same remains could just as well be (and probably are) the last remains of a dead or dying subculture. That is indeed how this author would interpret the facts. Anyway, it is suggested that the theory certainly deserves to be considered on a par with the currently accepted one.

On this question of climatological issues, studies in the field over the last fifty years have shown that microclimates are remarkably fragile and susceptible to disruption (and even wholesale destruction) by the side effects of human urban adaptation or farming practice. The main culprit seems to be overintensive agricultural activity, causing deforestation and accelerated soil erosion. As urban civilization depends for its very existence upon agriculture, it would seem that venturing beyond a certain critical population mass and density inevitably (and probably irretrievably) leads to the "ghost town" phenomenon. However, the limestone ground of the Western Desert area and the sandstone of the Eastern Desert could within the given time frame only have developed sufficiently to support "subsistence (mainly livestock) farming," because no adequate depth of soil would have been deposited to allow much else.

Deprived of human care and maintenance, even properly constructed urban environments decline very rapidly as elemental Nature takes back her own territory through decay, erosion, and gradual disintegration into an original, homogeneous state, leaving no trace of any former existence. By way of an example, if London were to be systematically deprived of its main cultural anchor—the institutions of state—over a period of, say, three hundred years, its architectural organization would probably be in ruins within a further three hundred years, as progressively occurred in the case of Rome when its political center of gravity was divided by Constantine in A.D. 264. Within a further thousand years, London would undoubtedly revert to the variegated system of villages and village subcultures (that still underlie it today) existing as separate social entities even two hundred years ago. A further millennium or so would ensure that less of its architectural heritage remained extant than is today the case with that of Imperial Rome. Thus, if within the space of a mere 5,000 years very little trace can be found of many major civilizations and their associated or antecedent cultures, what can we say about the rise and fall of possible civilizations prior to 3000 B.C.? From what archaeologists have themselves discovered, one civilization tends very often to build (or farm) directly upon the very foundations or ruins of another (even though its main politico-economic center may change), thereby concealing its prior existence. Mere villages would tend to just disappear.

Archaeological Evidence

Bearing in mind the Nile's characteristic annual flooding, one could well imagine that the governments (and even the populace) of even quite early dynastic Egypt saw domestic homes—built of materials that would not necessarily last very long—as having far less significance than the massive, stone-built temples that were constructed to last for millennia, notwithstanding the annual floods. Why, then, should archaeologists expect to find extensive evidence of ruins or foundations as the sole or even main confirmation required to prove an even more ancient civilization? Where metal artifacts are concerned, rust and atmospheric corrosion will destroy steel extremely quickly within a few generations, while copper, bronze and iron will survive only if protected from dampness and condensation. Wood will, of course, decay even faster in normal circumstances. Is it then surprising that archaeologists have not found any metal artifacts of any really great age other than in the drier parts of the Middle East?[29] The Bronze Age (bronze being a hard, water-resistant alloy of copper and tin, sometimes incorporating lead or zinc) in the Middle East is thought to have commenced about 6,500 years ago.[30] Yet the dating of the supposedly later (2000 B.C.–1500 B.C.) Iron Age is itself undermined by examples of much earlier use of the metal.

Perhaps one of the most striking examples is that of the iron plate found in 1837 by R. J. Hill, in the southern "ventilation shaft" of the King's Chamber in the Great Pyramid, as shown in a photograph in *The Orion Mystery*.[31] As we shall see in a later chapter dealing with the age of the Pyramids and Sphinx at Giza, such examples indicate that the technology of ancient civilizations, forgotten by subsequent and degenerate cultures, existed far earlier than our contemporary scientists are yet willing to credit, notwithstanding queries over inexplicably symmetrical, small bore holes also found cut in solid granite.

One of the more notable things that recorded history tells us about human nature is that, if the focus and impetus of a culture (and its tendency toward innovation and research) are lost, or if they relocate themselves, the previous urban environment will not continue at its original optimum level of self-maintenance. It will decline, using increasingly lower forms of technology and socioeconomic systems to support itself. Consequently, the archaeological record would tend to highlight the latter state of affairs rather than the former one—which would itself have either entirely disintegrated or otherwise been modified and thus subsumed in a different guise. This phenomenon is well recognized in our own times. Yet, how often (if ever) do we hear of archaeologists and anthropologists making due allowance for it in their assumptions and chronological calculations? The fact is that degeneracy is a cyclical phenomenon and fact of life in all areas of Nature, without exception. That being the case, how can these contemporary scientists reasonably argue that the evolutionary process follows a more or less sequentially upward linear curve? The few facts mentioned here demonstrate clearly that it does not.

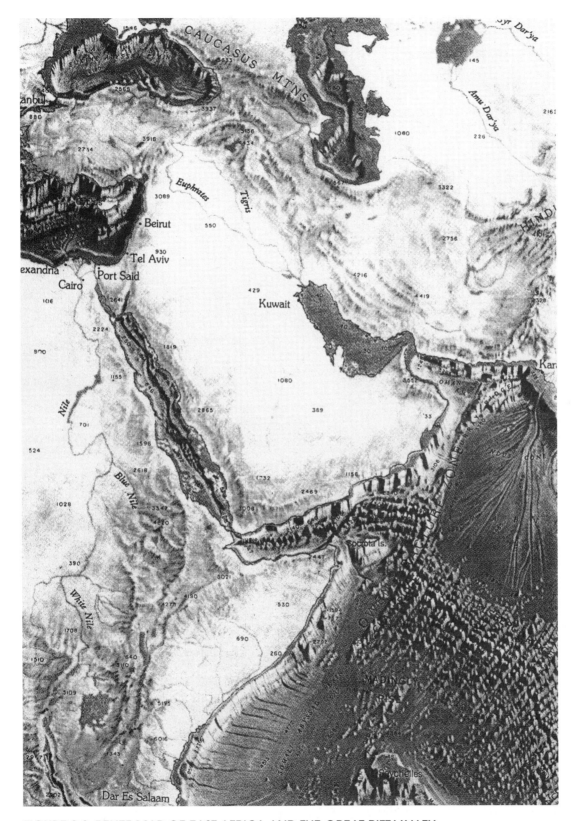

FIGURE 2.3. RELIEF MAP OF EAST AFRICA AND THE GREAT RIFT VALLEY

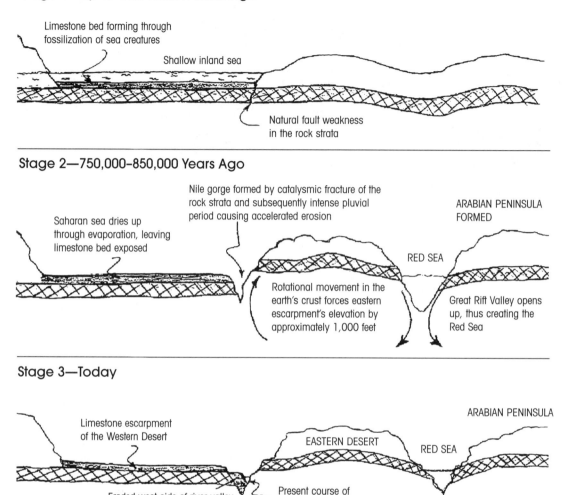

Stage 1—Up to One Million Years Ago

Limestone bed forming through fossilization of sea creatures

Shallow inland sea

Natural fault weakness in the rock strata

Stage 2—750,000–850,000 Years Ago

Nile gorge formed by catalysmic fracture of the rock strata and subsequently intense pluvial period causing accelerated erosion

ARABIAN PENINSULA FORMED

Saharan sea dries up through evaporation, leaving limestone bed exposed

RED SEA

Rotational movement in the earth's crust forces eastern escarpment's elevation by approximately 1,000 feet

Great Rift Valley opens up, thus creating the Red Sea

Stage 3—Today

ARABIAN PENINSULA

Limestone escarpment of the Western Desert

EASTERN DESERT

RED SEA

Eroded west side of river valley now covered by deep silt beds

Present course of the Nile River

FIGURE 2.4. THE GEOLOGICAL GENESIS OF THE NILE VALLEY

The Geology of Egypt

We turn finally and more specifically to the actual geology of Egypt itself, for this has several interesting aspects of relationship with the ancient culture of the early Egyptians. Although the river Nile was undoubtedly the critical factor in the existence and survival of their civilization, it was by no means the only one in their religion. The Nile Valley itself was created by the geological disruption in ancient times of a gigantic fault line running south to north from East Africa's Great Rift Valley all the way to Asia Minor. The Nile Valley fault is actually a subfracture, the main Rift Valley jinking northeast through Ethiopia (see fig. 2.3) and then running through the Red Sea and up into Palestine, where it created the Dead Sea. Flinders Petrie was himself of the opinion that the Western

Desert of Egypt "was largely a bay of the Mediterranean until the final elevation of the land to its present level."[32]

As we can see from figure 2.4, the geology of the Nile Valley consists of a sedimentary limestone sheet base on the west side and largely sandstone hills on the east side, with metamorphic rock (granites) in the area of Aswan southward. When the original fracture occurred, the eastern mass was pushed upward, thereby creating the present Eastern Desert.[33] At the same time (as we have already described), other geological events were taking place, causing the eastern Sahara to lose its covering of seawater from the Atlantic Ocean. Thus the Western Desert of Egypt came to exist. The rainfall of the Ethiopian Highlands (as the Blue Nile) then drained down into the newly formed Nile Valley Rift and this was joined by waters from the White Nile, emerging from the East African Rift. The Nile Valley then experienced a major flow of very fast-moving floodwater that, hurling large rocks along with it, gradually began to wear away the limestone-based western side to form a widening river valley. As the rate of flow decreased, however (which may itself have been the product of a cyclical climatic change), so there began to occur a deposition of silt—of crushed sediment gathered by the river in its higher reaches. This had two main effects. It eventually produced a fertile strip of land all along the river's course, which ultimately became useful for agriculture, despite the annual floods that seemed to occur when Sirius rose heliacally above the horizon. Second, it (much later) produced a vast area of rich land in the Delta, at the river estuary, where it joined the Mediterranean Sea. That itself eventually became the most highly populated part of Egypt because of its agricultural fertility. But again, how long ago did all this occur?

The Era of the First Colonizers of Egypt

The question is important because it may give us an indication of the earliest reasonable time that colonization of the Nile Valley and Delta could have commenced. The problem in arriving at an exact date, however, is that the various associated geological and climatological changes could themselves have taken (and almost certainly did take) many tens or even hundreds of thousands of years of adjustment and readjustment to settle into the present patterns after the major cataclysm. Notwithstanding that, it seems as though the original geological upheavals affecting a yet-to-be-colonized Egypt took place between 700,000 and 850,000 years ago and that matters then took perhaps another 300,000 years or so to settle down. It would very probably have been during this latter period that the basin of the eastern Sahara (present Libya) dried out and the Egyptian section of the Nile Valley underwent its formative genesis.

As we shall see in chapter 11, the fact that metamorphic Nature created the east bank of the Nile while sedimentary Nature created the west side seems to have played an important (although to us perhaps obscure) part in ancient Egyptian thinking. The reader will have to exercise some imagination and patience in accepting this, but the issue has to do with the fact that limestone—being derived from the calcified remains of plants and animals—relates to the organically evolutionary forces or influences in Nature. On the other hand, sandstone might be seen as the product of an inverse (or *involutionary*) influence in which elemental Nature first begins to individualize from an elemental mass of stone into cellular organisms. Granite was also regarded by the Ancients (for example, the Druids) as having its own peculiar (occult) characteristics, including the supposed first appearance of an objective "soul" nature (through an analagous metamorphosis).

As we shall also otherwise see, in chapters 10 and 11 particularly, the fact that the vast majority of original major temples dedicated to sidereal deities are to be found on the west side of the river, on the stone escarpments and plateaus above the river's silt beds, is highly important in the context of a progressive sequence of spiritual initiation in the Egyptian mystic culture. Those truly ancient temples found on either islands or the east bank have other, quite different (and very specific) connotations attached to them, even though they are also associated with the initiatory sequence.

THREE

THE DISAPPEARING "ATLANTES"

With regard to the primitive dolichocephalae of America, I entertain a hypothesis . . . that they are nearly related to the Guanches of the Canary Islands and to the Atlantic populations of Africa—the Moors, Tuaregs, Copts—which Latham comprises under the name of Egyptian Atlantidae. We find one and the same sort of skull in the Canary Islands, in front of the African coast, and in the Carib Islands on the opposite coast which faces Africa. The color of the skin on both sides of the Atlantic is represented in these populations as being of reddish brown.

—A. RETZIUS, *SMITHSONIAN REPORT* (1859)

The ethnological and ethnographical origins of the ancient Egyptians are subjects fundamental to the question of their cultures and civilizations. We therefore find ourselves having to take our research into these areas in order to understand more about their prehistoric society and its beliefs. That is despite the fact that current interest in DNA research has temporarily arrested any possible extension of nineteenth-century research into various human subtypes, by then already fast disappearing from the face of the Earth. Yet in tackling these subjects, we shall find ourselves inevitably crossing swords yet again with orthodox anthropology, and with paleontology on a second front.

The reason for this lies in the fact that these two sciences, following in the footsteps of Darwinian evolutionary theory,[1] regard man as evolved from the anthropoid, whereas all ancient (and some modern) philosophies and religions hold that man is a child of God or "the gods." To add insult to injury, these ancient traditions regarded the anthropoids and many of the Stone Age peoples as merely degenerate remnants of a very ancient human stock—hence their numbers being hugely limited by comparison with those of contemporary mankind. Whether the reader is open to such ideas or not, they are mentioned here and need to be adequately explained before we get stuck in the ethnology of the last few hundred thousand years, because the basis of the ancient Egyptian religious belief makes no sense at all without them. Having done so, we can move on to the issue of racial migrations over the last million years or so and see how they relate to the origins of Egyptian civilization itself.

Briefly, then, the ancient idea of man's origins was founded upon the concept of his being the "microcosm of the Macrocosm"—the same idea basically as found in Genesis that "God made man in his own image," although the latter sentence has been mistranslated. The true translation indicates that it was the Demiurge, or hierarchies of Elohim, which the Old Testament refers to as "the Creator"[2] of everything in the objective universe, on behalf of "the Ever Unknowable God." *Image* is also a poor interpretation of the original conception, for the Adamic rootstock was apparently an ethereally spiritual being (that is, a "soul") that apparently only later evolved the human type (as we know it) as an emanation of itself over a vast period of time. The impression derived from Genesis and other cosmogonical traditions might thus today be interpreted in terms of the human organism being merely a holographic projection of the soul's consciousness, only a fraction of the innate god-consciousness being manifested by it.

The essence of the concept of the "soul" as an evolving, potential god (as the ancient Egyptians saw it) was of the "inner Man"—an essentially divine entity—being regarded as having evolved above the animals by virtue of having two subsidiary soul-vehicles[3]—one spiritual (literally derived from sidereal substance and having a celestial origin), the other terrestrial (in the sense of being bound psychomagnetically to the earth's biosphere). These "souls" were themselves organized as ethereal intelligences, having spheroidally shaped body forms composed entirely of light.

That this was the concept shared by the Egyptians is clear from the Pyramid Texts,[4] where the gods are described as having been derived from "the breath of Ra" while Man (the divine being) was born amidst his "tears," interpreted by some as the "radiance" from "the Eye of Ra," as the luminous expression of his divine thought. Notwithstanding that such a concept might seem more alien to us than that of peculiarly shaped alien spacemen, we should treat it here with as much objectivity as possible.

Chronology of the Prehistoric Period

Further problems arise in the fact that paleontologists and anthropologists still believe that *Homo sapiens* evolved only about 100,000 years ago.[5] According to current theories, man—from his supposedly anthropoid start some four to five million years ago—eventually became a "hunter-gatherer" and then a pastoral farmer, eventually becoming intelligent enough to produce the first crude urban settlements only about 9,000 years ago.[6] However, the fact that Egyptian zodiacs depict the sidereal Annus Magnus of 25,920 years as having been recorded at least three times (that is, over at least a 78,000-year period) provides us with the first dent in these orthodox scientific theories.[7] Herodotus himself is on record as having been told by contemporary Egyptian priests that their written records went back no less than 12,000 years.[8] Eusebius, the early Christian bishop of Alexandria, calculated Manetho's recorded history as taking Egypt's civilization back 35,525 years (even after he had arbitrarily reduced the actual figures).[9] Other records (both cultural and historical) were far more ancient still, as already indicated.

There is no doubt that modern paleontological theory is itself currently in complete ferment as far as its chronology is concerned. The most recent discoveries (at Orce, near Granada in Spain, during 1995) involving Stone Age "tools" have been dated at between 1.1 and 1.6 million years old.[10] Until this latest discovery, scientists had believed that human types—Paleolithic man—had not begun to migrate into Europe until 500,000 to 700,000 years ago. Interestingly, H. P. Blavatsky, in her book *The Secret Doctrine* (first published in 1888), held that there were ancient records in the East confirming that Paleolithic

Cro-Magnon man (of pure Atlantean descent) began to migrate northward into Europe via Gibraltar between 1.25 million and 2.0 million years ago[11]—a suggestion that was utterly derided at the time by the orthodox establishment, although now apparently proved correct. Other human types have recently been confirmed by paleontologists as having inhabited the area between Pakistan and the Caucasus some 1.8 million to 2.5 million years ago, while supposed "protohumans" (Australopithecenes[12]) have been confirmed as inhabiting Ethiopia some 4.5 million years ago.[13] And so on. But all of these are based upon widely varying speculations over a very fragmentary selection of bones and partial skulls.

On a different front, certain of the Puranas (epic histories) of the Indian subcontinent otherwise appear to indicate the ancient origins of our present world culture extending back to a period even prior to 800,000 years ago, which, indicating a highly intelligent human civilization as it must, leaves Egyptologists with their civilization's genesis some 6,000 years ago indeed looking like "the poor relations."[14] Yet other traditions put the appearance of semi-intelligent, giant protohumankind as being far older still, coexistent with the paleontologist's "Dryopithecinae" (15 million to 20 million years ago).[15] However, such vast periods of time are in any case beyond the scope of this book.

Traditions of Giant Human Races in Prehistory

The Puranas—and various other written records and folk histories around the world (including the Bible)—confirm that "there were giants in those (ancient) days."[16] Scholars, however, find such ideas "embarrassing," presumably because such concepts conflict so fundamentally with their theory that early man was only of pigmy size and walked like a chimpanzee, with his hands on or next to the ground. But even paleoscience accepts that earlier humans (more than one million years ago) were often over six feet tall (averaging 1.8–1.9 m/ 5'11"–6'3") with a high, domed skull and a brain capacity superior to that of the modern European (that is 1,590 cc to 1,350 cc)[17] and also walked with as upright a stature as we do. Many bone fragments clearly suggest an even taller prehistoric mankind, but because such ideas conflict with the anthropologist's prejudices as to a simian ancestry, they are summarily rejected without further consideration.

At this point we might also mention the ancient tradition—itself found in widely distant parts of the world—of the four original races of humanity, the white, red, yellow, and black races.[18] It should be added that these were regarded as merely mortal races, preceded by three divine or semidivine races consisting of gods (the golden race), demigods (the silver race), and "heroes" (the bronze race). The four races, however, were referred to as "giants," and it seems likely from close study that they were intended to refer to the very earliest Atlanteans, far antedating the last one million years with which this book is concerned. However, it is interesting to note that the Egyptians regarded themselves as members of the "Red Race stock,"[19] akin to the "warrior" caste of the Indo-Aryan Hindus, whose own social class system was (and is still today) of a fourfold nature.

Evidence for Transatlantic Communication in Prehistory

In his *Atlantis: The Antediluvian World*, Ignatius Donnelly spent considerable time and effort in providing evidence from a wide variety of fields of study to support his case that the original continent of Atlantis had been located in the Tropics between West Africa and the West Indies.[20] Among other things, he described the multitude of varying skin colors, hair textures and colors, musculature and height, and so on among the many peoples living side by side on each of the great continents even today. Bearing in mind their common diet, environment, and climate, it was clear to him that some other differentiating factor was involved in such mixing and that it had to incorporate prehistoric movement of peoples across what are now oceans thousands of miles wide.

Donnelly's view was that migrations—such as those between Africa, Europe, and the Americas—must have taken place when Atlantis still existed (however many tens of thousands of years ago) and that it had then been possible to cross without undue difficulty from West Africa to the islands of the Caribbean and Gulf of Mexico (as well as Central America) via its landmass. Much to the shock and dismay of Egyptologists, Donnelly's theories as to an ancient transatlantic culture have only recently been given further credibility by scientists researching the biochemical constituents of 3,000-plus-year-old Egyptian mummies. The British *Sunday Times* of 1 September 1996 and a Channel 4 Equinox television program entitled *The Mystery of the Cocaine Mummies* reported the extraordinary and unexpected discovery by forensic scientists at Ulm University in Germany of traces of cocaine within the metabolically developed body material of the mummified corpses. Now, scientists themselves accept that cocaine has only ever been found (in the leaves of the native coca plant) in the Americas. So, how—and when—did it get to Egypt, bearing in mind that none of the most ancient known Egyptian records even implies such transoceanic contacts?

In addition to the cocaine, the same researchers found traces of Chinese silk in the hair of the mummies, which also clearly implies the existence of trading (and probably other) links between Egypt and China in ancient times, even though these too are not mentioned in any of the known records. However, the existence of Indo-Tibetan words used in the Egyptian religious culture (as described later in this and other chapters) in the earliest period recognized by Egyptologists adds further to the increasing certainty that a vastly extensive, yet historically unknown, trading culture must have existed in prehistoric times. Yet according to mainstream archaeological theory, the most sophisticated cultures in existence at such a supposedly remote time were little more than farming communities.

The Possibility of Asia Having Been Colonized by Atlantean Amerindians

Modern anthropology regards the Americas as having been only much more recently colonized from Asia via the Bering Strait during a period when the polar ice cap had receded very considerably.[21] This theory seems to be founded on the theory that "Peking Man"—believed to be far more ancient than the Amerindian stock—was of very short stature and grew in height and general size only when exposed to the better diet and environment provided by the Americas, once he arrived there. Donnelly's theory denies any such probability on a very much broader and better supported front that, if true, would tend to support the idea that it was, in fact, some of the ancestors of the Atlantean Amerindians who gave rise to the Eskimos and Sino-Mongolian stock, through migration in ancient times, possibly while retreating northward at a period when the sea level in the Tropics was rising threateningly high.

It is already recognized by modern science that the animal-human physique will always (quite quickly) tend to produce consistently smaller offspring when faced with persistent environmental and psychological deprivation. Conversely, even a congenial environment and wide diet will not by themselves cause a naturally small race to grow—as witness the peoples of Southeast Asia. Consequently, a redescending polar ice cap cutting off any retreat back to the North American mainland could well not only have isolated any such far-flung Atlanteans from their ancestral roots, but probably also led to their at least partial degeneracy amid a strange new environment. When one otherwise takes into consideration that archaeology and paleontology are currently talking about a period of anything between 20,000 and 40,000 years (with no great certainty in either direction) for the complete theoretical colonization of both North and South America[22] (from scratch), the fact of racial diversification into the multihued and otherwise physically characteristic ethnic types described by Donnelly is thrown into even sharper relief. Modern science's current view, when objectively considered, shows not only little common sense but also considerable partiality in selecting its evidence.

Origins of Indo-Aryan Humanity

This, however, in a somewhat roundabout way, brings us back to the ancient Egyptians, because the records of the Brahmans of India remarkably refer to the immediate ancestors of the Indo-Aryan peoples as having been evolved just over a million years ago from a rootstock (of late Atlantean extraction) located somewhere to the north of the Himalayas. At the same time, they refer to other human types (including giant Atlanteans) existing in far earlier ages still. Blavatsky confirmed these ideas from her own oriental sources in the 1880s (although they are elsewhere indicated in ancient texts) and also mentioned, as we saw in chapter 2, that the last really stupendous series of worldwide cataclysms had occurred some 850,000 years ago, evidently long after any such Atlantean exodus to Asia. According to her, these cataclysms—resulting from a reversal of the Earth's magnetic field—lasted about 150,000 years and altered the whole geographic layout of the various Atlantic seaboards and of Europe and the Mediterranean as well.[23] That such an event indeed took place around that time, although concluding many tens (or even hundreds) of thousands of years later, is now confirmed by the paleomagnetic record.[24]

Now, the great library at Alexandria, on the Mediterranean coast of Egypt, the repository of some of the ancient world's oldest records, was put to the torch not just once but three times—by Julius Caesar, by a Christian mob, and by an Islamic caliph. Most of the records are deemed to have been destroyed, although it seems that a few later found their way to Byzantium, and others may well have been stored safely elsewhere. However, the emperor Diocletian then had yet further esoteric works (again of the Egyptians) burned in A.D. 296, at both Alexandria and Byzantium. But if these ancient records had remained intact, and told the same story as the Puranas of India, or of an Egyptian civilization 100,000 years old, would they have been any more credible to modern historians? One doubts it. Manetho, Herodotus, Plato, and others of the soundest repute in their own time are branded by modern scholars as either imaginative retailers of "myths" or just "liars."

As Charles Hapgood reminds us in his *Maps of the Ancient Sea Kings,* the Romans in 142 B.C. also burned down the great library at Carthage, a repository containing half a million scrolls dealing with the historical, scientific, and other knowledge of the Phoenician peoples.[25] As they were generally regarded as the world's greatest seafaring nation of the time (3000 B.C.–2000 B.C.), doubtless with detailed records of voyages to all parts of the world, as well as associated maps, how much more knowledge was lost?[26] As Carthage (in modern Tunisia, facing Sicily) lay within the northwest African landmass of the Atlas Mountains, named after the Atlanteans (called by Homer the Atlantes in his *Odyssey*), how far back in time might its records have gone? The same might be asked concerning the records of the Central American Mayan peoples, ruthlessly destroyed by the Spaniards in the sixteenth century.

Still, notwithstanding that 95 percent of the ancient records may have been destroyed by the doyens of the emerging "civilizations" of our own millennia, we have to proceed on our retrospective quest with whatever information we can glean from other sources. As we shall see, there are (fortunately) several—not always exact or clear, but always definitely pointing in certain specific directions. To begin with, then, let us take the ethnography of Africa as a whole, as it stands today (see fig. 3.1). Its indigenous human stock might be described as comprising five main types:

1. The pigmy Bushman of western and southwestern Africa—a small and dwindling contingent, now nearing extinction;
2. The muscularly built native African type common to the whole of western Africa,[27] culminating in the Bantu stock of southern Africa, which also extends northward into East Africa. This is the largest single group, although itself highly mixed by local intermarriage with other racial types;
3. The generally taller and slimmer "Ethiopian" type, with a proud bearing and the sharply defined facial features commonly found on the Indian subcontinent;
4. The Indo-European peoples of the Sahara and northern Atlas area (the Mahgreb), including the Moors and the nomadic Tuareg and Berber peoples;[28]
5. The Semitic Arab, believed to have originated in Arabia, who (supposedly) only migrated westward (as the tribal Bedouin) across the Red Sea into Africa during the last 4,000 years or so.

Rather interestingly, the root language of the Bantu peoples has been traced by philologists (within the last twenty years) back to West Africa[29]—to the area between Senegal and Sierra Leone that stands due east of the Cape Verde Islands. Over what period the migration from there to southern, central, and eastern Africa took place, and in what numbers originally, it is obviously quite impossible to say. But a very ancient eastward migration there certainly once was. Where did the original peoples come from, however? And what made them move eastward?

On a slightly different and darker note, the Atlanteans had a darkly powerful reputation in some quarters for the practice of sorcery, and one legend has it that it was sorcery that led to Atlantis's downfall through some sort of semi-scientific interference in the bal-

Bushman   Congolese Bantu   Moroccan Moor

Semitic Arab   Eastern Tuareg   Ethiopian Type

FIGURE 3.1. THE ETHNOLOGY AND ETHNOGRAPHY OF AFRICA

These photographs are by A. J. Weber and R. Rahal and were published in L. Cabot Briggs, *The Living Races of the Sahara Desert*. See also *Papers of the Peabody Museum of Archaeology and Ethnology* 28, no. 2 (1958). Reprinted here courtesy of the Peabody Museum of Archaeology and Ethnology, Harvard University.

ance of Nature. Curiously, the one area of Africa best known for magic and sorcery (now known under the more general title of *voodoo*) is that part of West Africa which we have just been discussing. It was from this very area that such practices were transported across the Atlantic to the Caribbean and the Americas via the slave trade during the sixteenth to eighteenth centuries.

Atlantean Migrations and Continental Submersion

If such an inhabited landmass once existed in the general area between the Tropics, there would be little doubt or hesitation in labeling it as the original continent of Atlantis, in line with the description given by Blavatsky and suggested by others, such as Ignatius Donnelly. However, even from the Piri Re'is map, it is difficult if not impossible to point with sustainable logic to an obviously suitable location. So we are almost inevitably drawn back to the general probability of an at least originally large continental landmass (large enough to evolve such a racial type) in the mid- to western Atlantic, probably with colonies to the east and west in what is now West Africa and Central America. It is at least logical to assume that with the sudden or (more probably) progressive destruction of such a landmass (perhaps accelerated by sharply rising sea levels), any fugitives or colonists would have been forced to take shelter on high ground such as found in those same areas of Africa and America. Bearing in mind also how loath people are to leave their homes and country, even when faced with the most obviously imminent natural disaster (for example, California and the San Andreas Fault or Tokyo in our own era), we can safely assume that the ancient Atlanteans—wherever located—watched their civilization gradually disappear before their very eyes and then perished in the mass when escape ultimately became impossible.

If we look at a relief map of western and central Africa, we shall see that, if the southern Sahara Desert area is regarded as once having acted as a barrier (owing to its having been the bed of the eastern extension of the Atlantic Ocean at some past time), such a migration would have been forced to follow the line of the Central African Highlands due eastward, before being able to turn south toward the Congo and its huge river delta. The latter, at that time, may still itself only have been an open marshy landscape rather than the present, largely jungle terrain. Consequently, any further migration in a southerly direction might not have been possible for a considerable period of time, perhaps even tens of thousands of years—allowing plenty of time for degeneracy into Neanderthal man, or a western African equivalent.

Ethnological Relationships between Egypt and India

We turn next to northeast Africa, where we find the tall, smooth-skinned, and long-haired ethnic type whose features bear such a strong resemblance to either Indo-Caucasians or the Dravidian Tamils of southern and western India. As Margaret Murray put it in her book *The Splendour That Was Egypt*, "the type of the men of Pun(t), as depicted by Hatshepsut's artists, suggest an Asiatic rather than an African race; and the sweet-smelling woods (which they traded) point to India as the land of their origin."[30]

Herodotus referred to the people of Pun(t)—otherwise known as "the land of the gods"—as "eastern Ethiopians," and it is clear from the earliest Egyptian art and sculpture that the pharaohs and their retinues of the time were undoubtedly of this basically Indo-Caucasian stock, some of them even being shown as fair-skinned. There is no trace in these early depictions of either African or Semitic facial characteristics. Interestingly also, the Indus River is known along parts of its upper length as the Nilah, meaning "blue-black river"—presumably because of the silt content. Furthermore, the upper reaches of the Indus pass through the *Pun*jab, en route to Kashmir and the foothills of the western Himalayas—an area reputed even today to be the home of *mahatmas*—human beings who have become demigods through untold generations of highly ascetic spiritual training.

Aryavarta and the Cushitic Empire

It is otherwise recognized that there once existed a vast, apparently Indo-Aryan empire that extended all the way from the Caucasus Mountains (adjacent to the Hindu Kush range, at the western end of the Himalayas) to Nubia and Ethiopia.[31] Although the historical dating of this empire and its original culture are uncertain, it may in fact have been a late offshoot of Aryavarta, the land of the ancient Hindu Brahmans, far antedating both the Mesopotamian and Egyptian cultures known to modern archaeology.[32] The term Cushite is certainly to be found among the earlier Egyptian writings in relation to the "eastern Ethiopian" peoples, and it is also known that the ancient Pali language (directly derived from Sanskrit) is clearly evidenced in the derivation of the name Palestine, from Pali-stan. This implies that Sanskrit was already widely used throughout Asia Minor by around 4000 B.C. The biblical name Samaria appears to have been similarly derived—by Chaldeo-Assyrian colonists—from Sumer-Ea. The overall implication is thus that at some perhaps later stage in its chronological existence, Egypt was colonized (or recolonized) from the northeast and east by Indo-Aryan peoples, who probably migrated there via trading stations in the Levant, Arabia, and along the Red Sea coast. This is not to say that Egypt had not already been colonized from the west by others—but we shall consider that further in a moment.

The Semitic type (much mingled among Turks, Syrians, Hebrews, Arabs, and so on) also appears not to be indigenous to the African continent, being of a near-Aryan stock, although slightly different in facial features from the Indo-Aryan type already mentioned. And yet a branch of this same Semitic stock in the form of the nomadic Bedouin people is mentioned in the earliest records of the dynastic (human) pharaohs as causing problems with its marauding brigandage.[33] The (Hamitic) Berbers of the Mahgreb, however, are mentioned in the early Egyptian records as Barbaras—hence the Barbary Coast.[34]

So if, as seems possible from other sources, the Semitic stock had its genesis in Asia Minor, perhaps close to modern Turkey, it seems somehow to have managed to evolve (or to have been evolved from) a nomadic tribal offshoot some 3,000 miles away in northwest Africa at an indeterminate time prior to the earliest of Egyptian dynasties officially recognized by Egyptologists. How could this be so unless the Aryan rootstock was itself far older than imagined and had also already produced emigrant colonies? But were the original migrants seafarers, or had they managed to get to Libya and Egypt by land somehow? And what had happened to cut them off from their racial roots?

Was There a Worldwide Prehistoric Culture?

Professor Charles Hapgood suggests that there had almost certainly once existed (at least once) a worldwide civilization of some sort, "or a civilization that for a considerable time must have dominated much of the world in a very remote period."[35] As we saw in chapter 2, H. P. Blavatsky suggested that after the last major cataclysms of 850,000 years ago, only one northern Atlantean island (Daitya) of any real size remained (other than various scatterings of island chains) from the much larger original Atlantean continent that had originally spanned the present Atlantic Ocean from east to west. According to her, this vast land had been progressively destroyed by geopolar shift and consequent submarine earthquake activity over a prolonged period, while even Daitya had finally succumbed about 270,000 years ago.

Quoting her sources as being associated with a Himalayan esoteric school[36] that still retained connections with an esoteric brotherhood in Egypt (as does the Sufi tradition even today), Blavatsky further suggested that by the time of its final demise, Daitya had already developed or evolved a joint Atlanto-Aryan culture and civilization and that it was this that first colonized Egypt (progressively from about 400,000 years ago) and built the Pyramids over 100,000 years ago. She states: "So secret was the knowledge of the last islands of Atlantis on account of the superhuman powers possessed by its inhabitants . . . that to divulge its whereabouts and existence was punished with death." Her reference doubtless was to an advanced "scientific," or quasi-scientific, knowledge.[37]

In addition to what Blavatsky says on this issue, there are plenty of other references to be found of an Atlantean island civilization and/or continent, usually having connections with Egypt and even Asia. Homer himself—three centuries before Plato—spoke in his *Odyssey* of the "Atlantes" as a "people of west Africa." In Guatemala, there is still a Lake Atlan in existence today, while the Atlas Mountains of northwest Africa bear testimony to the ancient existence of such a people in that area long before the Greeks appropriated the name for one of their gods (the equivalent of the Egyptian god Shu[38]), who held up the heavens on his mighty shoulders. *Atl* (meaning "water") is still found linguistically widespread as both suffix and prefix throughout parts of Central America.

Transatlantic and Transcontinental Similarities in Ancient Names

The derivation of the name Atlas and its various offspring has puzzled scholars for well over a century, and the issue has still not been finally resolved by our modern philologists. However, bearing in mind the fairly universal basis of a creation myth in which we find "fallen angels" (or the near equivalent, "fallen gods"), a variety of different "heaven worlds," and a demiurgic creator, let us see how far we can cast our esoteric net.

In the Hindu Matsya Purana,[39] we find the tradition of seven archaic lands (planes of being represented as islands) called *tala*—Atala being the lowest, akin to an underworld, hence a perhaps unlikely suitor in the present context. But in the Hindu occult tradition, we also find that the teaching as to *talas* and *lokas* means higher and lower worlds—that is, states of being and consciousness composed of varying qualities of psycho-spiritual light-substance. In Lhasa, the capital of Tibet, we find the Dalai Lama's palace given the name Potala (or perhaps Ba-Tala?[40]); Lhasa itself appears to be derived from *lha-sa*, meaning "son of the Lha," *lha* being an Indo-Tibetan expression for one of the divine, demiurgic creator-hierarchies—that is, the Elohim. Thus the latter provides us with something of a clue, for Atlas seems quite logically to arise from the telescoping of the compound *ad-lha(s), ad* (as in Adonai, the followers of the archetypally original Divine Man, Adam) being a Sanskrit word meaning "firstborn," or "primordial." We may also recall that the mythical Adonis, lover of Aphrodite, died by being gored in the thigh by the god Ares (Mars) disguised as a wild boar.[41] As we shall see later, this is a highly important astronomical as well as mystical allusion.

The *lha,* or creative solar spirits—the origin of the Celtic Llyr (or Lyr) and the Roman Lar—which inhabited the Mayan paradise Tlaloca(n) (that is, Lha-loka), are quite clearly also the Semitic El or Al-lha (hence the later Moslem Allah). Adonis himself having been born in a tree trunk and subsequently forced to spend half the year in the underworld of Hades, the original Ad-Lha(nte)s are, by deduction, the demiurgic creator gods of several creation myths who "fell from Grace" into a cycle of objective existence as the divine *lha* (or Elohim) of our particular star and planetary system.

Interestingly, several other (by now well camouflaged) words seem also to have crossed the Atlantic between Africa, Asia, and the Americas. For example, the name Teotihuacan—given to the vast Mayan temple complex near Mexico City—is clearly derived from Tehuti-vahan (meaning the body, or vehicle, of Thoth, the Egyptian god) and has three pyramids matching those at Giza.[42] The Mayan serpent god Quetzalcoatl was given the title Kukulkan (*kuk-el-khan*, i.e., "head-god-chief/prince") of the Mayan people, while Khubilgan or Khubil-Khan *(khu-bel-khan)* is an Indo-Tibetan expression meaning "spiritual soul prince." Cuchulain (or *kuk-el-ain*) was an ancient Celtic demigod with a canine companion.[43] The combined phonetic and cultural cross-correspondences are too close just to dismiss. Thus, the inevitable overall impression derived from them all is that there is clear, inferential evidence to imply the prehistoric existence of an ancient, worldwide religious (or mystic) culture which extended all the way from Tibet (probably incorporating China, with its dragon cults) to Central America.

Ancient Colonization of Egypt from East and West

Now, whether one regards Blavatsky's story as credible or not, her same source of information nevertheless confirmed—over a century before our most up-to-date science could do so—that Paleolithic man (such as Cro-Magnon man) began colonizing Europe well over one million years ago and that a major geomagnetic shift had taken place just over three quarters of a million years ago. Lucky guesses? Hardly likely in the face of the withering scorn and skepticism such ideas faced in the 1880s when some Christian theologians still believed that the biblical Creation occurred in 4004 B.C.!

The fact remains that there is a greater similarity in the facial features of the native African (Bantu) type and the natives of Central America and (northern) South America than there is between either of them and the Indo-Aryan or Hamito-Semitic types that we find in northeast and northwest Africa. That quite clearly non-Semitic, Indo-European features were commonly shared by all the ancient Hamitic peoples of north Africa also raises questions concerning the origins and prehistoric extent of their own quite distinctively different culture and ethnic traditions. Is it then not probable that the ancient ancestors of the Hamitic stock were indeed the Atlanto-Aryans of Daitya mentioned by Blavatsky?[44] And had their eastward migrations originally extended so far up around the southern perimeter of the Mediterranean and across into Asia Minor that they ultimately met and mingled with the already mixed Dravidian and Caucasian rootstock to produce the Semites as a substock that then wholly absorbed them in this area? Is this why we find Atlantean ziggurats in Chaldea-Babylonia, matching those in Central America?

The Defeat of the Atlanteans by the Ancient Greeks

One of the other things related by the priests of Sais to Solon in the story told by Plato is that the Greeks of his day were but the puny remnants of a heroic Hellene stock that had lived in far earlier times when the Atlantes were busy tyrannizing the peoples of the Mediterranean generally.[45] So the story went, although severely outnumbered, the Hellenes fought and beat the Atlantes so convincingly that their power was finally broken and never

The photograph shows three of the ten statues of Guanche kings to be found in the town of Candelaria, in Tenerife, the largest of the Canary Island group. The figures are very tall indeed (totally unlike any local types in size and facial features) and otherwise possess the broad foreheads and the long (dolichocephalic) skulls usually associated by archaeologists with the Cro-Magnon type of humans, who lived well over one million years ago.

Origins
▲

FIGURE 3.2. THE HAMITIC GUANCHE KINGS

recovered. As a result, it seems that the Atlantes withdrew back to their own lands in the Atlantic and thereafter remained in relative isolation. Nothing further appears subsequently to have been reported about them, although there is some suggestion that pockets of them (described as "Libyans") came to live in northern Egypt, in the western Delta area. Sadly, no indication of the even approximate time spans involved appears to have been mentioned by the priests. However, if this part of Plato's story is true—and it has to be regarded as on a par with the rest concerning his Atlantean island itself—then it lends yet further credence to the suggestion of an Atlantean (or Atlanto-Aryan) colony in Egypt—or in Libya/Tunisia just to the west—the parent civilization of which had, for some reason, retrenched, leaving behind its giant temples and pyramids as mute testimony to its own prior existence.[46] The withdrawal of political and economic control over its Egyptian colony in such fashion would, however, have had exactly the same effect upon the local population as occurred in Britain and Gaul when the Romans withdrew to Rome after the Goths and Vandals attacked it. In that case, many Romans stayed behind (rather than return to Rome) and, through intermarriage, integrated both their families and their traditions completely with the local population. Now, much less than two thousand years later, just how much of the original Roman presence can be seen? In Britain, far less than in France.

The fact that the people of ancient Egypt seem to have spoken a Hamitic language adds further fuel to our fire. In addition—as we shall see in greater detail in chapter 4—Victorian ethnologists took the view from their own researches that there were distinct racial connections not only between the language of the natives of the Caribbean Islands and the Canary Islands (the Guanches) and that of the Basques, but also with the Hamitic and Dravidian tongues.[47] So, an indistinct but nevertheless obvious ancient trail seems to extend right across North Africa from the Atlantic to the Indian Ocean and also up into the heartlands of Asia Minor and thence to Tibet.

So what are we left with from all this? Central and southern Africa populated south of the Sahara (probably due to an ancient submersion of the latter) generally by a "proto-Bantu"-speaking, Atlanto-Negroid people whose roots appear slightly north of the equator, from a point on the Atlantic coast of West Africa; that Egypt itself appears to have been colonized from the west via Morocco, Algeria, and Tunisia by (northern) Atlantes speaking an utterly different Hamitic root language, like the Guanche of the Canary Islands, and having distinctively Indo-Aryan features; that it was otherwise (later) colonized from the east by other (Caucasian) Indo-Aryans via northwest India, the Levant and Ethiopia; that Egypt was undoubtedly colonized prior to 100,000 years ago by people with already highly advanced cultures.[48] Such a range of scenarios could hardly be more different than the prosaic one provided by contemporary archaeological theory, could it?

FOUR

The Appearance of Culture and Civilization

Diodorus Siculus (first century B.C.) was told by the Egyptian priests that the Gods and Heroes had ruled over Egypt for slightly less than 18,000 years, while mortals had ruled for just under 5000 years.

—C. H. OLDFATHER IN *DIODORUS SICULUS*, VOL. 1

In order to understand the historical development of both culture and civilization in prehistory, it is necessary to see them both as the Ancients themselves saw them—as products of a cyclically recurring spiritual impulse affecting humanity in general and their own culture in particular. For them, intelligence was the objective expression of spirituality, and they believed that at the beginning of each new cycle, or (zodiacal) age, the "gods" would themselves reappear to provide the new impulse and sense of future direction in line with Divine Purpose, with a resultant advance in human spirituality and overall human intelligence. Subsequently, after a while, so they also believed, the place of the "gods" would be taken by semidivine kings and leaders who, in turn, would later be replaced by "heroes"— spiritual adepts who, although themselves drawn from the ranks of the most spiritually evolved humanity of the time, had nevertheless been specifically trained and initiated by the demigods. After the heroes came the fourth and final period in each such cycle, when the adept-heroes themselves withdrew into the background, specifically to allow humanity in the mass to evolve its own sense of independence and to select its own kings and leaders according to its own best judgment.

Chronology of the Divine Rulers of Egypt

Such a succession is confirmed by the inscriptions on the Palermo Stone—a basalt stele dating supposedly from around 2400 B.C.—and the later document called the Dynasties of Manetho.[1] The latter was culled from the records of a priest of the temple of Heliopolis at the time of the Greek pharaoh Ptolemy, who was trying to resuscitate the cult of Isis. Manetho's succession is shown in figure 4.1, the dates shown, however, being those ascribed by modern Egyptologists, who seem to take a curiously selective view of his data. Egyptology now disregards all before Narmer (otherwise called Menes, the apparently first purely human pharaoh) as mere mystic fictions.[2] However, the chronological dating of Egyptologists has itself changed dramatically over the last fifty years. As of today's

NAME	DYNASTY	CHRONOLOGY
Gods (7)	First Divine Dynasty	12,285 years
Gods (9)	Second Divine Dynasty	1,196 years
Demigods (30)	Third Divine Dynasty	3,650 years
Hero-kings (10)	Fourth Divine Dynasty	350 years
Early Dynastic	I–II	3100–2686 B.C.
Old Kingdom	III–VI	2686–2181 B.C.
First Intermediate Period	VII–XI	2181–2055 B.C.
Middle Kingdom	XI–XIV	2055–1650 B.C.
Second Intermediate Period	XV–XVII	1650–1550 B.C.
New Kingdom	XVIII–XX	1550–1069 B.C.
Third Intermediate Period	XXI–XXIV	1069–747 B.C.
Late Period	XXV–XXX	747–32 B.C.

FIGURE 4.1. THE DYNASTIES OF MANETHO
(Amended to show the current Egyptological dating of the human pharaohs)

date, the first pharaoh is supposed to have begun his reign about 3100 B.C. In the mid-nineteenth century, this date was nearly 5000 B.C.[3]

Doubts were originally raised by archaeologists over a century ago as to whether Manetho's calculations were produced on the basis of ordinary years or "Sothic years" (cycles of 1,460 Earth years). Bearing in mind the altogether vast overall period involved using the Sothic-year calculations (over 25 million years), one can only assume that if Manetho intended that method, the original record must have purported to refer to periods associated with cosmic cycles. The number of years given for the Second Divine Dynasty, for example, indicates some considerable illogicality or discrepancy. However, it is known that Eusebius—one of the early Christian bishops in Egypt—spent some time "adjusting" the figures. As Eusebius was known as a general falsifier of records to suit his own ends, it is more than likely that these figures are not original anyway. Notwithstanding this, the Manetho chronology as given (as regards the period succeeding the divine dynasties) has played a major part in the belief systems of modern archaeology in relation to the likely dating of the various Egyptian pharaohs mentioned in the archaic records. The subject is still one of intense debate among scholars of the subject.

The opening quote from *Diodorus Siculus* shows just how far apart today's experts are from the priestly records of 2,000-plus years ago. It is interesting to note, however, that what the priests told Diodorus suggests that the "gods" began their cycle of influence, or "reign," at the very beginning of the present Annus Magnus—during the Age of Aquarius, some 25,000 years ago. Furthermore, these great beings (or their immediate agents) appear to have yielded sovereignty to "mortal kings" at the end of the Age of Gemini or beginning of the Age of Taurus; and that too is of considerable interest to us, for reasons that will become apparent later in this chapter.

That modern Egyptology should choose to be so arbitrary without caring to explore the matter in any great depth arises out of the fact that it agnostically refuses to entertain the practical possibility of there being a guiding spiritual impulse—a zeitgeist—for each Age, or of beings superior to our humanity. That in turn indicates its belief that the evolutionary process is itself the blind product of blind chance—as also, supposedly, must man himself be by a simple process of deduction. It has also resulted in Egyptologists' perceptions and chronological calculations of ancient history being entirely distorted, for reasons that we shall continue to outline in this chapter.

Traditions and Evidence of Divine Rulers in Ancient Egypt

Herodotus was apparently shown by the Egyptian priests the statues of their semidivine and adept-hero kings and supreme hierophants of the temples, all having reigned before Menes—and all supposedly "self-born," one from the other by mental self-projection, without the aid of the human birth process.[4] The statues were enormous colossi in wood (over 340 of them) and the priests assured him that no historian could ever understand such superhuman beings until and unless he first thoroughly understood all three dynasties preceding the human—namely, the gods, demigods, and heroes. Herodotus was himself able to confirm that the written history of the Egyptian priests went back some 12,000 years before his own time, and that their own traditions went back much farther still.

Now, again, all this might sound incredibly far-fetched. Yet all ancient cultures held to the tradition that at the commencement of each new sidereal (not zodiacal) age, the gods would briefly descend and walk openly among mankind, thereby providing an idealistic impulse and folk memory that would last until their next cyclical return. The very same idea is as implicit in the modern Christian tradition of "Heaven on Earth" as it was explicit 5,000 years ago in ancient Egypt. The corollary of this idea, however, was that toward the end of each such cycle, the larger proportion of humanity would lapse so far into materialism that it would forget or refuse to believe in its own divine origins. Hence a natural division would begin to show itself through spiritually degenerate behavior. As a result, the returning gods would then make a (presumably fairly straightforward) decision as to which among the "chosen" hierarchies (of souls, not human individuals) were suited to receive the impression of their nature, thereby accelerating their evolution during the remainder of the cycle in question. This effectively self-engendered "Judgment Day" would, so it appears, have automatically resulted in those of the spiritually oriented minority gradually beginning to segregate themselves from the rest. The remainder, meanwhile, presumably began to display varying degrees of corrupted intelligence, from thorough materialism to general inhumanity and even bestiality. Thus, even without knowing of the imminently dawning "Age of Aquarius," one might be forgiven for feeling increasingly certain of the old Age being close to its natural end! Notwithstanding this, the universal degradation referred to in the oldest traditions seems undoubtedly to refer to a specific part of the 25,920-year sidereal cycle, coincident with its "spring/summer" period.

An Ancient Concept of Human Spiritual Evolution

In figure 1.1, we saw the Annus Magnus depicted showing the four sidereal "seasons," each of about 6,500 years, with the associated celestial "equinoxes" and "solstices." By drawing direct analogies with the phenomena of our terrestrial Nature's own seasons, we also saw that we could perhaps derive some useful and informative ideas from it. One such idea evolved by the Hindus incorporated the conception of man evolving like the seed-essence of a plant—which they called the *saptaparna*, the "seven-leafed man-plant."[5] The "seed-essence" in question, however, was said by them to be the "spark" of Divine Intelligence that man has within his own nature, expressing itself specifically in the form of a self-conscious sense of idealism and altruistic responsibility—thus raising him above the beasts.

The concept—readily equated with the Egyptian "myth" of the Bennu (self-resurrecting phoenix)—is perhaps more easily understood if we think of an overshadowing divine consciousness "pollinating" the aspirations and ideals of those groups and individuals possessing a truly active spiritual orientation. Such individuals and groups had therefore to prepare themselves in advance by self-purification, ensuring that their idealistic aspirations really would "flower" in altruistic deeds and thoughts in order to attract the attention of the "gods"—just as plants produce flowers to attract bees and thereby ensure their own regeneration by cross-fertilization. This may well have been at the heart (originally) of the idea found in the East of building up karmic "merit" by good deeds. According to such ideas, the gods themselves apparently could not appear in objective form as such, by virtue of their very nature being too sublime (and too powerful) for them to do so. They were thus said to appear "by proxy" through the agency of the higher deva-daemons (appearing as literal "columns of light") or otherwise through demigods influencing humanity by overshadowing any particularly virtuous human consciousness.[6] In that respect, we may recall that one of the chief functions of the pharaoh and/or priestly hierophant was to prepare himself to manifest the god (for example, Horus or Osiris) through his own nature for the benefit of the populace. A distorted sense of this is to be found in the papal conception of infallibility when supposedly speaking "under the impression" (or ex cathedra) of Christ himself.

Invocation and Evocation of the Divine Presence

The central idea behind it all, however, seemed to be that the gods would literally (if properly invoked at the correct time) actually descend ("from the stars") and awaken the god-nature in man. That was deemed possible because man himself was but the outer, partial expression of a permanently self-existent god-nature. Although dormant during certain (astrologically determined) "seasons," so the Ancients believed, this god-nature in man could be stimulated into high activity, which then made it possible (subject to due preparation) for the god to manifest through the consciousness of the individual. A highly degenerate version of this is sadly to be found in the general run of shamanistic practice all around the world. This almost always involves possession by what the Ancients would have regarded as low-grade "daemons" and even "elementary" entities, none of which could be considered as even lesser "gods" at all, by any stretch of the imagination.

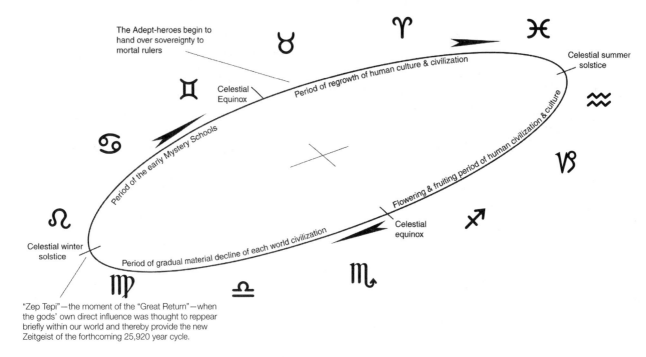

FIGURE 4.2. CYCLES OF INFLUENCE OF THE GODS, DEMIGODS, AND HEROES

The labels within the figure read:

- The Adept-heroes begin to hand over sovereignty to mortal rulers
- Celestial Equinox
- Celestial summer solstice
- Period of regrowth of human culture & civilization
- Period of the early Mystery Schools
- Flowering & fruiting period of human civilization & culture
- Celestial equinox
- Celestial winter solstice
- Period of gradual material decline of each world civilization
- "Zep Tepi"—the moment of the "Great Return"—when the gods' own direct influence was thought to reppear briefly within our world and thereby provide the new Zeitgeist of the forthcoming 25,920 year cycle.

The usually quiescent god-nature in man was then stimulated into high activity by the presence of those divine or spiritual entities already mentioned. But, as just described, these high, angelic intelligences were believed to appear within our world system only briefly during each sidereal "season," long enough merely to impress the purpose and idealism of the new age upon its most spiritually receptive humanity. Some of them (called *urshu* by the Egyptians) were evidently able to materialize human forms for their own use in direct dealings with human beings. However, Herodotus tells us that "during the space of 11,340 years they assert, no divinity has appeared in human shape"—which period of time takes us back to the Age of Virgo, close to the cusp with Leo.[7]

Although these periodically visiting high Intelligences were said to remain only temporarily in our world's atmosphere—commencing (it is implied) around the time of the "celestial winter solstice"—they would nevertheless leave behind them groups of lesser creative intelligences (demigods) to carry on their work. Thus, at or around the "celestial spring equinox," after initiating the new cycle, they would themselves withdraw, thereby taking no direct part in it. Hence there followed a natural burgeoning followed by an eventual (although not complete) regression in human civilization. The general idea of the progression is suggested in figure 4.2.

Appearance of the Gods Coincident with Astronomical Cycles

It thus becomes clear that the appearance and disappearance of these particular divine and semidivine entities was regarded as being directly connected with the occurrence of the celestial equinoxes and therefore also, necessarily, with the plane of the Galaxy. They themselves—being the very personification of light (the *shu* in *urshu* signifying the light of a god[8])—presumably could not venture beyond that state, for to do so would be to "fall from Grace" in a very literal sense. Consequently, they apparently had to await their own appointed hour before being able to appear within our world.

Now if there were any faint substance to these hallowed beliefs, it would clearly be easier to understand why exactly human civilization and culture should suddenly seem to appear or disappear with long intervals of thousands of years in between. That, however, is not to suggest that complete evolutionary inactivity would reign between the "celestial autumn equinox" and the corresponding "spring equinox." As in terrestrial Nature, this period (of some 13,000 years) would perhaps be expected to involve a cycle of synthesis and withdrawal followed by an equivalent period of karmic (that is, root) regeneration. Although some semidivine intelligences might then progressively depart our world come the "celestial autumn equinox," the spiritually perfected (but still semihuman) adept-intelligences left behind would (presumably) become responsible for preparing and hybridizing the next cycle's crop of human intelligence. Thus, when the "celestial winter solstice" was past, these same "specimen seeds" and "rootstock" (a spiritually initiated new "soul type") would be progressively "sown" and "planted" around the world.

All this might strike the average reader as so fanciful as to verge on science fiction. And yet it seems to be the way that the people of the ancient world actually saw the whole evolutionary process working. As far as they were concerned, nothing was left to chance in the cosmos. Everything functioned according to a divine economy and perfection of order in which a seasonally balanced cosmic harmony was the inevitable result. It followed that perfect cosmic order and harmony could not possibly occur by chance. The whole process had to be intelligent and guided by an ordered hierarchy of intelligences in such a manner that Earth's Nature mirrored cosmic Nature.

Ancient Origin of the Mystery Schools

As shown in figure 4.2, the "celestial winter solstice" would have heralded the regeneration of the new cycle of human psycho-spiritual evolution. From the period shown—the cusp of Leo-Virgo being implicit in the metaphor of the Sphinx—we might speculate that the Mystery Schools of our present cycle date from around that time. Interestingly, the submersion of Poseidonis seems to have occurred during the Age of Leo (if Plato's chronology is correct) and, so Blavatsky said, the Mystery Schools themselves then went progressively underground in order to preserve their secrets from corruption and misuse by spiritually uninterested and unregenerate mankind.

Now, as the priests of Heliopolis told Herodotus—and as otherwise seems to be confirmed by the Dendera zodiac—the full precession of the equinoxes had occurred at least twice within the period of their own records, that is, between 52,000 and 78,000 years.[9] In addition, the sheer cyclopean size and disposition of the main Nile temples implies that the original structures were built by a civilization (unknown to us) at the height of its powers. So, there seems little doubt that the Giza Pyramid and Sphinx complex itself was built at some epoch long preceding 10,450 B.C., perhaps coinciding with multiples of 25,920 years—that is, 36,370 B.C. or 62,290 B.C. or 88,210 B.C. or . . . However, if cosmic intelligences were involved in the original design and construction, our next question might perhaps hinge on what coincident but greater cycle might also have been involved. This is not an easy one to deal with but we can perhaps hazard one or two guesses as follows.

The Seven Races of the Present Greater Cycle

The Greeks (and others, including the Indo-Aryan Brahmans) believed that our present Great Age—which we take to mean the post-Atlantean era—has already seen several sub-epochs during which different races of mankind have appeared in the following sequence:[10]

1. The Golden Age—in which the greater gods "walked" the earth;
2. The Silver Age—in which the greater demigods took their place;
3. The first Bronze Age—in which the heroes were primordially active;
4. The second Bronze Age—in which mankind again reappeared;
5. The present (Iron) Age—during which mankind has itself begun, very gradually and tentatively, to show signs of recovering some degree of spiritual awareness.

Blavatsky interpreted these as a series of seven "subraces" within an Indo-Aryan (or Indo-European/Caucasian) "root race" that, starting just over a million years ago, succeeded an Atlantean "root race" (of giants). Her "subraces" in this present epoch then seem to last about 200,000 to 225,000 years, with every such "subrace" comprising seven "branch races," each lasting between 25,000 to 30,000 years, all fulfilling some purpose in the Divine Plan.[11] There is obviously very little that we can add to such ideas by way of comment, however, because of the huge time spans involved, plus the general dearth of reliable archaeological information. However, the way in which the "branch races" appear to correlate with the 25,920-year Annus Magnus suggests that the various archaic traditions that one finds scattered across several continents concur with these ideas, all thereby seeming to have a common astronomical source.

In the remaining sections of this chapter—bearing in mind what has just been suggested—we shall look a little more closely at the last cycle of 25,920 years, particularly the period since the beginning of the last Age of Leo. Astrologically, the latter is supposed to be associated with both individuality and "spiritual birth" as well as with children in a more general and mundane sense. But why should this be so?

The Gods Hand Over Responsibility to "Caretakers"

If what has been described concerning the celestial seasons has any truth in it, some of the demigods would already have begun to depart our earth in due cycle somewhere around 17,500 B.C.—the celestial autumn equinox—just as in Nature the tree begins to withdraw its sap, causing the leaves gradually to wither and fall. The obvious analogies are striking, as is the idea that, by this time, a new generation of "spiritually polarized" souls, or "seeds," had been developed and were then contained within the auric consciousness of the high adept-heroes, or demigods, themselves the literal "fruit of the vine" of the immediately preceding 25,920-year cycle. It seems difficult to conceive of it in any other way given the number of metaphors and allegories in that line found in so many ancient cultures. Anyway, on the basis that we are perhaps on the right track, the adept-heroes would have taken over full responsibility (as from around 11,000 B.C.) for the subsequent spiritual unfoldment and evolution of these same "seeds." Consequently, the prospective founding of the first Mystery Schools of our era during the Age of Leo seems very apposite. What Blavatsky had to say about the submersion of Poseidonis (circa 9500 B.C.) and the subsequent introspection of the Mystery Tradition also ties in.

To go back one stage for a moment, if humanity in the mass were to be regarded allegorically as the "leaves and blossom upon the tree" (of the civilization and culture between the equinoxes), the era around the Age of Sagittarius-Scorpio must in a very real sense have been a Golden Age. The idea that the consciousness of the gods and demigods was what actually gave rise to that also leads one to assume that their departure must have produced equivalent results. In other words, the worldwide culture and civilization of the time, suggested by Professor Hapgood, would gradually have disappeared, leaving only some isolated populations of "hardy spiritual perennials," to adapt a gardening term. However, the mass of human consciousness, having thus lost its universal sense, would once again instinctively have reverted to parochial forms of culture.

Chronological Synchronicities of History with Zodiacal Ages

Now, if we move historically backward to the last celestial spring equinox, around the beginning of the Age of Taurus (circa 4320 B.C.), we find that it rather interestingly approximates the period at which archaeologists believe our present human civilization commenced in Mesopotamia and Egypt. It also seemingly coincides with the long-delayed restabilization of the world's weather (after the cyclical Deluge commencing during the Age of Cancer) and the consequent reestablishment of extended social, cultural, and trading ties throughout the Mediterranean and Middle East. Perhaps this explains why, at this point, the reins of objective government should have been progressively handed back by the spiritual authorities to merely political ones. Such a scenario would indeed explain why and how these "original" cultures (of Sumer, Babylon, and Egypt) sprang apparently ready-made into existence, complete with sophisticated scientific knowledge and religious and administrative structures to match.

With regard to the issue of the Mystery Schools, however, it would seem probable that (in this cycle) they indeed first came into existence during the Age of Leo, but not just because of the submersion of Poseidonis. Entry to such schools resulted in "spiritual rebirth" (birth and childhood being associated astrologically with Leo and the fifth house of the zodiac), but it involved preliminary tests of courage and commitment before any occult information whatsoever was divulged.[12] The succeeding Age of Cancer—commencing about 8740 B.C.—seemingly associated by the Egyptians with the scarab beetle, seems to have been related to the Book of the Dead period of Egyptian mysticism. This appears to have involved the neophyte being introduced to the many-faceted aspects of the psychic nature associated with the Underworld, to which Cancer was traditionally "the gate." Consequently, the rituals and initiatory tests associated with this era seem to have involved experiences in caves and subterranean chambers or tunnels. The significance of this will become obvious in later chapters when we deal with the Osirian Mystery in greater detail. It will then be seen that there are perhaps unsuspected cosmic associations that tie in with the issue of initiation and the whole principle of sympathetic magic, on a hitherto almost wholly unrecognized scale. The subsequent Age of Gemini, however—commencing about 6450 B.C.—seems to have involved esotericism coming more out into the open again and becoming less secretive. It seems quite possible that this may have been the era when the "sacred groves" (or *ashras*—akin to the Indian *ashrams*) became the popular sites for the Mysteries among the Greeks. This era seems, however, to have been the last during which the adept-heroes remained in outward charge of the various nation-states then in existence.

By the time that the Age of Taurus—containing the celestial spring equinox—had begun to move toward its close (circa 2160 B.C.), an almost inevitable descent into materialism and religious sectarianism had already made its appearance. It was then that bull worship began to take a different turning, based upon absurdly literal interpretations of esotericism that led to the beginnings of live sacrifice and increasingly more ignorant attempts to propitiate "the gods" through fear and greed. It was purely out of these latter that religion gradually evolved the demonic "devil" figure that Christianity and Islam subsequently inherited from the latter-day Egyptians. One might also speculate that, notwithstanding Moses having been an entirely allegorical figure, the story of his having returned from Mount Sinai to find the "Children of Israel" worshiping "the Golden Calf" could from one angle be regarded as perhaps relating to such an epoch.[13] However, modern archaeological "evidence" that the period of cultural growth in the fourth millennium B.C. is when civilization and culture first commenced seems far more likely to have been the result of a merely long-delayed renaissance following the cataclysms affecting Poseidonis and Magna Graecia, as described by Plato, just as our own European Renaissance emerged after several hundred years of "the (cultural) Dark Age" following the fall of the Roman Empire.[14] It thus seems just as possible (if not more so) that the sheer extent of destruction plus trading and social disintegration caused by the cataclysms and subsequent pluvial period of the eleventh and tenth to the sixth millennia B.C. physically prevented such a renaissance before then.

The Origins of Modern Egyptology

The so-called prehistoric Egypt of the modern archaeologist has been largely derived from the work of Sir Flinders Petrie, whose pioneering approach was itself heavily based upon "sequence dating" of pottery.[15] He developed his ideas of Egyptian culture having evolved by about 3750 B.C. through five historic periods, which he called the "Tasian, Badarian, Amratean, Gerzean and Semanaian." However—as was widely acknowledged—Petrie was "largely unsympathetic" toward ancient Egyptian religion.[16] So, armed with willful ignorance on such a fundamental issue, how could he have had the faintest true understanding of what Egyptian culture was really about or where its roots might really have lain? But modern Egyptology has built its own temple of knowledge upon the foundations that Petrie constructed.

Present generations of Egyptologists, absorbing wholesale the view of anthropologists that only "hunter-gatherers" and pastoralists could possibly have existed in Egypt, Sudan, Libya, and Ethiopia prior to about 3500 B.C., have "logically" evolved the view that all the Nile temples, the Sphinx, and the Pyramids can only have been built since then. Yet as John Anthony West has already pointed out in following up the observations of Schwaller de Lubicz, the climatological erosion around the Sphinx's quarried enclosure and the Osireion at Abydos quite categorically confirms that such architecture preceded the extended pluvial period that commenced about the tenth millennium B.C.[17] In addition, the pottery and art found by Petrie has been shown quite clearly to be of a non-African type.[18] Thus, if Petrie's dating of the pottery sequence is correct, it would serve only to reinforce the idea that a new infusion of almost certainly Indo-Aryan humankind, in relatively modern times, merely reoccupied the architecture of a far more ancient and antecedent civilization.

Plant Culture Proves the Existence of Prehistoric Civilization

Quite apart from the question of metal artifacts and magical rituals, there are several other sources that show quite conclusively that human civilization must have antedated the dynastic Egyptians by untold millennia. One such area of proof lies in the perhaps unexpected realm of horticulture—the development of plant species—and perhaps the clearest examples of myriad such developments are to be found mentioned in Donnelly's book, *Atlantis: The Antediluvian World.* At one point he says (partly quoting Darwin himself):

> It is to Atlantis we must look for the origin of nearly all our valuable plants, as Darwin says: "It has often been remarked that we do not owe a single useful plant to Australia or the Cape of Good Hope (South Africa)—countries abounding to an unparalleled degree with endemic species—or to New Zealand, or to (South) America south of the Plata (River Plata); and according to some authors, not to America north of Mexico." In other words, the domesticated plants are only to be found within the limits of what I shall show hereafter as the empire of Atlantis and its colonies; for only here was to be found an ancient, long-continuing civilization, capable of developing from a wild state those plants that were valuable to man, including all the cereals on which today civilized man depends for subsistence.[19]

In addition to citing cotton, taro, red peppers, the tomato, wheat, maize, oats, barley, rye, the bamboo, guava, mango, and especially the banana (found on opposite sides of the world, yet having no seeds or bulbs and able to perpetuate itself only through suckers emanating from its perennial root) as examples of such provably cultivated plants, Donnelly made the point that all these have been scientifically shown as already extant at least 7,000 years ago.[20] More recent analysis of archaeologically derived samples takes us back much farther still. Pointing out that none of the historically known civilizations shows any indication of having pursued a scientifically based agronomy or horticulture (apart from China, to a relatively minor extent), Donnelly then asks how it is that many of these plants were to be found oceans apart even in prehistoric times if there had not already existed a vast and sophisticated civilization, scientifically interested in and also geared up to such development of plants from the wild state. It is a question that the science of our own century has still not been able to answer satisfactorily and which it carefully prefers to avoid. But why and how, in the face of such issues and such irrefutable facts, is the world of archaeology (and Egyptology) able to remain completely silent?

Inconsistent Scientific Views Concerning Human Intelligence

One of the other areas of extraordinary belief on the part of professional archaeologists is that related to the origins of metallurgy—the capacity to refine and/or combine mineral ores to produce metals. As things stand, the belief is that it all started around 7000 B.C., preempted by the first real farming culture in fixed communities around 10,000 B.C. Yet this view is held in the face of their own scientifically confirmed suggestions that *Homo sapiens sapiens* appeared just over 100,000 years ago, while *Homo erectus*—with a similarly sized brain (15 percent to 20 percent larger, in fact) and an often taller physique—was in evidence at least 1.7 million years ago (see appendix D). On their own terms, our modern *Homo sapiens sapiens* has managed to fly to the Moon within 8,000 years of its first metallurgical developments and yet it supposedly took at least one million years for man with a 15 percent to 20 percent larger brain to develop the intelligence and rationale associated with community farming instead of "hunter-gathering"! Basic common sense tells us that such a stance is both wildly untenable and totally absurd. But is this ever considered as such by the doyens of the archaeological Establishment? No. And why ever not?—because so-called material proof (notwithstanding the extensively incomplete, highly scarce nature and self-confessed unreliability of paleontological material and analysis) always takes precedence over common sense where "science" is concerned.

Further Evidence in the Field of Linguistics

We turn finally to the question of the spoken and written languages of "antiquity"—those derived from an alphabet—generally taken by anthropologists to indicate the quality of mental development and evolutionary sophistication of a culture. However, such ideas are based upon numerous assumptions that also need to be queried, particularly in view of our suggestion that science is tens (if not hundreds) of thousands of years out in its reckonings as to the origins and chronology of human civilization. As we can see from the fact that "classical English" is a relatively modern creature, formalized only during the last four hundred years from a mass of regional dialects and ad hoc spelling tendencies, a common cultural style and its widespread adoption can be seen (not least in its Sanskrit, Greek, and Latin roots) to trace its origins from over 4,000 years ago.[21] Yet the "flowering" and world-wide "fruiting" of English in our own day clearly still has far to go in terms of further adaptation. Could it not then be that each 25,920-year age produces its own seasonally predominant language, of which only the (naturally) degenerate remains can be seen in the next greater cycle?

We mentioned in chapter 3 that the fairly diverse Afro-Asiatic family of languages that one finds spread right across northern Africa from the Atlantic to the Indian Ocean seems to have been the ancient parent of the Semitic tongue.[22] Philologists have confirmed (see appendix F) that there appear to remain in existence today six main branches of an original "Hamito-Semitic" language, the Semitic being almost certainly the youngest, as well as the most widespread and culturally coherent. Does this not, however, imply that it is but the flower (or fruit) of the original Hamitic root language? And if so, from the seed of what pre-Hamitic language and culture did the Hamitic itself germinate and spread its branches from the Atlantic to the Indian Ocean and north to Asia Minor? Quite apart from its pan–North African spread in prehistoric times, the Hamitic tongue seems to have had definite connections with the (now extinct) spoken language of the Canary Islanders[23]—occupants of the small, Atlantic island group that could well have formed the southern flank of the island of Poseidonis—and as far afield as Tibet, southern India (the Dravidian culture), and Central America. How could this phenomenon possibly occur without (*a*) an internationally common written language in antiquity, long preceding the earliest Egyptian dynasties accepted by modern Egyptologists;[24] (*b*) a major focus of both civilization and culture which evolved it; and (*c*) an active, panoceanic network of international commerce and culture to support it?

If archaeologists have been unable to trace the focus of such a civilization—for there must originally have been at least one—there can be only one of two reasons for it. Either it disappeared among natural cataclysms or else it was so immensely ancient that time and tide have reduced most of its archaeological remains to indistinguishable rubble—which somehow seems unlikely given the size that such an urban environment must have commanded.

The Speed of Change in Spoken Language

Philological research over the last century and a half has confirmed beyond any shadow of a doubt that the pronunciation of most languages periodically changes (within a vibrantly active or fertile culture) at such a remarkably rapid rate that even well-known words and expressions can in one generation very quickly assume quite different inflections and meanings from those that an immediately preceding generation had taken for granted. For example, spoken English today is often very differently pronounced and spelled in different parts of the world. In fact, had it not been for the invention and spread of films, radio, and television, it would be easy to imagine that in distant parts of the old British Empire (such as Australia), the colloquial versions spoken today could be even more incomprehensible to a native Londoner after a mere two hundred years than they already sometimes appear.

The coherence of a language is very definitely the cultural product of a coherent national, racial, or other form of group consciousness. But when the sociopolitical or socioeconomic structure of such a group begins seriously to break down, the formally expressed versions of the spoken and written language quickly become casualties. In the world today English seems to have become the predominant tongue purely by virtue of commercial convenience and legal expediency of an international nature. As that commercial internationalization increases, we can perhaps expect (in due course of time) to see nationalism dealt a finally mortal blow by political and economic differentiation becoming irrelevant and also inconvenient. One of the things that we can already see looming on the horizon is that different currencies will also become increasingly irrelevant as some form of common exchange system (a sophisticated form of barter) assumes general acceptance.

Similarly, alphabetical language (already suffering) will increasingly give way in everyday usage to commonly understood icons (as in computer technology) with the result that language-oriented culture (among the masses) will itself become increasingly less evident in some places. All these changes are already (globally) well under way and, by now, seem unstoppable.

The point of mentioning all this, however, is to raise the query, What if something similar has happened (at least once) before, say, 25,000 years ago? What would have been the final result? Would it not have been, initially, a global civilization with no barriers to worldwide trade, generating enormous wealth plus widespread cultural diversity and scientific knowledge, inevitably resulting in an international redistribution of ethnic groups? But, then, what would happen to our own such society in the event of cyclical cataclysms of an extensive nature some 13,000 years hence? Could it not well tear the heart out of a complex web of civilization, including its scientific, manufacturing, trading, and cultural activities, so forcing an unexpected return to necessary self-sufficiency, much of it along the lines of an agrarian, or even "hunter-gatherer," society, because of a widespread loss of personal skills resulting from automation?

If such a thing were to happen, would we not see the rapid reemergence of tribalism and dog-eat-dog tendencies with a resultant general degeneration of both culture and human intelligence—unless of course advance steps were taken to avoid this by reasserting a common spiritual leadership and belief system? But such a quality of unifying leadership would need to be far in advance of any mere religion, with its instinctively divisive nature. However, if such a situation were conceivable 13,000 years hence, why could it not have happened 13,000 years ago?—and 39,000 years ago; and 65,000 years ago; and . . . ?

PART 2

TRADITIONS

FIVE

EGYPTIAN MAGIC AND THE LAW OF HIERARCHY

The ancient Egyptians were famed for their veneration of sacred animals, plants, and other objects and many absurd and ridiculous jests have been made on this account. Plutarch carefully explained the matter: "Nothing can be a god to men," says he, "that is either without soul or is under their power." But language is often mistaken in its purport, and symbolic language in particular. What the teacher utters as from his right hand, the hearer receives as with his left. Those who have not learned the true sense will also mistake in the things. In this way, statues and emblems have been spoken of as actual objects of worship, and animals that were only symbolic personifications of divinity have been asserted to be the real divinities that were worshipped. The intelligent worshipper had no difficulty in perceiving the real truth.

—A. WILDER, IN *IAMBLICHUS*

The ancient Egyptians and their more northern contemporaries in Greece, Assyria, Persia, and Babylonia-Chaldea all believed in the existence of One Universal Life—not as a concept, but as a practical, working fact of everyday existence that ruled every aspect of their lives.[1] With this recognition came the attendant perception that the infinite Consciousness of the One Life presented itself throughout the universe as a vast spectrum of Being. This was then seen to arrange itself into a natural and functionally ordered hierarchy of Intelligence—as "gods," generically referred to by the Egyptians as *neteru*.[2] This vast hierarchy of Being and Intelligence was seen in turn by them as constituting a "body of Light,"[3] containing within itself a whole spectrum of varying shades and colorings in the form of a hierarchy of lesser "gods" whose very life reflected itself in the stars. As both gods and demigods were regarded as being in a constant state of activity—hence the very rotation of the universe—so the stars were seen constantly to change their position. Thus cosmic patterns arose and gave rise to states of existence and associated consciousness. Within these, in turn, were evolved—through the magic of divine self-projection—all sorts of phenomenal forms, such as our planet and all its characteristic flora and fauna.

Gods, Daemons, and Souls

The Egyptian hierarchy of gods was thus recognized as having arisen out of the eternal patterns of activity in cosmic Nature. Emanating from a primeval state of Chaos, sometimes referred to as "the Abyss," these incessantly gave rise to the phenomenon of an organized, sentient, and seemingly interdependent field of universal existence.[4] According to the Egyptian hierophant Iamblichus, the Egyptians thus perceived the hierarchy of existence and consciousness as being apportioned among "gods, daemons, and souls," in that order. The hierarchical arrangement itself was seen as concentrically organized—that is to say, the highest or divine gods were recognized as intelligent states of Being that contained all other forms of existence within their multiform nature.[5] However, they themselves could not be perceived as discrete entities by virtue of their being composed of light itself. Notwithstanding this—light being electromagnetic in nature—their presence expressed itself in the form of a variety of definite positive-negative influences within a given field of consciousness. That duality was itself apportioned between the daemons and souls and, quite apart from giving rise to the instincts and evolutionary drive found throughout phenomenal Nature itself (toward stasis, repetition, or change), it later came to be perceived (by ignorant mankind) as either "good" or "evil."

The very qualities of the gods, their functions and force, were therefore to be found as "principles" (in relative proportion) in every noumenal and phenomenal state of existence and experience known to man, from the highest to the lowest. All phenomena, without exception (including all lesser entities), were thus expressions of these various divine or semidivine principles, although the question of relative "good" or "bad" inevitably remained a matter of interpretation according to Divine Purpose. This was the essence of Egyptian pantheism, and the way in which the Ancients adapted all knowledge and faculty associated with it came to be known as "Magic"—the "Great Knowledge."[6]

The Gods as Expressions of Perfection in Nature

Within this hierarchical pantheism, the gods—being regarded as the divine essences of all existence—were originally seen as the expression of completeness (or perfection) itself—and therefore also of all goodness. Being complete in their nature, they inevitably could not manifest anything other than a small and relatively localized demonstration of their quality and/or power at any one time—that is, outside of their autonomic nature within which the various kingdoms of Nature continued their daily function. All phenomenal activity in Nature, then—whether autonomic or otherwise—was magical and thus arose out of the stimuli provided by demigods, souls, and daemons. However, because the words *daemon* and *soul* have taken on a variety of ambiguous meanings in our own millennium, it would perhaps be sensible to pause a moment in order to explain what the Ancients meant by such terms.

A *daemon*, first of all, was not a devil or satanic entity in the much loved form espoused by the early and medieval Christian Church, but rather a "guardian spirit."[7] The expression was originally intended to describe a multiform hierarchy of entities, of an ethereal (semidivine) nature, each part of which was capable of manifesting a particular attribute or faculty of a given god. These beings were described as existing in two main groups, the one being subsumed within the other and emanated by it from its own essence. The natures of the two groups then gave rise to the distorted idea of "good" and "bad" daemons. In fact, the "good" daemons were originally seen as giving purposeful expression to the will of the god when in closely integrated association with the (Christian and Moslem) archangels and angels, or the (Indo-Aryan counterpart) *devs* and *devas*. They were then often referred to generically as "gods." The so-called bad daemons, on the other hand, were actually the entities of the elemental subkingdoms—"bad" because ignorant of the purpose of the god, through their own lack of evolutionary development, and therefore capricious and unreliable. These same entities (of Fire, Air, Water, and Earth) were often those ignorantly invoked by some medieval (and modern) alchemists, ignorant of the very real difference between them and their "parental controllers," the angels/*devas*. It needs to be stressed that the daemonic nature itself could function in the objective world only through combining itself with a soul-vehicle provided by the maternal *deva*/angel type that, in its totality, literally embodied the spiritual cosmos.

The Distinction between Daemons and Souls

Quite distinct from the entities associated with the daemon class were the entities known simply as *souls,* and in order to understand them, one must first comprehend the two distinctively different aspects of the mind of the god that both daemon and soul sought to express. Without going into immense detail, it would perhaps be easiest to summarize the nature of the pure *deva*-soul type as being the agent of the instinct of the god—that is, acting as the agent of the deific memory and subconscious nature. Their nature was thus purely repetitive and unable to exert an innovative personal choice. The daemon, on the other hand, represented the forward, or evolving, purpose of the god in the shape of the new ideas and perceptions beginning to take shape in his consciousness—working (in the lower register) through the plant, animal, and (particularly the) human kingdoms. In man, however, there inevitably existed the basis of friction, or conflict, between the two, and this had to be resolved by the work of the magus, or hierophant of the Mysteries, through the knowledge and practical (theurgical) use of High Magic. He had to resolve the daemon-soul duality in himself in order to demonstrate a full (and balanced) expression of the god—one of the main, practical aims of the initiatory process.

Within this field of activity, Man—the divine son of the god in his inner nature—was forced (through divine necessity) himself to adopt the guise of the "soul-body" in order to lead the process of divine thought and thus anchor the Divine Purpose consciously within the continuum of our world. This soul-body was recognized as spheroidal in nature and appearance, the (dual) divine Man necessarily possessing two subsidiary souls. The Egyptians called the lesser one of these by the general name *ba*, representing it as a small falcon with a human head, seen in temple hieroglyphs and in the Book of the Dead. They otherwise saw the soul nature in the universe as multiple, simultaneously divine (the "Universal Soul"), spiritual (the Oversoul of each kingdom in Nature, individualized in man as the *saha*), and terrestrial (or astral—the *ba*)—the parent of the objective body form.[8]

Linguistic Confusion among
Scholars and Theologians

Interestingly, the "Universal Soul" representing the overall Divine Purpose for our solar system in general and our planetary Life in particular, contained within the consciousness of our own demiurgic gods, the Elohim, was called the Ba-El (Bel, to the Assyrians). This was subsequently misunderstood and traduced as the absurdly satanic Baal of Christian theologians who had ignorantly misinterpreted (as supposed history) the allegory of the worship of the Golden Calf described in the Old Testament. The *ba* (or lesser soul) of the El(ohim) was in fact represented by the Egyptians as the "sky goddess" in the form of a great cow, whose milk was inevitably associated with the densely packed stars of the Milky Way. A related concept is to be found phonetically at the root of the Indo-Aryan god-name Brahma, from which is derived the name of the Greek god Prometheus (from *brahma-dhyaus* or *ba-ra[ma]-theos*), the bringer of the sacred fire (of cosmic Mind) to earthly mankind. A similar phonetic elision led to the misinterpretation by early Christians of Beelzebul as merely another alter ego of the Devil. Yet the name is derived from the Hebrew *baal-zeboul,* meaning simply "lord of the house"—the "house," however, apparently being an astrological one.[9] Thus the Ba-El of Zeboul seems to have meant the overshadowing soul-consciousness of that Elohim hierarchy temporarily in charge of a particular zodiacal house. *Zeboul* also means "a fly," used by the Egyptians symbolically to represent the volatile principle in Nature.

Religious and mystical history is absolutely littered with mystic double entendres and linguistic distortions of this sort from one end of the world to the other, and one could go on for pages reciting deific names that have been transformed by mere mispronunciation into almost unrecognizable versions of themselves, thereby completely losing the original meaning and force of the idea behind them. One highly peripatetic one that might be mentioned, however (evidently borrowed by the Hebrews from the Egyptians), is Zion, otherwise found as the sacred mount Sahon (*sah-on,* meaning "place of the descended spiritual soul"). Another is to be found in the "Stanzas of Dzhyan" in Blavatsky's *The Secret Doctrine* and otherwise as Shamballa (Dzhyan b'Allah), the "Sacred Island" of the Kabiri, which, according to many ancient legends, was supposed to have existed in what is now the Gobi Desert at a time, aeons ago, when the latter was covered by sea.[10]

The prefix *el*—generally associated with the Elohim and also the "Heavenly Bull"—is commonly regarded as of Semitic (that is, Chaldeo-Assyrian) origin.[11] However, the indications are that it was actually of Hamitic (that is, late Atlantean) origin, long predating the very existence of the Semites, who, we have already suggested in a previous chapter, are probably only a comparatively recent substock of an originally pure Hamitic type. As Ignatius Donnelly says in his book *Atlantis: The Antediluvian World:* "The great god of the so-called Semites was El, the Strong One from whose name comes the biblical name Beth-el, the house of God; Ha-el, the strong one; Elohim, the gods; El-oah, God; and from the same name is derived the Arabian name Al-lah."[12]

Egyptian Origins of Hebrew and Christian Theology

While the Hebrews appear to have borrowed most (if not all) of their mystical theology from the Egyptians and Babylonians at a time when a great deal of their esotericism remained intact, much of the earliest Christian theology seems to have been borrowed from it at a time when it had become degraded into a faint shadow of its former self. Such ideas came via the mystical traditions of what is now the Coptic Church, the Crucifixion of Jesus being seen by the latter-day Coptic priests of the first century A.D. as an almost perfect replication of what happened (in principle, at least) to Osiris, as Wallis Budge describes. Unfortunately, the idea was abstracted by evidently ignorant men quite willing to selectively distort ancient truths in order to ensure the perpetuation of their own cult beliefs and their own jobs. Human nature seems to change very little from age to age.

Now, where the practice of theurgy (or practical magic) was concerned, the Egyptian high priest Iamblichus is perhaps the best recorder of what the ancient Egyptians, Chaldeans, and Assyrians actually believed and how they used their occult knowledge. In his writings, Iamblichus shows quite categorically that the differing states and sequences of consciousness and activity within the vast hierarchy of Divine Consciousness were recognized as such by at least the initiated priesthoods of his time. He also explained how, when the manifold hierarchies and subhierarchies of daemons and souls remained uninvoked by the god in man, the superior consciousness and intelligence of the gods would lie fallow and relatively unrequited.[13]

The Underlying Rationale of Egyptian Magic

However, with that scientific knowledge of the underlying processes of Nature to which were later given the names *magic* and *alchemy,* forms of locally coordinated psychospiritual activity could be induced. In so doing, the attention and thus the intelligent force of the gods could be brought to bear and precipitated for the benefit of the population according to the latter's higher aspirations. One highly important point to remember in connection with this, however, is that the Magi (the priestly hierophants) realized how the energetic force of Divine Purpose or Divine Desire latent in the Divine Consciousness would often work out into objective expression via the lesser daemonic hierarchies, irrespective of whether specifically invoked by mankind or not. They believed that, because of mankind's ignorance, such daemonic activity would often manifest in an unforeseen and destructive way—unless the latent power was consciously absorbed and directed in a manner that was not only safe but also socially useful. Out of such necessity evolved rites of propitiation as well as of supplication in times of specific need.

It seems to have been as a result of these perceptions that the ancient theurgical schools came to be formed, with their strict rites of initiation to ensure self-discipline, altruism, and the necessary self-protection from the direct force of the Divine Power whenever evoked. The original public knowledge associated with this type of High Magic seems gradually to have fallen away since the submersion of Poseidonis in about 9500 B.C., since which time (it is understood)[14] the Mystery Schools themselves progressively went "underground." However, some of the occult knowledge (almost inevitably) "leaked" out over later centuries, much of it then (perhaps not altogether surprisingly) being misused and abused for selfish gain.

Arising out of this type of occult knowledge—supposedly given by cyclical revelation—the ancient initiates understood that within the multilayered consciousness of our planetary Life, functioning through both the phenomenal and the noumenal kingdoms of Nature, there existed a semidivine and spiritual hierarchy of rational intelligences above man in the evolutionary scale. They also understood that man himself stood above the lesser evolved kingdoms of Nature by virtue of his being able to express that very same evolutionary coordination of a higher consciousness within an objective form through the use of his rational mind. This was directly associated with the fact that the divine Man was regarded as having two subsidiary souls—the spiritual and the astral (the *saha* and the *ba*).[15]

Man, the True Hero, as a Spiritual Conqueror

It was further believed that man, once he had himself transcended the limitations of purely human self-consciousness, became a spiritually self-conscious intelligence—a "master soul" or initiated "adept"—known to both the Egyptians and the Greeks as a "hero"—that is, one who had achieved spiritual freedom through his own self-induced efforts. As such he was deemed to have the freedom of the higher and lower worlds of the planetary psyche, and was thus able to exert magical powers at will, although he still had to fight his way to the further attainment of fully conscious divinity, at which time he became a consciously Self-realized demigod, or "immortal." As we shall see in later chapters, this was the essential aim of the Osirian Mysteries.

Religio-Artistic Stylization of the Gods

Contrary to what seems to be commonly imagined among our modern generation of Egyptologists, the early Egyptians did not personalize their gods in the manner that, for example, orthodox Christianity seeks to.[16] Their gods and daemonic hierarchies were stylized pictorially in a manner that clearly distinguished between the two-dimensional subjective, or spiritual, state and the three-dimensional objective state. That many of the gods were depicted with a human body and an animal head was merely another stylistic technique—this time used to focus attention on a particular characteristic or function of the subjective, or higher, nature and the state in which it functioned—thereby confirming whether a god or merely a daemonic hierarchy was being symbolized. The fact that their deities retained a human body was intended to show that the human state was part of their consciousness. Consequently, humanity—the most evolved of the objectivized kingdom of souls—became in its subjective nature the outward medium of expression of the Divine Nature. The adopted human form was thus again but a metaphor.

In addition to this form of stylization, the Egyptians provided their depictions of gods, demigods, daemons, and so on with a definitely hierarchical form of headdress. Because they believed the field of existence beyond the physical to consist of divine, spiritual, and psychic (or cosmic, solar, and terrestrial) states, the headdress adopted in any particular depiction had to be specific to the state in which a given "happening" was described as taking place. As we shall see in a moment, the accuracy of such occult or esoteric metaphors was crucial to the practice of Egyptian theurgical magic.

Understanding the Hierarchy of the Egyptian Gods

We should perhaps next take a look at the fundamental basis of the Egyptians' god hierarchy because the apparent complexity of this has, on its own, caused immense confusion to scholars as well as to laypeople generally. It is, in fact, rather more easily understood if we always bear in mind the three following guidelines, which are themselves based upon the fundamental Hermetic principle, "As above, so below."

1. The Egyptians (as apparently the ancient world generally) regarded the very substance of the universe as the fundamental expression of the One Life principle—and also, therefore, potentially of a vast spectrum of Consciousness, all of which possessed the potential of intelligently coordinated function.[17]

2. The individually designated gods each relate to a specific (and thus sequential) phase or stage of the hierarchical process by which the universe unfolds from latency and subsequently returns to it. However, this has to be considered in both a macrocosmic and a microcosmic sense, for just as the objective stars appear out of apparent nothingness, so the atomic particles of our earth's own biosphere incessantly do exactly the same. Consequently, the "gods" can only realistically be considered as "universal principles" in Nature, whose consciousness gives rise to the serial emanation of forms of objective being. This nonlocational mutuality seems to be at the very root of the supposedly mystical idea that the flapping of a butterfly's wings can move a star.

3. Just as we see many different aspects of these principles interacting with each other simultaneously in our own planetary biosphere, so the Egyptians gave to these aspects (depicted as daemonic hierarchies) subnames of the god hierarchy of which they formed an integral part. Thus, for example, Set (the principle of self-centeredness) could be associated with Horus (the principle of consciousness) to produce the rather paradoxical figure of Horus-Set. One aspect of Horus, Herakhte, represented the consciousness of mankind as a whole, while several others represented the gradual spiritual independence of those individualizing from the mass. Ra, the principle of Divine Purpose itself, could thus be depicted in its wholly universal state as Amen-Ra, or else in its objectively ensouling function as Atum-Ra, or in its actively creative function as Ra-Tem—and so on throughout the whole of Nature.

Although every kingdom and subkingdom in Nature was regarded by the Ancients as being contained within the consciousness of a parental "oversoul" within the "World Soul," man was believed to have a (concentrically organized) triple soul-organism. It was this that enabled him to have both knowledge of higher worlds and also power over elemental Nature. As we shall see later on, this triple soul-organism was depicted by the Egyptians as the three uraei (serpents) mounted on the brow of the god Unas; for the unfurling of soul knowledge and its associated faculties was symbolized for the Ancients by the uncoiling serpent with the head raised and pointing attentively forward.[18] The single uraeus on the forehead indicated astral (that is, psychic) awareness having been attained to some extent, while the head of the vulture of Ma'at accompanying it confirmed that the faculty had been brought under the conscious control of the initiate's own higher Self. (The latter relates to the coordination of the brow and crown chakras.)

As a result of understanding all the various hierarchical classifications, the Egyptians were apparently able to devise (magical or alchemical) methods of combining them and/or separating them to produce specific, phenomenal effects. This, however, is no different in principle from the scientific processes that we ourselves follow today in chemistry, although we apply the method consciously only in the mineral kingdom. However, modern biochemistry is now learning to apply the very same principles in the plant, animal, and human kingdoms in a manner involving "sympathetic associations" that the Egyptians would readily understand from their own ritualistic techniques. But modern science does not like to believe that somebody else might have been there first!

FIGURE 5.1. THE MASK OF TUTANKHAMUN SHOWING THE SYMBOLIC URAEI ON THE PHARAONIC FOREHEAD

The Basis of Sympathetic Magic

While we shall deal more fully with certain of the various magical rituals of the Egyptians in chapter 8, it might be helpful at this point to tackle the subject of "sympathetic magic," the technique of theurgic association that they used to ensure that their invocations and evocations produced specific and controllable results, in a manner that would do justice to modern scientific principles. Sympathetic magic—the evocation of a potency in Nature by a ritualized, psychomagnetic stimulation of its likeness—is, perhaps curiously, based upon the principle of sacrifice. As Professor Raimundo Panikkar says in his book *The Vedic Experience:*

> By sacrifice, Gods and men collaborate, not only among themselves but also for the maintenance and very existence of the universe. . . . To perform the sacrifice is not to participate in a good act or to do good to the Gods, to mankind, or to oneself; it is to live, to "make" one's own survival and that of the whole universe. . . . The deterioration of this world-view begins when sacrifice is interpreted in a substantialized way, that is, when it is reified and thus permits the introduction of magical interpretations.[19]

It surely follows from this that the original attitude toward the practice of High Magic among the Ancients was that it comprised a fundamental part of humanity's normal, day-to-day involvement in ensuring that the world and universe continue in a healthy state of existence. As Professor Panikkar also points out, however: "Without Rta [self-sacrifice], the Vedic sacrifice would degenerate into a manipulation of the whole cosmic order by Gods or Men, and we would fall into a hideous world of magic, as men are sometimes prone to do"[20]—as indeed proved to be the case by late Egyptian/mid-Roman times.

Now, as has already otherwise been indicated, the Egyptians took the view that the essence of divinity—of a god—was to be found in all phenomenal existence, including the very materials used in their architecture and art. With that perception in the background, it was a short step to the view that a clear representation in the form of some idea contained (or could be made to contain) a concentrated amount of the essence of the god. The corollary to this was that because the noumenal nature of the god required a concentrated and condensed amount of its own lower nature in which to manifest, the representation—if properly and accurately dedicated by proper prayer and magical passes—developed a magnetic capacity of its own. This, then, in turn set up an immediate psycho-spiritual affinity with the noumenal essence and force of the god, thereby allowing something of its nature to "appear" within it.

Unconscious Magical Effects

All magical practice throughout the world involving the summoning or invocation of a noumenal entity seems to require (as of absolute necessity) the preliminary preparation of a field or vessel of limitation, or enclosure. The logic for this appears to derive from the magnetic polarity of the field or vessel. Without limitation, neither Mind nor Consciousness nor Power can manifest. In the selfsame way, from a scientific viewpoint, without resistance or inertia, electrical and mechanical energy can exert no force. The underlying principle looks to be exactly the same, although the doyens of modern scientific orthodoxy would again doubtless be most unhappy at the thought of admitting such a thing.

What would undoubtedly have caused some anxiety to the Ancients was that the phenomenon of concentrated magnetism sufficient to evoke the attention of a god could sometimes occur spontaneously without people being aware of what they had done to bring about such a situation. For example, swearing oaths or imprecations in anger, or threatening behavior, was abjured for this reason, and the doctrine of blasphemy was doubtless begotten in that manner. The idea also took shape that groups of human beings when gathering together with a particular, common aim in mind themselves automatically attracted the attention of a god (or, rather, a daemonic hierarch on the god's behalf). Thus it came to be that all undertakings—whether great or small—had first to be blessed by a priest. They were thereby given sanction and protection from any unwanted infiltration that might otherwise tend toward either subverting the original intent or otherwise harming the community from which it sprang. It is from this that the tradition of the "evil eye" seems to have sprung. Our own society today, of course, remains riddled with superstitious folk memories related to such issues, our instincts often telling us that there is something valid in them even if we cannot put our finger on what it might be. Is it not still common practice for people all over the world to call in the supposed efficacy of a priest to bless new undertakings by prior invocation and a passing over of hands? Belief in the "evil eye" is also still found throughout the world, as any reasonably well-traveled person knows.

Magical Artifacts in Theurgical Work

Turning to the issue of how a blessing could be administered by such a passing over of hands, it seems that the human individual—being the partial emanation of a god—was regarded as being able (with practice) either to project a spiritual "fluid essence" or to magnetically draw forth the latent divine essence within a talisman *(ushabti)* toward himself (the same principles being found in the practice of mesmerism and t'ai chi). In using mesmeric "passes," he was believed to magnetize and thus "supercharge" it, thereby giving it a temporarily attractive potency and individuality. In this way (as happens even today), icons became sanctified or "holy." However, according to one school of thought, a vast proportion of the supposedly continuing atmosphere of sanctity is provided by psychic effluvia generated by the devotions of the worshipers themselves.

No true sanctity, however, could be engendered in the *ushabti* or other object without a deliberate act of spiritual consecration involving (with total belief) the calling down of certain of the noumenal energies of the god, demigod, or daemon associated with the object of veneration, as already described. Behind this recognition lay the principle followed by the Ancients of blessing such amulets and other "charms," to carry a sort of personal, psychospiritual battery charge to supplement the faltering will of the individual. Inevitably, amulets and charms involving animal representations carried greater potency for the Egyptians because their very particularity signified greater concentration of a very characteristic type or quality of force. Thus, specifically different types of amulet and charm were considered much more efficacious than generalized ones. Following on in the same vein, increasing degrees of detail and complexity in the form itself signified increasingly greater potency.

The Rationale of Psycho-spiritual Magnetism

In considering the question of potency itself, a few words need to be said on the question of what supposedly carries the magnetism of the continuing psycho-spiritual charge. Although we have already suggested that a daemon of some or other evolutionary status was supposed to become present in the talisman by the priestly invocation, even the lowliest daemon needed a substantively energetic form in which to immerse itself. To have done so merely in the clay or metal of the model would have rendered it totally inert and impotent. This is also something that has not been generally understood by academics, who regard anything to do with magic as mere superstition. It is not understood, even in our own day and age, as a great many very intelligent people are prepared to testify.

The Ancients realized that because all material substance was a crystallization of light—the latter being the expression of the gods' intelligent consciousness—any localized concentration of that light gave rise to increasingly more inertial magnetisms and darker, earthbound forms.[21] Conversely, if at least some of the diffused light in the form could be induced to resonate and thus radiate its energy outward, an organically coherent magnetic field would be set up that resulted in the form being seen as emanating an ethereal "double," or *ka*. The principle is exactly the same as that involved in the use of an electrified wire wound around a bar of soft iron to create an electromagnetic field. Anyway, it was this ethereal double that then responded to all yet "higher" potencies associated with it by human magical evocation. Consequently, so it was believed, a daemon could be induced to enter this double (wholly or partially), thereby becoming anchored by and to it, so making it its own.[22] This is the essential nature of so-called elemental possession, although today's connotations of that expression tend to be associated either with the human personality or with a place infested with poltergeist or ghost activity. The latter are, however, a somewhat different class of phenomena.

It follows from all this, by implication at least, that the lesser type of daemonic (that is, elemental) entity invested in a minor personal talisman would usually be of a very different potency to one charged with, for example, guarding the tomb of a pharaoh. Yet each of these entities—being the emanated progeny of a *deva*-daemon—would itself bring to bear something of the nature of its parent as well as of itself. Bearing in mind that there were supposedly distinct classes of *deva*-daemons associated with each of the mineral, plant, and animal kingdoms, it follows quite logically that the quality of the elemental invested in a talisman had to be derived from the equivalent quality of the human invocation.

Human Motivations and the Angelic Hierarchies

For example—and the principle presumably holds just as well today in our own religious services—if the purpose behind an evocation were altruistic and relatively or entirely lacking in selfishness, the possessing entity would be of purer and more highly evolved quality, as would also its own *deva*-daemon parent. Consequently, the quality of psycho-spiritual magnetism evoked would tend to convey that characteristic quality as a psychic resonance to which the etheric "double" of the human being was itself sensitive.

At least one current tradition has it (and it seems to coincide with the ancient Egyptian train of thought) that it is as a result of human beings—through the use of their creative mental powers—finding phenomenal ways of fulfilling a sense of need on the part of others that the *deva* and elemental daemons are themselves said to evolve.[23] The idea seems to be that they do so through learning an intelligent response to enforced change. The Ancients appear to have recognized this and consequently took the greatest care not only to design the correct rituals to evoke the correct class of spirit entity, but also to ensure that such rituals were properly associated with the various seasons. These same hierarchies were themselves regarded as following cyclical patterns of activity and quiescence and, consequently, a highly accurate knowledge of such chronological associations was vitally important—hence, for example, the science of astrology. In a similar vein, when we look at the various hieroglyphic tableaux of the ancient Egyptians, we are initially staggered by the extent and complexity of their art, every hour of the day and night being accounted for in relation to the activities of the solar deity and his daemonic/angelic subhierarchies.[24] However, when considered in relation to their sense of need to coordinate their every routine with the natural cycles of the nether spiritual and divine worlds, this becomes readily understandable.

Egyptian Cultural Degeneracy

The unfortunate outcome of following this practice to the nth degree was that the ancient Egyptians of more modern times (under the human pharaohs) became increasingly rigid and atrophied in their political, social, and religious structures—as well as highly materialistic in their application of ancient symbolic customs.[25] Eventually, "the tail began to wag the dog," and the sense of an evolving Divine Purpose gradually dissolved. Then, as fear and acquisitiveness took hold of human nature again, the zeitgeist of Egyptian genius eventually withered away completely, leaving merely an institutionalized, bureaucratically ordered yet empty shell to provide mute testimony to the existence of a once magnificent civilization and culture. As Jane Sellers put it: "Depiction of strange mythological creatures proliferated; belief in magical spells and amulets seems to have completely overshadowed the often profound writings in the older texts. Egypt's splendid self-confidence, born partially of isolation from the rest of the ancient world, ended. . . . A wonderful culture slowly lost its nerve . . . and eventually lost its life.[26]

Notwithstanding this, something of the nature of the original civilization still seems to "hang in the air" in Egypt, in certain parts of which, it has long been noted, the light has a particular but indefinable quality of clarity to it. Bearing in mind the nature of a presumably continuing *deva*-daemonic association as described at some length in this chapter, the tangibly magic and echoing atmosphere of Egypt may perhaps be seen as exercising a continuing and resonantly magnetic fascination even in our own day and age.

While the sympathetic magic that we have described here has been loosely related to the issue of personal human aspiration, the ancient Egyptians otherwise adopted the very same principles on a truly grandiose architectural scale for their civilization as a whole—for example, with the Sphinx and Giza pyramids. Quite how and with what aims in mind we shall see in later chapters. However, before we get to that point, we must first have a look at the gods themselves and see how the Egyptians believed their very presence to be found throughout the length and breadth of their land.

SIX

TWO EGYPTIAN MYSTERY TRADITIONS RECONSIDERED

In all theurgic rites there is a double character put forward; the one as a human being, the other as participating of a superior nature and exalted as to the order of divinities. In the former, the priest makes the invocation as a man and supplicates the superior beings; in the other, he commands the powers of the universe, for through the ineffable symbols, he is in some manner invested with the sacred character of the gods.

—IAMBLICHUS, *THEURGIA*

Of the various allegorical stories related to the Egyptian tradition, two in particular stand out. The first relates to the death and mutilation of Osiris at the hands of his brother, Set, and his subsequent bodily reorganization by his wife, Isis. The second relates to the postmortem experiences of the human soul, leading to the "weighing of the heart" ceremony.[1] Both have suffered varying degrees of misinterpretation down the decades as a result of failure to appreciate, in advance, the significance of esoteric nuances. This chapter therefore aims to redress the balance. We begin with the Osirian tradition.[2]

In a very brief recapitulation of the story, the god Osiris (already king of Egypt) is first of all tricked by his brother, Set (who wishes to usurp his throne), into trying out a beautiful coffin for size. As soon as he lies down in it, however, Set and his accomplices nail down the lid and throw the chest into the river. It of course sinks, and the current eventually takes it down to the sea, where, on some lonely coast, it gets caught up in the branches of a tamarisk tree, which then over the years grows around and encloses it within its trunk. Isis, setting off in search of her husband, after much effort locates the coffin. However, the tamarisk tree has been cut down and its trunk used to support the roof of the local king's palace. By artifice, she at last manages to recover possession of the beam and, cutting it open, finds the dead body of her husband, which she then hides away "in a secret place." Unfortunately, Set comes across it and in fury he cuts it up into fourteen pieces that he then scatters all around Egypt.

Isis, on hearing what has happened, sets off again in search of her husband's dismembered body, but is only ever able to find thirteen pieces, the fourteenth bit (the phallus) having supposedly been eaten by a fish, the oxyrhincus. She turns to the god Thoth for help, and he then tells her of the magical processes she must use in order to make Osiris come back to life. These involve putting all the pieces together very carefully and then embalming the body, leaving only the head free of the wrappings. Once all such preparatory works are complete, she is then to repeat certain magical formulae and also to open the mouth of Osiris with an oddly shaped tool (called the *apuat*) so that his spirit—the very "Breath of Life"—will be drawn back into the body.

Having done all the initial work, Isis next makes up a mock phallus from one of the trees in the Delta and straps it to the body of Osiris. Thereafter she is made to take up the *apuat* instrument and, reciting certain magical phrases that Thoth has taught her, she arranges for Horus the Elder to open the body's mouth with it. At this, the spirit of Osiris is temporarily drawn back into the body, which has already been made ready to effect the act of procreation. Osiris's divine seed is thereby projected into her womb so that she conceives. As a result, a son (Horus the Child) is eventually born and grows to youthful manhood (as Horus the Younger), upon achieving which he goes off to do battle with Set in order to recover his father's kingdom and rule it himself.

Now, charming though this story might appear to be, it is quite clearly too far-fetched in almost all of its details to be anything but an allegory—but of what? Well, let us look at some of the details first of all. Perhaps the most curious is that Osiris (the archetypal man-god) seems to be depicted as a rather naive, albeit spiritual, figure. Why? Second, although usually described as the brother of Osiris, there is one tradition that associates Set with Osiris's firstborn son, Bebi, through an "unconscious" liaison with the goddess Nephthys.[3] She is clearly symbolic of the purely material side of Nature, just as her sister, Isis, represents the psychic side. So what is all this saying? Third, the various parts of this story seem to suggest a very definite and progressive sequence. Again, why?

FIGURE 6.1. THE OPENING OF THE MOUTH

This tableau shows Horus (symbolizing self-consciousness) "opening the mouth" of the Osiris figure (symbolizing the Osiris nature in man) using the *apuat* tool. This implement—as recognized several decades ago by the German Egyptologist Borchard—has an occult association with the circumpolar constellation of Ursa Minor. As the Osiris nature was also associated with the circumpolar stars, the implicit symbolism is that Osiris represents the individual's own inner (as yet paralyzed) semidivine nature, which has fallen from the divine state but which can be reawakened. The "mouth" symbolically refers to the crown chakra, which, when "opened," allows the spiritual "Word" to emerge.

Osiris as a Multiple Metaphor

As we have previously concluded, Osiris represents not only the phenomenal aspect of the great god Ra, but also the superior (that is, spiritual) intelligence of Man himself—the expression of his divine nature. At the commencement of the great round of existence, this newborn intelligence—although divine—lacked experience and conscious knowledge. He is shown as the potential ruler of all Nature (within the solar system as well as more specifically on Earth), yet he is apparently too naive to realize how to exercise authority and power properly. He is depicted as king inasmuch as he contains his kingdom within his own nature as the offspring of Ra.[4] This kingdom of his has four aspects to it—represented by Osiris himself, his "darker" brother (or first son), Set, and his two sisters, Isis and Nephthys, who incorporate the phenomenal side of Nature—its sensory faculties and powers—between them. All four, however, symbolize universal principles in Nature.

As suggested in previous chapters, every Egyptian allegory has to be interpreted on three quite distinct levels—corresponding with the fields of divinity, spirituality, and psycho-physical objectivity—that is, the cosmic, solar, and (astro-) terrestrial planes of existence. The cosmic, or universal, aspect will be dealt with in chapters 8 and 9, but here we shall touch on those aspects that relate more specifically to the sensory and psychological experience of our humanity. We begin with general consideration of what the five figures—Osiris, Isis, Nephthys, Set, and Horus the Child (later Horus the Younger)—symbolize from our own human viewpoint, both collectively and individually.

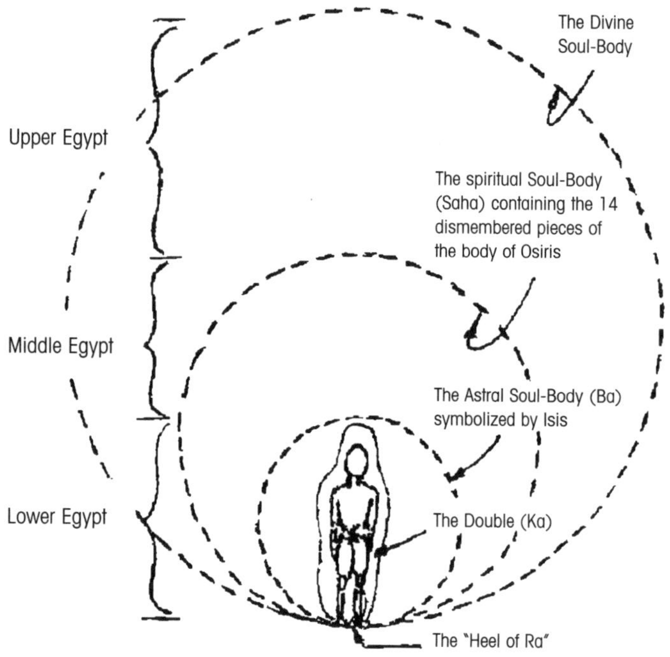

First of all, in a collective sense, these five represent the phenomenal body of either Ra or the divine Man—phenomenal in the sense of symbolizing the various aspects of his multiple soul nature. Readers more familiar with New Age philosophy will probably tend to recognize these quite quickly, because there are very distinct correspondences in the ancient Egyptian system, as we shall see. However, for those unfamiliar with such ideas, the following explanation is offered by way of an attempt to help simplify the general concept (see also appendix G).

In figure 6.2, we see the three primary "soul" aspects, the divine, the spiritual, and the astral, the latter two then comprising the respectively emergent worlds of noumenal and phenomenal Creation—esoterically symbolized by Middle and Lower Egypt. Initially, only the Divine Soul existed, and the four universal aspects of Creation remained in latent harmony. These four jointly born aspects—personified as Osiris, Isis, Nephthys, and Set—comprised:

FIGURE 6.2. THE THREE PRIMARY SOUL ASPECTS

1. The sense of a higher purpose (dharma);
2. The individualized senses of duty and necessity, that is, karma;

3. The instinct of self-sacrifice;

4. The principle of dynamic action and self-expression.

This state of heavenly equilibrium is now determinedly upset by the Set nature, which, however, is clearly to be seen as the mere *agent provocateur* of the unseen, parent Logos (Ra). The first effect of unleashing this drive toward outward incarnation is that the hitherto latent Osirian sense of higher purpose now "falls" into a state of active potential. It can fall no further, however, than the noumenal consciousness of the starry spiritual state (of the *saha*), where it is metaphorically depicted as "dead."

The Isis nature, on the other hand, falls further into generation—as the planetary *ba*, or astral soul—to become the future parent of the semidivine nature in the objective world system. The Nephthys nature—within the next lower octave of atomic matter—instinctively sets about assisting Isis by providing all necessary material support (as the *ka*, or "Black Virgin"). The Set nature, recurring in the lowest register of semi-intelligent, elemental consciousness, then blindly and self-centeredly seeks to appropriate, accumulate, and organize as much of this material as possible for its own use—that is, to produce a physical body form. So here, then, Set represents what the Hindus calls *kundalini*.

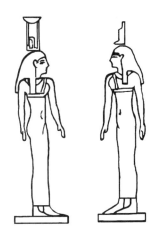

FIGURE 6.3. NEPHTHYS AND ISIS

In Egyptian esoteric symbolism, Isis represents the "astral" soul *(ba)* principle, while Nephthys represents the "etheric" double *(ka)* principle. Hence, these two are almost always found in functional tandem, whether in the cosmic or the terrestrial context.

Figure 6.2, showing the three-in-one soul nature, not only identifies the relationship between Isis and Nephthys, but it also depicts Set as the emergently blind life principle already mentioned, expanding centrifugally amid the *ka* of Nephthys with which it thus unites. However, we also see in Set that dynamic principle that ultimately unites all three soul aspects. Below him is the metaphorical "heel of Ra" that Isis arranged for a scorpion to sting in order to persuade Ra to confide in her his secret name, by which she could initiate a sufficiently powerful magic to bring her husband (the higher spiritual consciousness) back to life again.[5] The significance of the scorpion is an astronomical one, for, as we have already seen, the zodiacal sign of Scorpio is where we find the celestial autumn equinox, where Ra's influence naturally begins to recede. Consequently, the myth has Ra, at this stage, appearing "old and doddery." Isis, on the other hand, now armed with the knowledge of his sacred name, becomes the mistress of all of Nature's magical arts.

The allegory of the dastardly Set doing away with his brother, Osiris, is meant to signify that, within the cosmic round, there comes a period when the astral and divine natures become "separated" from each other, thereby creating an apparent duality of existence. The primordial Golden Age is over, and the as yet unself-conscious "spark" of Ra's will in the lower register of existence (that is, Set, the elemental nature in man) starts to carve out his own little "empire." In so doing he negates the influence of Osiris by usurping the Underworld (the astral psyche), over which Isis is then able to exert only a partial and indirect influence on behalf of her absent consort. Isis, however, finding that Osiris has been ousted from his active role as ruler of the kingdom, "wakes up," and after a "search" is reunited with his inanimate corpse. This refers to that point in the evolutionary cycle (of man) when the astral soul nature makes contact with the divine nature of the god-man, inert in its spiritual "coffin" (the *saha*). However, even though Isis finds the "body" and brings it back intact, because Set has assumed all power over the growth and expansion processes in the astroterrestrial world, or kingdom, the Osirian *saha* is depicted as being still unable to exert any active influence. Set then again removes the "corpse," but this time cuts it into fourteen pieces that he then distributes, apparently at random, around Middle Egypt.[6]

Interpretation of the Allegory

The underlying idea here—something that we shall deal with in detail in chapter 8—is that the fourteen pieces represent fourteen substates of consciousness separating the sevenfold astral soul from contact with the spiritual soul.[7] Isis, now representing the "higher" evolutionary orientation of the astral *ba*, sets about "finding" and coordinating the fourteen as yet chaotically distributed substates that (as the emotional and mental faculties) will eventually give rise to the distinctively human personality. However, the lowest of these substates (rather misleadingly represented as a phallus, because of its self-reproductive function) is then found to be missing, supposedly swallowed by the Nile fish, the oxyrhincus. The phallus is thus clearly a deeply esoteric metaphor, indicating that abstract archetype of human creative intelligence—the illuminating flash of "spiritual intuition."

Deprived of this self-creative psycho-spiritual function of the divine Man, Isis (the astral soul principle) seeks the advice of the divine Thoth-Tehuti (symbolizing the principle of higher knowledge and wisdom, fig. 6.4), whose advice that she must now carve out a facsimile of the missing phallus from the material of her Underworld kingdom

FIGURE 6.4. THOTH-TEHUTI, GOD OF HIGHER KNOWLEDGE AND WISDOM

means that the astral soul must develop its own invocative powers to draw down the desired spiritual influences. His further advice to her concerning the *apuat,* needed to prise open the "mouth" of the body so that the spirit of Osiris (the *kha* principle) may reenter, conceals yet more esoteric lore. The "mouth" is in fact another esoteric metaphor, this time representing both the highest mentality in man and its purely physical counterpart—the crown chakra. Once this is "opened," the spiritual ego (Horus) becomes manifest in the *ba* and also within the waking consciousness of its human "puppet."

Remembering that Isis represents the astral soul *(ba)* that potentially emanates and then continues to vivify the human consciousness out of its own nature, her/its fecundation by the higher energies obviously had a dual effect as far as the Egyptians were concerned. On the one hand, it actually gave rise to the reincarnation of the human entity itself by an emanation from the *saha* to the *ba;* on the other—later in life—it acted as the medium for focusing the higher energies directly into the waking consciousness of the aspirant to the Mysteries (via the crown chakra) when the proper methods of evocation had been learned and the associated faculties brought under control.[8] Thus the sense of spiritual awareness became permanent in the (initiated) consciousness.

Further Aspects of the Allegory

Now, remembering that Nephthys is the ever-present sister-companion of Isis, we find that she rather interestingly conceives Anubis at the same time that Isis conceives Horus (or shortly afterward).[9] But why should this happen unless the two events were intended to symbolize parts of an interconnected sequence? The fact that one tradition has it that Set was the involuntary result of Osiris having unconsciously made love with Nephthys seems to bear out this suggestion, for Set is clearly representative of the centrifugal energies of the chakra at the base of the spine, which energies unite with the "dark matter" of the *ka* to produce the (lesser) "spark of divine Intelligence" in the heart—the ancient Egyptian metaphor for the dog-headed Anubis. The two offspring (Horus and Anubis) are subsequently shown (once having reached maturity) setting out to marginalize the power and influence of Set—shown as a battle royal between the two—but, when this has been achieved, Set becomes reconciled with Isis, who therefore stops Horus from killing him—that is, from arresting the creative energies flowing through the base of the spine center. Horus, ablaze with anger, then tears off his mother's royal diadem. However, the god Thoth-Tehuti (with apparent insensitivity) turns up and replaces it with the head of a cow.[10]

This rather unflattering action toward one of the goddesses who is held in the highest respect also makes no sense unless treated as an esoteric allegory. What it actually signifies is that once the psycho-spiritual consciousness of Horus becomes united with that of the heart chakra, the astral soul no longer retains an independent identity. Instead—the cow being the ancient symbol of a perennial source of available psychic energy/sustenance—it becomes subservient to the Horus nature. Isis thus mutates into the cow goddess Hathor (derived from *hat-Hor*, the house of Horus).[11] In the purely human cycle, this appears to represent the child's first conscious sense of independence from its mother. That, in turn, has its own higher correspondences in the Mysteries, where the individual forsakes materialistic dependence for spiritual dedication. The reconciliation of Horus and Set in the human persona was thus depicted by the Egyptians as shown in figure 6.5.

**FIGURE 6.5.
HORUS AND SET
RECONCILED**
The combined Horus-Set represents the union of self-consciousness and self-centeredness in the human personality.

The Metaphorical Figure of Anubis

Just as Horus the Younger represents the *kha* (the psycho-spiritual "presence") of Osiris, so Anubis (fig. 6.6) represents the developing (purely human) sense of individuality, or independent intelligence, which constantly oscillates between the higher and lower aspects of human nature. Consequently, he is shown as the one who moves back and forth between the objective world and the world of the soul, as the messenger—like the Greek ferryman

FIGURE 6.6. ANUBIS, THE "OPENER OF THE WAYS"

Charon, who had his own canine companion, Cerberus. Although representative of man's higher and lower personal nature in the objective world, Anubis also symbolizes man's instinctive sense of gathering awareness (through curiosity). Hence, he has a human body with a canine head, rather than the other way around. Horus, on the other hand, has a human body with the head of a hawk—the implicit metaphor of flight being associated with the ascending and descending nature of the perceptual, self-conscious impulse.

Just as Horus and Anubis are shown curtailing Set's power, so Osiris is depicted going off on other "adventures" in Nubia, which is geographically to the immediate south of Egypt and represents the divine, or cosmic, world planes of existence. En route to Nubia, he encounters both Sebek, the crocodile god, and Horus the Elder—the latter having first teamed up rather curiously with Set to hold up a ladder by which Osiris is enabled to climb to the heaven world. In fact, that same ladder is to be found in the Hindu occult tradition of the *antahkarana*, which is itself designated as the subjective Path up which the initiate must travel to attain the higher Mysteries[12]—which we shall deal with in chapters 10 and 11. Interestingly, the "ladder" is described as being thrown down from a "great metal plate," symbolized as supporting the heaven world—something that we can immediately see to be representative of the World Soul from which the spiritual soul was emanated. That metal plate is also exactly the same as the "molten sea" that the Masonic Hiram Abiff attempts to cast for Solomon in the construction of his "temple" at "Jerusalem."[13] However, while providing additional indications as to where the Masonic ritual had its origins, further consideration of the allegory here would be a distraction.

We turn next to the tradition of the "weighing of the heart" ceremony, which was said to follow the death of each individual Egyptian, thereby ordaining his/her progress in the next world. Before we do so, however, we should perhaps preface what we are about to suggest with a few explanatory comments concerning the mortuary preparations of the physical body of the deceased—particularly in relation to the practice of embalming.

Egyptian Views Concerning the Dead Human Being

As we have already seen, the Egyptians regarded the dead body as merely a receptacle of the Life principle, although having important magnetic (and therefore magical) associations with the netherworld of the immediately postmortem state. The prime concern of the later Egyptians—so it would appear—was to use the *ka* (the etheric double) as a sort of telegraph mechanism between this state and that of the living so that a family or ancestral link could continue. Thus the spirits of the deceased could (through adopting the correct magical rites of invocation) continue to be exhorted to act in the spiritual world on behalf of the living, as intercessors with direct access to the "gods." Because of intending to use the *ka* in this way—it being known that the *ka* was the creation of the *ba*—it was considered crucial to ensure that it did not dissipate as it would tend to in its normal entropic fashion, thereby returning to the "mother sea" of the astral light, the realm of Nephthys.[14] If the *ka* remained coherent, so it was believed, the psychic link would continue to exist uninterrupted; and so all sorts of magical practices were evolved to ensure that this occurred. It was known, for example, that if the organs were allowed to remain in the body, the latter would degenerate very much more quickly than if they were rapidly removed. As the full separation of the *ka* from the dense body was supposed to take about three days under normal circumstances, it was therefore important to initiate the embalming process without undue delay, before the processes of degeneration really got under way. The organs were then stored in canopic jars in the funeral chamber, close to the body.

FIGURE 6.7. THE *BA* BIRD
Whereas Isis represents the *ba* principle as attendant upon the individual during waking consciousness (or upon Osiris in the greater cosmic context) the *ba* bird symbolically represents the function of "astral travel," when the *ba* is out of the body.

In relation to the physical body, it appears that the *ka* was also believed to be most closely related to the skin and the layers of flesh immediately underneath it. Thus, they reasoned, removing the organs not only retarded the natural processes of organic decay, it also (theoretically at least) ensured the continuing purity of the *ka* so that the skin correspondingly retained its state and texture for a very long time (even years) after actual death. The process of embalming was itself specifically intended to extend the natural life span of the flesh and skin even further, with the various herbs and chemicals used adding a continuing vitality and elasticity. Finally, the deceased body was surrounded (in the mortuary chamber) with endless mementos of his or her life. This was supposed—doubtless through collateral magnetism—to exert both an anchoring and a reenergizing link to support the continuing telepathic connection with the spiritual world beyond. The degenerate materialism associated with all this is very obvious, however, and it shows to what extent the perceived natural associations with the psychic world had turned into mere necromancy by the time of the purely human dynasties of Egypt, some 4,000 to 5,000 years ago, commencing in the latter part of the Age of Taurus.

The "Weighing of the Heart" Ceremony

Having set the scene, as it were, we now turn to what was actually depicted as happening "on the other side of the curtain." In order to follow what is now to be suggested, the reader should refer to figure 6.8, which describes the scene as the Egyptians saw it. That scene is dual in nature. The room on the left in the top row is the Chamber of Judgment itself, whereas the squared section to the right (often interpreted as a throne canopy) represents something quite different, as we shall see. The fact that Osiris is seen seated there in mummified costume provides us with the key, for on the far left of the tableau we find the deceased person waiting "on the threshold" while the (astral) soul of the deceased has flown on ahead to watch the ceremonial rites. Now, the deceased (being merely a corpse

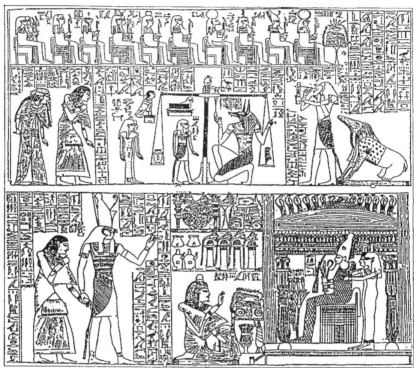

FIGURE 6.8. THE "WEIGHING OF THE HEART" IN THE CHAMBER OF JUDGMENT

The top sequence shown here is taken from British Museum papyrus no. 9,901. It shows the "deceased" (or rather, the neophyte in the Mysteries) entering the Chamber of Judgment (of the Soul) escorted by the lesser jackal god Anubis, holding the ankh of life, while the (higher) jackal god Apuat appears to adjust the balance—according to the relative imbalance between the feather of Ma'at (representing both truth and goodness) and the heart of the individual (contained in the small jar on the opposite side of the balance). Amemet, the "Devourer," looks away while watching Tehuti write down the judgment itself. Horus the Elder then shows the neophyte the mummified Osiris (symbolizing the as yet spiritually inert higher Self) attended by Isis and Nephthys (symbolizing the cosmic *ba* and *ka*), while seated on his "throne," which is itself represented as floating upon "water." At the very top of the tableau, we see an inset showing fourteen figures sitting cross-legged and looking backward—toward the objective, physical world from which the neophyte, or "deceased," has come. These represent the fourteen substates of his own human personality existence. The whole tenor of the picture (note in particular that Osiris, Tehuti, Apuat, and Horus the Elder are all completely uncolored) is clearly symbolic of the spiritually immature state of the individual here, as he passes through the repetitive cycle of reincarnation.

The lower two scenes, from British Museum papyrus no. 10,470—the lowest one being connected to the right-hand end of the middle one—are, however, just as clearly indicative of a much more spiritually advanced individual progressing positively through the postmortem transition state. For example, at the top we see twelve figures (a zodiacal association) facing in the opposite direction to the fourteen (i.e., that of spiritual evolution), while the combined Anubis-Apuat (representing the individual's own spiritual instinct) is himself checking a much more robust-looking balance with a much larger canopic jar and feather. Horus the Elder (now regally crowned and attired) is actively guiding the (suddenly much enlarged) deceased onward while his higher Self, shown kneeling before the throne of Osiris, clearly possesses an awakened crown chakra and an abundance of offertory "gifts." Osiris and his throne room are themselves now transformed by additional coloration and other symbolism, including firm fixings to the ground and his four sons also now facing him and not toward the lower "Underworld" of human existence.

previously vitalized by the astral soul) logically cannot attend the ceremony itself, for the Chamber of Judgment occupies a separate state of existence. Consequently, we may suggest, the human representation symbolizes not just the personality derived from the immediately past incarnation, but rather the product of the life's experience. Anubis, on the other hand, although usually (and misleadingly) referred to as "the god of the Underworld," here represents the "heart-centered" individuality of the deceased person, as we have just described. However, Anubis is also described as the "Opener of the Ways," which has caused some confusion because there is a second, smaller jackal-headed figure named Apuat (fig. 6.9) also holding that same title.[15] In fact, the problem is easily resolved because Apuat represents the faithfully trained *spiritual* memory (or higher intuition) while Anubis represents its purely psychoterrestrial counterpart.

FIGURE 6.9. APUAT, "OPENER OF THE WAYS"

The central part of the tableau shows the scales of justice around which are gathered several figures: Anubis; Thoth (the divine recorder); the smaller figure of the deceased, indicating his destiny, or next incarnation; the rather ungainly-looking composite animal called Amemet (the "devourer of the unjustified"). Thoth, as we have previously indicated, is the agent of dharma, or higher purpose, in the sense of acting as judge on behalf of the Universal Law (of Ra). He is shown without a crown, thereby indicating that his function here lies in relation to the objective world. Interestingly, neither Isis nor Nephthys plays any active part whatsoever in the Hall of Judgment; each merely stands passively behind the mummified Osiris.

Esoteric Interpretation of the "Heart" Metaphor

On the scales of justice (fig. 6.8) are seen, to one side, a canopic jar containing the heart of the deceased and, on the other, the "feather of Ma'at," representing Divine Purpose (or spiritual integrity in a merely human sense). The true interpretation of this metaphor is not the usual, rather simplistic one of the piety and purity of the heart being measured merely for evidence of any wrongdoing or wrong thinking. It is actually the establishment of what proportion of the spiritual soul's originating purpose in relation to the past incarnation has actually been achieved. The distilled essence of the spiritual achievement is then shown dripping from the balance point on the scales into a small jar held by Anubis. He here appears to symbolize the accumulated evolutionary essences of all previous incarnations.

While this weighing is taking place, Thoth stands to one side, noting down the achievement for the purely spiritual record. The "devourer" sits patiently next to him, awaiting the command to eat the remainder of the heart—that is, after the essence has first been removed by Anubis. The composite body of the "devourer" is yet another visual

FIGURE 6.10. HORUS THE ELDER

metaphor, comprising partial anatomies of three animals—the crocodile, the hyena, and the hippopotamus—representing the elemental substance of the mental, astral, and physical states in which the past incarnation of the deceased took place. The idea behind the metaphor, however, is that of restitution—clearly and accurately expressed for us in that part of the modern funeral litany that says "from ashes to ashes and from dust to dust. . . ." The usual interpretation of the scene is that Amemet would eat the heart only if it had been found impure, and, doubtless, by the time of the materialistically oriented pharaonic human dynasties, this is probably how it was rather simplistically viewed by those outside the priesthood. Such an idea does not, however, square with the very evenly balanced attitude toward spiritual development that the ancient Egyptians adopted.

On the left side of the bottom panel we see the deceased—now represented as a much taller person—being shepherded away by Horus (the Elder), who, representing the divine *kha*, acts as a guide for the spiritual Individuality in man. In other words, he is the agent of spiritual faculty that man has yet to learn how to use within the spiritual environment itself. This part of the tableau is usually taken as suggesting that Horus is in the process of introducing the deceased to Osiris. However, in view of the intervening figure of the deceased, now in a kneeling position before Osiris, with his hair whitened (a sign of wisdom) and a bulbous projection emanating from the top of his head, it obviously fails to explain everything. While Wallis Budge and other Egyptologists have preferred to suggest that they do not know the significance of this,[16] that it is the crown chakra is immediately evident to anyone these days who has even the very slightest knowledge of matters esoteric or occult—for example, in the field of complementary medicine.

The Significance of Osiris Being Shown as Still Dead

Finally, at the right of the bottom tier of the tableau, we have Osiris himself, depicted with blue-gray face and hands[17] while seated on a throne still ensconced in his funerary wrappings and held upright by Isis and Nephthys. That this is intended to signify him as being still "dead" is clear. Yet the fact that the spiritual Individuality of the deceased kneels before him (although not in worship) signifies something else.

Casting our minds back, we shall recall that the left side of the tableau showed the deceased as implicitly preparing to reincarnate. Yet we then see his expanded spiritual Individuality first being pressed onward by Horus, and then taking on an apparently holy appearance. There is clearly a progression involved, but there is no question of it happening as a single event. The ancient Egyptians believed in reincarnation—of that there can be little real doubt in anyone's mind.[18] Consequently, the progression that we see here has

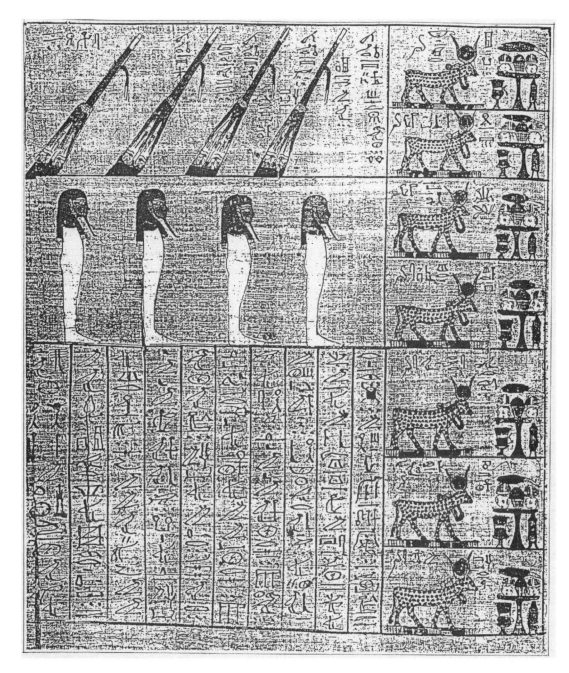

FIGURE 6.11. MAGICAL SPELL NO. 148 FROM THE BOOK OF THE DEAD

Although rather unimaginatively interpreted by Egyptologists as merely indicating the seven celestial cows which (with the "Bull of Heaven") provide sustenance for "the deceased," this magical hieroglyphic "spell" actually tells us far more. The seven celestial cows actually represent the seven states (of spirit and matter) within the octave of "the Underworld," through which the departing spirit of the individual has to travel en route back to the heavenly realms; for the cow symbolized the qualities of substance associated with each such state, or "plane." The top two planes represent the divine and semidivine states of existence, which govern or "steer" the "boat" of cyclic incarnation—hence the symbolism of the four rudders. The next two planes are those in which the "fallen" spiritual Man exists, symbolically incarcerated in mummified form. The lowest three planes are then those of the purely human sphere of existence—i.e., the psychological, psychic/astral, and physical states.

The sevenfold system of planes of existence and/or consciousness is dealt with more fully in chapters 7 and 8, plus appendices H and P.

to be a cumulative one, taking place at the close of each cycle of reincarnation and depicting a progression onward to increasingly greater degrees of holiness, until semidivinity itself is attained. However, even this is itself still shown as occurring within the Underworld—as symbolized by the "dead" body of Osiris apparently barring further progress even to the spiritualized individual. Thus, as the various rites make clear by referring to the deceased himself as Osiris, there is little doubt as to the overall allegory. The implicit meaning is that until the spiritual Individuality latent within the person has evolved (through reincarnation) back to a state of high holiness, the Osiris within him is esoterically considered to be "dead," because spiritually unawakened. However, once he has achieved that state of redemption, the "awakening of the god within" calls down the divine spirit of Osiris upon him. There is therefore considered to be a fundamental difference between the attainment of spirituality and the attainment of divinity, although both—according to the Egyptian rites—were possible given adequate personal effort. The fact that the latter-day Egyptian nevertheless still saw these psychological and psychospiritual aspects of his own nature as separate gods, to be feared or worshiped, again shows just how degenerate his religion had become during the later, pharaonic dynasties.

The complete inability of Egyptologists to perceive (or even be interested in) the inherent esoteric symbolism of such issues is again shown in relation to their interpretation of the papyrus extract shown at figure 6.11, the meaning of which is dealt with in the accompanying caption. The clearly self-evident probability that it involves an important sacred metaphor that pertains to the fundamental, sevenfold structure of cosmic existence within which Man functions is just brushed aside with the implicit suggestion that this is merely another expression of Egyptian superstition.

From these two traditional representations (figs. 6.8 and 6.11), then, we can perhaps see just how readily modern Egyptology has come to believe, quite wrongly, that the ancient Egyptians lacked any real sense of intellectual objectivity. It is entirely regrettable that modern scholarly orthodoxy makes no practical distinction between the perceptions of the initiated priesthood on the one hand and the uninitiated general populace on the other. That lack of distinction also extends to the perceptions and attitudes of these same two groups before and after the demise of the Old Kingdom—a differentiation which led to a gradually chronic spiritual malaise once Egypt became subject to intense mercantile interest outside its own borders (post–2500 B.C.) and subsequent invasion by a series of other nations from the Middle East.

The original seeds of materialistic thought and spiritual degeneracy in Egypt derived from various causes, one of these perhaps being the representational implication (during the Middle and New Kingdoms) of spiritual progress being reserved for those who were wealthy or influential enough to have such scenes portrayed for them personally. Because such representation in great detail was supposed to ensure success (through sympathetic magic) in things working out beneficially in the spiritual world, the inevitable implication was that the inability to have such a tableau prepared seriously increased one's chances of failure, or of being "found out." The original idea was, of course, that the process of spiritual evolution applied to all mankind equally.

One is therefore left with the impression that at least some of the later Egyptians were as naive on these issues as a present-day child who believes that Santa Claus is more likely to bring the right presents if a properly written list of preferred gifts is put in the fire and allowed to blow up the chimney on Christmas Eve. Out of such muddling of original ideas with personal hopes and fears superstition itself arises. When taken into consideration along with the extraordinary interchangeability and variation of alter egos among the Egyptian gods, it is perhaps small wonder that present-day Egyptologists have often taken the view that the Egyptians of the period 4000 B.C. onward must have progressively developed their religious ideas "on the hoof," as it were. However, to judge the whole of Egyptian society and its history on such simplistic grounds without taking into consideration the obviously conflicting implications otherwise thrown up by their scientific, legal, administrative, and moral sophistication itself leads to clearly unbalanced general assumptions and other distortions of presentation that we would not accept even of our own defective civilization and culture.

FIGURE 7.1. EGYPTIAN SYMBOLISM OF THE CREATION PROCESS

In the drawing, we see the androgynous godhead formed amid the "waters of space" by the Divine Purpose, thereby creating the necessary field of Mind-limitation from which the Divine ideation will eventually emerge. This encircle-ment symbolizes the Demiurge, or "creator god," whereas the eye within the field of Mind represents the nonmanifest aspect of the Logos. From the crown of the head of the Demiurge there is then emanated (like Athena from the head of Zeus) a female deity, who presents a portion of the diffused matter of space to the "cosmic dung-beetle," Kheper-Ra, who immediately rolls it into a spheroidal shape. He himself is supported by the twin sister goddesses Isis and Nephthys, the former being attended by five lesser deities, two of whom are responsible for guiding and propelling the "Boat of Ra," which is supported by the Titan god Nu, the positive or male aspect of cosmic Chaos. Nephthys, meanwhile, is attended by three other minor deities at the prow of the boat, representing the triple nature of manifestation in the objective universe.

The underlying meaning is fairly clear, but it is worth noting that there are, in total, eight "boatmen" gods. These appear to represent the very same "octave of manifestation" that we find in the septenary structures common to the Vedic Hindu and modern theosophical systems as "Universal Principles," although interestingly arranged here in a musical sequence (dominant fifth and dominant third), which we shall see recurring elsewhere, later on. The meta-physical sequence, however (from the stern, moving forward), involves the two steersmen representing the divine and semidivine principles (Adi and Anupadaka in the other systems); the next three standing behind Isis then seem-ingly correspond with the Hindu Atma-Buddhi-Manas triad. The three boatmen gods in the prow, behind Nephthys, then correspondingly represent the three planes of material objectivity—the mental, astral, and physical. Thus we may infer that Isis represents the cosmic Ra (the astral Soul of the World) while her sister, Nephthys, represents the tandem principle of the cosmic *ka* (or "double") and Kheper-Ra the instinctively self-regenerative urge in Nature. The boat itself symbolizes the Demiurge vehicle, carried along on the current of cosmic Chaos, represented by Nu.

SEVEN

Gods of the Abyss and Underworld

I am the Creator of what hath come into being and I myself came into being under the form of the God Khepera in primeval time and formed myself out of primeval matter. My name is AUSARES [Osiris] who is the essence of primeval matter. . . . I appeared under the form of multitudes of things from the beginning. Nothing existed at that time and it was I who made whatever was made. . . . I made all the forms under which I appeared out of the god-soul which I raised up out of NU, out of a state of inertness.
—FROM E. A. WALLIS BUDGE, *THE GODS OF THE EGYPTIANS*

The apparently common attitude among Egyptologists toward the original administrative and religious organization of Egypt is a rather curious one. It seems to involve a belief that the political setup was clearly and thoroughly put in place while the religious side was approached in a somewhat ad hoc manner. This seems to be based on the supposition that a varied mass of religious cults were all constantly vying with each other for supremacy on behalf of their particular god or gods.[1] While that may perhaps have been the widely degenerate state of affairs by about 1500 B.C., or perhaps even a little earlier, it certainly does not coincide with what is known about the prevalent attitudes and customs of even the earliest dynastic periods.

With that in mind, this chapter and the next set out to show that not only did the ancient Egyptians adopt a universally common theological system and pantheon from the outset, but that they also translated it into a literal and nationally coordinated scheme of religious architecture and layout, all based upon one overall plan. That they did so resulted (it is suggested) entirely logically from a deep knowledge of astronomy, a perception of "parent" star systems greater than our own, and, finally, a wish to give formal, objective expression to associated mystical ideas. It is consequently unsurprising—given their well-known wish to create a reflection of the heavens on Earth—that one would expect to find evidence of such a desire in sequences and forms of expression that were not only metaphysical in nature (involving a hierarchical system related to states of consciousness) but also architectural. Thus, provided that one knows exactly what to look for in the first place, it becomes possible to detect a very specific and progressive sequence that runs all the way from the northernmost to the southernmost perimeters of the country.

To begin with, it is not possible to understand anything of the essential nature of Egyptian philosophy and religion without first taking into account and consideration the concept of divine polarity (expressed in the form of male and female gods) plus a third, mediating principle of creativity responsible for the emanation of the phenomenal universe *ex nihilo* from "the Abyss."[2] It was from the latter primordial "stateless state" that the whole pantheon of cosmic gods was regarded as having appeared, self-engendered and already perfect, and to it they were deemed ultimately to return.[3]

While the teaching as to the Abyss is fundamental to the system of ancient Egyptian religion, many confusions have arisen in scholarly thought owing to the associated gods and states of being having been given a variety of confusingly half-similar names. These were supposedly donated by the various civilizations and cultures that occupied the Nile Valley over a period of many millennia. However, as we shall now try to show in general terms, the central idea in each of these (apparently different) pantheons was essentially the same, all being derived from a single, central scheme of unfoldment. But it will be more easily understood if we continue constantly to bear in mind that the Egyptians saw everything in a triple sense (fig. 7.2). Thus their pantheon and cosmogony simultaneously described essentially the same principles and pattern of unfoldment recurring throughout the universe, the solar system, and on planet Earth, each of these symbolizing an aspect of the god Ra.

Now, it may seem rather extraordinary to suggest that the ancient Egyptians had clear concepts of the solar system and our galaxy. After all, how could they without a highly

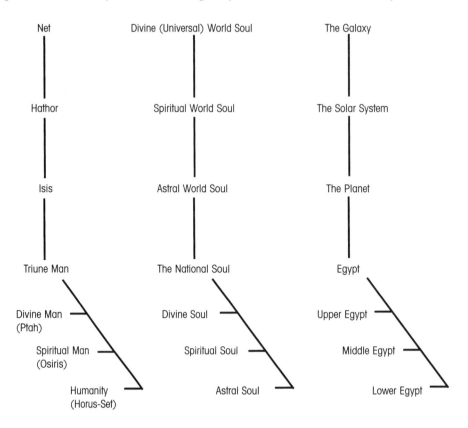

FIGURE 7.2. AN EGYPTIAN VIEW (IN OUTLINE) OF THE TRIPLE FIELD OF EXISTENCE
In this depiction we see the macrocosmic trinity of divine, spiritual, and astral "world souls" and their microcosmic counterparts, the latter showing the progressive evolutionary individualization of the "divine spark" from the mass "world soul" through which it originally came into existence.

advanced technology? Yet they did, and these next two chapters will endeavor to confirm that very fact.

The Gods and Their Associations with Particular Temples

While, as a general rule, all the other temples in Egypt were associated with a triad of gods, Heliopolis boasted a triple triad (or ennead) of nine gods, all co-related in one family as a single, coherent pantheon. They are as shown in figure 7.3.

In addition to the nine gods of the ennead, the Heliopolitan pantheon included Horus, the falcon-headed god (son of Osiris and Isis), and Anubis, the jackal-headed god (son of Set and Nephthys, although Osiris is sometimes shown as the "inadvertent" father of Anubis). There is a very specific reason as to why Heliopolis alone should have nine gods as opposed to the usual three, however, and that reason is outlined in appendix A. At this stage we shall content ourselves with suggesting that Tum/Ra-Tem, in representing the unfoldment of the objective universe, or solar system, symbolizes the lowest of seven cosmic planes of existence. Thus the other god-principles of the Heliopolitan pantheon shown as emanating from him are to be regarded as contained within his cosmic body-form. The latter—otherwise depicted as the Duat (or Tuat)—was both spherical and

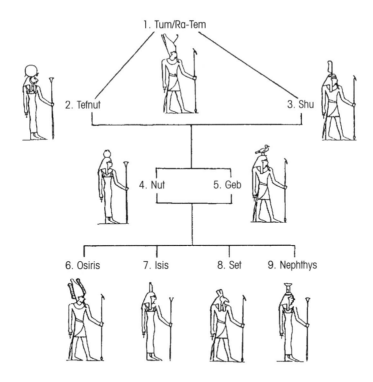

FIGURE 7.3. THE HELIOPOLITAN ENNEAD OF GODS

Strictly speaking, the Heliopolitan ennead appears somewhat arbitrary, because it omits Horus the Elder (represented as a brother principle to the quartet of Osiris-Isis-Set-Nephthys and "born" at the same time as them). It also comprises five dualities—namely, Atum-Ra and Temu-Ra; Tefnut and Shu; Nut and Geb; Osiris and Isis; and Set and Nephthys—while also failing to include Horus the Younger and Anubis. The ennead is less important in purely structural terms than the sevenfold heptad in the Egyptian system, as confirmed by the fact that, of the two, only the heptad had a specific deific figure representing it—the goddess Seshat.

wave-shaped (taking the form of a river valley)—a fact that we shall find to be of very profound significance. However, before going into further detail in that respect, let us briefly draw certain comparisons with the rather better-known Greek cosmogonical system, at the same time bringing into our considerations the Hindu pantheon as well.

The Egyptian Origin of the Greek Theogony and Pantheon

The Greeks admitted quite openly that their own cosmogony and pantheon had been entirely borrowed—largely from the Egyptians, so it would seem, but also in part from the Indo-Aryans and (Hamitic?) Semites of Assyria, Mesopotamia, and India, who themselves shared much common religious imagery with the Egyptians.[4] In the Greeks' Orphic cosmogony, Night (the primordial state of undifferentiated universal existence, otherwise known as Chaos) became active and emanated from within itself the hitherto quiescent creative principle Eros.[5] Thus, this primordial and eternal duality—the "Eternal Father-Mother" of so many ancient religious systems—was regarded as a divine Unity with a dual polarity.

In the Egyptian scheme, the very same bipolar principle is found, although described in somewhat greater detail. The state of eternal passivity of both substance and the creative principle was known as Nu-Nun (infinite space—the Nirguna Parabrahman of the Hindus), and when this began to awaken from its state of dormancy, it automatically transformed itself into Amen-Ament (the Hindu Saguna Parabrahman).[6] This, however—the state of Amenti—was a still as yet invisible state of dynamic cosmic Chaos in which No-thing (that is, no differentiation) as yet existed, not even the gods. Unfortunately, it is usually mistaken to mean "the Underworld" (which it certainly was not) because few seem to realize that it (Amenti)—being the primordial state out of which all ordered existence was emanated—was held to underlie every single possible state of phenomenal existence in the cosmos. It is akin to what the Hindu system of thought calls *akasha*, which is itself, seemingly, synonymous with the "intelligent chaos" of modern quantum theory.

Anyway, as divine wakefulness began to be resumed, the principle of divine self-existence began to reassert itself and the universal Will-to-Be returned to our part of the cosmos—the future universe of our galaxy, the Milky Way. This all-pervasive influence was represented by the ancient Egyptians as the primordial, abstract trinity of Amen-Ra (Universal Life), Mut (Universal Consciousness), and Khonsu (Universal Creativity)—i.e., Eros.[7] The way in which our universe later unfolded and took on a progressively phenomenal existence was then depicted in sevenfold terms as various aspects of Ra in his greater, cosmic manifestation. These were as follows:

1. Kheper-Ra — the self-created Demiurge;
2. Amen-Ra — the fallen Cosmic Mind principle, or "Causeless Cause";
3. Menthu-Ra — the "Breath (or Presence) of Ra";
4. Net/Neith — the "wife" or *"ka"* of Amen-Ra, or "Eye of Ra";[8]
5. Sebek-Ra — Universal Mentality, creator of diversity and repetition;
6. Khnemu-Ra — the god of the "Waters of Space"; the "desire of Ra" (for objective self-existence);
7. Atum-Ra — the phenomenally manifesting universe.

First of all, Kheper-Ra (symbolized by the scarab beetle) was depicted in Egyptian mythology as creating two fields of self-limitation.[9] One is represented by his own spherically or oval-shaped body; the other is the mass of chaotically diffused cosmic substance (symbolically represented as a "dung ball") that he gathers together from space (Mut). It is this that then becomes the mass of the future universe—our galaxy—as we shall see, and in it Kheper-Ra lays his "eggs." As Kheper-Ra is himself a metaphor for that aspect of Ra that creates fields of consciousness by virtue of willed self-existence, the "eggs" too are thus clearly metaphorical.

FIGURE 7.4. KHEPER-RA

Now, Atum-Ra's body (the Duat) was symbolized as a river valley between two mountains—reminiscent of the modern scientific image of space curving downward in an electromagnetically induced "sag" that causes sidereal bodies to orbit around a central point.[10] It would otherwise appear from a contextual interpretation, however, that Atum-Ra might be said to represent the generalized field of consciousness of the "cosmic dung ball" in which Kheper-Ra lays his seeds, the latter being the latent divine "sparks" of his own creative Life-force. Quite why this should be so we shall see in a few moments. However, Atum-Ra was also depicted as an alter ego of Ra-Tem (the two names being dual aspects of the World Soul), who was the chief god (also possessing a dual aspect) of Heliopolis, widely worshiped in the form of a serpent, as Budge himself confirms.[11]

FIGURE 7.5. THE ORPHIC EGG
(from Bryant's *An Analysis of Ancient Mythology*)
The primeval "Egg of the Universe" is an esoteric metaphor for the Universal Oversoul, the "egg" being that field of limitation which is contained by the serpent-soul-being of ancient knowledge, symbolic of the Elohim themselves. This same metaphor is found all over the world in different ancient cosmogonical systems, thereby clearly indicating a common, worldwide spiritual culture back in the mists of prehistory.

Creation Myths Always Involve Battles with Serpents

Interestingly, one of the most universally recognized creation myths involves God (or his archangels) having to do battle with a serpent before his Divine Will and Purpose can be made manifest throughout the universe. In the Gnostic system, the serpent was called Ouroborous (clearly derived from Aura-Bur-Eos); in the Mayan, Quetzalcoatl; in the Hindu, Nag; in the Egyptian, Nak. But the meaning inherent in this image is always the same, for the coiling of the serpent was seen to give rise to the principle of limitation, thereby resulting in the appearance of a spherical, or egg-shaped, field of existence (fig. 7.5, depicting the Greek "Orphic Egg of the Universe"). The underlying principle—as with the activities of

Kheper-Ra—involves the creation of an archetypal field of objectivity through privation, or apparent isolation from the One Life. As already stated, the primordial form thus created was in fact that of the spherical, or ovoid, soul, itself synonymous with the archetypal mythic serpent of all religions. Moreover, the Egyptian version of this symbolic serpent was itself threefold—given the names Nak, Sebau, and Apep (the Greek Apophis). Although appearing to be separate, they are nevertheless to be regarded as three concentrically organized aspects of the same underlying universal principle. Thus it is that Nak represents the cosmic or divine Oversoul (which contains the seven solar systems of our "home universe"), Sebau the spiritual Oversoul (which contains our solar system), and Apep the terrestrial (or "astral") Oversoul, the latter containing our planet and otherwise also representing (initially) the "innocent virgin" mentality in man. The idea of the serpent being "conquered" by the forces of Ra has, however, to be viewed in the sense of its consciousness submitting to the Divine Will and so creating the universe (out of its own substance) so that Ra can project his own intelligent Life-force into it.[12] Thus the serpent (or soul principle) is clearly seen to represent the Oversoul principle as Demiurge, and it is this collective entity that we find in the Old Testament is given the name Elohim. Consequently, every possible plane or state of consciousness in the cosmos was regarded as contained within the nature of this great hierarchy of beings, themselves always referred to as "gods."

Origin of the Concept of the "Fall from Grace"

The essence of the idea was that the purposefully evolving aspect of the Ra-nature was projected into the consciousness of certain of these great cosmic beings but not into others. Those that were impregnated in this way allegorically "fell from Grace" for their pains and were thereby "forced" to create their own organic worlds. It is these that—as individual solar systems—came under the generic name Atum-Ra. Interestingly, we find precisely the same idea in other cosmogonies, also in the form of allegories. For example, Krishna (Ra's alter ego in the ancient Hindu pantheon) says of himself in the Bhagavad Gita, "With a fraction of myself I invest the universe. Yet I remain (apart)."[13]

Atum-Ra, therefore, is the Elohim-Soul of our solar system, the objective part of which—despite its vast entirety—is merely contained within an imponderable field of intelligent existence that extends halfway to the next nearest star. There is then that aspect of Atum-Ra that "falls into generation" (in the lower Underworld), and it does so as two great hierarchies of lesser intelligences, according to the Ancients. One was that of the *devas* (the *neteru*)—the organic life- and form-building consciousness of the solar Elohim. The other was that of "evolving daemons"—the objective expression of which was to be found in the human kingdom. These two streams of life were generically referred to by the Ancients as "Angel" and "Man," respectively. The former is represented by Sebek-Ra, the latter by Horus the Elder, this fact being found clearly expressed in the deities worshiped at the Upper Egypt temple of Kom Ombos. The actual creative impulses behind them, however, were symbolically and respectively depicted by the gods Khnemu and Ptah. Together, they respectively represented the principles in Nature of its unfolding forms and its unfolding consciousness.[14]

Sebek-Ra was depicted as the offspring of the union of the goddess Net (wife of

Amen-Ra) and Khnemu-Ra, the god of the watery vortex or cosmic cataract. The implicit metaphor of Sebek-Ra's cosmic function lies in the terrestrial crocodile's hunting technique of lying in wait just below the water's surface, then leaping out and dragging its prey under water, where it tears it to pieces. If one considers the way in which the human mind works when searching for new ideas within the "waters" of its own consciousness, the meaning stands clear. However, in the cosmic context, the "ideas" comprise Divine Man "falling" prey, as one complete hierarchy of cosmic Being, into the "Underworld" of the World Oversoul below, where it is forced into a cycle of evolutionary differentiation.

Cosmic Archetypes and Their Imperfect Reflections

Before turning to the internal unfoldment of the solar system itself, as seen by the Egyptians, we should perhaps spend a moment or two considering the archetypal figure of Sebek-Ra (fig. 7.6) because he plays such an important role in the Egyptian myth. That role—like so much else, unfortunately—has been widely misunderstood as some sort of demonic figure and, as Sebek, being a mere associate of Set.[15] The esoteric meaning is far more subtle, despite his indeed being a macrocosmic counterpart.

FIGURE 7.6. SEBEK-RA, THE COSMIC CROCODILE

To begin with, Sebek-Ra should be regarded as an emanated aspect of Atum-Ra rather than of Amen-Ra.[16] To understand why, it is important to bear in mind that the faculty of ideation implicitly represented partiality and, with the gods being complete and perfect in their own nature,[17] this meant artificial segregation, diversity, and also, therefore, error or ignorance—the root of so-called evil. Amen-Ra, Kheper-Ra, and Mntw-Ra (or Menthu-Ra) seem to represent the three main triadic archetypes of divine perfection. Atum-Ra, Khnemu-Ra, and Sebek-Ra therefore represent a mere (and thus imperfect) triadic reflection of them within the phenomenal universe, striving toward the achievement of a better representation. However, as this recognition of the archetypal Divine Nature is itself then only *partially* apprehended within the bounds of each individual solar system (that is to say, within each further stage of unfoldment), the basic degree of error, ignorance, and cosmic confusion is compounded. It is from this that the Ancients derived the idea of "imperfect gods."

The name Sebek signifies the "seventh (and highest) soul"—the soul being that principle in Nature, as already suggested, that contains the manifesting Life. Yet Sebek is also clearly associated with the "higher death"—either that resulting from the highest spiritual achievement leading to a quite natural, evolutionary withdrawal from the objective field of existence or that involving the unseen World Oversoul seizing its (divine) prey and dragging it downward into the waters (of local space), where it becomes enmeshed in the demiurgic Creation process and so enters a completely new field of (cosmic) activity.

FIGURE 7.7. THE SEPARATION OF NUT AND GEB BY SHU

While the larger, upper picture is perhaps the better known in relation to this concept, the smaller, lower one is particularly interesting for a number of reasons. First of all, it depicts two sky goddesses rather than just one, each being quite distinct from the other. The greater (i.e., cosmic?) goddess has two flying disks within her body, but no stars—the latter first appearing only within the "space" occupied by the two goddesses. Here also we find two quite distinct types of flying disk: one having two stars above it and the other having seven.

The male Earth god figure is evidently common to both the sky goddesses, and the globes that he holds (spheres of existence?) are located between the two goddesses' legs, on the one hand, but beyond the hands of the greater goddess on the other. The polar positions of the globes at the lower and upper ends of the goddesses' bodies are significant in that respect.

Finally, the single human figure in the picture is to be seen extended between the hands of the two goddesses while all the rest of the "action" takes place within the center of the picture. The stars themselves, throughout the picture, probably represent specific god hierarchies, each with its own significance.

As we shall see in a moment, Sebek is associated with such activity as a cyclic impulse (but see appendices J and L).

The Creation and Organic Evolution of Our Solar System

From the general context of the manifest universe in its entirety, we move on to the more specific field of Ra's self-limitation (as Atum) within our own particular solar system. However, the selfsame principles of unfoldment continue to apply. Just as in the Greek system the localized versions of Chaos and Eros were Gaea (female) and Ouranos (male)[18]—both being aspects of the solar Logos and not just of the earth—so the Egyptian equivalents were Tefnut and Shu.[19] In the Greek system, Gaea (probably derived from the amalgamated Ka-Ea) was a localized form of Chaos (Ka-Eos), the vitalized but still as yet wholly unorganized substance of the solar system. Ouranos (wrongly interpreted as "sky"), on the other hand, is the principle of limitation (like Atum-Ra) that "creates" the solar system by enfolding Gaea within its embrace.[20] This is quite evident from the triple root of the name—that is, Aura-Nous—*nous* being the principle of abstract mind. Anyway, once this phenomenal limitation had been achieved, Ouranos emanated his creative alter ego— Eros again (corresponding with the Egyptian Ra-Tem)—thereby fecundating the contained field of Gaea, so rendering the intelligent, atom-shaped soul-principle universal throughout it and also endowing every such entity with the triple principles of function— namely, Life, Consciousness, and Creative Instinct. Here, therefore, we have the reflective microcosm of Amen-Ra, Mut, and Khonsu. Consequently, the Egyptians were able to regard Amen-Ra himself (symbolizing Divine Purpose) as being omnipresent within (and without) our solar system and investing it with his infinitely conditioning Life-force.

In the Egyptian system, Tefnut and Shu, the self-created "lion gods" who take the place of Gaea and Ouranos, emanate two "children"—Nut and Geb. These two, however, are the expressions of bipolarity within the Gaea substance of the solar system. As such, they represent what we ourselves call "spirit" and "matter." In one of the best known of all the examples of Egyptian art (see fig. 7.7), they are shown as the goddess of the star-spangled sky (Nut) and the recumbent god Geb (or Seb) with the figure of their father, Shu, standing on Geb and supporting Nut in a semi-upright, arched position. Egyptologists generally interpret this in a merely literal sense as Shu forcing the "lovers" apart from their embrace without taking into consideration the allegorical significance of what symbolically underlies the imagery. In fact, Shu is an alter ego of Ra and here he represents the principle of both manifest (cosmic) intelligence and phenomenal light within the solar system.

Unfortunately, because the metaphysical approach of the ancient Egyptians has not been properly understood by most Western scholars, the tableau has been subjected to widespread misinterpretation (as is also the case with Gaea and Ouranos), which tends to depict the Egyptians as hidebound by mythological superstitions.[21] This—as far as the real ancient Egyptians were concerned—is quite wrong. Their whole metaphysical system— like a biblical parable—was meant to be interpreted at various "levels" according to the insight of the listener. The most esoteric secrets thus remained concealed by their obviousness.

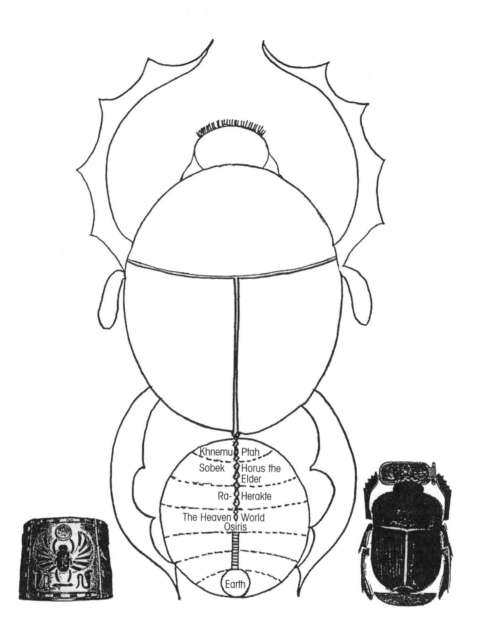

FIGURE 7.8. KHEPER-RA AND THE COSMIC DUNG BALL

Kheper-Ra effectively represented the creatively self-awakened, noumenal Mind principle as far as the Egyptians were concerned. The concept is somewhat akin to the Cartesian "I think, therefore I am." The sequence of mental creation necessarily involves, first of all, self-limitation—the isolation of a "field" of proposed creative activity within the over-all consciousness. Only then can the intuitive seed-thought be projected into it with any real hope of development, or unfoldment. Because of this association with the very creation of self-awareness, the Egyptians also associated Kheper-Ra (hence also the Chaldeo-Babylonian Kabir) with a continuity of personal self-existence. In a cosmic sense, therefore, Kheper-Ra represented the self-engendered (higher) Mind of the Logos. The Sphinx, however, symbolically represented the merely lower, or dualistically personal, Mind function that (as the *akhu*, or "Ego") simultaneously identifies itself with the senses (and thus the Underworld) while still, unconsciously, harnessing the Creative (higher) Mind faculty to produce objective phenomena.

The Origin of Light in the Solar System

The selfsame idea can otherwise be seen in the imagery of the opening of the "Eye of Ra." Here Tefnut represents the subconsciousness of Ra, while Shu represents his waking consciousness. Nut and Geb then become his upper and lower eyelids, respectively, which Shu pushes apart, enabling the light and life-force of the waking Ra to radiate out into the world. Osiris then takes the part of Ra's eyeball, Isis the iris, Nephthys the pupil, and Set the outgoing light and returning image resulting from the projection of the visual faculty. Here too, however, the image of the eye is symbolic, for, as we saw earlier, Osiris represents the spiritual soul (saha), while Isis represents the astral soul (or ba) and Nephthys the "dark light" of the etheral "double" (ka)—this latter symbolism being later reabsorbed into the fringes of Christianity as the "Black Madonna."

We now progress a stage further from the general scheme of unfoldment in the universe and solar system to the complementary esoteric structure and dynamics of the evolutionary scheme as the Egyptians saw it. In order to deal with that as graphically as possible, the whole process of Creation is described for us in figure 7.8. Here we see the symbolic representation of Kheper-Ra as the coordinated states of cosmic consciousness, with the seventh and lowest such state depicted as the "dung ball" of cosmic substance from which each solar system is to be formed. Once created in this way, Kheper-Ra projects his "seed" into the lesser sphere, the point of insemination being represented by the watery vortex of the cataract and also the laterally curling horns of the god Khnemu, the presiding deity at Elephantine.

Khnemu and Osiris

Now, the name Khnemu (meaning "to unite") is supposedly of Nubian origin and intended to signify Osiris as the prototypical solar man-god.[22] Although often simplistically referred to as a "water god,"[23] we can see here that this expression actually signifies the "waters of the cosmic river"—akin to the Greek Okeanos. The associated symbolism, however, is clearly that of Khnemu appearing immaculately conceived and self-born from Chaos (of which the Cataract is a metaphor). Khnemu himself is described as having a specifically septenary nature,[24] which is described by Wallis Budge as follows:

1. KHNEMU-NEHEP   The Creator
2. KHNEMU-KHENTI-TAUI   Governor of the Two Lands
3. KHNEMU-SEKHET-ASHSEP-F   Weaver of the Light
4. KHNEMU-KHENTI-PER-ANKH   Governor of the House of Life
5. KHNEMU-NEB-TA-ANKHTET   Lord of the Land of Life
6. KHNEMU-KHENTI-NETCHEM-   Governor of the House of Sweet Life
   ANKHTET
7. KHNEMU-NEB   Khnemu, Lord[25]

Clearly, then, Khnemu is derived from Khnemu-Ra, who (fourfold in nature, as is also Sebek-Ra,[26] both being principles of cosmic manifestation) represents the "desire of Ra"—that is, for objective self-existence. It is this that is inseminated into the field of phenomenal

FIGURE 7.9. THE GOD KHNEMU CREATING MAN
Khnemu is accompanied by the god Tehuti, confirming man's intended life cycle.

FIGURE 7.10. ISIS AND PTAH-SEKER-AUSAR
The "risen" god Osiris represents the successful initiate in the higher Mysteries.

existence represented by the solar serpent Sebau (Ra-Tem). Once within the field of the solar system, the insemination redivides into three elements—represented by Sebek, Ra-Herakhte, and (implicitly) Osiris.[27] Given the inherent limitations of a two-dimensional drawing (fig. 7.8) to depict a metaphysical concept, we have next to imagine that the small sphere at the base of the "dung ball" represents the densest aspect of the solar system—that is, a planet (which incorporates its atmospheric elements as well as its terrestrial form). This then is the "dead" Osiris, whereas the Osiris shown resurrected in the heaven world simultaneously represents the "germinating seeds" of Kheper-Ra. It must be remembered, however, that the Ptah and Khnemu principles are essentially associated with pansolar consciousness, whereas the quartet of Osiris, Isis, Nephthys, and Set was clearly symbolized by the Egyptians as being particularly associated with our planetary existence.[28] Hence the composite Ptah-Seker-Ausar (see fig. 7.10) symbolically represents the Self-realized and Self-creative Buddha nature, which has completely liberated itself from the thrall of merely planetary existence and now has the "freedom of the solar system" within which to express that nature in its fullest sense. In the picture, Isis represents the cosmic *ba* principle.

As already indicated, the small, lowest sphere intends to depict Nephthys as the astral light, or *ka* of the planet. This, then, is the biosphere-supporting element that is contained by the *ba,* or astral soul of Isis—the latter seeming to equate with the planetary ionosphere. Set then represents the evolving "spark" of life (in the mineral, plant, and animal kingdoms) that has to emanate through all these various states of existence. Consequently, Set can be seen as the lowest (that is, elemental) aspect of the Will-to-Be of Ra, dispersed throughout the universe but, because of its instinctive drive for self-fulfillment, shown as "ousting" Osiris and esoterically "killing" him, as described in the last chapter. The ladder depicted in figure 7.8 symbolizes an evolving path of consciousness leading from the objective (astral) world up to the spiritual soul of the "dead" Osiris-consciousness. Consequently, once this ladder is scaled, man re-becomes the germinal "son of Ra." The "seed-casing" (of the merely spiritual consciousness of the adept-hero) itself eventually fragments and the consciousness then emerges as semidivine—a demigod.

Terrestrial Representations

Now, when we translate this symbolism onto the ground in the land of Egypt, a number of things very quickly become apparent. We have already mentioned the correlation between the sixth and seventh cosmic planes as being symbolized by the First Cataract and its presiding god, Khnemu. The whole of the seventh (and lowest) cosmic plane then becomes the land of Egypt, while south of the Cataract, the temple of Abu Simbel clearly represents the cosmic aspects of Ra—and, as we shall see later on, has nothing whatsoever to do with Rameses II! The four massive seated god-figures outside the "male" temple were thus doubtless intended to represent four primary aspects of the man-god in his outermost *cosmic* manifestation (as the multi-aspectual cosmic Osiris), with Ra-Herakhte (the principle of the hovering divine consciousness) evident in the central relief above the temple doorway (see fig. 0.1).

In figure 7.8, we can also perhaps now see the implicit triple nature of the serpent-soul. The divine, or Universal Soul, is represented by the body of Kheper-Ra—which is contained by Nak. The spherical soul of the entire solar system (i.e., of Atum-Ra) is correspondingly contained by Sebau, the solar serpent, while the lower (astral) World Soul is contained by the terrestrial serpent Apep (the Greek Apophis). The immense importance of this in the ancient psychology and metaphysical system of thought will become clear in the next two chapters.

One other point that emerges with clarity from all this is that Khnemu's association with both Ptah and Osiris is self-evident. Osiris is himself depicted as the triple *objective* form of the consciousness of Ra. The consciousness contained within the astral soul is symbolized by the "dead" Osiris in his funereal wrappings. The spiritual consciousness is symbolized by the resurrected Osiris, while the divine Creator-consciousness is symbolized jointly by Khnemu and Ptah. In the macrocosmic sense, the Atum-consciousness then becomes that of the greater astral *ba* of Ra himself, while the spiritualized consciousness of the reborn Osiris (as Horus) symbolizes the *kha* within the *ka* (see fig. 7.10). Again, these facts are of extreme importance in the context not only of personal initiation into the Mysteries (as we shall see in chapter 11) but also of the very existence and cultural coherence of the ancient Egyptian people and their civilization. To many readers, all this may seem unduly complex. There is, however, a very real order in the complexity, of a type clearly unrecognized by the majority of Egyptologists. It is perhaps most simply summed up in the paraphrased words of the divine Thoth-Tehuti (Hermes Trismegistus), "As above, so below."[29] As we shall see in this final part of the chapter, this axiom was taken quite literally by the ancient Egyptians in a manner that remains barely visible in the ruins of their culture.

Now, although the description of the various gods of the Abyss is one of divine principles as "Powers," they were also seen by the Egyptians as supporting the phenomenal existence of our own planet Earth, and of Egypt in particular. However, what was understood as such by the highly advanced priesthood of ancient times was almost certainly not perceived by the lay population. Consequently, for the abstract ideas associated with the divine cosmogony to have any semblance of relevance to the uninitiated populace, the whole mystical allegory had to be psychologically "anchored" by associating it very specifically and visually with the chief life-giving feature of the country—the river Nile.

The Esoteric Significance of the Nile

The allegorical importance of the Nile cannot be too heavily stressed because of its many metaphysical and cosmological associations with both the Milky Way and the constellation of Draco, the Dragon, or "flying serpent." As we shall see in greater detail in chapter 8, this is particularly the case in relation to the sequential apportionment or allocation of administrative zones along the river. These zones—called *nomes* by the Egyptians—each possessed a major temple (of the equivalent status of a cathedral in many cases) dedicated to a particular deity, indicating its overall hierarchical significance.

The reason for this significance is that the nomes themselves represented the various "states" or "planes" of being through which the evolutionary process was believed to run, as we shall show in chapter 8. Through recognition of the sequence and the various mystical or religious associations attributed to it, ordinary humanity supposedly evolved through a constant subliminal association with Divine Order, in which it constantly absorbed the essence of each deity. As a priest or priestess, the individual actually took conscious part in the mystical ceremonial and so came gradually to understand the inner significances that led to initiation into the higher Mysteries.

Quite apart from such man-made significances, the fact that the Nile had two original sources—the Blue and White Niles, one originating in the Ethiopian Highlands and the other in the volcanic folds of the Great Rift Valley of East Africa—also had great symbolic importance, because—as we have already seen—the manifest universe was regarded as having arisen out of a great primeval duality involving the two streams of cosmic Life—Man and Angel *(deva)*. Interestingly, it may well be that the curious straight and curling lines depicted under the Eye of Ra symbolized this unified duality, as well as other things.[30] The fact that the Nile otherwise inundated the valley plain once each annual cycle, thereby reemphasizing the virility of Ra (in the guise of the river god Hpi), reinforced the sense of a mystical association that must have been based upon much more than mere economic hopefulness. All of these things and many more provided such a constant barrage of evidence that Egypt was indeed the expression on Earth of the order in Heaven above that the religion of its inhabitants could hardly fail to coincide with such a grandiose concept. Associated with the idea of a progressive spiritual evolution through increasingly more refined and powerful states of being and consciousness, it was hardly surprising that the Egyptians regarded themselves quite literally as "the Chosen People," long before the Hebrew people even appeared.[31]

The Importance of Particular Temples and Their Geographical Siting

When considering the question of why and how the geographical nomes were associated with the various planes of existence, certain factors stand out quite clearly, and we can recognize these by looking for various correspondences associated with the temples (as we shall see in chapter 8). For example, Osiris in one of his aspects was regarded as "King of the Underworld"[32] and the temple most clearly dedicated to his worship was at Abydos, which was itself regarded as providing one of the entrances to the lower Underworld.[33] Interestingly—because Osiris was also given the title "Lord of the Two Lands"[34]—Abydos is exactly halfway between Abu Simbel and Heliopolis, measured along a north–south line of longitude. In addition, the First Cataract is exactly halfway between Abydos and the original location of Abu Simbel. Heliopolis, on the other hand, was dedicated to Ra-Tem, the most objective aspect of Ra. The implication is thus that from Abydos to Heliopolis was to be regarded as metaphorically representing the lower Underworld—the planes of objective matter in the body of Atum-Ra—while the area southward from Abydos to Abu Simbel represented the planes of spirit, ascending toward imponderable divinity, symbolically beyond the First Cataract. When we look at the various temples between Philae-Elephantine and Dendera, we find that they too all appear to be equally spaced by geographical distance measured along the river. The distances between Thebes-Dendera and Thebes–Diospolis Parva are also equal. Now, as regularity and symmetry were absolutely vital in the Egyptian religious scheme—as already described—this can be no mere coincidence and lends further support to the idea of nomes symbolizing progressive planes of consciousness throughout the Duat.[35] A similar progression is noticeable between the various temples between Abydos and Heliopolis. However, the significances are somewhat different.

Where particular temple arrangements are concerned, we see extensive further symbolism. For example, on the midstream island of Philae (generally regarded as the most holy of all the Nile temples) there are six interconnected temples, the name of the associated god being regarded by Egyptologists as uncertain, although assumed to be Isis.[36] The next temple complex heading north—Elephantine, also on an island—is dedicated to Khnemu, who, as we have already seen, is sevenfold in nature. This symbolism separates at the next temple (Kom Ombos—which may also once have been an island) into a true duality, for it is dedicated jointly to Sebek and Heru-ur (Horus the Elder).[37] Interestingly, given the geological associations (see chapter 3), Sebek—representing the demiurgic hierarchies—is given the east bank, while Horus the Elder (representing the hierarchy of evolving souls) takes the west bank.

Significant Questions to Be Answered

There were only two really dominant temple complexes on the east bank—at Thebes (governed by Amen-Ra) and at Heliopolis (dedicated to Ra-Tem, the polar opposite of Amen-Ra), both of these being associated with very important crossing points of the river.[38] Why? The only pyramid on the whole east bank is at Kom el-Ahmar, which is exactly halfway between Abydos and Heliopolis. Why? Was there a particular religious reason for the priests of Amen-Ra at Thebes reacting so very dramatically to Akhenaten's supposed "heresy" in building his new city and temple to the Aten disk at Tell-el-Amarna on the east side of the river, rather than on the west side? All of these involve important issues that can be properly addressed only in the context of the esoteric symbolism of Egypt's temple layout and system of dedication. The latter is not the ad hoc jumble that some Egyptologists tend to make of it, and in chapters 8 and 9 we shall see precisely how and why that fact is confirmed beyond doubt.

EIGHT

The Ancient Esoteric Division of Egypt and the Significance of Its Main Temples

Aaru, or Sekhet-Aaru, was divided into a number of districts, the chief of which was called SEKHET-HETEPET, i.e., "Field of Offerings," or SEKHET-HETEP, i.e., "Field of Peace," and was presided over by the god SEKHTI-HETEP. To the south of this region lay SEKHET-SANEHEMU, i.e., "Field of the Grasshoppers" and in it were the Lakes of the Tuat and the Lakes of the Jackals. In the waters of Aaru, or Sekhet-Aaru, Ra purified himself and it was here that the deceased also purified himself before he began his heavenly life.

—E. A. WALLIS BUDGE, *THE GODS OF THE EGYPTIANS*

As we have to some extent already seen in previous chapters, the land of Egypt in its totality was regarded by its ancient peoples as symbolizing the field of Creation itself—hence it was that incarnation involved a literal "captivity in Egypt." Curiously, the boundaries of the country appear to have remained pretty much intact from ancient times right up to the present day. The southernmost perimeter—most of it comprising a horizontal straight line at latitude 22 degrees north—leaves Abu Simbel (and the new Lake Nasser) immediately to its north. However, as we shall see in a moment, Egypt possessed an internal pattern of organization that provided full support for its cosmogonical myth-allegory.

Many people interested in Egyptian culture have simplistically associated the idea of Ra, the solar Logos, with the Sun itself—a fundamental error also indulged in by the "heretic" pharaoh Akhenaten.[1] As we have already seen, however, the Logos was that which *contained* a universe, solar system, or planetary existence within the field, or aura, of its own consciousness. Humanity does not exist "inside" the Sun, even though the latter is at the center of the solar system. Humanity does, however, exist "within" the field of our planet and of the solar system too. Thus, as the Creation process ever seems to work from the periphery inward to the center, the biblical concept of a "Fall" from a primordially divine state looks to take on a quite literal dimension. The concept of an "Underworld"—combining both a terrestrial and a spiritual state of existence in parallel with each other—derives from the same source, because it is seen from the viewpoint of the originating divine state and not the human state, as is commonly supposed to be the case.

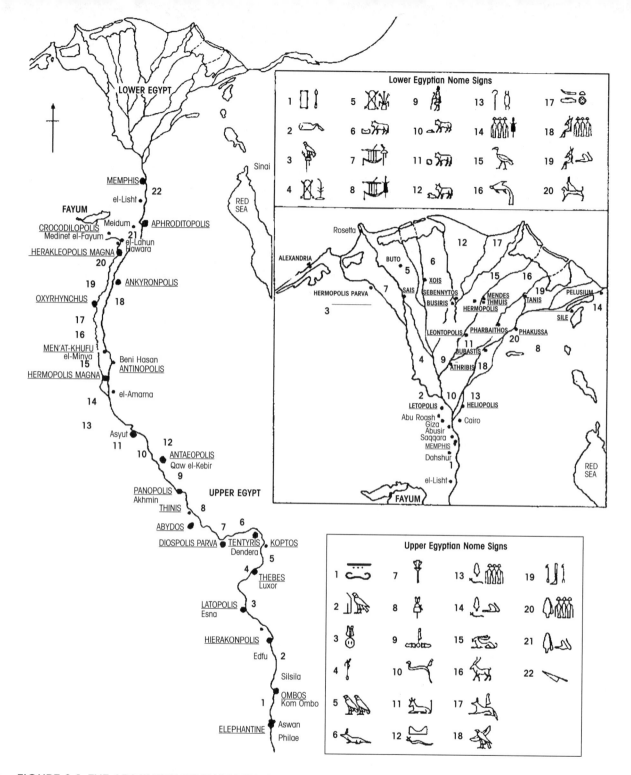

FIGURE 8.1. THE ADMINISTRATIVE NOMES OF EGYPT

Ancient Egypt is generally regarded by scholars as having had the First Cataract (at Philae) for its southern boundary. The architectural and esoteric indications, however, are that it extended all the way to at least Khartoum, to the southeast of which lay the Island of Meroë, the fabled (greater) Meru, where lived the highest of the gods. In view of the generality of the Egyptians' sevenfold metaphysical system, it can surely be no mere coincidence that the Nile has six cataracts and that the confluence of the Blue and White Niles with the tributary known as the Black Nile lies in between the Sixth Cataract and the Island of Meroë (which separates them). Thus Egypt to the north of the First Cataract would have represented only the seventh and lowest of seven macrocosmic states of being. (Nome capitals are underlined where known.)

How the God Ra Manifested Himself in the World

The whole essence of Creation symbolism was that Ra (as the sun god, or solar Logos), in projecting a proportion of his divine Life-force down to Earth, "peopled" the land of Egypt with it. This "peopling" (of serried ranks of man and angelic beings) gave rise not only to the world of form but also to the phenomenon of consciousness. Thus duality and conflict were born—epitomized in the allegory of the constant struggles between Horus (in his various aspects) and Sebek, the lord of elemental Nature.[2] By far the most important aspect of the tradition, however, dealt with the fact that man came into existence in a state of ignorance via a particular process, and subsequently had to recover a knowledge of his divine origins in full self-consciousness, through undergoing a graded sequence of tests, or "initiations," resulting in expansions of spiritual faculty. (These are dealt with more fully in chapter 11.) What is not so well recognized, however, is the fact that the geographical siting of the various main temples seems to have played a crucial (and sequential) part in the allegories of the outward creation and also of the actual process of "redemption," or return to the state of divinity. But how else could it be so if the Egyptian "Heaven on Earth" were to have a fully functional existence? Consequently, we can suggest with good reason that the temples must have been directly associated with representing a progressive process of spiritual emanation and corresponding spiritual reabsorption. That progression—as in other such systems in different cultures—was of a septenary nature overall, as we shall see here.

The Sequence of Temples along the Nile

Over the last few years, the particular suggestion that the sequential location of temples along the Nile represented a progress through planes of consciousness has received increasingly greater recognition. However, the idea that the siting of all the temples is generally connected with the sequence of chakras found in the human psychomagnetic (or etheric) field is only a partial truth, as we shall see in a moment. In fact, as we have already mentioned, there is a much more obvious connection with the "planes of consciousness" extending between the divine and terrestrial states of being. To support this thesis, the reader's attention is drawn to a number of important points, which we might list as follows:

1. Taking the temples of Abu Simbel and Heliopolis as extremities of the land from the point of view of a purely solar influence, the Delta beyond was regarded, we might suggest, as being under planetary (and especially lunar) influence. The really particular significance of this is to be found in the idea that the astral soul of Egypt was ruled by the priests of Ra-Tem at Heliopolis, which was the chief religious center for the Delta as well as being the first of the sidereal temples of the Upper Nile. This may perhaps sound a little enigmatic, but it should become clearer when we deal with the subject of initiation into the Mysteries.
2. Whether or not the geographically central location of Abydos is regarded as a mere coincidence, the First Cataract (with its temples of Elephantine and Philae on either side) is situated exactly halfway between Abydos and Abu Simbel.

The Ancient
Esoteric Division
of Egypt and the
Significance of Its
Main Temples

▲

119

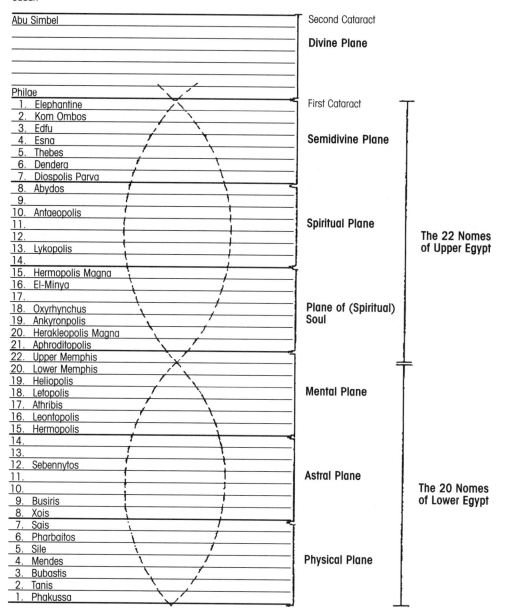

FIGURE 8.2. THE ESOTERIC DIVISION OF EGYPT

The original nome capitals of Middle and Lower Egypt are not all known. Those shown for Lower Egypt (below Memphis) are thus not necessarily given in the correct order.

    With regard to the question of the esoteric symbolism of the dawn in Egypt, it has to be remembered that it is only because of Earth's own counterclockwise orbital rotation around the Sun that the latter appears to rise "in the east." However, the spiritual progress of the initiate—himself a reflection of the sun god—necessarily follows that of Earth and also of the Sun in their own orbits, because he is no longer subject to such material illusions. The position is clarified for us by Jeremy Naydler: "A person standing and facing south is in the 'archetypal' position by which the ancient Egyptians oriented themselves in 'the Beloved Land' *(ta-meri)*. One of the terms for 'south' is also a term for 'face,' while the word usually used for 'north' is related to a word that means 'back of the head.' The word for 'east' is the same as that for 'left'; likewise the word for 'west' and 'right'" (*Temple of the Cosmos: The Ancient Egyptian Experience of the Sacred* [Rochester, Vt.: Inner Traditions, 1996], p. 9). Hence, geographically speaking, the left (east) bank of the Nile symbolized to the initiated consciousness the "involuntary" descent into the material Underworld, whereas the right (west) bank signified the ascending (evolutionary) path. For the uninitiated, the reverse was the case. Egyptologists have so far failed to appreciate these paradoxical distinctions and the reasons for them.

3. To make matters even more interesting, the geographical distances between Philae, Kom Ombos, Edfu, Esna, Thebes, and Dendera, and also between Thebes and Diospolis Parva, are all apparently equal.

4. To cap even this—as the sharp-eyed will already have noted—there are exactly seven progressive stages involved in the northward movement from Philae to Abydos, thereby producing a complete set of "harmonic tones" in this esoteric "octave." This is then confirmed in relation to the various administrative nomes (see fig. 8.1) or districts into which the region was divided. As we can see from the map, there are twenty-two such nomes in Upper Egypt, of which exactly fourteen were located between Abydos and Memphis.[3] In addition, however, there were another twenty nomes in Lower Egypt.

5. Next, let us hypothetically regard each nome as perhaps being esoterically symbolic of an astrological decan. As thirty-six decans would thus represent the completion of a cycle (the 360-degree zodiacal cycle), if we count the twenty nomes of the Delta and continue moving southward, we find the thirty-six-fold cycle itself concluding at Dendera. This is of the most profound significance in relation to the Mysteries, as we shall see later.

6. As we can also see from the plan, the twenty nomes in Lower Egypt plus the twenty-two in Upper Egypt produced an overall total of forty-two.[4] Now, bearing in mind our contention that the nomes esoterically depicted a progressive sequence of (septenary) planes of consciousness within the Duat, there is a quite distinctly curious synchronicity and an apparent significance about these latter numbers as well. That is because (relative to the overall septenary system shown) the apportionment as between Upper and Lower Egypt is three and one-seventh to two and six-sevenths.

New Age Synchronicities

Following on from that, it may seem a quite extraordinary coincidence, but at least two branches of the modern New Age movement—in also adopting a septenary system of planes of consciousness[5]—apply exactly these same proportions between what they regard as the three planes of spirit and the three planes of matter (the mental, astral, and physical), as shown in figure 8.2. The first curiosity is that twenty-two is a solar number associated with the Greek letter pi and the mathematical factor of 3.142 that we use to calculate all the characteristics of a circle. The second curiosity is that in the New Age system referred to, this same apportionment point is used to depict the evolving "spiritual Ego" that coordinates the liaison between the human personality and the consciousness of the "spiritual Self." That, however, also coincides exactly with the geographical and nome relationship between Heliopolis and Memphis, as we can also see from figure 8.2. As we shall see in the next chapter, this has a very particular significance in relation to the Egyptian Mysteries and the process of initiation at Giza. However, one other remarkable feature of this septenary scheme of psycho-spiritual consciousness is that it was introduced into the West in the 1870s by H. P. Blavatsky, who claimed her source as being an "ancient esoteric school" led by "Mahatmas" (spiritual Adepts) located in the Himalayan region of northern India, on the borders of western Tibet.[6] Now, we have already pinpointed this general area as the "land of Pun(t)," which the Egyptians regarded as the "land of the gods." The clear implication is, therefore, that this same esoteric school may have already existed in very ancient times. Furthermore, it would perhaps explain why the two septenary schemes of consciousness (New Age and ancient Egyptian) seem to coincide so precisely.

Important Facts Related to Specific Temples

We have already mentioned in chapter 7 certain characteristics of the First Cataract area in connection with the Egyptian concept of "the Abyss" and their allegory of Creation. What we can next progress to is a preliminary consideration of certain characteristics of the temples themselves, first of all at Philae, which, we may recall, was situated on an island at the southern end of the Cataract. In fact the temple now stands on a different island from the original one, archaeologists having relocated it owing to the damage being caused by constant flooding from the first Aswan Dam.

As Margaret Murray confirmed, the Great Temple complex at Philae actually consisted of six interrelated temples, each separately dedicated but with one overall, presiding female deity and an apparently significant association with childbirth.[7] That the layout is not arbitrary, but rather metaphorical in nature, is clear; for the number six, when compared to the number seven esoterically, denotes the multiform vehicle of the goddess minus the objective presence of the god (i.e., Ptah). In other words, it is here representative of the immediately prebirth state. Consequently, one might suggest that the originally presiding deity is likely to have combined Ta'Urt (the goddess of pregnancy) with Hathor but not Isis. These latter two are recognized by Egyptologists as having quite different maternal functions. However, when we move downriver, just past the Cataract to the next main temple, at Elephantine (also an island), we find the sevenfold principle translated into actuality through dedication to the water god Khnemu, regarded—as Budge himself says—as the "god of the Cataract par excellence."[8] As we mentioned in the last chapter when we described the sevenfold nature of Khnemu in detail, this god is regarded (jointly with Ptah) as the first self-engendered (i.e., immaculately conceived) and self-contained, objective manifestation (within the solar system) of Ra himself. In that sense, Khnemu can surely be seen as the Demiurge (during the "Fall from Grace"), for the sevenfold nature of the god undoubtedly represents the seven planes of existence (of Man's active presence within the solar system). In other words, Khnemu-Ptah is Osiris in his primordial, pregenetic nature, whereas the Osiris of Abydos is but the spiritually objective "shadow."

The Association of the Cataract with the Cosmic Birth Process

The fact that Philae and Elephantine were located so close together, separated only by the Cataract, is extremely important. The Egyptians symbolically represented the Cataract as being the point at which the floodwaters of the Nile rose (like the breaking of the waters during the human birth process), while Khnemu was held to be responsible for holding them in check.[9] In the last chapter we mentioned the Cataract itself being symbolized in the horizontal, wavy horns of Khnemu, the self-created "Creator of man," from out of the vortex of matter, drawn inward from space. Thus, we suggest, that which lay beyond Philae correspondingly represented the maternal "womb" of the cosmos—hence its suggested association with Hathor. We might otherwise mention here, in passing, that Khnemu's female counterpart at Elephantine—the goddess Sati (a compound of Isis-Hathor, but whose own name was associated with the "throwing of seed")—was specifically connected with the star Sirius.[10] The goddess Anqet was the third member of the divine triad at Elephantine, she being identified with the goddess Nephthys.[11] The underlying symbolism thus appears to be of these two goddesses as "midwives," the progression northward up the Nile producing various allegories to confirm that.

We come next to Kom Ombos, which, from the present course of the river, suggests that (now on the east bank) it too may once have been an island. Here the temple is found to be jointly dedicated to two solar gods[12]—Horus the Elder and Sebek—who are commonly regarded as adversaries from the viewpoint of Egyptian religious folklore but who, in the esoteric sense (as already described), are to be regarded as the complementary "poles" of objective existence within the land of Egypt as it allegorizes the "heavenly fields." Now, Horus and Sebek here represent the next onward progression in the unfoldment of consciousness and form, respectively. Whereas Ptah and Khnemu are concerned with the demiurgic act of Creation in these two fields, Horus and Sebek may be said to immediately precede them as the actual initiators of the process.[13] Sebek symbolizes the constant sequence in Nature that instinctively seeks to "imprison" the subjective cosmic Life (the Verbum) in a phenomenal form. That is why he—as the crocodile-headed god—is depicted as seeking to drag the individual (the divine, or "cosmic," Man) down into the "waters" of phenomenal space. Horus the Elder, on the other hand, represents the principle of divine consciousness that seeks to liberate the divine Man from within the imprisonment of worldly existence. That is why (a constant source of puzzlement to Egyptologists) he is described in the Pyramid Texts as often working with the supposedly evil Set (however, this is the higher, cosmic version of Set) to help Osiris climb back to the heaven world on a "ladder."[14]

The East and West Banks of the Nile at Thebes

Now, before we move on northward to the sequentially next main temples, at Edfu and Esna, we need to jump ahead a little bit in order to understand where these two temples—situated on the west bank as they are—fit into the sequence of evolutionary progression. We move straight on, therefore, to the temple of Karnak at Thebes, which is dedicated to Amen-Ra,[15] here curiously represented in the form of a curly-horned god (like Khnum at Esna, rather than the wavily horizontal horns of Khnemu at Elephantine), with subsidiary dedications to Mut and Khonsu, the other two members of the divine Theban Triad.[16] Bearing in mind that the only temples dedicated to Ra himself are to be found on the east side of the river—at Thebes and Heliopolis—there has to be an underlying reason, and that, we suggest, is to be found in the temple rites associated jointly with Luxor and Karnak and the temples on the other (western) side of the river—for example, the so-called Ramesseum. The ram-headed symbolism is also important because it always appears to represent the point of (simultaneous) origin and completion of a cycle.

The temple arrangements on the east bank at Thebes are clearly dual—the two huge temple complexes at Luxor and Karnak are quite separate—and that in itself is highly suggestive. Karnak is north of Luxor and all the indications are that it was associated with creation of the material world and its mundane rulership or governance, while the much smaller and less grandiose temple of Luxor was concerned with onward spiritual evolution—that is, divine governance. In that respect, the peculiarly skewed orientation of the western end of the temple at Luxor has already been associated by others (notably Schwaller de Lubicz) with the figure of a man whose left leg is advanced in front of the right—thus suggesting forward movement. Whether this is so and therefore perhaps symbolic of onward spiritual progression is nevertheless unclear. However, following the sequence of Khnemu's sevenfold aspects northward from Elephantine, it does appear clear that (east-bank) Thebes undoubtedly represents the seat of the "Lord of the Land of Life."

One further observation is perhaps worthwhile making in relation to the temple at Luxor. It concerns the massive outer pylon on which is sculpted in huge panoramic detail the "Battle of Kadesh," in which Rameses II (according to Egyptologists) glorifies himself in a virtually single-handed victory over an army of his enemies (supposedly the Hittite Kheta) after the god Amon/Amen has "overshadowed" him. The battle itself, however, bears a more than passing resemblance to the entirely allegorical Battle of Kurukshetra in the Indian Bhagavad Gita, in which the hero-initiate Arjuna ultimately defeats his "enemies" (a metaphor for his own lower nature) by calling upon the help of the great god Krishna (a metaphor for the highest Self in man). In addition, Kadesh (an ancient city north of Damascus) looks remarkably like the Hebrew word *kodesh* (as in *Ruah ha Kodesh*—the "Holy Spirit"), which would indeed make it a "holy battle" of the spirit-Self. Bearing in mind also the physically impossible way in which the conduct of the "battle" is described, one cannot help but feel that it too was (at least originally) entirely oriented toward the "Path of Initiation."[17]

On the western side of the Nile at Thebes, the temple rites (for example, in the Ramesseum) seem all to have been associated with death—the death and burial of the pharaoh and, undoubtedly also, of all who were regarded by the Ancients as having reached a certain high point of psycho-spiritual evolution in which they were esoterically regarded as "rulers" (i.e., of the mortal world).[18] To understand the metaphor and allegory here, we need to recognize that the Path of Initiation, per se, involved a stage when the individual was regarded as having completely conquered his purely human nature—the personality—with all its selfish desires and aspirations. While he still had far to go in a purely spiritual sense, at this stage he was required to show that his achievement to date metaphorically involved him "dying" to (i.e., renouncing) the material world that he had conquered. In order to do this ritualistically, the individual had to cross the river (of Consciousness) itself, symbolizing the divide between the spiritual world and the world of human psychosensory perception (i.e., that of "the dead"), and be crowned (and thus divinely reborn) on the east bank, at Karnak, under the direct auspices of Amen-Ra (or at least those of his priests). After the ceremonials were completed, he would probably then return to Heliopolis or a designated temple complex in which he, as a member of the priesthood, would have a new and more senior official role.

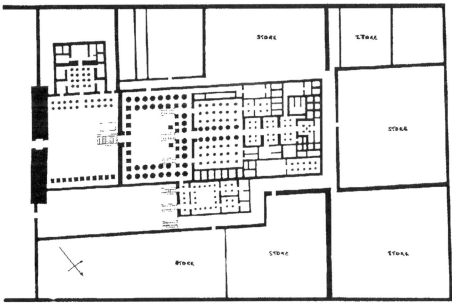

FIGURE 8.3. THE RAMESSEUM AT THEBES

To summarize, then, this all-too-brief section, Thebes appears to represent a definite point of beginning and end in the symbolic journey of the (astral) soul. The 360-degree cycle represented by the thirty-six nomes that conclude at Dendera seem clearly to be associated with the zodiac (as we shall see in a moment) and thus also with the precession of the equinoxes. This is why, it is suggested, we find Amen-Ra, Mut, and Khonsu here

The Ancient
Esoteric Division
of Egypt and the
Significance of Its
Main Temples

▲

125

FIGURE 8.4. THE TEMPLE AT ESNA
An imagined reconstruction of the interior of the temple, showing a religious procession (from Denon's *Description de l'Egypte*, 1798)

on the east bank at Thebes (but not on the west bank) as the initiating deities in relation to the Underworld cycle. Interestingly, there is a suggestion that Menthu- (or Mntw) Ra may have been an original deity here. However, the name Mntw itself represents repetition and fiery periodic initiation of activity, so the underlying principle remains the same.

As the zodiac and repetitive precessionary round involved the purely human cycle of "fall" and subsequent evolutionary "individualization," the association of west-bank Thebes with death clearly represents the natural conclusion of that lower cycle of experience, for the astral soul now becomes redundant. It is therefore the earthbound astral soul that "dies." The conquering spiritual individuality is thus either "reborn" in the temple of Luxor (if progressing onward) or "crowned" at Karnak in recognition of the achievement of total domination over the "lower world."

The Sequence of the Initiation Process in the Mysteries

As we shall see in chapter 11, the initiation just referred to as being represented in the rites at Thebes was the third in a series of seven, although all the actual initiations undoubtedly took place at Giza. The fourth of the initiation series was represented symbolically in the temple at Esna (fig. 8.4), called by the Greeks Latopolis and otherwise known as "the Sekhem in which Osiris lives." This religious center, dedicated to the god Khnum[19] (another form of Khnemu), was represented by one of the species of Nile fish, and the metaphor associated with it seems to have revolved around the initiate of this particular grade or stage of development being, like the fish, free to swim alone in the river (of Spirit) in either direction.[20] The "fish" (as in the later, Christian tradition) was thus a metaphor for the "spiritual soul-body" in which the initiate was now able to function consciously, thus advancing his own higher and further evolution.

Here in Esna we find the temple otherwise dedicated to the lion-headed goddess Menhyet, who, like her alter ego, the goddess Net (or Neith), was associated with weaving by virtue of the shared emblem of two crossed arrows in front of a shield. Now, as we have already noted, this emblem's esoteric significance relates to the "weaving" of light, and here at Esna it has, we suggest, a very particular significance. First of all, Esna is the fourth temple downstream from (and including) Elephantine, where the principal god is Khnemu, whose fourth aspect, as we have already seen, is quite categorically referred to as "Governor of the House of Life"—this translation being that of the perfectly orthodox Egyptologist Wallis Budge. In addition, however, the fact that Esna was called "the Sekhem in which Osiris lives" confirms our proposition beyond any shadow of a doubt, because the Sekhem was indeed the "House of Life"—the "body of light" of the spiritual Self according to the Egyptians; and the wrappings around the mummy of the deified god were a visual metaphor for exactly that.

We next return to Edfu, where we confirmed the temple as being dedicated to the deity Heru-Behutet, the "son" of Ra-Herakhte.[21] This temple, then, appears to be oriented toward the plane of "pure Spirit"—the zodiacal sign of Aquarius being representative of that—and to the fifth of the seven earthly initiations.[22] The metaphor of the hawk (the usual form in which Horus is depicted in Egyptian religious art) thus appears related to the fact that the initiate at this stage was regarded as a "pure divine breath" whose conscious existence could soar beyond even the limitations of a "spiritual soul-body." Quite what this involves is not altogether clear, although with Horus being representative of the consciousness of Ra within Egypt, it does suggest the faculty of what is sometimes called "universal consciousness" within that greater field of limitation. The implication (drawn from other philosophies sharing the same system of initiations) is that the consciousness of the initiate, being no longer earthbound, was now free to roam the bounds of the solar system (the body organism of Atum-Ra) at will. This seems to be entirely consistent with the nature of the adept-hero, for at Edfu we also find the Shemsu-Heru (Companions of Horus), who, represented as "blacksmiths," literally fashion the "celestial metal" (light).[23]

That takes us back to Kom Ombos and Elephantine in the southward sequence, presumably representing the sixth and seventh initiations in the series, of which we can know nothing. However, by virtue of the known relationship between Khnemu and Ptah—depicted as together building the edifice of the material universe,[24] we would hazard a guess that Elephantine is therefore also in some way jointly dedicated to the great god Ptah as the "Great Artificer" (or "Great Architect") who fashions within his own nature

FIGURE 8.5. THE INTERIOR OF THE MAIN TEMPLE AT ABU SIMBEL

To either side of the interior are four facing pairs of giant Kabiri—the eight lesser Titan gods of the underworld uni-verse—those on the left wearing the crown of Lower Egypt and those on the right wearing the crown of Upper Egypt. At the far end, within the innermost sanctum, sat four aspects of man himself—Ptah, Amen-Ra, the Initiate (as king), and Ra-Harmachis. Although interpreted by our modern Egyptologists as a temple to the glorification of Rameses II, the esoteric indicators clearly indicate that this is wholly inaccurate.

and then scatters the fertile "seeds"[25]—symbolically represented as "Man," the "Divine Spark"—into the septenary Duat.

The Cosmic Question Mark over Abu Simbel

That leaves us, finally, with Abu Simbel, which is as far removed in distance from Philae as Philae is from Abydos. Philae would logically represent an eighth stage of the initiation process that must relate to an even more inconceivable state of (cosmic) consciousness subsuming all the others. Then Abu Simbel—if associated with the process of initiation too, as we must assume it to be—is the ninth in the series, thereby reflecting the ninefold nature of the already known ancient Egyptian pantheon, or "divine ennead." The temple at Abu Simbel, which has been curiously and unimaginatively designated by Egyptologists as built by Rameses II in self-glorification, is dual in nature. On the outside (see fig. 0.1) we have the well-known façade showing four huge, seated god-figures, with a dozen much smaller and lesser goddess figures standing immediately in front of them. Inside we have eight huge, standing god-figures, facing each other in pairs (see fig. 8.5) and a further (seated) human-sized quartet in the inner sanctum.

Egyptologists are fairly certain that while the temple as a whole was dedicated to Amen-Ra, Ra-Herakhte, Ptah, and Rameses II, the four seated giant figures are but different representations of Rameses II. However, bearing in mind that the creation myth is clearly indicated here (as we shall see in greater detail in the next chapter), it is apparent that the idea of the original builders having included a mortal pharaoh in the external symbolism is utterly misconceived. In addition, we believe that this temple, along with all the other main Nile temples, was built tens of thousands of years before the time of Rameses II. Taking into consideration what we have already said about Philae and Elephantine, and also bearing in mind that the gods Khnemu and Sebek were both regarded as somehow containing within themselves the four gods Ra-Tem, Shu, Geb, and Osiris[26] (the four male aspects of the Creation process), it seems fairly clear that Abu Simbel (originally adjacent to the Second Cataract) must, in fact, have symbolically represented that point at which the very conception of the gods symbolically occurred.[27] The fact that the (female) temple of Hathor—the wife of the great god Atum-Ra—faced the (male) temple of Abu Simbel at such close quarters suggests that it was at this location that the marital union of the pharaoh with his consort always (originally) took place. Precisely why this should be so we shall also see in chapter 9, but we can nevertheless suggest in the meantime that such a union would have been seen by the ancient Egyptians as symbolizing the astronomical "Great Return."

That the pharaoh was already universally regarded as the incarnation of Ra would have made it quite easy for an apparently successful and confident warrior-king like Rameses II to have himself symbolically deified by adding his own inscriptions to the temple at Abu Simbel, as also elsewhere throughout the country. If it is remembered that he (in the thirteenth century B.C.) was supposedly responsible for driving all invaders out of Egypt and returning the country to an indigenous Egyptian rule, this is to some extent understandable, even if less than laudable. It does, however, confirm the total degeneracy of Egyptian religion by then, for no priesthood really believing in the magically invocative (and therefore inviolable) nature of the sanctuary would have dared or dreamed of allowing such wholesale desecration.

The Nile Temples North of Thebes

At this point we return to the lesser atmosphere of the temples north of Thebes, because these were undoubtedly more closely associated with the lower strata of initiation into the Mysteries and also with rituals concerning deities very much more familiar to the general population of Egypt outside the priesthood itself. Immediately next in line above Karnak stands Coptos, which, however, stands on the east bank of the river, just before its large and dramatically sudden westward bend toward Dendera. While interesting in other respects because of its associations with the beginnings of Christianity (which took a large proportion of its theology lock, stock, and barrel from the Coptic priests), it does not in any way appear to be associated with the issue of initiatory progression in the Mysteries.[28] Rather, to the contrary, its deity—the ithyphallic god Min—directly associated with fertility (and thus with Eros), represents the outward emanation of the divine Life-force. Margaret Murray cites the ritual of this temple involving a running dance performed by the pharaoh (in front of the god's image) while carrying a single oar, although she is unclear as to the underlying meaning behind the symbolism.[29] Perhaps we can help. The most obvious interpretation, it is suggested, is that of a superior being trying to steer something that is weaving and bobbing all over the place in an altogether unpredictable fashion. The esoteric implication is that of the higher mentality, or spiritual Ego, trying to control the lower self, like a boatman or puppeteer, "through a glass, darkly." This would also account for the association with fertility, because the cyclic phenomenon of human reincarnation is supposedly due to the regenerative urge of the "higher Self" in response to Divine Purpose.

It is otherwise worth remembering that Victorian anthropologists saw the Copts as a branch of the Atlantidae—the Hamitic race of northwest Africa. If that is indeed so, it might otherwise imply that the (evidently tenacious) Copts hold—or at one time held—the key to religious continuity between the lattermost Atlanteans and ourselves. Quite how any ancient Atlantean knowledge might have interacted with the ancient Egyptian form of religion, however, remains obscure.

Moving onward to Dendera, we find there one of the most impressive of all the Nile temples. It is dedicated to Hathor, the Egyptian mother goddess figure most often worshiped in the form of a cow—thereby signifying her importance as a constant source of readily available (spiritual) sustenance. However, there are a variety of other symbolisms in evidence here that make Dendera even more significant as a highly important temple in the sequence of initiatory progression.

First of all, as Margaret Murray also confirms, the ceiling decoration of this temple is entirely astronomical (it is here that we find the famous circular zodiac), while the appearance of Nut the sky goddess in her well-known arched position confirms that the "spiritual sustenance" comes from the starry regions of the heavens.[30] Second, Hathor (the wife of Atum-Ra) is here shown "married" to Horus of Edfu, there being also in evidence their infant child, Hor-Samtaui, shown as in a cradle. Now, Horus of Edfu, as we have already seen, represented the semidivine Self of the individual (the adept-hero).

Consequently, the symbolism may be regarded as representing the birth of a spiritual consciousness in the neophyte that is destined to be brought about through achieving dominion over the lower self, which comprised the various aspects of the purely human personality.[31]

The Temple Ritual at Dendera

In addition to this, Murray tells us that "the famous Ritual of Dendera . . . was performed as a mystery play with puppets; the size and material of each figure is given in full detail and the prescribed attitudes shown, beginning from the time when the body of Osiris lies stark and dead upon the bier, till the moment when the god springs to life protected by Isis, who shields her eyes from the exceeding great glory of the risen deity."[32] The fact that Osiris is actually shown here as springing to life clearly indicates that the initiation associated with this temple involved the first true (and retained) spiritual awakening, rather than the mere "stirrings" associated with the next succeeding temple, at Diospolis Parva.

Now, Diospolis Parva (the "city of the double god") has an importance that will become clear in chapter 9 and so we shall leave it there (with the passing suggestion of an association with the first of the sequence of initiations) and pass on to deal with certain astrological associations. Before we do so, however, it would perhaps be useful to provide a short synopsis of what we have just described over the last few pages, by way of brief descriptions of the esoteric associations of the temples between Abu Simbel and Abydos:

ESOTERIC ASSOCIATIONS OF THE TEMPLES BETWEEN ABU SIMBEL AND ABYDOS

Temple and God	Manifesting Impulse	Returning Impulse
1. Abu Simbel (4 Creator gods)	urge to create/reincarnate	withdrawal
2. Philae (the World-Mother)	the womb/field of limitation	synthesis
3. Elephantine (Khnemu-Ptah)	conception	resurrection
4. Kom Ombos (Sebek/ Ra-Herakhte)	duality of form and function	achieved coordination of spirit-matter
5. Edfu (Heru-Behutet)	Self-existence (as light)	spiritual Will (enlightenment)
6. Esna (Khnum)	spiritual "birth" in the soul-body	spiritual Self-consciousness
7. Thebes (Amen-Ra)	unfoldment of Egoic individuality	focused spiritual mentality/ independence
8. Dendera (Hathor)	karmic awakening and desire for objectivity	spiritual Self-dedication

Astrological Issues

The temple at Diospolis Parva being associated with the first main initiation in the series, what are we to make of Abydos? Is it not also associated with the process of initiation as part of the spiritual evolutionary process known in Egypt? The answer is, of course, "Yes

FIGURE 8.6. THE EGYPTIAN REPRESENTATION OF GEMINI AT DENDERA

it is." However, Abydos seems to represent a "threshold" to the process—a definite "doorway"—apparently direct from the Underworld to the spiritual plane (see again fig. 8.2) from which the impulse toward reincarnation emanates into the field of objectivity symbolized by the zodiacal signs again, but this time on a lower turn of the spiral.

This time, therefore, we look at it from an astrological angle, again focused around the Nile itself, which from one point of view, as mentioned in an earlier chapter, metaphorically allows it to represent the ecliptic—the path of our solar system in its 25,920-year round, relative to the Milky Way, the plane of our galaxy. Now, remembering what was said in this connection in chapter 2, if we next take Philae as our starting point and work sequentially northward, we find the following astrological associations:

Philae   Scorpio
——The First Cataract (representing the ecliptic crossing the celestial equator)——
Elephantine   Sagittarius
Kom Ombos   Capricorn
Edfu   Aquarius
Esna   Pisces
Thebes   Aries
Dendera   Taurus
——————The ecliptic again crosses the celestial equator——————
Diospolis Parva   Gemini
Abydos   Cancer

FIGURE 8.7. TAURUS

The house of Cancer is regarded by astrologers as one of the "Gates of Death" in the cycle of the soul as it cycles downward into the material worlds, and so it is perhaps entirely as expected that we find the temple here dedicated to Osiris in his position as king of the Underworld.[33] We might also suggest that the modern crab glyph associated with the sign of Cancer is itself a metaphor indicating the "twin souls" of Egyptian theology—the "spiritual soul" and the "astral soul," to use modern terminology. The Egyptians used the symbol of the scarab beetle, but the essential symbolism is precisely the same, for the spiritual soul "pushes" the astral soul around its lesser cycle. Similarly, the earth itself is "pushed" backward around the precession of the equinoxes.

Following the same astrological progression northward through the various main temple complexes, we eventually find a direct association between Memphis-Heliopolis and the zodiacal signs of Leo-Virgo. That

FIGURE 8.8. CANCER

in turn, however, brings us to something else of a quite extraordinary nature, for the "head" of the Nile (i.e., the Delta) is clearly shaped like the head of a cobra. In addition, its waters discharge into the Mediterranean via the Rosetta and Damietta branches, which remind us of the two fangs of the cobra.[34]

FIGURE 8.9. VIRGO-LEO

As we saw earlier, the cosmic serpent (Nak) was metaphysically equated by the Egyptians with the Demiurge (i.e., the Elohim) and it was this that (Atum) Ra "conquered" in order to bring about the objective manifestation of his divine Will and Purpose in the form of the universe. Bearing in mind the cycle already described as existing between Heliopolis-Memphis and Philae-Elephantine, we can perhaps attribute this section to the form of the solar serpent Sebau. Correspondingly, the lesser cycle incorporating the Delta and concluding at Heliopolis-Memphis represents Apep/Apophis, the merely terrestrial serpent. His head is thus symbolic of the elemental nature of the objectively manifesting universe.

Why the Creator Serpent-God Has to "Die"

Now, in order to subdue the serpent, Ra—like other "mythic" solar gods, such as Hercules—had to metaphorically "cut off its head," for it was in the head that existed its memory and its faculty of instinctive repetition (of Nature's incessant self-re-creation of old forms) to the potential exclusion of the new Divine Purpose. Until this was done, the new Divine Purpose could not be set in motion, for the serpent's magical knowledge would otherwise prevail. Once the head was severed, however, the body would itself automatically coil, thereby creating the necessarily finite field in which the process of divine manifestation and evolution could then take place.[35]

The fount of magical knowledge (of how to remanifest oneself at will) was symbolically held by the priesthood of Ra-Tem at Heliopolis, where we also find the *benben* obelisk representing the self-resurrecting phoenix.[36] Here also—according to the Book of the Dead—were "two turquoise-colored sycamore trees" (dedicated to Nut) at the foot of which Apep was slain "by the Great Cat Ra"[37]—a clear metaphor relating to the (etheric) spinal channels of kundalini yoga, or the Masonic pillars of Jachin and Boaz.

There exists a considerable variety of similarly esoteric metaphors and allegories associated with Heliopolis and they are well worth studying with care for the insights they provide as to the Egyptian Mysteries as a whole. One of these stories has the god Geb—in the form of a goose—laying the "Egg of the World" there, following his union with the goddess Nut.[38] At the same time, we also find a clear association of the *benben* bird (the Egyptian phoenix) with Heliopolis, for it too is said (cyclically) to lay its fiery egg there. But in order to understand how the various myths tie up (something that Egyptologists refuse to believe is possible), we perhaps need to bring in some "foreign" associations. By juxtaposing the Egyptian and Indian metaphysical systems, we thus obtain the following.

Close Correspondences between the Egyptian and Indian Concepts

Ra-Tem—the downward-pouring "serpent fire" from the solar heaven—divides itself as Tefnut and Shu (synonymous with the Indian "etheric" spinal channels of *ida* and *pingala*)—the self-born "lion-headed gods." These then coil around each other in their downward "embrace" until they reach the lowest (and thus the closest) point of their cosmic union, where the "egg" (their united offspring, Nut and Geb) is laid. Here, there suddenly arises between the latter the centrifugal solar kundalini (represented as their father Shu) that pushes them apart, thereby creating the duality of Heaven and Earth, plus phenomenal fire—light and creativity. This outward surge is caused by the "egg" breaking and the indwelling phoenix emerging—the infant "rising sun," Herakhte (Horus of the Horizon). Thus the new sun is born from the "ashes" of the "dead" setting sun—Ra-Tem.

From all this it becomes rather more clear that Herakhte (otherwise Heru-khuti) represents the returning divine consciousness of mankind as a whole. Then the subsequent differentiation of that same consciousness—as Heru-Behutet (the "son" of Ra-Herakhte, also represented as a winged disk)—involves the spiritual/semidivine individualization of the human soul, which thereby joins the ranks of the Shemsu-Heru, the "Companions (or Followers) of Horus." The complete progressive sequence is entirely self-consistent.

It is this same visual imagery of a massed, creative descent (of consciousness) followed by intelligence (symbolized as light) rising up out of the depths of matter that we otherwise find in the guise of the Sphinx, dedicated to Ra-Temu-Khepera-Heru-Khuti.[39] The latter confirms to us the triple creative impulse; for Ra-Tem—as the descending and reascending cosmic kundalini projected by the demiurgic Atum-Ra—gives rise to the instinct to produce out of its own nature a field of prospective self-manifestation, organized by Kheper-Ra (the principle of Self-regeneration). Out of this, in turn, then springs forth the phenomenal, fiery principle of an intelligent consciousness (Heru-Khuti) throughout Nature. The associated principles can be interpreted at a variety of "levels."

On a macrocosmic level, Geb may himself be regarded as the lesser counterpart of Kheper-Ra, for, in accordance with the Egyptian love of wordplay and consequent double or even triple meanings, *Geb-Ra* and *Kheper-Ra* are clearly synonymous. Thus the cosmic dung beetle that rolls together the chaotic substance of space to create the spheroidal form of Tum (i.e., the god Atum-Ra), formed by the helically compressed coils of the cosmic serpent Nak, otherwise mutates into the goose (Geb) that lays the "egg" of the solar system. Inside this is then found another (winged) creature—a serpent, or a bird representing the god Thoth-Tehuti (the principle of Knowledge), and so on.

We may nevertheless suggest that, while (by implication at least) the process of theoretical education into the Mysteries clearly had good theological grounds for taking place in the priestly college at Heliopolis, the metaphorical "severance of the serpent's head" would symbolically have taken place in the initiation rites and tests of the pyramid complex at Giza. There being three serpents in the Egyptian myth, it logically follows that the sequence of initiation at Giza also had to involve a triple progression—hence the three pyramids. However, we shall deal with this in greater detail during the next few chapters, when we shall also examine a number of associated astronomical corroborations—one of which will confirm precisely why Memphis came to be selected as the historic seat of government for the whole land of Egypt.[40] We shall also explain a variety of associated astronomical issues that demonstrate exactly why and how the original ancient Egyptians managed to synchronize their terrestrial landmarks with cosmic phenomena.

The Ancient
Esoteric Division
of Egypt and the
Significance of Its
Main Temples

▲

135

PART 3

KNOWLEDGE

NINE

COMPLETING THE "JIGSAW PUZZLE" OF ASTRONOMICAL METAPHORS AND ALLEGORIES

When each of the stars necessary for the constitution of Time had obtained a motion adapted to its condition, and their bodies bound or encompassed by living chains, had become beings possessing Life, and had learned their prescribed duty, they pursued their course [in space].

—PLATO, *TIMAEUS*

It is not uncommon amid conversation about ancient Egypt to hear people refer to "the Egyptian pantheon." Yet most Egyptologists will tell you quite categorically that there is no such single pantheon, but rather several—all of them very confusingly cross-related in a manner that defies a universally coherent, hierarchical classification. The fact that several of the gods had half a dozen or more alter egos with different animal heads or crowns or other headgear, and apparel to match, is itself a source of endless confusion to the uninitiated. It is also of endless fascination to the professional Egyptologist whose forte lies in the field of unraveling such mysteries and classifying everything as neatly and tidily as possible. To date, this has always been done either by grouping together the related god figures themselves or by otherwise relating them to the city or nome specifically dedicated to their worship. Unfortunately, neither of these two approaches provides any real sense as to why such a complex approach to their religion should have been adopted by the Egyptians. In fact, even eminent Egyptologists have so far given up trying to resolve the problem; they have in most cases opted for a choice between mere animism and the idea that a specific deity must have been named after a real historical figure whose personality and exploits only subsequently became "mythologized." From such limited vision and understanding is historical chaos itself derived.

The Consequences of Ignoring Ancient Philosophy

Had Egyptology not divorced itself from ancient philosophy a century or so ago, there would undoubtedly be far less confusion and narrow thinking today. Modern science alone and unassisted (when starting from the assumption that ancient knowledge was far less extensive than our own limited perceptions of how the universe works) is almost forced to deal with everything it meets in a purely literal sense, for that is its method. Because of this literalness, however, it becomes wholly incapable of telling us anything about the actual beliefs and rationales of those ancient cultures that it is supposed to be studying. It also results in immediately denigrating them, at the very least by implication. That is particularly so where the Egyptian system of deities is concerned, for without each of these deities being treated as a metaphor and only then allocated a proper hierarchical status, the whole pantheon becomes little more than a colorful jumble, lacking even the natural pattern of a kaleidoscope. However, in order to provide such an allocation, we suggest that it is essential to start with the "core" idea of differentiating them into cosmic, solar, and terrestrial groups. This chapter aims to show why such a division is so very important.

The present confusion has arisen largely from an assumption by Egyptologists that the mystical and mythical concepts of the ancient Egyptians were originally based upon an "ad hoc" type of star worship, allied to the natural superstitions of an as yet unobjective and unscientific mentality. Yet, as we have already seen, the very sophistication of Egyptian religious and metaphysical thought (as well as their technological genius) flatly denies such a scenario. The "Establishment" response to Bauval's idea that the pyramids at Giza are a perfect geographical-astronomical replication of Orion's belt, as well as a "star clock," has been almost predictable—near total silence and a refusal to even consider the implications.[1] Yet Bauval's theory has merely exposed the tip of a gigantic iceberg that must eventually force modern scholarship to recant its arrogant complacency and so recast its whole chronology of Egyptian civilization.

In this chapter we intend to travel a great deal further along the path that Bauval has exposed and, in so doing, to examine in greater detail the extent of the ancient Egyptians' astronomical knowledge of sidereal movements within our galaxy. We shall aim to do so by showing how such knowledge was contained in allegories related to the various gods and their interrelationships. However, we do not propose to go through either detailed astronomical data or the various characteristics of each god in turn. There are dozens (if not hundreds) of books already in existence that do the latter quite capably, with associated translations direct from the Pyramid Texts or other original sources. Our concern here is rather to consider the astronomical context—in line with what we have already said in other chapters—so as to relate discernible allegory and metaphor not only to some of the main gods and their temples, but also to the whole field of human psycho-spiritual experience as the ancient Egyptians saw it.

A Brief Recapitulation

So far, we have outlined the Creation process as it commenced from an ex nihilo state in the Abyss. We then showed how the First Cataract allegorically represents the point at which Egypt (symbolizing the manifold states of being comprising both the solar system and our world—and thus also the "body of Ra") takes on a phenomenal existence. We saw that this field of existence is essentially dual (hence the Egyptian name Duat), from one angle comprising the world of Spirit and the complementary world of Matter—these, however, being co-arranged into one sevenfold sequence of states of being. The lowest of

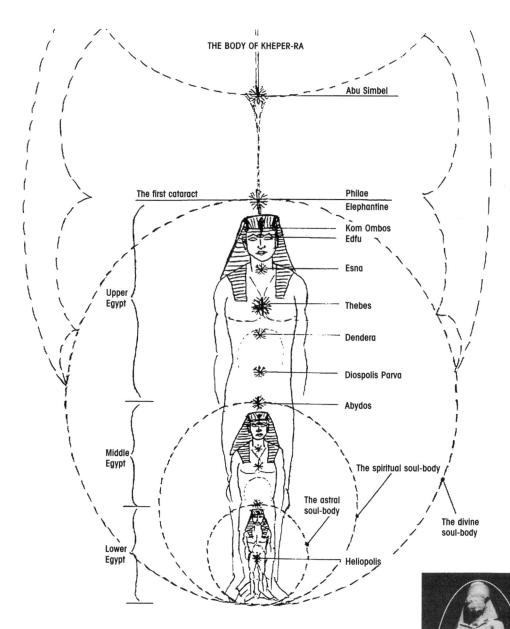

THE BODY OF KHEPER-RA

Abu Simbel

The first cataract
Philae
Elephantine

Kom Ombos
Edfu

Esna

Thebes

Dendera

Diospolis Parva

Abydos

Upper
Egypt

Middle
Egypt

The spiritual soul-body

The astral
soul-body

The divine
soul-body

Lower
Egypt

Heliopolis

FIGURE 9.1. THE NILE TEMPLES AS DIVINE FORCE CENTERS IN THE EGYPTIAN RELIGIOUS SYSTEM

In several of the Nile temples we find statuary such as that pictured in the inset in the lower right, where a small figure is shown standing on or next to the feet of the giant figure. Egyptologists are wont to suggest that these are merely indicative of the pharaoh's children or wives. However, the giant figures are esoteric metaphors representing the god-nature or divinity in man, while the smaller figures are symbolic of the lesser aspects of man (for example, the astral soul) that are esoterically reliant upon the background stability provided by, and the protection of, their spiritual or divine "parent." The primary part of the figure is intended to embody the same basic idea, correlating it with the idea of man's various, concentrically organized soul-bodies plus the progression of Nile temples as correspondences to the chakra system in the human being.

See also appendix O concerning the meanings associated with multiple image statuary like this, such as found at Abu Simbel, Karnak, and (West Bank) Thebes.

these states geographically—commencing at Heliopolis—then gave rise to a separate field of existence, symbolized by the Delta.

We otherwise saw that Khnemu—the sevenfold god worshiped at Elephantine—evidently represented the archetypal form-creating aspect of Osiris, as the outward manifestation of Ra. Correspondingly, the Osiris worshiped at Abydos represented Ra's "alchemical" Purpose—hence Osiris being regarded there as "king of the Underworld" and Abydos itself being represented as an entrance to the Underworld. Such an undoubtedly complex metaphysical concept is perhaps more easily understood if graphically presented, as in figure 9.1. Here we see the triple aspect of Ra, who (as an amalgam of Khnemu and Ptah) incorporates within his lower nature Osiris, who, in turn, incorporates within his own lower nature Man himself. Although the drawing is meant merely to indicate the general concept, it is noteworthy that the proportions of the smaller figures relative to the largest ones coincide with those in the rock sculptures at Abu Simbel and other temples possessing huge god statues with lesser deities standing between their feet.

The Nilotic Centers in the Body of the Triple Osiris

Now, as we can see from figure 9.1, the "body of Osiris" symbolizes the whole of esoteric Lower Egypt from Abydos right down to (and including) the Delta. The latter is represented by the divided legs of the lower half of the human figure contained within the astral soul. Bearing in mind the divisions of the Nile (as at Rosetta and Damietta) that discharge their waters into the Mediterranean, this is clearly logical. The association of Ra-Tem (the lowest *evolutionary* aspect of the triple Ra) with Heliopolis and his depiction and worship as a serpent also become rather clearer.[2] The symbolism relates to the lowest point at which the evolutionary kundalini ("serpent fire") reaches its farthest point (as man) in the downward cycle before beginning to rise and return (southward) toward its point of origin. The symbolism of the downward-flowing serpent fire represented itself to the Egyptians as the mass of undifferentiated "Divine Sparks" that subsequently had to go through the process of developing astral (i.e., terrestrially bound) souls, thence differentiating, or individualizing, through experience to become man.[3]

The Return of the "Prodigal Son"

From the angle of spiritual evolution of the individual human being, however, in order to follow the "Path of Return," man had then to cross over the "River of Life" (symbolized by the seaward-moving Nile, representing the natural, precessionary flow of ordinary human experience) and so permanently cut himself off from all previous personal associations. He apparently did so (progressively) through the initiatory process that undoubtedly took place in the three pyramids at Giza. Thereafter, he had to travel southward (esoterically "homeward," against the tide of precession) by land, progressing from temple to temple according to his (spiritually) hierarchical status and obligations as a neophyte. From this we can begin to understand exactly why Heliopolis was such an immensely important spiritual center and also why it was symbolically associated with the Bennu (the phoenix), representing the reconstitution, or remanifestation, of the god-man within. The

Completing the
"Jigsaw Puzzle"
of Astronomical
Metaphors and
Allegories

▲

141

FIGURE 9.2. THE PYRAMIDS AT GIZA
This photograph was taken from the south, with the Menkaure pyramid and its three small "satellite" pyramids in the foreground. To the distant right of the Great ("Khufu") Pyramid (in the far background) can be seen the other small pyramid trio. The Sphinx is out of the picture, to the right. The central "Khafre" pyramid, although the same size as the Great Pyramid, appears taller because of the perspective and also because it sits on a slightly higher part of the Giza plateau. At the top of the "Khafre" pyramid can be seen the remains of the limestone casing with which all three pyramids are believed originally to have been completely covered.

priests of Heliopolis (the city known to the Egyptians as Anu, or Annu) appear to have had the sole responsibility for the "screening" process of selecting and then training suitable candidates for the priesthood from among the general population of Egypt, preparatory to rites of initiation and induction (at Giza).[4]

Absurdity of Regarding the Pyramids as Tombs

Rather pointedly, the pyramids at Giza have no clearly evident god associated with them by depiction, although—again, contrary to what Egyptologists seem to think—their names (Khufu, Khepren, and Menkaure) imply definite respective relationships with the three highest ensouling aspects of Ra—that is, Amen-Ra, Kheper-Ra, and Menthu-Ra. None of these pyramids possessed any internal wall inscriptions or murals whatsoever, the clear implication being that they were very definitely intended to be completely free of any associated psychic influences. As all the more important tombs and mortuary temples in Egypt were covered prolifically with murals and hieroglyphs, the insistence by Egyptologists that the Pyramids were merely funereal chambers falls flat on its face. The further issue of the

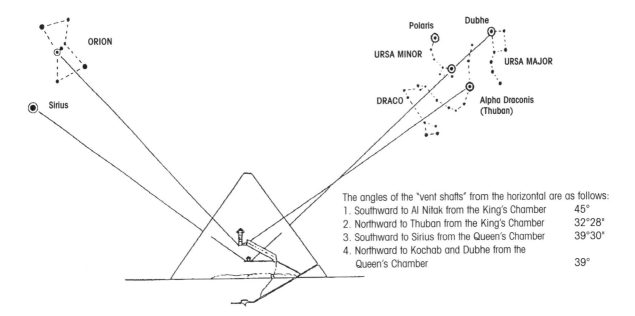

The angles of the "vent shafts" from the horizontal are as follows:
1. Southward to Al Nitak from the King's Chamber   45°
2. Northward to Thuban from the King's Chamber   32°28"
3. Southward to Sirius from the Queen's Chamber   39°30"
4. Northward to Kochab and Dubhe from the
   Queen's Chamber   39°

FIGURE 9.3. CELESTIAL ORIENTATIONS OF THE GREAT PYRAMID

Neither of the two vent shafts from the Queen's Chamber actually reaches the outer surface of the Pyramid, which seems to indicate that the candidate for initiation was (at this point in his progress) at an intermediate stage (i.e., a "threshold"), having almost but not quite achieved the outer (i.e., "higher") consciousness. The fact that the line of sight of the northern vent shaft passes through Kochab (the seventh star in Ursa Minor) and also Dubhe (the seventh star in Ursa Major) is highly significant, because it appears to relate to the first of the seven initiations of the "Upper Way." Dubhe was itself associated by the Egyptians with "Ak" (the Eye) and was otherwise known as "Heaven's Pivot" by the Chinese.

The line of sight from the King's Chamber northward to Thuban (Alpha Draconis—known by the Chinese as "the right hand pivot of the upper heaven world") passes en route through the "neck" of Draco, thereby "severing" it. It also then appears to pass immediately through a point akin to the equinoctial pole, just behind and to one side of the "cobra's hood." The same line of sight continues onward to the sixth star in Ursa Major (Mizar), which is a binary, its companion being Alcor. Interestingly, one ancient Arabic story has Mizar as mother of the heavenly child while the seventh star, Alkaid, was known as "the destroyer" and was specifically associated with the Ursids, a rich meteor stream emanating cyclically from it during the zodiacal month of Scorpio. The symbolism of heavenly procreation is unmistakable.

clearly evident astronomical associations of the "vent shafts" in the Great Pyramid—which Bauval confirmed, as shown in figure 9.3—has also reinforced objectively intelligent opinion that Egyptologists have been utterly wrong over this issue for well over one hundred years.[5] Their insistence, therefore, upon pursuing such an obviously far-fetched idea, even in the face of their own criteria disproving it, demonstrates yet again the ostrichlike mentality of academia when left entirely to its own introverted speculations.

The Associated Symbolism of the Sphinx

The Sphinx, while clearly associated with the dual god Ra-Tem (and thereby with Heliopolis as well), very definitely represented man as an emergent god.[6] The symbolism of the pharaonic headdress with a mounted uraeus on the forehead, surmounting a specifically leonine (not merely animal) body, represents the divine intelligence emerging from the purely limited sensory capacities of the astral soul in conjunction with a zodiacal cycle. The emergence from a primitive mentality is implied in the backward-sloping forehead of the sculpture, the latter feature having also been confirmed by John Anthony West in conjunction with Frank Domingo, a forensic expert from the New York City Police Department.[7] However, mainstream Egyptology continues to reject such ideas, showing just how little it really tries to understand ancient Egyptian mystical thought on its own terms.

The onward progression to Abydos from Giza (still within the field of the Underworld) itself appears to have been triple in nature, as we can see from careful consideration of the map of Egypt in relation to the various chakras shown in figure 9.4. As we have already noted, the number of nomes involved in this same progression is fourteen, Abydos being the main city of the fourteenth nome (from Memphis). As we shall see in a moment, that is of major importance in the Osirian Mystery allegory of his body having been cut up into fourteen pieces by his brother, Set, for Set (as we saw in an earlier chapter) represents the ignorantly (i.e., spiritually) blind "Divine Spark."

Evolutionary Progression through the Underworld by Association

In order to understand the symbolism of "the Underworld" of the Egyptians, we must bear very clearly in mind the question of zodiacal associations. Just as the Heliopolitan Ra-Tem contained and distributed the millions of "Divine Sparks" that constituted the god-self of the humanity of the cycle, so every star in the universe was an organically Janus-like Atum-Ra (just like our own solar system) at some or other stage of cosmic evolution. The spiral-cyclic movement of our solar system during the 26,000-year Annus Magnus was thus believed to expose the millions of our earthly "Divine Sparks" to the influence of their own higher correspondences, thereby subliminally encouraging their evolutionary progress en route to an even greater "global" sense of absolute divinity.

It would appear that the main temples between Heliopolis and Abydos were therefore specifically designed to reflect definite zodiacal associations. Consequently, by taking part in the particular rituals of each such temple, the individual would automatically absorb an increasing degree of the nature of its particular god. We shall take a closer look at this in the next chapter. However, the general issue is of importance here because the higher initiations were deemed to be influenced by both the zodiac and certain of the other constellations or stars—Ursa Major, Ursa Minor, Sirius, and Draco in particular.[8] It is perhaps also worth reiterating that the temples in the Delta were mainly oriented toward planetary influences and the worship of their associated gods and goddesses. Abydos, however, was of crucial significance in the Egyptian Mysteries. That is because the Osiris god-man within the consciousness of each neophyte was deemed to continue "dead" until and unless awakened by the higher influences of the polar constellations. In regard to that, we turn back to the story of Isis trying to resuscitate Osiris by using the *apuat* tool in the "Opening of the Mouth" rite. By now turning the map of Egypt upside down (see fig. 9.4), a really startling picture emerges to throw the whole allegory into sharp relief.

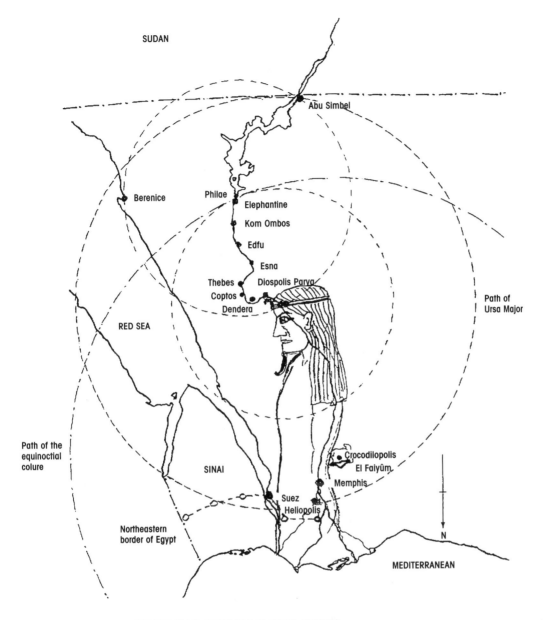

FIGURE 9.4. THE AWAKENING OF THE NILOTIC OSIRIS

As we can see, Crocodilopolis (ancient Arsinoë) is located at a point representative of the pivotal "small-of-the-back" position in the human body. The cosmic (i.e., astronomical) symbolism is self-evident. In addition, the figure shows the spherical arc of travel of the Ursa Minor–shaped portion of the Nile between Diospolis Parva and Philae, with Philae as the focus and representing the star Polaris.

Significance in the Shape of the Nile

As we can see in figure 9.4, the shape of the Nile between Diospolis Parva and Philae exactly fits not only that of the *apuat* tool but also of the constellation Ursa Minor, while that part of the Nile between Abydos and Heliopolis becomes the mummified upper body of Osiris. The *apuat* approaches the top of the head of Osiris, however, and not the physical mouth, despite the misleading name of the ceremonial rite. The "mouth" is

Completing the
"Jigsaw Puzzle"
of Astronomical
Metaphors and
Allegories

▲

145

therefore confirmed as referring esoterically to the crown chakra, for it was through it (and through it alone) that the influence of the spiritual soul (or *saha*) could be regarded as being able to regain access to "the Underworld" contained by the astral soul. Correspondingly, it is via this same point that yogic philosophy tells us that the consciousness escapes in order to unite with the "higher Self." In that respect, the Greek tradition comes to mind of Pallas Athene springing forth from the head of Zeus after Hermes (the Greek version of Thoth-Tehuti) has cleaved it with a "hammer and wedge."[9]

If we look again at the planisphere, we shall see quite quickly that the star at the end of the mouth-opening "hook" of the *apuat* is Kochab—the same star at which the northern "ventilation shaft" from the Queen's Chamber in the Great Pyramid is pointed. The star at the other end of the "handle" of Ursa Minor is, of course, Polaris, which currently stands at the celestial North Pole. This, however, equates with the location of Elephantine-Philae when related to the map of Egypt, as we shall see in a moment.

Involvement of Other Circumpolar Stars in the Drama

Now, the constellation Draco has sixteen stars in it, and as Ursa Minor swings around in its natural orbit (as shown in fig. 9.4), it comes close to the ninth star counting from the end of its "tail." By counting the equivalent major temples from Philae, it becomes obvious that Abydos coincides geographically with that same star.[10] Consequently, the *apuat* esoterically divides the serpent in two (or else esoterically unites itself with it), substituting itself for the lower body and tail of Draco[11] and thereby creating the Duat—Spirit and Matter, Heaven and Underworld (see fig. 9.1)—but there is still more. In chapter 8, we mentioned Ursa Major as the great cosmic Bull (of which only the hind leg is shown as manifest in the heavens—see the Dendera zodiac, appendix E.1), which, following its own natural orbital path around the pole, esoterically cuts off the head of Draco between Memphis and Heliopolis—i.e., at Giza—or which is otherwise "bitten off" the constellation of Taurus by the head of Draco. From the planisphere, we can also see that Ursa Major's orbital path is dictated—in relation to Ursa Minor—by their apparent joint progression as seen from any particular point along the path of the ecliptic. But the apparent path of the celestial pole during the 26,000-year Annus Magnus is itself dictated by the equinoctial pole—which we find located just to one side of the "neck" of Draco (just behind the "cobra's hood").[12]

The "Mill of the Gods"

Here, therefore, appears to lie the center of the "spindle" upon which our local universe is turning—that having been recognized by the ancient Egyptians and represented by them as Horus the Elder stabbing an elongated spear through the rear part of the head of the great dragon-cum-crocodile god (Sebek), which Draco represents. This all takes place under the aegis of Sebek-Ra, the "Lord of Darkness and Diversity" (the galactic macrocosm of Set), whose lesser self—Sebek—performed the same centripetal function within the solar system. Bearing this in mind, and remembering that the Delta resembles the downward-pointing "cobra's head" at the foot of the Nile, it becomes clear by deduction that the equivalent geographical location of the equinoctial pole was in the Faiyum.[13] Obligingly, it is here, at Crocodilopolis, that we find the main temple clearly dedicated to Sebek.

FIGURE 9.5. THE "WORLD MOTHER" GODDESS TA'URT

(concubine of the cosmic Set)

Bearing in mind the Egyptian love of double entendre, there are fair grounds for speculating that the name Ta'Urt might well be closely related to Tehuti-Thoth—the god of knowledge and wisdom. The underlying esoteric metaphor here is thus doubtless intent on indicating the principle of Divine Wisdom keeping the activities of the Ur-Shu and the *neteru* constrained by a path of Divine Purpose. In addition, the dual metaphor of Ta'Urt herself as both World Mother and the goddess of pregnancy happily tends to reinforce an implicit idea of containment.

Interestingly, we discover in the Hindu Vedas the phonetically very similar Sanskrit word *rta*, meaning quite literally "Self-sacrificing Cosmic Order"; it is from this, according to the ancient Brahmanical scriptures, that the "firstborn" gods emerge, or are self-emanated.

We also find *rta* concealed in the Greek god-name *Rhadamanthus*. However, in the Egyptian it becomes Rta-Mntw, an aspect of the god Mntw-Ra. But Mntw—from which comes the French word *manteau*—has the significance of a surround, or some sort of cloaking garment (esoterically, a body of Light). The combination of the two—*rta* and Mntw—then appears to confirm that these "Firstborn Sons of Cosmic Order" are essentially none other than the hierarchies of the Self-limiting Demiurge, or Cosmic Oversoul.

Here, symbolic representations of the circumpolar and near circumpolar constellations show Sebek (Draco, the dragon-headed crocodile) climbing on the back of Ta'Urt (representing the Oversoul of our local universe), who holds the northern pivot (the Pole Star) in thrall while the latter, in turn, holds fast the tail of the cosmic bull (symbolizing Taurus).

FIGURE 9.6. HORUS THE ELDER AND THE CELESTIAL BULL

Here the figure of Horus the Elder is stabbing a spear downward through the head of the Celestial Bull (representing the zodiacal constellation of Taurus). As our solar system appears (at least by inference) to be part of Taurus, the implication is that the spear here represents the "spindle" around which our immediate, local universe turns, within the yet greater celestial sphere upon which Draco sits, at its northern pole.

By straight deduction, it becomes fairly certain that the goddess Ta'Urt (the name literally meaning "provider of coffins") here represents none other than the divine Oversoul of our local universe (see also appendix L) in its appointed role as the Demiurge, conceiving (i.e., providing "soul-bodies" for) the divine As-r's that karma has decreed must "fall from Grace." The depiction of Ta'Urt chained to the incomplete bull of Taurus in figure 9.6 then confirms the unbreakable bonds of relationship between the two (with Ursa Major doubling up as the Celestial Bull's missing leg) and their probable cyclic conjunction in the heavens.[14] That Horus is shown spearing the forehead of Taurus otherwise suggests that the Pleiades (located in that spot astronomically) are also directly involved in the underlying metaphor of this unfolding cosmic drama.

The Hidden Cosmic Bull Becomes Manifest

Now we next return to the orbit of Ursa Major, specifically in relation to the *apuat* of Ursa Minor, for here lies one of the greatest cosmic associations of all. In so doing we find that as the latter comes into the celestial position mirrored by the Nile between Philae and Diospolis Parva, so Ursa Major relocates (see fig. 9.4) not as the "hind leg" of the bull god Hapi but as the replacement phallus of Osiris himself![15] Consequently, we can now see why it is that the capital of Egypt was located at Memphis—something that has puzzled scholars for well over a century—and why Memphis itself was dedicated to Serapis and the god Ptah—the "Divine Craftsman" who "fashioned" Man upon his potter's wheel. Memphis actually represents the divine sacral chakra (*chakra* literally meaning "wheel") in the body of Osiris, while Heliopolis is thus confirmed beyond doubt as representing the base of the spine chakra on behalf of the "fiery serpent" Ra-Tem. That, in turn, may perhaps serve to confirm the significance to the Egyptians of the often mentioned ancient city of Kadesh, for the latter's astrogeographical location appears to coincide with that of the star Arcturus (see fig. 9.7).

The Symbolism of Cosmic Fertility and Re-creation

While all this occurs at one end of the elliptical path of the Annus Magnus, it is the general reorientation of stars as seen from the other end of the 25,920-year cycle that completes the picture and the overall allegory. In fact, there appear to be two possible alternatives, both of which have exactly the same meaning. The first involves Ursa Major appearing to merge partially with (or join to) the "tail" of Draco. The four stars forming

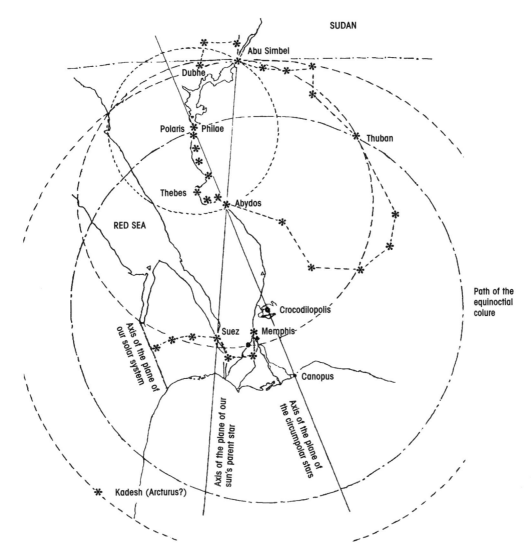

FIGURE 9.7. SIDEREAL CONVERGENCES OVER EGYPT

(see also appendix M)

1. As the solar system's path in space takes it below the plane of the Galaxy, esoteric symbolism has it descending into the Underworld, the crossing point being at Abydos. It then passes back through the same equivalent point.
2. The orbital paths of both Sirius and Orion appear to be associated with the cyclical movements shown.
3. The northeastern boundary of Egypt (running from the Gulf of Aqaba to the Mediterranean) appears to run parallel to the axis between Philae and Crocodilopolis.
4. The four colossi at Abu Simbel appear yet again to be confirmed as associated with Amen-Ra, this time as the four stars in the head of Ursa Major, which is also the head of the cosmic serpent Nak.

its "bucket" then become the "head" of the cosmic serpent Nak, whose body can thus be seen to extend the full length of Egypt. The second alternative involves Draco itself being seen to swing southward until it reaches an equivalent position at the far end of the great orbital cycle. But in either instance, there are four stars that focus on the equivalent geographical position of Abu Simbel.[16]

Much of the associated symbolism appears fairly clear. The fact that the cosmic serpent has a head at each end of its body signifies either a complete major sidereal cycle (i.e., the Annus Magnus) or Eternity itself. From one angle, the head of the cosmic serpent—representing the divine intelligence and knowledge of Ra—reproduces itself in our world through the agency of its alter ego, the Osirian phallus. From another, the fire of ultimate divinity (the very Life-force of Amen-Ra) descends serpentlike through the various planes of being until its furthermost point is reached (in the base chakra of man, and thus also symbolically at Heliopolis), whereupon it turns "homeward," ultimately to remerge with (and refertilize) the One Source from which it was originally emanated. In the latter case, the significance is clearly one associated with procreation because the spherical orbit of Ursa Minor represents the "divine ovum." Ursa Major in turn represents the "divine spermatazoon," the head of which breaks off once it has penetrated the ovum and then bursts apart in a shower of "sparks" of creative Life-force.

Two Significant Geographical Axes

Rather critical in all this is the already established fact that Polaris—the first star in the "handle" of Ursa Minor, esoterically oriented on Philae-Elephantine—is another binary star, just like Eta Draconis at Abydos. However, as shown in figure 9.7, if we now produce a straight line between Philae, Abydos, and Crocodilopolis (which interestingly extends directly through the ancient coastal temple of Canopus[17]), as well as between Abu Simbel and Abydos (extended through the city of Suez), we find that we are looking at two highly important axes. We nevertheless need to bear in mind that what is depicted has a simultaneously dual interpretation, consistent with the Egyptian predilection for (at least) double meanings in everything.

First of all, Crocodilopolis would seem to represent not only the ecliptic pole, as we have already established, but also the central focus of the vertical axis (Philae-Canopus) of our particular sidereal system, or constellation. The other axis then (Abu Simbel–Abydos–Suez) presumably represents the plane of our sun's parent star. Rather remarkably, the angle between these two axes is exactly the same as that of the ascending and descending passages in the Great Pyramid. But by turning the drawing on its right side, we suddenly find that another, quite separate picture presents itself, for the body of Osiris with its erect phallus is transformed into the recumbent figure of the god Geb. The symbolic place of the phallus is then taken by Shu, the god of light, holding up Nut, the arc of the heavens above the plane of the Galaxy—represented in the diagram by the path of the celestial pole, looking eastward.

The Astronomical Movements of Ursa Major and Ursa Minor

From these few observations alone we can see that we have thus wandered into a truly vast field of cosmological significances on which an encyclopedia could be written—and probably one day will. Quite clearly, there is no way in which we could do the subject full justice in this book and we must therefore limit ourselves to considering a few of the more immediately significant points associated with it. In doing so, however, we need to reiter-

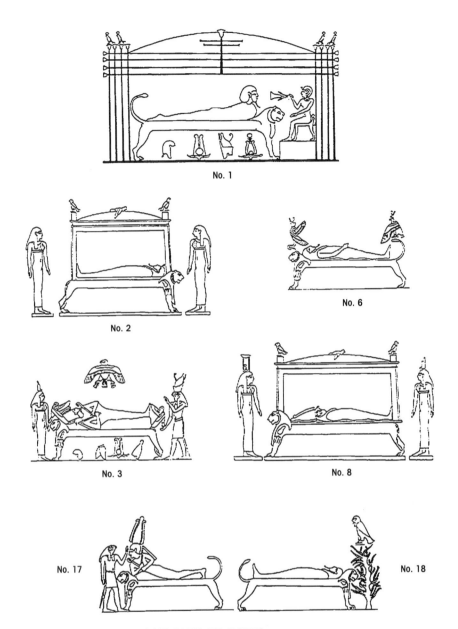

FIGURE 9.8. THE "FUNEREAL POSITIONS" OF OSIRIS

These pictures are taken from the temple of Dendera, and they have caused real puzzlement to Egyptologists for over two centuries. Why would Osiris be shown in so many different death positions? Well, if we take Osiris as a metaphor for a celestial figure that appears to revolve in the heavens (owing to the epicyclic movement of our own solar system and the earth within it), it would make perfect sense, because it would refer to the earth's own relative observational position within that sidereal cycle—perhaps the 25,920-year cycle of precession.

ate that the allegory of the death and resurrection of Osiris is triple in its interpretation. It relates primordially (as far as humanity, at least, is concerned) to the zeitgeist of the 25,920-year sidereal cycle of the Annus Magnus, secondarily to the process of spiritual initiation that is nevertheless closely connected with the Great Year (as we shall see in chapter 11), and thirdly to the religious and administrative organization of the Egyptian state. Yet there

Completing the
"Jigsaw Puzzle"
of Astronomical
Metaphors and
Allegories

▲

151

is more still, for as the celestial revolutions take place, two very important associated phenomena evidently occur in the heavens, as seen from Earth.[18] First of all, the "head" of Ursa Minor dips into the plane of the ecliptic at its highest emergence from the Milky Way, the "celestial Nile," where we find the "submerged" cosmic equivalent of the "dead" Osiris—hence, perhaps, the many depictions of his body as wave-scaled. Second, Ursa Major itself appears to descend in due cycle into the plane of the Milky Way, thereby becoming "fastened" to the cosmic corpse in readiness for the "impregnation of Isis" and the "conception" of Horus the Child.

Now, there is far more to this than just a question of cosmic imagery, amazingly well coordinated though it may be with the actual movements of other constellations in the Galaxy. But before we go into that in further detail, let us first examine some of the various other pictorial symbols that the Egyptians used to both describe and conceal the whole process. Perhaps the most informative is a sequence of twenty-three scenes on the walls of the temple at Dendera, depicting Osiris on his funeral bier.[19] The fact that there are only twenty-three shown implies that there is an esoteric twenty-fourth. In other words, a complete 360-degree circuit of the precessional path is being described, using 15-degree intervals to describe the relative locations of various stars and constellations.[20]

The Celestial Revolutions of Osiris

In connection with the cosmic associations just mentioned, Osiris on his funeral bier is shown in a variety of different and very intriguing positions and poses (see fig. 9.8). Sometimes he is face up, sometimes face down; sometimes with his head at one end, sometimes at the other; sometimes in funereal wrappings, sometimes not; sometimes bearded, sometimes not; sometimes wearing a Horus mask or crown, sometimes nothing. The general implication, therefore, taking into account a probably sequential progression, is that the symbolism refers to the axial rotation and orbit of our solar system, relative to the plane of its parent star, or even the Galaxy itself. Second, Isis and Nephthys (or Isis and Horus) alternate their respective positions at the head and foot of the funeral bier, thereby confirming the suggestion of an implied orbital aspect of the Great Sidereal Year within the plane of the ecliptic. That is because Isis and Nephthys appear, in one sense, to represent the path of the celestial pole (which is parallel to the celestial equator), while the figure of Horus seems to point to the constellation Aquila (the Eagle), through which the celestial equator passes (see the star map at fig. 1.3). The occasionally appearing figure of Anubis would then coincide, we suggest, with the cyclical incursions of Sirius.

That in turn leads us to the triple constellation Orion (generally understood to form the belt of Orion-Osiris "the hunter"). As Bauval and Gilbert point out in *The Orion Mystery*, this constellation follows a rising and declining arc from the southeast to the southwest horizon looking southward (as seen in Egypt).[21] That, in turn, suggests its location relative to the axial path of our solar system, for (according to his description) it rose above the eastern horizon on its lowest arc—coinciding with the line of sight from the King's Chamber—in about 10,450 B.C. and every 25,920 years before that date as well. At such times, our solar system would thus appear to be at the highest point of its own axial path (i.e., aphelion to its own parent star), equivalent to the "celestial winter solstice."

The Cosmic "Opening of the Mouth" Ceremony

If, as Bauval further indicates in his photographic plate no. 15a, it is at this point that Horus (Aquila?) appears to take hold of the *apuat* of Ursa Minor in its lowest position in the sky, the symbolism stands out clearly. As the equatorial revolution takes place, Orion (representing the triple soul) passes through and out of the body of Osiris (lying within the plane of the Galaxy) and flies back to "the Chamber of Judgment"—the celestial aphelion. It is, however, at the time of the celestial winter equinox (i.e., its perihelion) that our solar system begins to turn in its axial path, back toward the plane of the Galaxy, thereby recommencing the cycle of regeneration with the "impregnation" of Isis. At the same time, so it would appear, the zodiacal constellation of Leo appears on the eastern horizon, directly facing the Sphinx. Then, at the time that Ursa Minor descends back to the plane of the Galaxy, thereby making ready to "open the mouth" of the dead Osiris, the cosmic *ba* reenters "the body" of Osiris, thereby revivifying it.

When Orion appears at its furthest point away from the plane of the Galaxy—remembering that this occurs twice, at sidereal "aphelion" and "perihelion"—he is either "dismembered" by Set or "reconstituted" by Isis, minus his phallus, the latter symbolizing his creative (divine) intelligence. Consequently, it is at this latter point that Isis (the evocative nature of the psyche) fashions the "wooden phallus" (symbolized by Ursa Major), attaches it to the body of Osiris, and so impregnates herself. When Orion returns to the plane of the Galaxy, the infant Horus is then "born" and the cycle of regeneration is completed. However, it seems that the whole sequence will be clearly perceived only when the twenty-three stages depicted at Dendera have actually been worked out astronomically to show the progressive positions of the various constellations during the Annus Magnus.

The staggering breadth of astronomical knowledge necessary to put together such an accurate cosmic allegory is in itself amazing. But what had been described so far merely covers a few of the phenomenal aspects of the interrelationships of the cycles associated with our solar system and the surrounding universe. The most important part of the allegory lies in relation to what it signified to the ancient Egyptians in terms of the very process of evolution of our planetary Life and how that same evolution was regarded as inextricably linked to the ever-changing divine influences that it cyclically meets.

The Real Significance of the "Great Return"

While many readers might well be prepared to recognize and admit the astronomical allegories just described, experience leads one to believe that much less credence will be given by the scientifically sophisticated minds of the intelligentsia of our time to the practical aspects associated with "soul evolution." Almost certainly in the train of what has just been suggested here, we shall now experience a plethora of authors confirming that it is at these cyclical periods just mentioned that "spacemen" arrive from other, more advanced solar systems in order to further the evolution of our mentally or spiritually backward humanity. While such a materialistically literal interpretation can hardly be avoided as a product of our times and will thus just have to be accepted, we make the point here very firmly that this is not what the ancient Egyptians (whoever they were) were intent on putting across in their metaphors and allegories.

Not only did the Ancients—as we have otherwise seen—believe in the actual existence of gods, daemons, and souls as entirely real entities, but they regarded them as the very core of their philosophy of life as well. Without them—as we said at the very outset—their culture makes no sense whatsoever. In addition, there is absolutely no doubt as to their belief that the periodic return of the gods—as divine influences—was not only a matter of fact, but that it was also entirely dependent upon a synchronicity of sidereal cycles. To imagine then that such a civilization—whenever it existed—could put together a vast, exactly working model of our local universe without a highly meaningful spiritual rationale, allied to a huge amount of detailed scientific knowledge, and instead suggest that they merely indulged in fantasy about the spiritual life animating and guiding the mechanism of the universe, is plainly fatuous. What we see in their stupendous allegory is a gift of information and prophecy to future generations of humanity who would be able to perceive its hidden meanings. Of that there can be little doubt. For in none of the historical records of the last 6,000 years or so is there any indication whatsoever of anything even nearly approaching such an intelligent civilization in existence on the face of the earth. That alone leads one to surmise that theirs had to be a far more ancient culture and civilization than is presently recognized, and that it almost certainly disappeared by prior design, at its allotted time, in conjunction with the conclusion of a major sidereal cycle, as we endeavor to describe in chapter 10.

That leads us directly back to the idea of "seasonal" cycles affecting the growth and decay of human civilization and culture. It also answers the paradox of advanced scientific knowledge being found in the hands of young civilizations that could not possibly have derived it themselves from mere personal observation and empirical rationalizing over the period of a couple of thousand years. It also otherwise leads on to the supposition that even though the mass of highly evolved mankind may depart this planetary sphere in due cycle, some must remain behind, somehow, in order to maintain the continuity of existence and the natural momentum of the evolutionary process. That in turn implies that the dynasties of Manetho are no work of fiction after all; that his dynasties of gods, demigods, and heroes actually did exist; and, furthermore, that they will continue cyclically to reappear on Earth.

How Do the Gods Supposedly Reappear on Earth?

But, we might reasonably ask, what is the mechanism of appearance and disappearance of these seasonally returning hierarchies of hugely intelligent, spiritual or divine beings? If they come to Earth and take a phenomenal form (perhaps sometimes akin to our own), surely they must travel in some or other form of spacecraft. In fact, the answer is a quite categorical no! The traditions of the Egyptian priesthoods give us the answer to the question in the form of the soul-bodies (the *saha* and *ba*), which have for so long been regarded as almost if not entirely mythical entities—or, if not mythical, so ethereal as to have no existence in our physical world. But, as we suggested in a previous chapter, it is the earth-bound astral soul that was regarded as the true reincarnating entity, the human form that it animates being merely a holographic projection—hence the Egyptian priests referring to the soul and the objective forms of the gods as "bodies of light substance."[22]

In order to help explain the rationale of the mechanism of appearance (as light and

FIGURE 9.9. THE AURORA BOREALIS
(copy engraving from drawings made by the French Arctic expedition of 1839–40)

color) of the hierarchies of deity, it seems that we have to point to the aurora borealis as the most obvious single, local example available to us. While to some this suggestion might seem to take our examination of this subject irrevocably beyond the bounds of sanity, we believe that it will be found to tie in exactly with what we have already said here and in chapter 1.

Harald Falk-Ytter, in his book *Aurora*, describes a great many of the characteristics of the so-called northern lights.[23] While we cannot cover them all here, we can perhaps remind ourselves of a few that seem particularly specific to what we have been discussing. Thus, in relation to the field of the solar system as the spiritual body (*saha*) of Ra, Osiris is the cosmic symbol, while the *macrocosmic* Set, we suggest, is correspondingly representative of the "group personality" of the Divine Man. Our planet's ionosphere (its *ba*, or astral soul) is symbolized by Isis; the lower atmosphere as the planet's *ka* is symbolized by Nephthys; while the physical earth itself becomes the domain of the *microcosmic* Set.

The various related issues have already been recognized by science. The first is that the main cycle of activity of the aurora borealis is itself determined by electromagnetic effects generated in the ionosphere by energetic projections from the solar photosphere (resulting in the solar wind phenomenon) and sunspot cycle, with a secondary activity determined by Earth's position relative to the Sun in its annual orbit. Second, it appears to arise through the constant electromagnetic interaction between the ionosphere and Earth's core, the former itself responding to a fluctuating pattern of electromagnetic stimulation from the solar wind, which we described earlier as the "breath of Ra." Third, the aurora consists of an arc or ring of electromagnetic force (fig. 9.9) encircling the Pole, ascending and descending in pleated (i.e., serpentine) curtains of light and color. It often seems to do so at terrific speed (up to hundreds of miles per second), extending right down into the body of the planet or right up into the highest atmosphere.

The Aurora's Traditional Function

The fourth point is one that our modern science would probably not wish to verify and which will almost certainly draw laughter on the grounds of our being absurdly seduced

Completing the
"Jigsaw Puzzle"
of Astronomical
Metaphors and
Allegories

▲

155

by old superstitions. However, old superstitions often have a hidden germ of truth in them. Anyway, at the risk of such derision, the point to be made lies partly in relation to the tradition that the aurora brings groups of souls down to Earth and also removes them after death, thereby suggesting that it is fundamentally intelligent. Such a sense of Divine Purpose would otherwise imply an association with the "angels of birth and death" of several ancient traditions.

While there have been several stories of subfolds of auroral light actually approaching human beings—as Falk-Ytter relates[24]—in such a manner that suggests a reactive sense of curiosity, our concern lies rather more specifically with the issue of the apparently literal "transportation of souls" and whether such an idea seems really rational. On the grounds that the astral soul of the human being is a definite entity, comprising some sort of psychomagnetic field capable of emanating a subfield of light (or *ka*) within itself, one might perceive a rationale for Earth's ionospheric sheath to be regarded as the World Soul. This, however, would then imply that there is a guiding hierarchy of intelligence within (or enclosing) the ionospheric sheath of the planet and that it periodically emanates "electromagnetic cells" (which we call *souls*) that then give rise to the various kingdoms of Nature. If so, could this be the reason for the obviously coordinated order and intelligence found generally throughout Nature?[25] And could it not also be that a correspondingly cyclic "Fall into Generation" (of the *saha*) occurs from the electromagnetic sheath surrounding our solar system, just as its lesser counterpart (the *ba*) might do in relation to the ionospheric sheath of our planet?

Parallel Traditions in Other Religions

Bearing in mind what we have already suggested concerning the spiritual relationship between the ancient Egyptians and the semidivine "adept-heroes" of the land of Pun(t) in northwestern India, it is also worthy of note that there are exact associations between the astronomical correlations just described and the cosmic allegories of the Hindu Puranas and Vedas. For example, during the Hindu creation story, the "fallen *asuras*" (direct counterparts of the Christian "fallen angels") are said to be emanated "from the thigh of Brahma."[26] As Brahma was often depicted as a bull, the association with Ursa Major is self-evident.[27] Additionally, As-r (the Egyptian form of "Osiris") bears an extraordinary philological resemblance to *asura*, while other kindred associations could be drawn in relation to "Ursa" and the "Ur-shu," the "beings of light" recognized by the Egyptians.[28]

We otherwise find Krishna (the Hindu equivalent of the solar Logos-Kristos) in the Bhagavad Gita saying: "All beings, O Kaunteya, enter my lower nature at the end of a World-Age; at the beginning of a World-Age, again I emanate them. . . ."[29] As Santillana and von Dechend also remind us in *Hamlet's Mill* when talking of Krishna in his manifestation as the Kristos-Redeemer figure of the avatar of Visnu: "He [Krishna] was delegated from higher quarters to free the Earth, 'overburdened' as it was with Asura."[30] Does this not perhaps imply some sort of "Judgment Day" at which the "unworthy" (i.e., as yet inadequately evolved *asuras*) are temporarily withdrawn from the cycle of objective existence?

The Union of Philosophy, Science, and Religion in One Concept

No matter how bizarre all this might seem to us, it merits careful consideration. The concept of personal reincarnation is already widely accepted, and yet our knowledge of what supposedly lies between one lifetime and another appears largely conjectural, even if rooted in ancient philosophies and traditions. But why should there not occur a cyclically determined yet progressive reincarnation of whole spiritual hierarchies in which the individual soul takes part? Such a concept does not actually conflict with any of the various ancient teachings, and it also rationalizes a (potentially scientific) cosmic connection that may not be so readily ascertainable from other angles.

For example, the essential idea behind the whole process of spiritual initiation that the Egyptians (and other ancient peoples) followed is that the spiritual soul—bearing the real Man—would eventually recognize its own reflection in the astral soul, rather than (as hitherto) believing itself to *be* the astral soul. As a direct consequence, it would dissociate itself from the further projection needed to create the physical human being and, in so doing, it (and that generation of humanity) would disappear from this field of phenomenal existence altogether. Such a concept is readily found in one or another local guise in several philosophies around the world. In addition, historical stories concerning demigods, or adept-heroes (like Apollonius of Tyana), being able, apparently, to appear and disappear at will, or even to appear in two distant places simultaneously, also fit in with this idea.[31]

Such a range of suggestions may appall some readers (as much as it intrigues the author himself) and strike them as palpably impossible—and they have every right to their views. However, all we are doing here is examining the background of ancient Egyptian belief and bringing together other diverse strands of thought that have hitherto been regarded by formal science and scholarship as either unconnected or pure mystical fantasy. If the "myth" of self-creation by the gods is anything to go on, however, it is clear that intelligent light (of some or other evolutionary quality) is the sole possible creative phenomenon in the universe. That is a sobering thought, but, when considered "in the light" of our most modern technology and quantum science, it suddenly begins to look not only highly logical, but also decidedly feasible.

We shall touch again on several of these issues in chapter 11 when we discuss the actual processes of spiritual initiation, as found in the various rituals and tests associated with the pyramid complex at Giza.

Completing the
"Jigsaw Puzzle"
of Astronomical
Metaphors and
Allegories

▲

157

TEN

SACRED GEOMETRY AND THE "LIVING" ARCHITECTURE OF EGYPT

The Egyptian priests were accustomed to exhibit simulacra of the gods in circles and globes as symbols of the uniform principle of Life. Hermes Trismegistus compared Divinity to a circle, and the sublime description will be remembered, that its center is everywhere and the circumference nowhere. The Pythagoreans regarded the circle as sacred and considered it as the symbol of the highest spiritual truth. It also represents very aptly all human progress, which is never in straight lines, but in circles returning on themselves as if advancing in ascending spirals, or retrograding in vortices tending downward.

—IAMBLICHUS, *THEURGIA*

Following in the wake of our previous comments that the ancient Egyptians did nothing without it having an esoteric or religious significance, we must apply the same principle to their architecture. By that we do not mean just the aesthetic design of their temple buildings but, much more significantly, such characteristics as relative proportion, acoustics, lightness and darkness, numbers of supporting columns, and general configuration of the internal layout.[1] Each aspect looks as though it should perhaps tell us something about the nature of the associated divinity and the way in which it was to be worshiped. In this chapter we shall be taking a fairly general introductory look at a few of these issues. However, there are two distractions to be dealt with before we start out on this particular quest.

The first lies in the fact that while most temples have fallen partially or wholly into ruin over the last two millennia (since the Romans left Egypt), many appear to have been extensively rebuilt and/or otherwise added to by various generations during the preceding two millennia. The second lies in the fact that the pharaohs of the later dynasties (supposedly between 3150 B.C. and 30 B.C.) appear to have suffered from the self-indulgent habit of serially erasing whole areas of previous hieroglyphics in order to attribute the appropriate religious devotion or details of battles won specifically to themselves, their families, and their court retinues.[2] This habit has caused untold havoc with the historical record, and it is partly because of it that Egyptologists over the last century have found it so difficult to date any dynasty back any further than about 4000 B.C.[3] Fortunately, our concern here lies not at all with the hieroglyphics of the temples.

Knowledge

▲

158

God as Number and Geometer

What we shall particularly concern ourselves with in this chapter derives mainly from numerological/architectural associations because these were intrinsically of a magical nature as far as the Egyptians were concerned. Number denoted potency, and potency was associated with particular hierarchies of gods and *deva*-daemons within the framework of Creation. While the idea of numerology in relation to architecture might perhaps seem somewhat curious to some readers, we shall be touching upon the issues only in very general terms here. We do so in order to convey something of the sense of atmosphere that is vital to understanding the extent to which strictly ordered ceremonial organization affected the ancient mystical piety felt by the Egyptians toward their deities. This involved a deep reverence that was remarked upon even in later days by visiting Greek historians and tourists such as Herodotus.[4]

To begin with, everything originated and finished with the circle, for, to the Egyptians, the circle represented the completeness of a god-soul and all such souls were regarded as concentrically contained within yet greater god-souls.[5] As everything that could take place did so within the soul consciousness of one or other god (all being subsumed within the Universal Soul of Ra), the circle and its microcosmic correspondence, the metaphysical Point (the Pythagorean Monad), were regarded as the origin of all form (seen as a group of relationships), all knowledge, and all faculty. For them the whole evolutionary process involved the Point (or Spark) of Life-force emanated from the Eye of Ra, diversifying and expanding its potential until it returned to fuse and thus became consciously reunited with its parent god-soul.

However, as we ourselves know, the circle also represents infinity and is itself but a point within a much greater circle. So knowledge and faculty were themselves regarded as infinite, and the "Great Work" of alchemical transmutation in relation to man consisted of bringing about his evolution from a tiny "spark" of semi-intelligence to god consciousness itself. This was the basis of the work of the Mystery Schools and from it was derived the associated knowledge of how the universe itself functioned. That knowledge was accordingly based upon mathematics, which is essentially derived from the active and static interrelationships of "points of force," all of which express value—or potency—according to their hierarchical function.

The Egyptian Approach to Defining Time and Space

The Egyptians (like the Chaldeans) calendrically divided the circle into 360 degrees.[6] But while we now split each degree into sixty further parts of itself (a "minute"), which we then further subdivide into sixty segments (seconds of arc), the most important part of the circle for the Egyptians—in the sense of relationship to the evolutionary process—was the decan, and its numerological counterpart, the decad.[7]

The reason for this was that each decan or decad itself represented the completion of a circle—and even more importantly, a cycle. However, in order to understand the reasoning behind their approach, we have to know something of the detail concerning numerological associations. That is because their hierarchical potencies provide the underlying basis of both sympathetic magic and the very process of evolutionary transformation (i.e., alchemy),

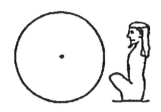

FIGURE 10.1. THE ONE IS SYMBOLIZED BY THE POINT

This Egyptian symbolism is clearly of a man in meditation upon the "sphere of Ra"—the inner soul consciousness.

which is itself a fundamentally magical process. As we proceed into the chapter, the reason for tarrying to deal with this preliminary issue will become more obvious.

Like the Ancients, we begin with the zero, which (being the circle too) symbolized the universal and consequently complete consciousness and faculty of a god. It accordingly also represented either the divine soul, the spiritual soul, or the astral (terrestrial) soul—the field of existence and influence of which remains ever unmanifest except as an indefinable "presence" when in its active state, accessed through meditation, as shown in figure 10.1. It is symbolic of Amen, or the state of Amenti. The "Circles of Ament," primordially created by Ra, are themselves the unseen outer auras, or spheres of psycho-spiritual influence, of the god-souls behind all manifest existence.[8] As such, they are "no-thing" and represent a relative infinity, a "stateless state" of potential consciousness. The same concept is to be found in the Brahmanic philosophy in the form of the *akasa*, or ring of Divine Fire, the Ka-Eos from which all cosmic Order emerges by virtue of Divine Law. This is also the essence of the idea of creation ex nihilo, a concept that has puzzled Christian theologians for two thousand years.

The One is symbolized by the metaphysical Point, the first emanation of life itself, which, as "the Eye of Ra," is opened by the efforts of Tefnut and Shu. The allegory relates, however, to the awakening or revivification of the body of the universe by the Universal Oversoul. The consequent duality represented by Tefnut and Shu is related to what we might then call the "Universal Subconscious" and the merely objective Universal Consciousness.

The Two is otherwise found in the various dualities of, for example, Spirit and Matter, the Duat (Heaven and the Underworld), Osiris and Isis, daemons and souls—all representing the separative sense that itself paradoxically gives rise to the sense of mutual association that we call "relationship," or "belonging."

The Three (the triad, or trinity) was perhaps the most significant and widely used of all the numbers employed by the Egyptians in their culture—except for the Seven. In the symbol of the "Eye of Ra" (where "cosmic" consciousness is concerned), Nut is the upper eyelid, Geb/Seb is the lower one, and Shu is the awakening intelligence that causes them to part so that the "Divine Eye" becomes objectively revealed. In a yet wider sense, the triplicity (within the unity) represents the universal principles of Life, Consciousness, and Creative Instinct, which act as the fundamental Cause behind all manifest existence. It follows that, as all gods were essentially souls, the coordination of the duality of "spirit" and "matter" would inevitably, ad infinitum, give rise to the creation of lesser souls. Hence the idea that evolution as a process was essentially concentric and that it progressed in ninefold cycles.

The Quadrature as Form Leading to Sensory Function

The Four was representative of the four aspects of the animal form, or body, within the ensouling sphere of consciousness (see fig. 10.2). Thus Osiris, Isis, Nephthys, and Set

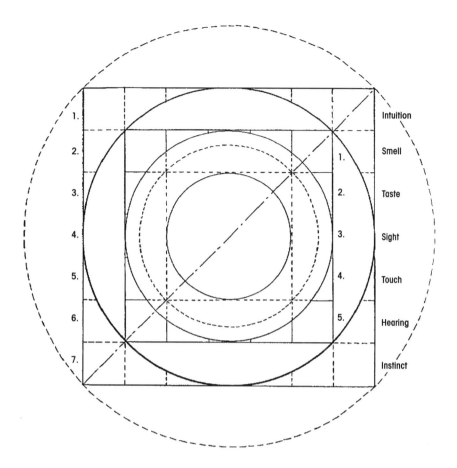

Labels on diagram (left side, top to bottom): 1. 2. 3. 4. 5. 6. 7.

Labels on diagram (inner right, top to bottom): 1. 2. 3. 4. 5.

Labels on diagram (outer right, top to bottom): Intuition, Smell, Taste, Sight, Touch, Hearing, Instinct

FIGURE 10.2. THE ESOTERIC RELATIONSHIP BETWEEN THE CIRCLE AND THE SQUARE

The Ancients regarded this relationship as expressing that between god-consciousness and form. The Circle represents the Consciousness of the enfolding Soul nature (typified by the Greek god Ouranos), which, by limiting the portion of the universe (Gaea) in which it seeks to manifest itself, induces the "trapped" Matter to generate out of itself specific points of active potential and relationship. It is these interrelationships that then produce the world of Form—the objective universe—symbolized by the Square. The diagram otherwise shows that there is always a 7:10:22 relationship between the side of a square, its diagonal, and the circumference of the lesser circle bounded by that square. Hence, these numbers in particular assumed immense significance in the eyes of the Ancients, from whom Pythagoras understandably derived his certainty that "God geometrizes" and that "the universe is founded upon Number." From the diagram it also becomes clear why all the ancient philosopher-metaphysicians regarded the universe (in both microcosm and macrocosm) as being essentially sevenfold in its combined noumenal and phenomenal structure.

The (also Pythagorean) association with the "Music of the Spheres" is clear from this as well, for, as John Anthony West so succinctly puts it: "Consider a string of a given length as Unity. Set it vibrating; it produces a sound. Stop the string at its midpoint and set it vibrating. It produces a sound one octave higher. Division in two results in an analogue of the original unity. . . . Between the original note and its octave there are seven intervals, seven unequal stages which, despite their inequality, the ear interprets as 'harmonious.'" *Serpent in the Sky*, p. 49.

together symbolized the coherently organized, objective body of Ra (and the senses of hearing, touch, sight, and taste) but without an accompanying higher Intelligence. From the viewpoint of the overshadowing soul, therefore, this state was one of death—hence the Underworld. Interestingly, the structure of a pyramid—four equal triangles on a common, square base—represents these four fields of awareness arising out of the fundamental body-form. The same idea is symbolized in the cross, although the ankh or "ansated cross" of the Egyptians (and as modified by the Celts) gives a better symbolism of the astral soul's presence in the loop of the uppermost arm. The ordinary cross represents material existence, pure and simple.

The Five represents the same objective body-form of the god plus the fifth sense (smell), which invoked the presence of the overshadowing soul nature and its higher Intelligence. Thus it is that we see Horus the Child being added to the company of Osiris, Isis, Nephthys, and Set. These five therefore symbolize the reflection of the god Ra within the field of Matter and that is why five (as half of ten) has apparently always been regarded by Hermeticists and esotericists generally as the number of common humanity. One might speculate further on this in relation to man's five limbs (including the head), but we do not have the time to do so here. Interestingly, stars were themselves always depicted in Egypt as five-pointed and were called *dwa*. Bearing in mind that the Sanskrit pronounciation of *deva* is *dewa* and that the five Universal Elements and five Universal Senses are supposed to be *deva* faculties, this further correspondence between the Egyptian and Hindu Vedic traditions is striking.

The Six represents the existence of two souls (hence two concentrically organized circles) as yet uncoordinated within the overall consciousness of the god. It thus symbolized man (as neophyte) as aspirant to the spiritual way of life. The symbolism is evident in the way in which the pharaoh is shown in Egyptian art with his arms folded across his front in the shape of a Saint Andrew's cross, holding the symbols of his power and knowledge—akin to the scepter and orb of the British monarchy.

The Seven represented the same two souls (spiritual and astral) now coordinated by an intervening *ka*. This number therefore signifies initiation as a result of dominion over the principle of Matter and the sensory faculties of the objective body. It is otherwise signified by the so-called Star of David, which implicitly involves the containment of the astral soul by the spiritual soul, as shown in figure 10.3. In addition, the Seven was regarded as playing such a fundamental role in bringing about the very fact of ordered existence that it was regarded as having divine significance. Hence it was that the seven sacred vowels of the kabbalistic alphabet enabled speech and language to be derived through their dissemination among the twenty-two consonants. It also had another vitally important mystical significance, expressed by the Pythagoreans in their philosophy, as we shall describe in a moment.

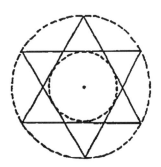

FIGURE 10.3. THE SIX AND THE SEVEN

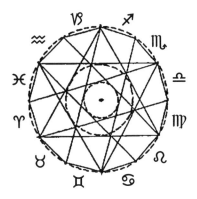

FIGURE 10.4. THE TRIPLE SOUL

Pictured here are the esoteric connections and correspondences between the zodiacal Oversoul and the lesser Oversouls contained by it through the influence of the triadic faculties.

Transcending the Octave of Phenomenal Existence

While the Eight represented the consciousness of the individual being fully absorbed into the spiritual or divine soul and thus (in a Pythagorean sense) being able to sound the note of its octave, in and beyond this lay a wholly noumenal state of functional existence. Within it, the Nine and the Ten followed on in the same sort of progression so that by expanding the consciousness of the spiritual soul, the Intelligence would ultimately arrive at union with the divine soul. This was done by resolving the six faculties symbolized in the "Star of David" into a series of originating dualities and triplicities, as shown in figure 10.4. Hence the consciousness of the divine soul was associated with the "cosmic consciousness" latent in the zodiac. This relativity is the very essence of the Pythagorean "divine dodecahedron."

This whole issue of resolving the "spark" back into the primal unity of Amen-Ra is highly important, and in order to understand it fully, we must remember that the decennial cycle just described had to be completed thirty-six times before the primordial cycle was concluded. If we then recall that 360 degrees is itself composed of four triune quadrants, each representing a cosmic god, it then surely becomes apparent why the temple at Abu Simbel has four massive representations of the god Ra outside its entrance. This divine quartet then clearly represents the Egyptian counterpart of the four archangelic "governors" at the "corners" of our local universe. Now one might say, "All very well in relation to the occult philosophy of the Egyptians, but how does this translate on to the ground other than in relation to the Pyramids at Giza?" Well, the answer—as Pythagoras found out—lies in the "music of the celestial spheres" and the way in which this was geometrically represented in the siting and architecture of the temples all along the Nile—which we shall now deal with, albeit again in necessarily general terms.[9]

Psycho-sensitive Architecture

First of all, we might suggest that the architecture of the temple was specifically designed to produce its own set of psychomagnetic tensions—the Egyptian equivalent of feng shui—to work upon the subconscious nature of the individual. It was, however, subconscious purely in a nominal sense, for this architectural feng shui was (and is) believed to be directly perceived by the astral soul, which responded to the evocative nature of the whole temple geometry. The human consciousness then reacted to this purely in the secondary sense of being aware of the "atmosphere" thus generated. Exactly the same principle applies in our own day and age, for the ability of human beings to respond to such atmospheres (particularly in places of worship) is timeless.

A structural engineer, by studying the size, composition, weight, and disposition of structural elements in a building, can tell you where the major stresses and tensions lie. He will also tell you that the essence of a structure is to convey load safely and evenly down to the ground that supports it. Consequently, as far as he is concerned, the stress remains (or, at least, should remain) comfortably within the structure. At the same time, the engineer acknowledges the fact that certain tensions generate vector (directional) force which, in turn, carries a restrained angular momentum, or "kinetic" energy. This itself tends to generate rotational (or spiral) torque, which carries degrees of force called "moments."

What the average structural engineer will not so happily accept, however, is that such "moments of force" seem to have an actual phenomenal existence in the air (the "ether," rather) around the structure and that this can be clearly felt (sometimes even seen if powerful enough) by those people who are sufficiently sensitive in that manner. But such appears to be the case and the fact that most ordinary people are, to some extent, capable of responding to such "atmospheres" confirms that these phenomena are no mere illusion.

The Energetic Distribution of Load and Force

The main weight of a temple's upper structure is carried on its load-bearing columns and outer walls, and, consequently, one would expect the downward force to be greater in these areas. But, in fact, the walls support what are called "dead loads" for, if properly arranged, very little—if any—lateral torque arises in them. The major tensions occur under massively large structural spans—which itself appears to point to one of the "secrets" of the Pyramids—as, in those areas, varying degrees of force of a particular psychic quality can apparently be generated and/or tapped, given certain other psychic conditions—as they seemingly also can in a church or cathedral.

What has otherwise been noted is that the very shape of the structural members themselves appears highly significant in generating a particular quality of psychic force. A spiral shape—as expressed in a tubular column—actually distributes a variable load far more effectively than a square one would, and, indeed, it possesses an elasticity in it even when made of stone. Consequently, rounded pillars—such as the massive ones found in the temple of Hathor at Dendera (see fig. 10.5)—could possibly be regarded as having generated a constantly fluctuating vertical force. The shape of the fluting along the sides of these columns (also geometrically varied) seems to have a definite significance as well.

Now, the ancient builders of the Nile temples did not need to build them quite so massively purely for support, even though they had to be of a sufficient size and grandeur to reflect the nature and force of their particular gods. However, it is worthwhile considering certain of these structural elements because of their dual function—the one aspect being purely structural and the other occult.

The main lateral and vertical supports were both of stone. The lateral ones—the lintels—were rectangular in profile in contrast to the rounded vertical columns. Yet this appears not to have been purely a question of aesthetics or mere structural necessity. In order to understand the underlying issue, we have to come back to the idea that the physical shape somehow conditions the nature of an energy's phenomenal expression.[10] A tubular shape (like a column) connected at either end can apparently—under certain circumstances—be induced to resonate within a given range of frequencies, whereas the rectilinear lintels resting upon them will allow merely a linear transfer of energy and a single sound frequency.

Given this suggestion, a massed congregation chanting or singing in unison might be expected to cause the columns to resonate at a certain frequency. If so, this tensile energy would then transfer itself (as an alternating current) to the continuous line of stone lintels above. These would then act in unison as the psychic equivalent of a giant electrical accumulator, or battery. Correspondingly, does it not make entirely logical sense that the immense potency of a concentrated divine Presence would require an equivalently massive

FIGURE 10.5. FAÇADE AND INTERIOR OF THE TEMPLE AT DENDERA
(from Denon's *Description de l'Egypte*)

field of inertial resistance through which to resonate in response? Thus the "temple battery" would become a "spiritual transformer" as well.

The Use of Sound to Create a Specific Atmosphere

It has been found during scientific experiments (by engineers working on their own outside "the Establishment") during the last few decades that the pitch and particularly the frequency with which sound is projected into a contained environment can result (quite inexplicably as far as scientists are concerned) in the generation of an even greater amount of energy emerging from it, apparently ex nihilo. This appears on the face of it to deny that law of thermodynamics which says that it is impossible to get more out of something (in the way of energy) than is originally put into it. Thermodynamicists, however—although accepting the existence of what is called "zero-point energy" latent in the atmosphere—do not (yet) admit that this de facto confirms the existence of a universal "ether" from which all energy and force are drawn in the first place.

The point is made here because the spontaneous generation of energy in this way is understood by New Age researchers into technical aspects of occult science to generate a plasmic "atmosphere," or "ozone" (i.e., an "ether" in all but name), that exhibits all the qualities of a potential electromagnetic force field. Fairly logically, the generation of energy in this way would also attract the earth's own geomagnetism upward, so that the latter's own force was added to it. The columns—of varying number and diameter (and undoubtedly of differing stone as well)—would (according to this theory) produce a varying range of resonances, thereby resulting in ethereal chords being sounded in a definite rhythm. The effect upon human emotions and senses created by response to particular forms of music under such circumstances is, of course, already well known even though the underlying mechanism may not be properly understood by researchers using merely orthodox scientific methods.

Angelic Involvement in the Ritual

Now, this in itself sounds interesting enough, but the intention in ancient Egyptian times would certainly not have been merely to generate a "psychic buzz" in which the congregation could join. The whole purpose was undoubtedly invocative—intended to attract the attention of the superior angelic hierarchy of *devas* believed by them to be associated with the particular god (or gods) of the temple, so that these entities would then themselves descend into the psychic force field thus generated and join in the ceremonial. The whole point of the operation would then have involved inducing these powerful entities to condition the psychomagnetic field, or "atmosphere," with the spiritual quality of their own intelligence in such a manner that it would then result in a general precipitation of "Grace." The whole congregation would thus benefit from this by association, and their increased spirituality would inevitably spill out across Egypt as a whole.

The carrying out of such ceremonials on a regular basis would inevitably have had a cumulative effect upon the "magnetism" of the temple structure as a whole, and so it too would gradually have built up its own permanent and highly characteristic psycho-spiritual "atmosphere." The very fact that the whole of Egypt was so carefully coordinated to coincide with the natural revolutions of the cosmos, as described in the last chapter, must thus have rendered the whole country immensely invocative in an entirely spiritual sense—as the Egyptians themselves believed it to be.

The "Pregnant" Emptiness of Egyptian Temples

Walking around the temples of Egypt sometimes gives one a feeling akin to that associated with the *Marie Celeste* mystery—as though the whole ship is miraculously sailing on although all the crew and passengers have somehow, inexplicably disappeared. It is almost as though at some distant point in ancient time the whole organization of Egypt and its temples had been set up specifically with that departure in mind—presumably to coincide (at least eventually) with a very powerful and critical moment in one of the great sidereal cycles.

Several authors have speculated that the ancient Egyptians and the ancestors of the Central American peoples left their gigantic architecture either as a memorial to their own existence for later generations (prior to their civilization's own natural decay) or as a warning of some sort. Those keen on the latter theory have further speculated that such a warning can only have been related to an anticipated (and perhaps cyclically returning) era of major cataclysms, resulting in wholesale destruction in Nature and the wiping out of human races. The more one considers the ethos of the ancient Egyptians, however, with their total focus on a practical mystico-religious culture and, through it, the achievement of spiritual and even divine evolution, the less likely seems mere anxiety over cataclysms—even serious ones. There is no doubt that the temples were intended for practical use. The only query is, When were they actually used? As we have already otherwise suggested, Egyptian zodiacs suggest an absolute minimum of some 78,000 years, and the other information mentioned in previous chapters suggests a period far anterior to even that.

The Internal Layout of the Temple

Where the internal layout of the temples is concerned, we find sometimes widespread variation. However, all the most important temples appear to be designed around a quite definitely sevenfold plan—as is the case with those plans shown in figure 10.6. As we can see, no pillars are to be found beyond the third section of the temple. The architectural distinction between the third and fourth areas moving inward thus clearly seems to represent an esoteric or mystical divide, and the innermost areas of the temple could only be approached through it, each part thus acting as a sort of "filter." It was, however, the sixth area—the "sanctum sanctorum"—that alone contained the focal point of the divine Presence and the association with a particular star god. Into this area, only the pharaoh or hierophant (an adept of at least the fifth degree) would have been permitted access. Anybody else doing so would probably have been instantly put to death for such violation of the innermost sanctuary, specifically designed as the point at which Divinity and semidivinity were brought into holy communion. Notwithstanding this, other initiates would have been allowed access, progressively, into those inner areas of the temple that were associated with their particular degree. Thus the courtyard, plus the first and second areas, would have been accessible to "spiritual probationers" and first- and second-degree initiates, respectively. The next area—without pillars—would have been accessible only to initiates of at least the third degree; and so on.

From these coordinated architectural and mystical arrangements we can perhaps see the extent to which modern religious ritual has changed. For example, the "holy of holies" (i.e., the altar) in the non-Orthodox Christian Church is in plain view of all the congregation, and anyone may approach reasonably close to it if they have been "confirmed" into the Church—a rite that recalls but the first degree in the ancient tradition.[11] The usual Islamic temple does not go even this far in having a central architectural focus of direct association

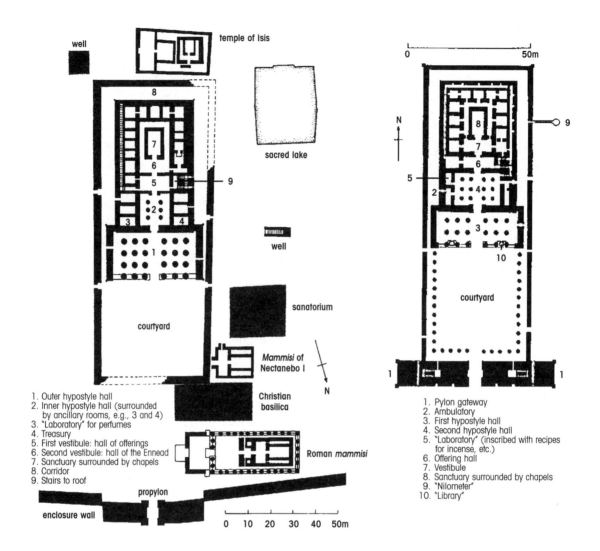

FIGURE 10.6. FLOOR PLANS OF THE TEMPLES OF DENDERA (LEFT) AND EDFU (RIGHT)

with God, because of the orientation toward Mecca. However, as a general rule, the mystic aspects of initiatory ceremonial are, these days, paid little more than "lip service" throughout most of the world's religions anyway. Consequently, the once universal and very real sense of a central "Mystery tradition" is very rarely these days to be found within the portals of orthodox religion—a fact that seems to be subconsciously realized by the majority of the lay public, who nevertheless seem to return in great numbers for major ceremonial occasions. As a result of this lack of faith in the very real presence of Divinity, the quality of priesthood throughout the field of orthodox religion has also deteriorated dramatically. The belief of the priesthood in actually being able to invoke the angelic agents of the divine Presence is thus rarely found and even more rarely practiced.

With regard to the association of a particular temple with any particular initiate, we might perhaps surmise that at least two factors were involved. First, there could well have been merely local (family) or even personal astrological connections. Second, there would

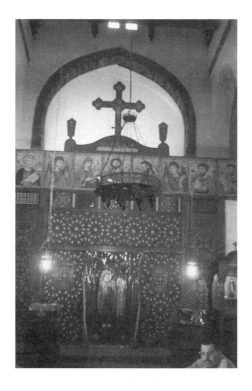

FIGURE 10.7. THE "HOLY OF HOLIES" OF THE MODERN ERA IN EGYPT AND EUROPE

Above, interior of an Egyptian Coptic church showing the "Holy of Holies" behind a permanently fixed high screen, beyond which only the priests may pass and behind which, in strict privacy, the sacred icons are kept. *Right,* a typical early Victorian high church, the general interior style of which has remained unchanged since pre-Norman times, in the early Middle Ages. The altar plus all the iconography are in plain view of the congregation.

be a logic in any particular initiate within the priesthood itself perhaps having to spend time at each of the main temples as part of his progressive training, thereby coming under the sequential influence of a series of star gods. Having thus been "apprenticed" to the temple god in question, he may well have had to be formally released later on from that particular relationship before he could actually progress through the next stage of initiation. Thus due ritual propitiation would have had to be made and the initiate may even have been ceremonially "cast out into the wilderness"—but this is mere speculation.

Coherence of a Civilization Must Be Based Upon a Central Ideal

The Egyptians realized that all real power—whether in the outer or the inner world—derives from the general acceptance of a properly structured hierarchy, plus regular rites of passage and ceremonial to confirm it—hence the critical importance of their temples. They also recognized that hierarchy itself is derived from a sense of unified purpose associated with a central divine ideal and that without this, the whole structure and fabric of a civilization would, without question, decay and finally collapse. As religion—the belief in a greater, spiritual existence common to all—is really the one and only perennial means of expressing such an innately subjective perception, the greatest civilization would automatically derive its power from the most universal religion. And what could be more universal than the quite literally universe-wide religion of the Egyptians?

These few comments merely skim the surface of information concerning the Egyptian temples and their rites of worship. However, as we said at the outset, our intention here has

Sacred Geometry and the "Living" Architecture of Egypt

▲

been merely to provide a soupçon of the aims and atmospheres once associated with them. The rest of the chapter will be devoted to the sacred geometry and related esotericism of the pyramids at Giza and of the Great Pyramid in particular. Before we proceed with that issue, however, we should again reiterate that the concept adopted by Egyptologists of pyramids having been designed for use as pharaonic tombs is wholly unsupported by the available evidence. We shall therefore regard them in the manner for which we believe they were truly intended—jointly as temples of initiation and cosmic invocation. Although Bauval's theory about the three pyramids at Giza being a representation of Orion's belt has, we hope, been given considerable further support by what has been suggested in this book, much else needs to be said about the Giza complex as a whole.[12] While our chapter 11 will actually deal with that as far as the question of rites of initiation is concerned, we shall now take a preliminary look at the Great Pyramid itself to see if anything more can be deduced (over and above what has already been suggested) as to any esoteric meaning that it may perhaps conceal. In particular, it would be interesting to know why the three inner chambers are located where they are and thereby deduce whether any further chambers remain to be discovered—as Edgar Cayce seemed to believe was so.[13]

The Sacred Masonic Geometry of the Great Pyramid

Figure 10.8 provides us with an indication of why the Great Pyramid alone has a flat top at the particular height shown. The sides of the pyramid, when connected to the equilateral triangle formed by its base as a chord within a circle, describe a gigantic set of compasses. It does not take a genius to understand its metaphorical significance as representing the "Great Architect of the Universe" of the Masonic movement. However, it also symbolizes the forward- and downward-looking "all-seeing Eye of Ra," because all things were deemed to have come into existence through the creative visualization of Amen-Ra on behalf of the One Unknowable God. The flat, apexless platform at the top of the pyramid then represents the point at which the "upper eyelid" crosses the axis of triangulation.

A great many other esoteric symbolisms can be derived by exploring the associated geometrical relationships between the pyramid and the equilateral triangle, as shown in figure 10.8. Not least of these are the sacred Tetraktys of Pythagoras (clearly borrowed from Egypt) and the Kabbalah, which can also be shown quite simply to be of Egyptian origin. The location of the pyramid's entrance, chambers, and passageways can themselves be shown as following points or lines of horizontal, diagonal, vertical, or radial coincidence and association, all related to hierarchically organized spheres of influence—as we shall see further in chapter 12.[14]

As we have already suggested elsewhere, the three Giza pyramids appear to represent the three aspects of Ra (as Osiris) in cosmic, solar, and terrestrial substance, and also as divine mankind, spiritual mankind and also hu-mankind. The Great Pyramid clearly represents the first of these—which inevitably brings the product of the evolutionary process back to Ra (the Logos), its point of origin. In fact, the exoteric pyramid "footprint" itself symbolizes the Masonic square always seen in conjunction with the compasses. The square (as we have already seen) represents the form, or material side, of existence—hence the quartet of Osiris, Isis, Nephthys, and Set—while the compasses represent that which gives expression to divine Purpose by describing the "sphere of limitation" (i.e., the soul) within which that great Purpose is to manifest itself. Here again, then, we see the influence of the number seven. When we come to the various chambers of initiation, however, we find ourselves having to take into account the four "levels" derived from the interlaced triangles around which the Great Pyramid is designed, the so-called Star of David thus formed clearly being yet another device acquired by the Semitic Hebrews from the Egyptian Mysteries during the period of their historical "captivity" in Egypt.

Now, the question of whether there are any other chambers appears to be answered for us by the design of the so-called King's Chamber. This consists not only of that large chamber specifically—in which the adept-soul was raised as a fully fledged "Master Mason" from within the sarcophagus (symbolizing the coffin in which Osiris was imprisoned by Set)—but also of five other, much smaller ones within the structure immediately above it (see

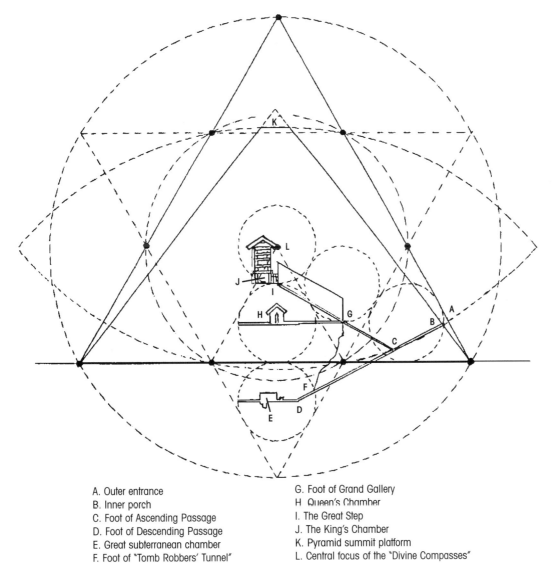

A. Outer entrance
B. Inner porch
C. Foot of Ascending Passage
D. Foot of Descending Passage
E. Great subterranean chamber
F. Foot of "Tomb Robbers' Tunnel"
G. Foot of Grand Gallery
H. Queen's Chamber
I. The Great Step
J. The King's Chamber
K. Pyramid summit platform
L. Central focus of the "Divine Compasses"

FIGURE 10.8. THE MASONIC PYRAMID (AS THE "EYE OF RA")

again fig. 10.8). Of these, only the last—directly under the inverted V-shape of the roof—is actually located above the center point of the equilateral triangle forming the outer profile of the "compasses." These latter chambers are dealt with at further length in chapter 12.

The initiation of the "Raising of the Master" is regarded in some occult and esoteric circles as the third in a series of seven, and by others as the fifth in a series of nine.[15] We have adopted the latter schema for reasons to be more fully explained in the next chapter, but fundamentally associated with the ninefold nature of the Egyptian ennead. The tenth and highest chamber then represents completion of the whole evolutionary process and consequent reassimilation back into the subjective nature of Ra. On that basis, it seems a little unlikely that there are any further initiatory chambers in the Great Pyramid.

While certain further suggestions are made in the next chapter as regards the third to fifth initiations, already known symbolically in the Masonic rites (which clearly had their genesis in ancient Egypt), we do not propose to add anything more concerning the sacred geometry of this pyramid, other than in relation to the two southern "vent shafts" leading upward from the King's and Queen's Chambers. These—so sacrilegiously adapted recently for use with air-conditioning equipment—have, as already noted, been clearly associated with Orion's belt and Sirius in Bauval and Gilbert's book *The Orion Mystery*. All we would add here for the moment lies in relation to a query concerning the reason for the small fetus-shaped recess in the wall at the foot of the Orion shaft.[16] Bearing in mind that the "Raised Master" is, in one sense at least, synonymous with Horus Behutet—the "child" of Ra-Herakhte—the answer appears, after all, perhaps fairly self-evident.

ELEVEN

THE ESOTERIC SIGNIFICANCE OF THE SPHINX AND PYRAMIDS

The representation of the Divine Essence as a supernal luminescence is universal. The passage in the proem of the Johannean Gospel has been the philosophic dogma of all periods: "In the Logos, or Divine Reason, was Life and the Life was the light of mankind." The Chaldean Oracle also says: "When thou shalt see a very holy fire without definable shape, leaping as it shines, hearken to the Voice of the Fire." Moses and Zoroaster both professed to hear the words of the Deity spoken out of Fire. . . . Pure fire unmingled with material particles is not visible to the human faculty of sight. This explains satisfactorily the apparent contradiction in which the Supreme Being is depicted as Light and likewise as enveloped in clouds and thick darkness.

—IAMBLICHUS, *THEURGIA*

The idea fostered by orthodox archaeology for so many decades that the Pyramids at Giza were giant pharaonic mausoleums has by now been ridiculed on such a wide front that it surely cannot expect to keep its head above the ramparts of academia with a straight face much longer.[1] That these great buildings have no internal hieroglyphic inscriptions like the mass of Egyptian temples and mausoleums on its own sets them apart. That there never was any evidence whatsoever of funerary articles within them tends to speak for itself as well. But the clearest testament to their raison d'être undoubtedly lies in the astronomical associations confirmed by the pioneering work of Robert Bauval—latterly in conjunction with Graham Hancock as far as coordinating research on the Sphinx is concerned. From this research has come increasingly conclusive evidence as to the Great Pyramid and Sphinx having been designed and constructed specifically in relation, respectively, to the circumpolar stars and to the precession of the equinoxes.

Out of the initial research came proof that the "vent shafts" in the Great Pyramid cyclically pointed directly at Orion, Sirius, and the circumpolar stars Kochab and Alpha Draconis, and that the Giza pyramids themselves were terrestrial representations of Orion's belt. Out of the latter research has arisen the clear indication that the ancient Egyptians saw in them a definite mystical association with the ecliptic and the ring of circumpolar stars. From this we may ourselves infer that the whole Giza complex—Pyramids

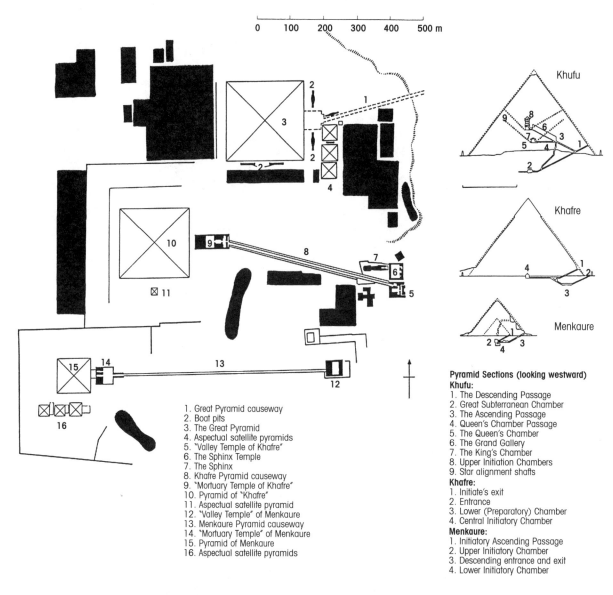

FIGURE 11.1. SITE PLAN OF GIZA, INCLUDING SECTIONAL DRAWINGS OF THE PYRAMIDS

1. Great Pyramid causeway
2. Boat pits
3. The Great Pyramid
4. Aspectual satellite pyramids
5. "Valley Temple of Khafre"
6. The Sphinx Temple
7. The Sphinx
8. Khafre Pyramid causeway
9. "Mortuary Temple of Khafre"
10. Pyramid of "Khafre"
11. Aspectual satellite pyramid
12. "Valley Temple" of Menkaure
13. Menkaure Pyramid causeway
14. "Mortuary Temple" of Menkaure
15. Pyramid of Menkaure
16. Aspectual satellite pyramids

Pyramid Sections (looking westward)
Khufu:
1. The Descending Passage
2. Great Subterranean Chamber
3. The Ascending Passage
4. Queen's Chamber Passage
5. The Queen's Chamber
6. The Grand Gallery
7. The King's Chamber
8. Upper Initiation Chambers
9. Star alignment shafts
Khafre:
1. Initiate's exit
2. Entrance
3. Lower (Preparatory) Chamber
4. Central Initiatory Chamber
Menkaure:
1. Initiatory Ascending Passage
2. Upper Initiatory Chamber
3. Descending entrance and exit
4. Lower Initiatory Chamber

and Sphinx—was designed (and probably built) at one and the same time in accordance with a single, overall master plan. That plan—so it would appear from the oft and clearly quoted intent of the Egyptians themselves—was to make Egypt into an infinitesimally accurate representation of the sidereal heavens. However, that intent was not limited to the monumental symbolism of Giza alone, as we have seen in preceding chapters. Nor was it intended as a dead-letter representation (for mere worship), for the Pyramid Texts make it absolutely clear that the very real ambition of the Egyptians involved their souls returning to their heavenly home in the circumpolar stars.[2] Consequently, astroterrestrial synchronicity was absolutely essential to coincide with cycles of actual celestial opportunity.

Now, bearing in mind that their souls were regarded as having become (through spiritual immaturity and consequent ignorance) "captive in Egypt"—that is, within our world system—such a return necessarily had to be preceded by a long round of experience, followed by a sustained effort at respiritualization and the consequent gaining of a self-consciously divine maturity. The confirmation of success in that same (progressive) effort could take place, however, only via the sequence of psycho-spiritual education and subsequent testing (i.e., initiation) provided by the Mystery School. Consequently, it is highly probable that the whole life experience of those among the ancient Egyptian people selected (in childhood) for "fast-track" spiritual streaming was treated as being dedicated to the fulfillment of that ambition; and, as we shall see in this chapter and chapter 12, the associated sequence of tests clearly took place at Giza. That is because the architectural design of its monuments (both internally and externally) had been specifically coordinated to achieve the best possible results through accurate psycho-spiritual correlation of the individual's evolutionary status with the astronomical alignments of the time.

As we can see from figure 11.1, of the three Giza pyramids, only that of "Khufu" possessed "vent shafts." Hence, we suggest, the Great Pyramid alone was capable of providing the symbolic association with the circumpolar stars, plus the psycho-spiritual connections with Orion and Sirius. This leads to the further suggestion that the rites and initiations carried out in the other two pyramids had to be associated with mere preparation before any thought of a "return" became feasible. That, in turn, seems to be confirmed by the orientation of the Sphinx toward the ecliptic and its particular association with the second ("Khepren") pyramid; for the ecliptic—being at an angle to the celestial equator (the plane of the heaven world)—represented spiritual deviation and a consequently involuntary but incessant cycle of reincarnation for the soul until the path "homeward" could be discovered.

Initiation and the Mystery Schools

So much has been made of the issue of initiation in the Mysteries that people tend to forget about the very necessary and very extended prior training, the latter in itself being no guarantee of success for the individual. While we have perhaps no clear model to go on as far as Egypt is concerned, it would not be altogether unrealistic to consider parallels in the Indian, Tibetan, and Japanese systems. It appears fairly certain from scholarly research that these various "schools" have been in existence for several thousand years and follow pretty well the same methods today as they did many millennia ago. All seem to follow the same basic principle that any secret or sacred teaching would be given only to those who had proved their prior fitness (in conduct and psychological capacity) to receive it. As there is clear evidence of Chinese, Tibetan, and Sanskrit words being used by the Egyptians, it seems probable that the common approach to spiritual teaching and testing throughout the whole area derived from a single source.[3] That, in turn, suggests not only a common spiritual culture, but also the probability of widely common ties of civilization. However, to return to the subject of Egypt in particular, we shall now take a closer look at what we suggest was the actual sequence of initiations in the Giza complex and how the symbolism of the architecture appears to confirm it. We begin with the generality of there being three pyramids. Why three, apart from the fact that the belt of Orion has three stars in it? And how is Sirius involved?

Judging by the triple divinities found in so many religions around the world, the common significance of such a triad is that it always represents a dark (male) creator god, a dark (female) mother goddess, and a third (often hermaphrodite) child-god who combines in himself the essential nature of the other two and otherwise contains the whole of phenomenal Creation within himself. It is perhaps more readily understood if we substitute the expression *soul-principle* for *god*. The three stars of Orion then—as the divine soul, spiritual soul, and astroterrestrial soul—represent the upward evolutionary progression of consciousness that takes place from the mother principle (universal Nature) to the Son principle (the psycho-spiritual world) to the Father (representing pure divinity).

Second, the fact that the triple Orion is clearly associated with the celestial equator is self-evident from the planisphere. But the direct association of Isis with Sirius just because the rising of the latter is a useful pointer to the cycle of the Sothic Year (as it ties in with the Annus Magnus) and the rising of the Nile seems far-fetched, particularly as the latter is not entirely regular anyway. It would have been easier in many ways for the Egyptians to have attributed such issues to a male god, especially as the fecundity of the Nile was associated with Serapis[4] (Asr-Hapi), the generative aspect of Ra. The mother goddess, however, fulfills a much more specific role in the Egyptian mythology, and we have already shown this as being representative (in the case of Nephthys and Net) of the *ka*—the "light-web" of either the human "etheric double" or the shimmering stellar structure of the Galaxy. Sirius, however, cannot possibly be the "trigger" for the whole plane of our galaxy to become "pregnant" with returning gods, and so we can only assume that its association with our particular solar system is much more specific.[5]

Historical Celestial Orientations

Third, we have also seen that, just as the Celestial Thigh of the "Bull of Ra" (in the form of Ursa Major) "cuts off the head" of Draco at Giza, so the *apuat* of Isis further divides (or merges with) its Nilotic body at Diospolis Parva—associated with the star Kochab in Ursa Minor. And as Bauval and Gilbert point out in *The Orion Mystery*, the northern "ventilation shaft" of the Queen's Chamber in the Great Pyramid pointed directly at Kochab in about 2450 B.C. (and cyclically every 25,920 years before then as well).[6] They also confirmed that the northern "ventilation shaft" of the King's Chamber pointed at that same time to Alpha Draconis (Thuban), while the southern "ventilation shafts" of the two chambers pointed to Sirius and Orion, respectively[7] (see also fig. 9.3).

Fourth, it would appear that, coincident with all these other astronomical convergences, the zodiacal sign of Leo was to be found on the eastern horizon, looking across the Nile (here symbolizing the Milky Way)—seen from the location of the Sphinx.

"All very well," you might say, "but where does it all lead?" Well, the answer is complex but it is again inextricably linked to the precession of the equinoxes and its objective path—the ecliptic. That in itself should tell us that the "Path" of the higher initiations is to be entered at a certain point once the "river" of Life and Death has been crossed, the individual having made the irrevocable commitment to follow the Way of spiritual individualization. Bearing in mind that the deviant path of the ecliptic represents the "cycle of necessity" (of automatic reincarnation for mankind in general), this might make for more sense. The fact that the ancient Egyptian population as a whole (so it seems) regarded themselves as "sons of God"—hence the "Chosen People"—would imply that they felt that they had some sort of responsible destiny or divine role to fulfill, perhaps at some time in the far distant future.[8] One might deduce from this that the evolutionary "spiritual Path" involved a progression in that very direction (notwithstanding that progress by our own humanity seems pitifully slow). If this is accurate, however, then Giza undoubtedly represented a "forcing house" for spiritual development through certain crises of awareness engendered by the initiation process devised by the ancient Egyptian priesthood—as we now believe to be the case.

That being so, the rites of the Giza pyramids might be said to represent the (progressive) severance of the individual from the mass of humanity in order to tread the spiritual Path. The final step in that direction was symbolically taken (as we shall see in a moment) by the individual on the cusp of Leo-Virgo, the point of zodiacal "birth," for Virgo represents the Virgin Mother and Leo the infant (or fetal) child. And yet the symbolism was related to the Great Sidereal Year and humanity in general, as well as to the solar year and the individual incarnation. The initiate, therefore—in order to learn at firsthand of his own higher nature—had to be made to see that Man was triple in aspect, consisting of spirit, soul, and body, thereby exactly reflecting the nature of the great god Ra. As a consequence, the initiatory tuition and tests would have been geared accordingly and in specific sequence. But the real spiritual tests were reserved for the Great Pyramid, and we shall take a look at these in a moment. Before we do so, however, we must first of all take a general view of the "astroterrestrial" landscape from Giza, because there appear to be a number of correlations with the myths we have discussed in previous chapters.

Representative Orientations Relative to Giza

If we look at the general architectural arrangement on the ground (see fig. 11.1), it quickly becomes obvious that if the Giza pyramids are synonymous with Orion's belt, the Sphinx should itself represent something in the heavens. However, there is no star in the appropriate place. Nevertheless, the star map shows us that the position coincides exactly with the path of the celestial equator and that, as we have previously suggested, was symbolized by the ancient Egyptians as the "great metal plate" of the heaven world. Moreover, the eastward orientation of the Sphinx faces directly toward that point in the heavens where the celestial equator and the ecliptic path cross each other—that is, the celestial spring equinox. Consequently, the associated symbolism appears to involve the correlation of the equinox with the corresponding winter solstice. As far as the individual candidate for initiation was concerned, the underlying meaning must surely therefore have involved confirmation of spiritual "rebirth" through being able to look back at the point of "breakthrough." The elevated angle of the causeway to the second pyramid seems to confirm the question of choice—whether to continue yet further on the upward path.

As Bauval and Hancock have pointed out in their latest book, *Keeper of Genesis*, the three causeways from the Giza pyramids pointed eastward to specific points in the annual cycle.[9] That of Menkaure pointed due east and was in perfect alignment with sunrise on the horizon at the spring and summer equinoxes. The "Khufu" causeway, on the other

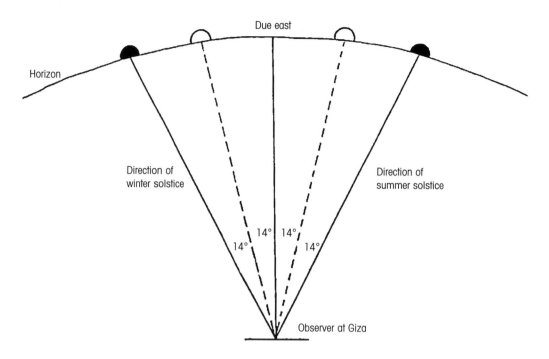

Due east

Horizon

Direction of
winter solstice

Direction of
summer solstice

14° 14°
14° 14°

Observer at Giza

FIGURE 11.2. VARYING POSITIONS OF SUNRISE DURING THE YEAR, LOOKING EASTWARD FROM GIZA

hand (or what is left of it), faced a point exactly halfway between due east and the summer solstice sunrise, while that of "Khepren" faced a point exactly midway between due east and the winter solstice, as shown in figure 11.2.

The associated implication—by virtue of the winter solstice referring to the moment of the Great Return, as we have otherwise seen—is that the Khepren pyramid and the Sphinx are united in the process of spiritual conception, whereas the Great Pyramid is associated with spiritual (re)birth. Again, we see that the furthermost swing, or oscillation, from the central plane—whether the Sun's equator or the celestial equator—enables the incarnate intelligence to come into contact with a wider and greater field of influence. The first contact with this (at the winter solstice) causes a subliminal recognition of what will eventually reach sufficient maturity (at the summer solstice) to become fully conscious, although not yet fully developed through mature experience. So yet again the underlying idea follows exactly the same pattern that we have described from a variety of other perspectives in earlier chapters.

Now, Bauval draws our attention as well to the interesting right-angled triangle formed between the Great Pyramid, Letopolis (due north of it in the Delta), and Heliopolis.[10] If translated onto the star map in figure 1.3, we would find that this same triangle seems to equate with the positions of Orion, Sirius, and the star Procyon, in Canis Minor (the Little Dog). But the interpretation of the intended metaphor surely lies with Procyon, for it (as another "Opener of the Ways") represents the *apuat* of Isis from a slightly different angle to that already described. Meanwhile, Sirius/Letopolis is confirmed as representing Anubis, the "lesser" counterpart temporarily stuck in the Delta, itself representing the objective world, as we have already seen. The fact that Procyon and Sirius face each other across the plane of the Galaxy completes the picture; for Procyon represents the celestial "Chamber of Judgment" (a metaphor for the priestly college at Heliopolis) to which Anubis "leads" the human soul in order to face Thoth, the Hierophant-Recorder. Thereafter, the "neophyte soul"—if found worthy—is taken back across the Nile to Giza to meet Horus the Elder or the "dead" Osiris, face-to-face in the initiatory chambers of the Pyramids of Ra-stau.

There is, however, another ancillary aspect to the same metaphor, because the reincarnating astral soul, upon reaching the Chamber of Judgment at Procyon-Heliopolis, is forced back into the cycle of necessity (which we have already equated with the path of the ecliptic) that it rejoins in the adjacent zodiacal sign of Cancer, the "Gate of Death"— as far as the soul is concerned anyway! It then follows the path of the ecliptic until this again coincides with the celestial equator (see fig. 1.3) on the cusp of Virgo-Leo. If it then chooses this latter "path" (another metaphor signifying the awakening of the higher consciousness during the physical lifetime), it eventually "meets" with the star Altair in Aquila (symbolized by Horus the Younger, or Elder, as the case may be) as it passes through the plane of the Galaxy. Horus then leads the soul back to the "house of initiation" at Giza. Alternatively, soul "death" recurs on the cusp of Pisces-Aquarius, effectively representing the "Judgment Day." The whole process is repeated ad infinitum, the lower aspect (or astral soul) always following the ecliptic path while the higher Self (or *saha*) opts for the path of the celestial equator, synonymous with the "heaven world."

The fact that Procyon provides a double association with Ra-Tem and the *apuat* of Isis is entirely self-consistent with the underlying symbolism, as is also the fact that Heliopolis is the place to which the Bennu phoenix bird always returns in due cycle to lay its periodic "egg"—the "Anu." In the Mystery Schools, "death" and "rebirth" were regarded as immediately consecutive parts of the cycle of experience of the soul, which always involved a transition through the "gates of fire" in order that the process of spiritual purification should be carried through. Only with that ritual preparation having been duly made could the candidate for initiation be brought safely before his own higher Self.[11]

The Aim of the Initiatory Process

Now, in order to understand something of the process and ethos of occult initiation of the time, we have to bear in mind that the aim was to help produce a spiritually self-conscious and self-sufficient individual. In order to achieve that, the individual had to be a well-equipped "all-rounder." The idea of candidates being selected purely for development of their occult powers—as some seem to believe occurred—is absurd and does not coincide with the attitude to such things held by the Ancients (or their modern counterparts among the true gurus and Zen masters of the East). For them, spirituality had to express itself in a universally beneficent Intelligence (not intellect, or power) and thus the initiatory training in its earlier stages would almost inevitably have been akin to a collegiate education. But not all undergoing such an education would have proved to be the right sort of material for the more advanced spiritual Path.

Because of the self-evident existence of a septenary metaphysical system in ancient

Egypt (as already described in earlier chapters), it seems clearly logical (in fact, unavoidable) that the initiatory process had also to be septenary by way of direct correspondence. As the essential idea behind this involved a conscious reascent through the seven planes of matter in the Duat, so seven initiatory expansions of consciousness needed to be achieved, commencing with the physical state and conquest, or transcendence, of the purely physical senses. Once the seven planes had all been transcended individually, the (by now highly advanced) initiate then had to complete the entire octave of experience by finally transcending even the synthesis of their simultaneously coordinated entirety.

The sequence of initiation also seems to have followed the musical principles inherent in the octave itself, insofar as the latter was divided into the dominant third and dominant fifth—as we shall see in relation to the Great Pyramid. The "dominant third" corresponded with the three substates of the Greek "Hades," while the "dominant fifth" involved the capacity to resonate with the higher (i.e., spiritual) Intelligence of the Divine Man. The lower three thus involved "initiations of the threshold," while the higher five involved the true spiritual "Higher Way." At the same time, this musico-mathematical correlation found its further expression in the temples of Upper Egypt themselves.

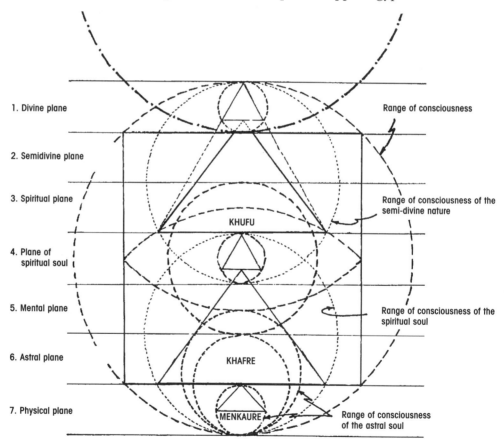

FIGURE 11.3. THE SYMBOLIC ASSOCIATION OF THE PYRAMIDS WITH THE SEVEN PLANES OF SELF-EXISTENCE

The *vesica piscis* is clearly of Egyptian origin and symbolically represents the "Eye of Ra." The five central planes of consciousness represent the five universal senses—hence being bounded by the square, which represents the field of perceptual existence within the seven planes of self-existence.

The overall integration of the temple system throughout Egypt is not properly understood today, and yet, at one stage, judging by its overall structure and distribution, it must have been very centrally administered. We need to think of all of Egypt functioning as one great coordinated whole if we are to understand her historically. We cannot separate her religion from her politics or even her socioeconomic activities. Although far more spiritually and religiously inclined than our present civilization, the Egyptians were essentially trying, like us, to maintain a single, coherent culture. With that in mind, therefore—and with our feet planted firmly on the ground rather than in glamorized flights of New Age fantasy—let us have a general look at the Giza complex itself, prior to considering the sequence of actual initiations that is perhaps represented there.

The Combined Abstract Symbolism of the Giza Pyramids

First of all—remembering that to the Egyptians the sequence of presentation of Divine Order (Ma'at) was of paramount importance—we should perhaps look for an arrangement, or pattern, in the general disposition of the Giza complex. Second, also remembering that to the Egyptians a star was the phenomenal expression of an atom-shaped sidereal body—a "soul"—and that the Divine Man or incarnate Logos (Ptah) was their symbol of perfection and completion, we can perhaps look for an abstract representation of such issues here. But this would be difficult, if not impossible, without a dogleg into the world of metaphysics, which to most people probably conjures up images of boring intellectual polemics between theologians. However, that sort of thing is not our concern here. What actually interests us is that if the three pyramids represent the three "soul" aspects of the Divine Man—the divine soul, the spiritual soul, and the terrestrial or astral soul—everything else related to them must have to do with description either of soul characteristics or of the type of activity expected of the soul. To try to put this into a readily understandable modern context might not appear altogether easy, and yet an effort must be made to see if it can be done. Taking figure 11.3 as our model, therefore, there are a number of aspects that we can fairly quickly equate with the site arrangements at Giza. We shall endeavor, however, to keep our analysis as broad as possible without losing any of the essential significances.

To begin with, the Divine Soul may be said (in one sense, at least) to incorporate the whole complex and, as we can see at a glance, the complex itself is septenary in nature—there being seven minor pyramids attached to the main three. It is also dual, the upper (northern) half being "spirit" to the lower half's "matter," each overlapping half also being represented as a limited field of consciousness. The upper half is dedicated to the Great Pyramid, while the lower half is dedicated to the influence of the "Khepren" pyramid, with which the Sphinx is particularly associated. Both of these spheres of influence, or consciousness, are depicted as being the same size—as indeed are the two pyramids themselves. In the lowest (seventh) substate of the overall Divine Soul, we then find its own (again septenary) microcosm. This, however, is one quarter the size of either the "Khufu" or the "Khepren" fields and—looking at the site plan of Giza—we find that the "Menkaure" pyramid is indeed one quarter the size of the other two. Now, the Great Pyramid and the Menkaure pyramid both have three small accompanying pyramids alongside them (see again fig. 11.1). Interestingly, the Menkaure pyramid also comprises a pyramid within a pyramid for, as we can see from the sectional drawings, the inner core—following exactly the same outline and of exactly half the size of the outer pyramid—is made of red granite. This is a metamorphic rock as opposed to the sedimentary outer casing—in other words, representing the *ka* of the human being encased within the "cloak" of the astral soul. Interestingly, this also appears to be symbolic of the concealed Masonic square, which, as already stated, we know to represent the sensory consciousness of the objective world.

Menkaure Represents the Purely Human Entity

The name Menkaure (the telescoped form of Men-Kau-Ra) indicates a relationship with the problematic "first pharaoh" Menes, who was referred to by Herodotus as Min.[12] The ithyphallic Min is supposed to have founded the Memphite bull cult in which the god Mntw (the lesser form of Menthu-Ra) was also involved. However, as we suggested in an earlier chapter, Min—the main deity at Coptos—appears to be a metaphor for the psycho-spiritual ego in man. Thus the supposition as to the nominated deity of the smallest pyramid having been a pharaoh looks not so much unlikely as thoroughly irrational. Bauval has already otherwise pointed out[13] that the idea of a self-seeking pharaoh being willing to build his own "tomb" right next to those of two preceding pharaohs whose own are four times larger

FIGURE 11.4. THE SPHINX

is patently ludicrous. If our own deduction is correct, the three small Men-Kau-Ra mini-pyramids can be defined, we further suggest, as symbolizing the sensory, emotional, and mental-intellectual aspects (hence, perhaps, the multiple *kau*?) of the human being (or, rather, the astral soul).[14] The Great Pyramid's three minor pyramids might then be said to represent the three higher correspondences as expressions of deity—what the Indian esoteric system refers to as Atma-Buddhi-Manas—and what we might translate either as spiritual Will, spiritual Consciousness, and spiritual Mind, or as the Will-to-Be, the Will-to-Know, and the Will-to-Create or Act. As with the Menkaure pyramid, these minor pyramids are to be regarded as the emanations of the archetypal parent pyramid alongside which they stand. What then goes on within the parent pyramid represents the entirely subjective nature of that particular "soul," as dealt with in the associated rites of initiation.

The Second Pyramid

That then leaves us with the so-called Khafre or Khepren pyramid, which, as we can see in figure 11.1, has but one subsidiary pyramid—a much smaller one than any of the other six subsidiaries. In addition, the causeway linking this particular pyramid to the Sphinx complex is unique. Neither of the other two pyramids is shown as being associated with the Sphinx by such a linkage. But why? Well, the answer takes us right back to the metaphorical symbolism of the Sphinx, where the lion body represents the courage of the aspirant to the Mysteries while the human head (with its pharaonic headdress and uraeus) represents the "seeker after Truth." The fact that the long causeway from the Sphinx leads only to the second pyramid is because the latter represents the archetypal spiritual soul, which is regarded esoterically as mediating between god-consciousness and the human consciousness inherent in the astral soul (represented by the Menkaure pyramid). The very small subsidiary pyramid on the south side of the "Khepren" pyramid thus appears to symbolize the evolving spiritual Ego—the phenomenal spiritual individuality that retains the highest essence of each cycle of reincarnation, as we saw in the chapter dealing with the "Weighing of the Heart" ceremony. Thus the spiritual Individuality (i.e., the Egyptian *akh*) appears to become a sort of microcosmic Kheper-Ra.

Now, if we look again at the Giza pyramid complex as a whole, certain other apparent oddities come to light. For example, the main parent pyramids are internally approached by entrances on the north side, despite their associated temples being on the east side. Why? The Menkaure pyramid is exactly one quarter the size of the Great Pyramid. Why? The causeways leading to each of the pyramids are at different angles to one another. Why? The ancient Egyptians—bearing in mind their philosophy of life (as already described)—were incredibly careful in all such matters of geometrical arrangement because each characteristic line and linear pattern (like feng shui) was regarded as carrying its own magnetic potency. But notwithstanding this, there still appears to be some sort of variable geometry that one can sense about the whole orientation of the Giza complex, irrespective of the refusal of archaeologists to countenance such an idea. Therefore, to try to find any perfect symmetry would appear to be a waste of time because of the very potency that one senses would lie in its progressive, or dynamic, nature. Thus the sole answer has to be, we suggest, that the orientation is entirely astronomical.

The "Ritual Geometry" of the Giza Complex

Having considered some of the general issues related to the site complex, let us now turn our attention to certain more specific issues related to the rituals supposedly associated with them, linking each pyramid in turn with the raison d'être of the whole complex. We start with Menkaure, representing the nature of the astral soul and physical man. Here, through cross-correspondence of ideas associated with the theme of progressive initiation, we would expect to find some symbolism showing the animal-human senses being disciplined as an absolute prerequisite of progress on the spiritual Path—represented by the "Khepren" pyramid.[15] Bearing in mind that the whole Giza complex seems to have been oriented toward the triple expression of divinity—through achieving self-consciousness in body, soul, and spirit—the rites of Menkaure (involving a single chamber below ground level) were undoubtedly intended to instill in the individual qualities of courage and self-control over his personality nature—physical, emotional, and mental. As we have already suggested, without such a proven degree of self-control on the neophyte's part, any attempt to introduce him to the psycho-spiritual rigors of the real initiations would have proved worthless and also fraught with extreme danger for the candidate's own personal sanity. The so-called Valley and Mortuary temples of Menkaure may thus be seen as probably having involved rites of a solemn but not particularly extraordinary nature—perhaps incorporating prior preparation and then subsequent ceremonies of anointing and reclothing.

The rites associated with the "Khepren" pyramid, on the other hand, would probably have been rather more dramatic, commencing with the underground passage from the riverbank (if Edgar Cayce was correct as to its existence), opening out into the chamber directly under the Sphinx. From here, the neophyte would again emerge into the open air, prior to preparation in one of the temples, before proceeding up the causeway to the pyramid itself. As the second stage of the occult Mysteries involved what was called "discipleship," it seems very likely that this particular pyramid's rite involved acceptance into the priesthood following its various tests. It is also noteworthy that while the passage within the Menkaure pyramid proceeds from the "above" to a cavernous "below," perhaps representing "Hades" (see fig. 11.1), its upper extension leads to a dead end at the junction with the "inner pyramid." The passage within the "Khepren" pyramid, on the other hand, proceeds first underground to the central axis of the pyramid (where the chamber itself remains significantly at ground level) and then returns to the open air via an upward-leading passage that itself mirrors the entrance passage in the Great Pyramid. Hence we get the impression of the priest-to-be emerging from the Sphinx and proceeding to the "Khepren" pyramid, where he symbolically went down into the Underworld and then later reemerged into the daylight above the point at which he entered.[16] The symbolism is self-evident, particularly as the Menkaure pyramid has but one entrance that also doubles as an exit. Quite what the detail of the associated rites involved is relatively unimportant. The crucial issue in each case would have involved what overall impression was left in the psyche of the individual undergoing the rite and its associated tests. And, of course, the potency of the complex as a representation of the Divine Order in the celestial heavens would itself have been invoked by the very ceremonials thus enacted.

The Significant Individuality of the Great Pyramid

Now, when we get to the Great Pyramid, we find a very different set of circumstances indeed. This pyramid seems to have involved the tests associated with the higher initiations, leading to a sequence of experiences fitting the individual to be regarded finally as a hero (an adept, or master soul), one who had conquered the material nature of existence in the Underworld in its entirety and was thus on the way to semidivinity.

As we shall see in a moment, there appear to have been three obvious initiations associated with the Great Pyramid (each related to the three known chambers), but the tests and rituals were of an apparently different nature to those experienced in the other two pyramids. First of all, it will be noticed that the causeway to the Great Pyramid is far less clearly defined than the others, and the temple that one would expect to find at the base of the pyramid is not there—and, we would suggest, never was. The explanation implicit in these factors was that the initiate in these final stages had to abjure the world of even the priesthood and now travel entirely alone and without recognition, finding his own "way"—his "temple" being his own inner nature.

Quite how the initiate was expected to climb up to the main entrance of the Great Pyramid (some thirty feet above ground level)—given its polished limestone sides—is not altogether clear. But there is little doubt that the very minimum of assistance would have been given by the hierophant and senior priests responsible for this particular pyramid. One is almost left with the feeling that the only available method must have involved self-levitation! However, the probability is that a ladder of some sort was used, a symbolic ladder itself being mentioned in the Pyramid Texts as used by Horus the Elder and Set[17] to allow Osiris to climb up to the heaven world, and two senior priests would doubtless have represented them.

FIGURE 11.5. ANCIENT MAIN ENTRANCE TO THE GREAT PYRAMID
(drawn by Richard Dalton in 1749)

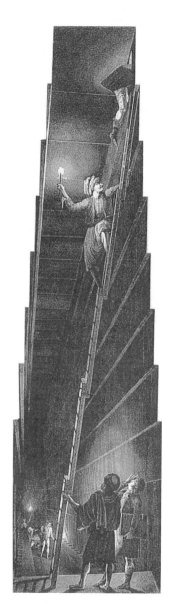

FIGURE 11.6. VIEWS FROM THE FOOT AND SUMMIT OF THE GRAND GALLERY

(from Denon's *Description de l'Egypte,* 1799)

Although perhaps not entirely clear because of the depth of shadow in the drawings, the visual perspective from either end of the Grand Gallery has a particularly powerful effect on the psyche when seen for the first time, particularly in a half light. The right-hand picture, looking down the Grand Gallery from the Great Step, gives perhaps the better sense of a yawning, cavernous drop, not least of all because the stepped ceiling and inwardly corbeled walls also produce a sense of being upside down.

The gallery itself is full of symbolism. For example, there are ten courses of stonework to the side walls above the ramp, although only the upper seven are corbeled. This, it is suggested, is yet again symbolic of the planes of consciousness—something that otherwise needs to be considered from the upside-downward as well. In addition, the rectangular holes in the side ramps may well have been intended as mountings either for holding statues of gods/daemons (e.g., the 42 Assessors of the Dead in the Chamber of Judgment) or for holding plaques with symbolic art and inscriptions on them, before which the candidate had to pass.

We move next to the question of the actual initiations associated with the Great Pyramid, and to understand these it is necessary again to follow the symbolic guidance provided by the sequence of internal passages.

The Main Passageways in the Great Pyramid

There are three main passageways (see again fig. 10.8)—the Descending Passage, the so-called Tomb Robbers' Tunnel (which is considered to be both original and quite deliberate), and the Grand Gallery, leading to both the Queen's Chamber and the King's Chamber. We shall deal with each in turn in a necessarily generalized fashion because the broad issues of their raison d'être in the initiation process are of the main importance. For greater detail concerning the technical measurements, the reader should consult such books as Peter Lemesurier's *The Great Pyramid* and Peter Tompkins's *Secrets of the Great Pyramid*.[18]

The first thing to bear in mind (as we shall see further in chapter 12) is that the Descending and Ascending Passages appear to represent the spiral movement of the ecliptic relative to the plane of the Galaxy, the latter itself being represented by the difference between external ground level and the slightly raised plateau within the base of the pyramid. The Great Subterranean Chamber at the base of the "plumb-line" forming the central axis of the pyramid probably symbolizes the lowest limit of the ecliptic path and thus also the very depths of "hell" from the soul's viewpoint, from which it had to make good its escape, although without being sucked back into the same cycle of existence as before— hence the reason for the Tomb Robbers' Tunnel. The "grotto" within the raised plateau can thus be seen as representing the point of decision as to whether to return back down the serpentine Tomb Robbers' Tunnel or to press on upward, a metaphor related to the plane of soul, the "Chamber of Judgment," and the urge for reincarnation.

The Queen's Chamber passage and the foot of the Grand Gallery then look to represent that level of ascent in the higher progression of the initiate's consciousness corresponding with the "upper celestial tropic" confirmed by the fact that it was built at the same level as the external entrance to the pyramid, from which the access ladder was dropped. Finally, the "Great Step" and the level of the King's Chamber floor symbolically stand at the very top of the "higher Path," from which the Great Return begins. However, the fact that the Ascending Passage and Grand Gallery lead in the opposite direction to the Descending Passage further indicates that the "Upper Way" was no longer subject to the backward pull of the equinoctial precession.

The Initiations of the Great Pyramid

Now, it would appear (from highly fragmented hearsay evidence) that there must have been definite preparatory and accompanying rites of a ceremonial nature associated with each of the Great Pyramid initiations.[19] Without attempting to hypothesize as to specific details, we might suggest—from some knowledge of the requirements of each of these initiations in other traditions—the following (speculative) descriptions, remembering that the only obvious access to the interior was via the raised main entrance and the Descending Passage.

First of all, there are only three chambers in evidence. However, immediately above the King's Chamber and within its "roof" structure there are five further chambers at least symbolically represented (see again fig. 10.8). Yet again, therefore, we find a representative octave divided in the ratio of 3 to 5, equivalent to the major third and major fifth in the harmonic scale. This can surely be no mere passing coincidence any more than the others were. The fact that the higher five chambers are not so immediately accessible as the lower three matters not, for the magical force of initiatic transmutation lies in the symbolism of the associated architectural arrangement. The essential theme of the initiatory sequence in any case had the "Raising of the Master/adept-hero" from the tomb as the highest of the purely human rites. Consequently, those involving further experience entirely in the spiritual world would have required only a representative presence, even though this would itself produce an overshadowing influence upon the candidate in the sarcophagus. Having mentioned these background issues by way of perspective, let us now have a look at the individual progressions leading up to the final achievement.

The First Great Test of Courage

The first of the initiations in this pyramid (perhaps corresponding with the "dark night of the soul") would have involved a transmutation of psychological will into a real spiritual certainty through a literally harrowing ordeal, requiring great personal courage—almost certainly involving escape from the Great Subterranean Chamber upward through the absurdly named Tomb Robbers' Tunnel. The latter is some 170 yards in length, ending in a section of some 70 feet comprising a near vertical section followed by an almost sheer wall some 30 feet in height. Bearing in mind that this would have had to be negotiated in total darkness (the tunnel itself being completely unventilated and rarely more than three feet wide) with complete ignorance of its length and not knowing what to expect en route or at the other end, one can perhaps understand the strength of mind, persistence, and sense of purpose required of the individual undertaking this test. The essential nature of the trial, however, seems to have involved him symbolically breaking away from the ecliptic path (and thus the "cycle of necessity" and constant human reincarnation) in order to make his own way back to the point of originating spiritual equilibrium—and, from there, onward and "upward" back to his divine point of origin. The moment of success facing the initiate would then perhaps have involved an exhausted and very brief vision of the (probably dimly lit) Grand Gallery, before being taken away by the priests and gradually resuscitated. The momentary perception of the "Upper, Lighted Way" would of course have been intended to evoke a sense and memory of the potential next stage of the initiation process, although when that test came it would hardly have been so simple as involving a straight climb through the Grand Gallery!

The initiate of this degree (the third in the series of seven) was now numbered among those to whom the innermost Mysteries could progressively be made known, and it would seem that the educational process associated with that may well have taken place in the temples of Upper Egypt, south of Thebes. These, as we have already seen, were regarded as being far more holy than those of Lower Egypt by virtue of being nearer the mystical source of the Nile. However, it also seems likely that before leaving the Queen's Chamber, some other drama would have first been played out, involving the sidereal influences of Kochab and Sirius emanating (latently) into the room via each of the two "vent shafts."[20] From inference, it presumably involved the activation of the neophyte-initiate's crown chakra, so that his "higher Self" could enter the body consciousness, thereby linking it up to the spiritual planes (and thus "transfiguring" it) via the descending, divine influence from Kochab, while Sirius-Anubis controlled the balance.[21]

The Way of the Higher Death

The next great initiation test must have involved yet another display of courage and determination, for the strange design of the Grand Gallery induces a sense of complete disorientation between visual perspective and natural sense of horizontal balance. It is possible that the candidate may have had to pass up it naked (if the Masonic tradition is anything to go by) while assailed from both sides by an assortment of either seductive or death-dealing influences (or both) symbolically representing elemental forces that he had to conquer by passing through with complete impassivity. Only when he had reached and surmounted the Great Step at the top end of the Grand Gallery could he be regarded as having succeeded, and even then his instructions may well have been not to look back.

Having passed from the Grand Gallery into the small antechamber separating it from the King's Chamber, the initiate would doubtless have had to utter (or be given) certain mystical "words of power"—hence the Masonic "passwords." He would also have been made aware of there being another chamber beyond, involving the next stage of the initiation process, although whether access was allowed at this time for a preliminary sight of it is unknown. The design of the antechamber suggests that heavy, vertically sliding gates (possibly of some heavy wood such as cedar) may perhaps have been inserted in the niches on either side. If so, it may have been that it was the task of the initiate facing the next degree to raise these before (or after?) being able to gain access to the King's Chamber.

The initiate of this (fourth) degree now stood on the Great Step, behind him "the pit" of darkness that the descending Grand Gallery represented. The associated symbolism seems that of having emerged into a transitional stage, or state, from the Underworld of human physical and psychological experience, which he had just left behind. The intensity of the imagery must have been extraordinary, as also the sense of knowing that he perhaps had to pass and repass that same way constantly en route from the spiritual world to the outer world in order to help other "spirits lost in hell" find their way back as he had done. Yet his own personal task was far from finished.

Return to the Outer World

We might speculate that among the magical "words of power" now his to command were those that enabled him immediately to quell the elemental forces associated with the "rite of passage."[22] But we can only speculate. It is nevertheless certain that he had to return the same way he had come, and this poses for us a question because it seems highly unlikely (although not altogether impossible) that the achievers of either the fourth or fifth initiation returned to the outside world via the Tomb Robbers' Tunnel. It is possible, however (again, judging by similar traditions in other ancient cultures), that it was required of the initiate of the third degree.

This suggests one of two things. Either there is a separate, concealed exit from the Grand Gallery or the Queen's Chamber or the massive granite "plugs" blocking the passageway between the Grand Gallery and the Descending Passage had to be moved. Of the two, the latter somehow seems the more likely even though modern engineers have stated quite categorically that they could not now be shifted because of the snugness of their fit within the tunnel. Which, then, is it?

If the alternative of a secret passageway were to prove the true one, any clue as to its whereabouts should theoretically be consistent with the geometry of the chambers and passageways. It could not be arbitrarily positioned, however, because that would, in turn, upset the fundamental feng shui of the pyramid and so destroy its very potency. We are thus drawn to the conclusion that such a secret passageway would lead back either to the main entrance or downward to an underground passageway. The latter would then open out elsewhere on the plateau—perhaps under the Sphinx itself?

The other possibility—which many would consider thoroughly far-fetched—involves levitation of the "plugs" and their withdrawal up the passage in some hitherto inconceivable fashion. To students of the occult sciences, used to concepts of "the ether" and to the idea of sound somehow being used either to produce an "ozone" (a layer of ether) capable of supporting huge weights or of causing the blocks to become literally much lighter in weight, such ideas might not seem so bizarre. To others, the matter must remain a complete mystery and that is how we must tantalizingly leave it here, although some further ideas are provided in appendix Q.

Parallels with the Christian Mystery Tradition

Before we move on, however—bearing in mind the previous suggestion that much of the early Christian tradition was borrowed from Egyptian sources—we might do well to consider momentarily the fact that there is yet another interesting parallel here to the story of the death of Jesus. The Grand Gallery from one angle is not unlike the Via Dolorosa leading to Golgotha, and the antechamber "portcullis" is easily compared to the rock placed over the entrance to the tomb of Jesus in the Garden of Gethsemane. The possibility thus suggests itself that the fourth and fifth initiations (as supposedly in the case of Jesus) followed immediately one upon the other and that, if this was indeed the case, the initiate of the completed fifth degree (the "Raised Master") had himself to move aside the immediate obstruction in order to demonstrate the power of his spiritual Will over matter before reemerging into the outer world.[23] It is an intriguing thought that the story of the Crucifixion and Resurrection of Jesus—whether historically factual or not—may perhaps represent a deliberate public reenactment of what had hitherto remained among the highest of secrets in the Egyptian Mysteries. However, that is pure speculation.

We come next to the fifth initiation itself, which—taking place in the King's Chamber—inevitably had to involve certain events of a truly cosmic nature, as we shall see. The initiate presumably had to lie down in the sarcophagus and put himself into a state of the deepest meditation—akin to catalepsy—which would last for some extended time (perhaps three days?). It seems likely that fellow priests would probably have taken the parts of Set and his accomplices in "sealing the chamber" by erecting the immensely heavy portcullis barrier in front of it, thereby making it impossible for the candidate for initiation to get out of his own accord before "passing" the initiatory test.

During the period of the body's catalepsy, the spirit of the initiate presumably left it and then underwent an experience involving such complete transcension of the human state that he was said to become fully self-conscious on the spiritual plane of existence. Thus he was deemed to have "died" to human existence altogether in one sense, through now functioning entirely within his *saha* (spiritual-soul vehicle). In so doing (following the same line taken by the biblical version of the death and Resurrection of Jesus), he would have "descended into Hell" (i.e., the triple Underworld of human earthly existence). There he would have had to demonstrate to his peers and superiors of the Egyptian Brotherhood that he could now not only create a transient body form by pure mental projection and the use of his spiritual Will, but also invest it with his own higher consciousness.[24]

The Celestial Dimension

The architecture of the King's Chamber implies that a great deal more was involved than just this, however, because the twin "vent shafts" leading from it and pointing due north and south (cyclically toward Alpha Draconis on the one side and Orion's belt on the other) undoubtedly determined the exact time at which the initiate "died" to one plane of existence and simultaneously began the first phase of a higher, celestial evolution. If one remembers that the "soul" of the individual was considered akin to the ovum within the maternal womb that presents itself for conception, the metaphor behind the "ventilation shaft" will become immediately apparent. This perception was first voiced by Robert Bauval and Adrian Gilbert in *The Orion Mystery,* although their idea focused solely on the concept of the pharaoh's soul being thus transported to the stars.[25] However, we shall look at such ideas in greater detail in chapter 12.

There are several other "pointers" associated with the King's Chamber, but it would take far too long in this book to go through them and so they must be left for a later volume. There is, however, at least one further initiation that must be mentioned, for it was said to complete the Master Soul's transition into the Divine world, thereby making of him a fully incarnate demigod—one of the Shemsu-Heru.

As is by now well known, the sides of the Great Pyramid were originally of polished limestone and therefore unclimbable. It has also been a much speculated upon tradition that the pyramid once had either a copper or a gold capstone (of the same shape as the pyramid) sitting upon what is now the horizontal platform of its truncated top. Yet why should there necessarily have been any such physical finish when the whole raison d'être of the three pyramids was to demonstrate, or aid, an evolutionary spiritual progression that concluded in divinity? It is therefore suggested that the deliberately missing capstone was intended to depict the fact that the god (almost certainly as Ptah himself) had to manifest there before the progressive, triple cosmic cycle was complete.[26] Consequently, we might perhaps suggest—and one can only speculate at this point—that the final terrestrial initiation (inevitably a highly rare occurrence) could have involved the most advanced initiate-soul appearing on or above the capstone platform in all his aurically radiant glory as a transfigured human form enclosed in a blazing sphere of light. In this manner the (original) pharaoh, as king-hierophant, would have been regarded literally as the direct manifestation of the god, demonstrating himself in full glory, power, and majesty to the assembled priests and people of Egypt.

TWELVE

THE INTERNAL GEOMETRY
OF THE GREAT PYRAMID

Bearing in mind that over the course of the last century there have been several ingenious (but often theologically prejudiced and otherwise flawed) theories concerning this particular subject, one hesitates to leap out of the frying pan into the same fire by adding another. However, as we know that the ancient Egyptians possessed an advanced astronomical knowledge, it seems very probable that the internal architecture and proportions of the Great Pyramid as a whole should reflect this right across the board. We ought perhaps, therefore, to begin this chapter by mentioning the work of the late professor of ancient history at Paterson College in New Jersey—Livio Stecchini—whose exhaustive work on the mathematics of the Great Pyramid is described in the appendix to the book *Secrets of the Great Pyramid,* by Peter Tompkins. Stecchini ultimately concluded that the Pyramid represented the Northern Hemisphere of our planet, while its perimeter represented the equator and its apex, the North Pole.[1] In addition, he discovered that the associated scale of construction was 1:43,200 (of which the latter figure is notably one tenth of the ancient Hindu meta-physicists' period for a "minor" Age of 432,000 years, and also twenty zodiacal Ages, each of 2,160 years). Further discoveries included these facts: The length of the perimeter = 2π times the height; the "golden mean" (phi) was fundamental to the construction (it was otherwise confirmed that pi also was); the Pyramid's design itself showed a clear and precise knowledge of the precession of the equinoxes.

Bauval and Hancock have more recently confirmed certain additional astronomical facts to us concerning the angular inclinations of the "vent shafts" and their stellar orientations. This chapter therefore aims to follow further in their footsteps, although it will be seen that there are one or two areas of difference with them as regards interpretation. That is because we believe that the idea of the pharaoh alone "returning to the stars" fails to address the whole question of the initiation process in the Mysteries being open to all candidates worthy of meeting its trials. It also skirts the issue of the Pyramid perhaps providing a general indication of stellar movements in our part of the Milky Way galaxy. Before we commence with our suggestions as to the question of interpretation, however, let us briefly remind ourselves of the following salient facts, which we can quickly relate to figure 11.1.

1. Both the Descending and Ascending Passages are inclined to the horizontal by an angle of 26°19'—almost exactly half that of the external sides of the Pyramid.

2. The Queen's Chamber passage is exactly on a level with the original entrance to the Pyramid.

3. The maximum altitude above the horizon (during the cycle of precession) of the constellation Orion is 58°14' when it rises almost due east at azimuth 91°. The correspondingly lowest altitude in the sky, seen from Giza, is 9°20', when it rises in the south at azimuth 169°.[2] This latter position was apparently last achieved in about 10,450 B.C., at which time the zodiacal sign of Leo was to be seen exactly on the eastern horizon. We now know this era to have been synonymous with that of "the Great Return," called by the Egyptians *Zep Tepi.*

4. The lines of sight of the two southward "vent shafts" from the King's Chamber and the Queen's Chamber describe angles from the horizontal of 45° and 29°30', respectively. Bauval confirms these as having pointed at Zeta Orionis and Sirius, respectively, around 2450 B.C.[3] This date has so far been given no particular astrological significance by him, however, and he has apparently assumed that it must ipso facto relate to the actual date of construction. On that, however, we must agree to differ because if the Pyramid is indeed intended to fulfill one function as some sort of "star clock," it seems far more likely that the orientation of the vent shafts is related to the celestial equinoxes and solstices. In fact, Bauval and Hancock confirm in their latest book, *Keeper of Genesis,* that Al Nitak in Orion actually crossed the north–south meridian at 38°08' altitude in alignment with the southern shaft of the Queen's Chamber circa 3850 B.C.[4] Now, if 10,450 B.C. was indeed the approximate era of the celestial winter solstice (the beginning of "the Great Return"), the era of the celestial spring equinox would have occurred at around 3950 B.C.—which (given the very brief period between these two rough dates) probably then clinches the relationship between the southern shaft and the equinox. It also suggests that, rather than the celestial winter solstice occurring precisely on the cusp of Virgo-Leo, it actually occurs at least 300 to 400 years into the 2,160-year Age of Leo.

5. The lines of sight of the northward-facing "vent shafts" from the same two chambers have been confirmed as describing respective angles with the horizontal of 32°28' and 39°. Bauval confirms these as having pointed at the stars Alpha Draconis (Thuban) and Kochab (in Ursa Minor) in about 2450 B.C.[5] Again, he surprisingly suggests no particular significance in these associations, although the Egyptians would undoubtedly have had something firmly in mind.

6. In about 2500 B.C., when the alignments of the "vent shafts" were exactly focused on Orion and Sirius, Orion rose at Azimuth 106°, its maximum elevational angle in the southern sky being 45°.[6]

For What Were the Various Shafts Intended?

The natural corollary of all these, we might perhaps suggest, is that the line of sight of the Descending Passage indicates that it was intended to track the path of the ecliptic at all times during the Annus Magnus. Correspondingly, the metaphor of the Great Pyramid representing the lower face of the "divine compasses," as shown in figure 10.8, implies a navigational (i.e., forward) progression of our whole local celestial universe. This seems to be confirmed from a number of angles, at the back of which stands the ever-present cosmic metaphor of the "Eye of Ra" (see again fig. 10.8), which (like our own human eye) is clearly threefold in appearance. The pupil represents the impenetrable darkness of the divine state itself, from which all gods (and thus the source of all light) emanate into the field of semidivinity in their quest for knowledge and experience—and to which they must ultimately return with their evolutionary harvest. The iris then appears to represent the downward progression from the semidivine to the spiritual state, while the "white of the eye" correspondingly represents the progression from the spiritual to the psychoelemental state. The latter is itself bounded by the lower eyelid, which thereby symbolizes the upper perimeter of the Underworld.

In that latter respect, it is particularly noteworthy that the Descending Passage runs at a tangent to the curve of the eyelid, one third of the passage being exactly at, or slightly above, the level of its "horizon," while the other two thirds descends progressively below it. As the ecliptic path produces this same effect as between the zodiac and the plane of the Galaxy—Cancer, Leo, Virgo, and Libra appearing to be "above" the celestial horizon—the metaphorical association between the ecliptic path and the Descending Passage seems to be highly probable, if not certain.

The Great Axis of the Ecliptic

Bauval and Hancock make the point that the three stars of Orion adopt a varying angle to the horizon according to the point in time of the vernal equinox during the cyclic precession of the equinoxes.[7] Thus at Orion's lowest point in the sky (9°20'), the "belt" is closest to being horizontal. Correspondingly, at its highest angular position, the belt is closest to being vertical. What has curiously not been deduced from all this is that these various angles provide us with a clear picture of the elliptical movement of our solar system cyclically up and down an inclined axis, or plane, like a gyroscope. At the top end of this ellipsoid movement not only is Orion to be seen at 9°20' above the southern horizon; Leo appears simultaneously at the vernal equinox on the eastern horizon. As we have outlined in previous chapters, this same point represents the beginning of the "Great Return," equivalent to the "celestial winter solstice"; and, indeed, we can immediately see why that should be so and why the Egyptians would have credited it with such immense significance and importance.

Symbolism of Polar Reversal

Now, by virtue of the cycle of precession, at one end of the ellipse formed by the ecliptic path our solar system faces in the opposite direction to the other. In one sense, east becomes west and west becomes east. The overall movement thus described helps us to see that the consistent orientation of our own planet toward a circular path of changing pole stars is derived clearly from the ecliptic path (pursued within the Sirian system) and owes nothing to an arbitrary scientific "wobble." As already indicated, the Descending Passage

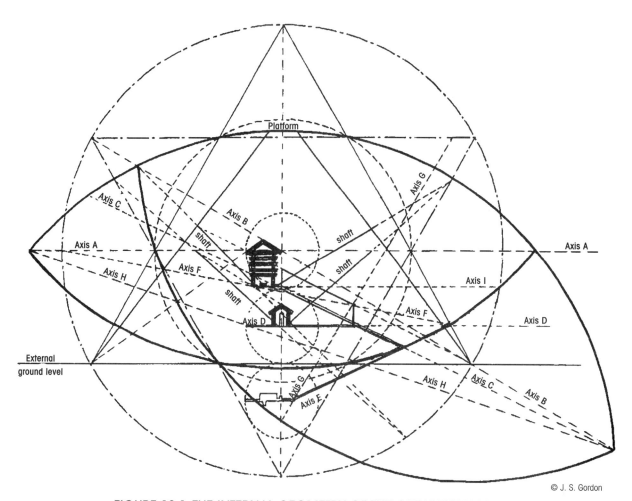

FIGURE 12.1. THE INTERNAL GEOMETRY OF THE GREAT PYRAMID

© J. S. Gordon

in the Great Pyramid bears a striking resemblance to this same axis. However, if we describe an inward line at an upward angle of 9°–10° from the outer Pyramid entrance, we find that it appears to pass through both the ceiling-wall junction at the lower end of the Grand Gallery and the base of the southern wall of the King's Chamber. If we next describe a line upward from the foot of the Descending Passage at an angle of 58°–59°, we find that it passes through the very same ceiling-wall junction in the Grand Gallery, immediately beneath which point we also find the well access to the Tomb Robbers' Tunnel and the junction between the Ascending Passage and the Queen's Chamber passage. Thus, from the zenith and nadir of the apparent precessional axis, it looks as though the two angles associated with Orion define the commencing point and height of the Grand Gallery, perhaps, as well as pointing to a variety of other "secrets."

A Wealth of Further Hidden Significances

Even more extraordinary and extensive cross-correlations come to light when we begin to extend the various alignments of shafts and passages generally throughout the Pyramid as shown in figure 12.1. While it would perhaps be tedious to go through each of these individually, there are one or two of which we might take particular note in passing. For example, if we extend the 26° line of the floor of the Ascending Passage right through the Grand Gallery and the King's Chamber and then out the other side of the latter, we find that it appears to intersect with the southern shaft from the Queen's Chamber exactly on the inner plane of the "divine compasses." Precisely the same is true of the Grand Gallery ceiling line and the southern vent shaft from the King's Chamber. Elsewhere, the small "door" in that shaft discovered by Gantenbrink's robot, Upuaut, appears to be located at the junction with a horizontal line through the center of the "pupil" of the "Eye of Ra," as though this horizon was itself acting as some sort of barrier to further progress. The northern vent shafts from the two chambers otherwise intersect exactly on the arc of the upper eyelid of the "Eye of Ra." And so on.

While we have already noted (in fig. 10.8) the *vesica piscis* that frames the "Eye of Ra," the various cross-axes shown in figure 12.1 produce another, even larger *vesica* that possesses some interesting characteristics of its own.[8] Among these is the longest axis (Axis B) in the diagram, running between the top left "arm" of the six-pointed star and the extreme right end of the *vesica,* passing en route through the very center of the Eye, along the "roof line" of the King's Chamber gable and also through the lower right leg of the star. It is suggested that there is a clear esoteric implication contained in this. The implication is thus of two sidereal systems, seemingly with a common focus—and that in turn (in an astronomical context) suggests a binary star system. Inevitably, Sirius springs immediately to mind and the fact that the southern vent shaft from the Queen's Chamber terminates at Axis A seems suggestive. However, there is more to this than meets the eye (no pun intended!), for while the northern shafts of the two chambers converge above Axis A and the outer face of the Pyramid, the two southern shafts converge well below ground level, perhaps at the level of the natural water table (perhaps also pointing to something else?).

The further implications of these orientations are that the southern vent shafts are concerned with downward movement while the northern ones are concerned with upward movement. The former would thus focus on inward impression, or "fertilization" of the initiatic consciousness, as Bauval has suggested,[9] while the latter would appear to focus on outward expression, or spiritual emancipation. As Sirius was representative of Anubis, the combination of Sirius and Orion would then imply the metaphorical return of Osiris to the objective plane of existence, at one or another level of consciousness. The vertical axis from the point of fusion is worth noting in this respect because it appears to pass right through the junction of the Ascending and Descending Passages, and also through the junction of Axis G on the periphery of the iris in the Eye. As Axis G rises from the lowest point on the ecliptic path (symbolized by the foot of the Descending Passage), the synchronicity is staggeringly perfect.

A Combination of Uses for the Pyramid

The idea that the "vent shafts" were intended merely to point exactly at specific stars at one particular time during the Great Sidereal Year seems somewhat questionable in light of all this. Given the idea of a permanent "house of initiation," one might be forgiven for supposing that the building should have been in perennial use. If not (that is, if once in

25,920 years is what was intended), the only reasonable supposition is that such a coincidence of time and architecture must have been aimed at some sort of profound cyclical regeneration in Nature—which would again tend to point toward the celestial spring equinox. But why should the intention not have involved a simultaneous focus on both aims? Quite clearly, if the latter suggestion is accurate, we need to work out a clear understanding of the "paths" followed in the heavens by the sight lines through the various shafts. This has not yet been comprehensively done because the suggestion of our solar system following an angled, elliptical path in space, relative to the plane of Sirius, has not until now been seriously considered—or, if it has, it has certainly not been followed through. While we must therefore await detailed astronomical calculations to support the theory, we shall return to the internal geometry of the Pyramid generally to see if we can find what else might perhaps suggest itself.

Delineation of the Lower Cycle

Turning back, therefore, to the Descending Passage and the Grand Gallery, we next concern ourselves with linear proportions, as these also seem to provide us with all sorts of esoteric pointers. These again bring into consideration the association with both the ecliptic path and the orbital pattern of movement of a binary star. To explain:

The Descending Passage, first of all, is seen to be divided in half at that point corresponding with external ground level—which symbolically suggests that the ecliptic passes through an equivalent celestial "plane." But if we then take the three granite "plugs" at the foot of the Ascending Passage (where it intersects with the Descending Passage) as another symbolic marker, we find that it divides the Descending Passage in the proportions of 1:2, or, for purposes of zodiacal analysis, 2:4. Now, it has been assumed for the last

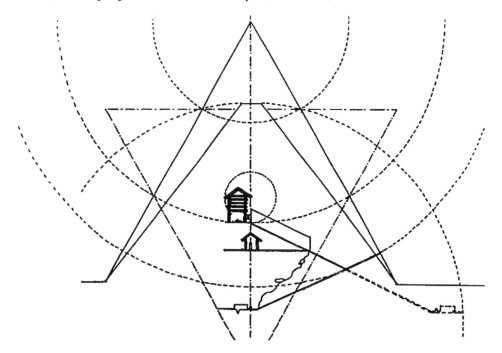

FIGURE 12.2. THE "ROTATIONAL" ORIENTATION OF THE DESCENDING PASSAGE

several centuries that the orientation of the Descending and Ascending Passages (the latter leading to the Grand Gallery) was originally designed to follow a fixed north–south line. Yet, closer examination of the visual metaphor (incorporating the profile of the Great Pyramid as the "divine compasses") suggests that this might not in fact be so. For example, if we treat the three granite "plugs" as a metaphor for an astronomical "hinge" (or pivot), it becomes possible to rotate the Descending Passage axially around it so that the Descending and Ascending Passages actually align and coincide with each other. As a consequence of this (see fig. 12.2), a single axial gradient becomes cyclically evident, leading up from the Great Subterranean Chamber in a straight line to the Great Step at the top of the Grand Gallery.

The implications arising out of this (to this author, at least) appear to be that the Descending and Ascending Passages are clearly confirmed as a visual metaphor for not only the ecliptic path (and thus the zodiacal progression) but also for the orbital path of Sirius A. Correspondingly, the Grand Gallery would appear to provide a mutually interactive metaphor for the axial path of Sirius B. In producing this single alignment, it becomes clear that the three granite "plugs" lie at the midpoint between the Great Step and the foot of the Descending Passage. They also lie exactly one third of the way down the Descending Passage, which, in zodiacal terms, appears to represent the location of the sign of Cancer, the traditional "Gate to the Underworld." The very restricted profile of the Ascending-Descending Passage and the immensely high profile of the Grand Gallery—if representative of the paths of Sirius A and B—then suggest that the two stellar paths might be connected like a chain link in a horizontal–vertical sequence. The symbolism of the granite plugs would otherwise suggest itself as representing the three aspects (divine, spiritual, and astral) of the Osirian figure entombed in a mummified (or coffinlike) position through which no return access is possible. In other words, the visual metaphor involves the compound soul-principle/entity having been dropped into a permanent position (like a "fixed star") immediately "overshadowing" the ecliptic "Wheel of Necessity" (the cycle of constant reincarnation) at this point. In addition, the granite plugs are located just above the lower eyelid of Ra, implying that whatever they represent is unable to "fall" any further from the "state of Grace"—i.e., the Inner Eye.

An Alternative Route

If such access to the "Higher Path" is rendered impossible via this route, there should logically be another, and, if we look to the bottom end of the symbolic ecliptic path, we surely find it in the shape of the so-called Tomb Robbers' Tunnel (sometimes called the "Escape Shaft"). This is found, not precisely at the bottom of the Descending Passage but slightly up it, at a point that appears to be equivalent in zodiacal terms to the cusp between Aquarius and Capricorn. That is of esoteric interest because, to astrologers, Capricorn (representing the Goat) symbolically involves the neophyte in the Mysteries having to find his own individual way back up "the mountain," there being no formal path after a certain point is reached. This way has traditionally been regarded as "steep, stony, and treacherous," requiring great personal courage and fortitude. By his supreme effort in climbing the winding tunnel back to the foot of the Grand Gallery and the "upper lighted Way," the candidate for initiation would then bypass the "dead Osiris," who seemingly therefore represents the static nature of the accrued spiritual faculty of his own previous (purely human) lifetimes. This tortuously individual path of course leads him to the very summit of the symbolic ecliptic path—the opening of the "Escape Shaft" at the foot of the Grand Gallery. Having achieved this, he must climb the Grand Gallery itself and, at the top of it, he—the lion-hearted initiate—is shown as symbolically passing beyond the zodiacal sign of Leo. This he now represents in a truly spiritual sense, for the axis of the upward path (i.e., Axis C in fig. 12.1) passes through the vertical axis of the pyramid and it also puts the initiate on a level (see Axis I) with the pupil of the Great Eye, representing the divine state from which the gods themselves emerge.

Geographical Associations

Continuing our analysis of the linear apportionments within the pyramid, we find that if the granite "plugs" at the intersection of the Ascending and Descending Passages represent Abydos, there are two further symbolisms immediately ahead. The distance from this intersection, rising right through the Grand Gallery and the King's Chamber and meeting the outer face of the equilateral triangle enclosing the pyramid as we see it today (see again fig. 12.1), is exactly bisected by the Great Step. Now, as we saw in an earlier chapter, the distance from Abydos to the First Cataract is equal to the distance between the Cataract and Abu Simbel. Hence we may perhaps infer that the Great Step symbolically corresponds with Elephantine, while the King's Chamber, so-called, corresponds with Philae, the latter itself (as we also saw earlier) representing the divine "womb" in which the Master soul, or semidivine Man, is conceived (or reborn). On this basis, the outer face of the equilateral triangle perhaps symbolically represents the southernmost boundary of Egypt, the borders of which, as already seen, appear to have been originally defined by astronomical orientation. Now, if these mathematical ratios and coincidences are correct, it clearly indicates that the intersection of passages and tunnels at the foot of the Grand Gallery symbolically corresponds within the pyramid to what Thebes represents on the ground outside. (The ratio of distance between the Grand Gallery and the Ascending Page is 4:3, akin to the temples between the Cataract and Abydos.) In fact, there is even a suggestion that the winding route of the Tomb Robbers' Tunnel appears slightly akin to the bends of the Nile, ending in the "steep" climb from Dendera to Thebes. As the Nile symbolically represents the body of Draco, the esoteric meaning surely again stands clear.

Can Further Verification Be Provided?

While our figure 12.1 to some extent graphically confirms the incorporation of the phi ratio, its orientation—if indeed related to our sun's parent star—suggests that there are geometrically and mathematically consistent correlations between the orbital paths of all heavenly bodies in space. Without detracting one whit from the work done by Stecchini, the ancient Egyptians would thus seem to have extended their range of mathematical knowledge far beyond the bounds of Earth's biosphere, while also being able to perceive the selfsame principles operating universally at the smallest and really quite insignificant levels of terrestrial existence. That is itself entirely consistent with their religious philosophy and tradition, however—hence the universally well-known axiom of the ancient analytical method (still followed by the modern esotericist), "As below, so above" (or "As above, so below"). However, the unavoidable conclusion arising out of all this (associated with that most abused of New Age expressions, "cosmic consciousness") is that such an extended range of "inner vision" surely means that, unless the ancient Egyptians (and all the other millions of people of their time) were suffering from a vast, mass self-hallucination, there must indeed exist a factual divine hierarchy of being and capacity extending far beyond the purely human state. If so, the Inner (or Divine) Man (being perhaps a "linchpin" in that same hierarchy?) would indeed have a crucial role to play in the fulfillment of Divine Purpose, through the agency of our own humanity.

There are doubtless many who will say that this author is projecting far too much of his own wishful thinking into all this associated symbolism. However, mathematical, geometrical, astronomical, and astrological cross-correlations cannot be dismissed or treated lightly where the Mystery Tradition is concerned. Bearing in mind the sheer extent of cross-correlations in this particular instance, no reasonable person could seriously suggest that mere coincidence is involved throughout. That being so—and as we know, sympathetic magic was the very basis of ancient Egyptian religion—there are indisputably conclusive grounds for supporting the case that the Great Pyramid was, simultaneously, a vast temple of (permanent) divine invocation and of initiation into the Higher Mysteries, and also a "star clock."

It is not proposed to go any further into such issues in this book, as one must regard the original thesis on which it set out as having been reasonably demonstrated (if not proved beyond reasonable doubt) by circumstantial evidence from a wide variety of angles. Some may still stubbornly disagree. Others will doubtless take the matter even further and work out many more remaining correspondences so that the final jigsaw-puzzle picture stands complete. Perhaps with the benefit of any such findings they may also stumble across the network of underground passages that, some have speculated, cross the Giza plateau between the Pyramids and Sphinx. That in itself, however, may not incontrovertibly prove (to the complete satisfaction of professional archaeologists, anyway) the existence of a scientifically sophisticated predynastic civilization. The weight of circumstantial and deductive evidence needed to do so will probably have to extend into many other areas first. This book has merely attempted to open up a few of these for further examination.

THIRTEEN

REFLECTIONS

Well, where do we go from here? It seems less than likely that many professional Egyptologists will have read their way right through this book—even if they deigned to pick it up in the first place—because of the dreaded word *Atlantis* in the title. Experience leads one to believe that many scholars and scientists paradoxically often disdain the merely unpalatable, preferring instead to continue living off the truly indigestible. Consequently, the empirical body of suggestions and associated evidence that this book has gathered to support its case—as to a far more ancient humanity and culture than anthropology will currently entertain—we expect to see treated with the usual range of suspicion and disdain that so many academics and scientists regrettably tend to display when their own natural well of human curiosity has become clogged with prejudice.

Having criticized the often thoroughly inflexible attitude of mainstream Egyptology, we must point out that its restricted views are not by any means universally shared among its own fraternity. Graham Hancock mentioned in *Fingerprints of the Gods* the feelings expressed by the highly respected Dr. Jane B. Sellers that Egyptologists would be unwise to discount the importance of astronomy in the original foundation of ancient Egyptian thought, a feeling intensely (and frequently) echoed in the also highly regarded book by Santillana and von Dechend, *Hamlet's Mill,* although little or no attention has been paid to any of these authors by their own intellectual community.[1] From our own limited experience, we feel that they are by no means alone in expressing such sentiments, in this or in other related areas of scholarship and science. However, "peer pressure" makes it very difficult (if not impossible) for any dissenters to speak out categorically for fear of professional ostracism and consequent loss of jobs and influence—a sad comment indeed upon the unprincipled character assassination and manipulation of human intelligence and creative thinking that so often seem to take place behind the scenes. It is for this very reason that most really new thought in the world inevitably comes from dedicated amateurs working on or outside the fringes of the recognized Establishment. Unfazed by threats of potential peer pressure and job loss, they are ever the true pioneers of lateral thought, willing to "think the unthinkable." The world of formal science (if Egyptology could actually be considered as such, which seems a little doubtful), however, usually tags along later (once the body of evidence becomes too strongly incontrovertible to do otherwise) to "put flesh on the bones" and work out the details plus the formal rules, or "laws."

Although the bastions of orthodoxy are gradually being broken down by interdisciplinary thinking, many scientists and academics still twitch visibly at the mere thought of any form of spiritual belief infiltrating their bespoken patch of ground. However, as priests of the orthodox Christian faith adopted the same attitude up to a mere century and a half ago, we can perhaps regard this as mere scholarly repartee and of no great consequence. The fact remains, however, that the intelligent lay public (on a broad front) increasingly finds the whole trend of modern science and academic research—dependent as it usually is on political support and commercial funding—disturbingly and materialistically self-serving. The fact that it also seems unable or unwilling (through fear or arrogance) to entertain even the possibility of a coexistent spiritual dimension attached to its field of endeavor makes the general concern even greater—and understandably so in a world fraught with every sort of apparently fratricidal tendency. That spiritual beliefs are clearly regarded by many scientists and Egyptologists as having no particular working relevance to their area of concern, or that such interest constitutes a potential threat to "scientific rigor" (on the basis of what the Christian Church did to early scientists, or how similarly minded "fundamentalists" would like to interfere today), does not necessarily mean that such an idea is even remotely applicable or accurate in a modern context.

Having said as much, there are areas where one must feel some genuine sympathy for professional Egyptologists. On the one hand, there are Islamic fanatics who would dearly (and misguidedly) like to reduce every vestige of Egyptian art and architecture to rubble, as the idolatrous products of "heretics." On the other, there are constant hordes of camera-happy tourists to be catered to (to satisfy politicians and generate revenue), even though their depth of interest in the subject is, in the main, highly limited. Quite apart from these, there seems to be an increasing number of New Age weirdos (and some really are weird) to be found infesting the temples, trying to summon the spirits of the gods or to regress their own consciousnesses back to previous incarnations in ancient Egypt. And then, to cap it all, there are other, impertinent types who actually have the temerity to question the interpretations of the professionals themselves. Where will it all end?

Well, the short answer to that must surely be, "When the mainstream body of archaeological scholarship recognizes and admits that, in relation to ancient mysticism and its real meanings, it is largely (often deliberately) illiterate and that others might perhaps have a much better understanding of such things than it does itself." In the meantime mavericks like us must continue reviving long-undisturbed bodies of esoteric knowledge with their attendant shades of occult interpretation to hover over the heads of scientists and scholars and haunt their working hours.

Rather fortunately, perhaps, there is a large and ever growing community of intelligent and widely read people among the lay public, most having a catholic interest in the origins of human civilization and the true nature of its ancient spiritual beliefs and ideals, many of which they intuitively agree with and share. This growing band—with an increasing number of scientists and scholars joining it—refuses to be fobbed off with Establishment insistence on a conventional wisdom that clearly defies both reason and sheer common sense. It is largely for such folk that this book has been written. However, notwithstanding that the book may have broken some fresh ground, there is still a great deal more to be learned, and it is here that all the work already done by Egyptologists in collecting, coordinating, and cataloging information over the last century and a half actually proves of great help. This author freely admits that had such not already been available, his task in detailing the conclusions described here would have been rendered considerably more difficult and time-consuming.

The foregoing, however, covers merely general outlines of the overall scheme of the ancient Egyptians, while acknowledging that the knowledge of the priesthoods of Egypt was already in serious decline by about 2000 B.C.—as was observed by Wallis Budge.[2] However, until the whole issue of the ancient chronology is fundamentally reopened and reassessed against the background of ancient astronomical metaphor, no orthodox Egyptologist, we suggest, would really be able to comment properly upon the nature and extent of such errors and general degeneracy. But the prime obstacle to that is the still entrenched idea that urban culture could not have existed before 10,000 to 8000 B.C. when there are so many indications as to a "prehistoric" civilization culture that extended from (at least) northwest Africa to the Caucasus and the Indus Valley.

Until archaeologists openly concur with the findings of professional geologists that the Sphinx's quarried enclosure and the Osireion at Abydos had been seriously eroded during at least the last major pluvial period following the eleventh millennium B.C.,[3] and until they take people like Schwaller de Lubicz seriously, it just will not be possible to move beyond the present impasse. However, a protracted failure to heed the clearly argued opinions of such bona fide researchers will itself succeed in merely undermining the public standing of archaeologists in general—which could hardly be in their best interest, or that of their own academic discipline. But merely pushing back the date of the supposedly first Egyptian civilization to the tenth or even thirty-sixth millennium B.C. will not by itself suffice. Serious regard must be given to the various other issues that this book and others have raised, ranging from astronomical factors to horticultural and ethnographical ones, and many more besides. However, the really crucial issue that will ultimately have to be faced relates to the question of the possible validity of the ancient Egyptians' belief (as of all other ancient cultures) in the cyclical return of a divine "influence" to Earth—something that will undoubtedly cause our literal-minded and dyed-in-the-wool scientific and academic friends (and many orthodox priesthoods too, perhaps?) to shudder inwardly. However, as long as they refuse to entertain the suggestion that there might be a scientific rationale to the idea of such a cyclical zeitgeist and to there also being psycho-spiritual states of existence that substand (but still interact with) the physical one, they will (by default) leave the field of spirituality and mysticism to an often less than fragrant potpourri of myopic priests, religious fanatics, woolly minded mystics, and impressionable would-be occultists, with all the attendant and volatile dangers implied by such a situation. These are already all too visible in our modern world, as well as having highly unpleasant historical antecedents.

It is unavoidably clear that there is a very real and worldwide "spring tide" of public interest in spiritual existence today, as well as in mysticism and the occult by association. If not adequately recognized by scientific and academic communities the world over, the latter will find themselves eventually buried either by merely superficial aspects of it or by blind fundamentalism as this toxic weed continues to proliferate; for politicians—upon whom they ultimately rely for support—will always bow to the duress of mass public opinion and interest long before they show support for an apparently expendable minority group of scholars. It is therefore crucial, we suggest, for all the associated issues to be as objectively and openly addressed as possible (no matter that final answers may be inaccessible at this stage), irrespective of how problematic they might at first appear.

Quite apart from the issue of the "seasonally returning gods," certain of the points raised concerning the background of the Christian Dispensation and of the origins of Hebrew culture will hardly, we suspect, have endeared us to some of the more extreme followers of these two faiths. However, facts tend to speak for themselves and, as we said at the outset, nothing suggested in this book is really new, even though it has perhaps been long forgotten. Respected authors in other fields are also currently commenting upon these issues and one would hope to see, as a direct result, much greater theological clarity and honesty eventually emerging right across the board. Finally, as far as Atlantis is concerned, one can only suggest that the subject is also due for a thorough, global reappraisal—preferably by an open-minded science willing to take into consideration all the related and relevant factors in a multidisciplinary approach. Only then are we likely to be able to assess the probability factor in a truly objective manner. If that could be done, we might indeed find ourselves rewriting the history of our world and its humanity.

APPENDIX A

THE RELATIONSHIP BETWEEN THE SOTHIC YEAR AND THE ANNUS MAGNUS

While the relationship between these two "years" is perhaps not immediately obvious, it is nevertheless very real. It confirms with mathematical exactitude not only the rate of precession as it affects the earth, but also a major reason why the Ancients regarded our otherwise apparently insignificant planet as the microcosm of a vast sidereal macrocosm.

First of all, the result of merely dividing the 25,920 years of the Annus Magnus by the 1,460 years of the Sothic cycle is that we find ourselves with the apparently unremarkable ratio of 71:4. However, let us imagine that two entities both set out at the same speed in space, at exactly the same time—one following the path of the ecliptic and the other a spiro-elliptical path around it, using the ecliptic path as its focus. The effect would be roughly as shown in figure A.1.

Figure A.1 shows the 360-degree cycle of the Annus Magnus subdivided into its own thirty-six decads, or decanates, each of the latter taking (theoretically) 720 years to complete.

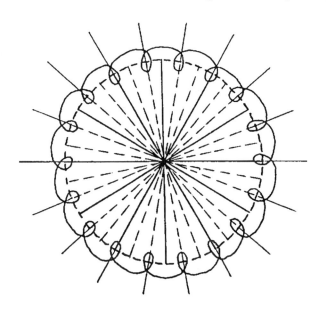

FIGURE A.1. THE THIRTY-SIX DECADS IN THE CYCLE OF THE ANNUS MAGNUS

The Relationship
between the
Sothic Year and
the Annus
Magnus

▲

205

Nevertheless, because our solar system cycles constantly around this path, completing one orbit every 1,460 years, when it has completed two decanates (i.e., 20 degrees), it then finds itself twenty years "behind schedule." This (mathematically) amounts to:

$$\frac{1460 - 1440}{1440} = \frac{1}{72}$$

By the time the solar system has completed eighteen Sothic cycles, it will have taken 26,280 years instead of the "scheduled" 25,920 years, the disparity between the two being exactly 360 years—that is, $\frac{1}{72}$ of the Annus Magnus. However, as we saw in chapter 7 of the book, the fact that there are nine Sothic cycles moving out from the start point and a further nine involved in the return to the point of origin from the celestial aphelion was dramatized by the ancient Egyptians in their pantheon.[1] The divine ennead of Heliopolis, which thus depicts the return cycle and the tenth god—Horus as the son of Isis and Osiris—can consequently be seen as a metaphor for the commencement of the new Annus Magnus. He himself—in one of his many guises—always commences and concludes the cycle, which, in its entirety, the Egyptians referred to as the maternal goddess Hathor—itself derived from Hat-Hor, the "house of Horus."

The Relationship
between the
Sothic Year and
the Annus
Magnus

▲

206

APPENDIX B

From Plato's *Timaeus*

"Thereupon, one of the priests, (of Sais in the Egyptian Delta) who was of very great age, said, 'O Solon, Solon, you Greeks are but children and there is never an old man who is a Greek.'[1]

"Solon, upon hearing this, said, 'What do you mean?'

"'I mean to say,' he replied, 'that in mind you are all young; there is no old opinion handed down among you by ancient tradition, nor any science which is hoary with age. And I will tell you the reason of this: there have been, and there will be again, many destructions of mankind arising out of many causes. There is a story which even you have preserved, that once upon a time, Phaethon, the son of Helios, having yoked the steeds in his father's chariot, because he was not able to drive them in the path of his father, burned up all that was upon the Earth and was himself destroyed by a thunderbolt. Now this has the form of a myth but really signifies a deviation from their courses of the bodies moving around the Earth and in the heavens, and a great conflagration of things upon the Earth at long intervals of time. When this happens, those who live upon the mountains and in dry and lofty places are more liable to destruction than those who dwell by rivers or upon the sea-shore; and from this calamity the fact that we live on the low-lying land by the Nile, which is our never-failing savior, saves and delivers us.

"'When on the other hand the gods purge the Earth with a deluge of water, among you herdsmen and shepherds on the mountains are the survivors, whereas those of you who lie in cities are swept by the waters into the sea. But in this country, neither at that time nor at any other does the water come from above on the fields, having a tendency always to come up from below (i.e., via the source of the Nile) from which we are also secure as the floods of the Nile are always predictable, for which reason the things preserved here are said to be the oldest.

"'The fact is that wherever the extremity of winter frost or of summer season does not prevent, the human race is always increasing at times and at other times diminishing in numbers. And whatever happened either in your country or ours, or in any other region of which we are informed—if any action which is noble or great, or in any other way remarkable has taken place, all that has been written down of old and is preserved in our temples; whereas you and other nations have just provided yourselves with letters and the other things which States require. And when the stream from heaven descends like a pestilence and leaves only those of you who are destitute of letters and education; and thus you have to begin all over again as children and know nothing of what happened in ancient times, either among us or yourselves.

"'As for those genealogies of yours which you have recounted to us, Solon, they are no better than the tales of children; for, in the first place, you remember one deluge only whereas there were many before that; and in the next place, you do not know that there dwelt in your land the fairest and noblest race of men which ever lived, of whom you and your whole city are but a seed or remnant. And this was unknown to you because for many generations the survivors of that destruction died and made no sign. For there was a time, Solon, before that great deluge of all, when the city which is now Athens was first in war, and was pre-eminent for the excellence of her laws and is said to have performed the noblest deeds and to have had the fairest constitution of any of which tradition tells, under the face of heaven.'"

Comment: There are three main points particularly worthy of note in connection with the context of this book. The first is that Phaethon also otherwise represents divine Mankind as one celestial entity, "falling from Grace," his "death" representing man's resultant ignorance of his divine origins, just as Osiris is depicted as having been "killed." The second is that the season of "ekpyrosis," or "celestial summer," clearly results in widespread death from an excessive increase in solar radiation, rather than from volcanic action. The implication is that really major volcanic activity is perhaps not so much associated with the 26,000-year Annus Magnus as with the greater cycle of which it itself forms a part. Similarly, the "kataklysmos" or "deluge period" might be perceived as associated with sustained heavy rainfall and flooding, with consequently higher sea levels. Major continental rises and falls, on the other hand, would be entirely due to radial expansion or contraction of the earth's crust during the greater cycle.

The third point is that the Egyptian priest seems, somewhat curiously, to have been unaware of the pluvial period affecting his country during the period between the tenth and fifth millennia B.C. even though he was aware of many cyclical "deluges." However, his relaxed attitude could well be due to the existence of (the man-made) Lake Moeris itself, in the Faiyum. Some 350 miles in circumference and capable (via a highly sophisticated system of canals and locks) of storing an immense volume of surplus river water (in readiness for times of drought) by siphoning off excess floodwater when the Nile was in full spate, the engineering arrangement may even have been esoterically designed to mimic the human kidney functions (see fig. 9.4).[2]

APPENDIX C

ON GEOLOGY

The Geological Chronology

Years Ago	Epoch	Period
To 6,000	Historic	
6,000+	Prehistoric	QUATERNARY
To 1.6 million	Pleistocene	
To 5.3 million	Pliocene	
To 24.0 million	Miocene	
To 37.0 million	Oligocene	TERTIARY

The western Mediterranean area was a single landmass (called Tyrrhenia by geologists) until about 1.6 million years ago, when violent tectonic movement caused the progressive severance of the Calabro-Sicilian mountain arc that had, until then, connected the Italian Apennines to the Atlas Mountains. It appears that this protracted cataclysm may in fact have resulted from the Earth's polar reversal preceding the last one some 800,000 years ago (i.e., about 1.6 million years ago), and that it was the cause of the original flooding of the western Mediterranean. It was seemingly also the cause of the Alps being pushed up toward their present height. The cataclysm involved a 30-degree shift in the Calabro-Sicilian and Pyrenean chains, these two twisting in apparently opposite directions to each other, thereby suggesting a massive rotational movement affecting the Earth's crust.

Regarding the Concept of Plate Tectonics

Because of their conviction that the core of the earth has to be of iron in order to produce the phenomenon of terrestrial magnetism and gravity, geologists remain of the opinion that any significant radial shrinkage of the earth would not be feasible. As the only other conceivable mechanism that could generate sufficient mechanical energy to produce the violent upthrust of mountain chains and seabeds, plate tectonics was evolved as the only reasonable alternative concept to explain massive landmass movement, notwithstanding the fact that it still fails to answer many fundamental questions.

On Paleomagnetism

When rock is liquefied, it becomes nonmagnetic. However, once it has cooled to "Curie point" (580°C), it develops not only a magnetic state, but also a characteristic orientation of polarity consistent with the magnetic field of the Earth at that time. The actual intensity of magnetism depends upon both the speed at which the liquified rock (lava) cools and its chemical constituents. Thus it is that palaeomagnetic scientists can (in theory) deduce the location of the Earth's poles at any given time in prehistory. Curiously, however, rocks with an inverted polarity possess much stronger magnetism (ten to one hundred times stronger) than can be accounted for by the Earth's magnetic field on its own. Consequently, one is drawn to the implication that our planet, at specific periods in the cycles of the solar system, has been exposed to a vastly superior electromagnetic field. Contact with the opposing polarities at either side of the electrical field of the Galaxy itself would be consistent with such an experience.

On Radiocarbon Dating

This method of dating was developed in 1947 by W. F. Libby of the University of Chicago. It is based upon the fact that cosmic rays hitting the upper atmosphere force nitrogen atoms to break up into hydrogen and radiocarbon (C14). The radiocarbon thereby becomes unstable by virtue of having two extra electrons.

The radiocarbon is then precipitated in rainfall and, as it falls to Earth (most of it actually falls into the sea), some of it mixes with organic carbon to produce carbon dioxide, which then enters into plant structures and, via them, into the food chain. Plant and animal cells contain roughly the same amount of radiocarbon throughout their life cycles because of constant absorption and emission. However, when the body of which they form part dies, no new radiocarbon is absorbed and the existing balance decays in sequences called half-lives.

The problem with this dating technique is that the amount of cosmic radiation impacting upon our planet undoubtedly varies quite substantially and, without knowing why or when these variations occur, scientific analysis becomes increasingly less accurate the further one goes back in time. It seems that the pattern of cosmic radiation has been roughly steady for the last 20,000 years or so. However, could the current enlargement of the polar "ozone holes" indicate that we are nearing a period of cyclical increase associated with the "celestial summer" of the Annus Magnus?

APPENDIX D

FROM SCHWALLER DE LUBICZ'S *SACRED SCIENCE*

"The latest discoveries in nuclear physics endow geology with several means of dating: *the strontium method* has permitted evaluation of the age of the oldest formations, those which go back more than three billion years; *methods using lead* (uranium, etc.) reveal the age of non-sedimentary rock between the Precambrian period and the Tertiary era, which began seventy million years ago; *the method based on isotopic relationships* pertains to marine sediments; and lastly, *the radioactive carbon-14 dating method* makes it possible to estimate the age of organic substances, but the latter procedure [which has not proved reliable in all cases] cannot date back further than 30,000 years and therefore only concerns our immediate prehistory.

CRO-MAGNON
MAN
(Homo Sapiens)

NEANDERTHAL
MAN

"It has therefore been possible to determine the beginning of the Quaternary sequence at approximately one million years ago but it is precisely the chronology of that era which, even today, it is most difficult to establish."[1]

"Thus one fundamental point is established: During the first half of the Quaternary, there existed beings strongly resembling apes and men, and presenting morphological characteristics common to both apes and men, so that a common stock would seem to be implied. It is impossible, however, to consider *Australopithecus,* still animal and of too-recent geological age, as a direct ancestor of *Pithecanthropus,* or *Archanthropus.*

"Proof therefore now exists to the effect that man does not descend from the great anthropomorphic, tree-dwelling apes, nor from the bipedal *Australopithecus.* Man and ape form two distinct branches. . . ."[2]

FIGURE D.1. CRO-MAGNON MAN AND NEANDERTHAL MAN

"... Neanderthal man differs completely from all human races, even the most primitive now existing; nor can he be compared to types very close to our present races, types which almost immediately succeed him. ... From a morphological point of view as well as judging by their industry and art, these highly evolved [Grimaldi-Negroid, Cro-Magnon, and Chancelade] men who almost coexisted with Neanderthal man, could be considered his descendants *only by admitting a mutation so considerable as to be absurd*. ...

"... [Thus] the Neanderthals ... consequently cannot be the ancestors of *Homo sapiens* but should be seen as a human offshoot representing rather, a degeneration, as their sudden disappearance at the end of the Mousterian [circa 100,000 years ago] would seem to confirm."[3]

"[The Cro-Magnon] race was of great stature (1 m. 80 to 1 m. 90). Their dolicocephalic [long-headed] skull had a high dome and a brain capacity superior to that of a modern European [1,590 cc to approx. 1,350 cc]. 'The skull presents to a marked degree all the characteristics considered as indications of an intellectual development of the most advanced kind.'"[4]

Note: Since Schwaller de Lubicz wrote *Sacred Science* in the 1950s, the commencement of the Quaternary has been pushed back by palaeontologists to 1.6 million years ago. Temporarily deterred by having to admit that *Homo sapiens,* instead of having emerged only within the last 100,000 years, actually existed as far back as the beginning of the Quaternary, paleontology has since recovered its scientific equilibrium by creating *Homo sapiens sapiens* to take its place (and save its own face). However, paleontologists still have to explain how and why it is that the brain capacity of the supposedly much more intelligent *Homo sapiens sapiens* has actually diminished in size, thereby undermining the much vaunted Darwinian theory of evolution upon which all their own theories of physiological-intellectual definition are based.

The very latest discoveries in Australasia (Papua New Guinea) threaten to overturn even the well-embedded idea that *Homo sapiens* came out of Africa while, at the same time, pushing his origins back to well over 200,000 years ago. The fact that the American archaeologist Virginia Steen McIntyre (in the 1960s) discovered remains over 200,000 years old in Central America has already upset orthodox opinion to such an extent that academia destroyed her career rather than face the radical implications. But the discoveries will undoubtedly not stop here.

From S. A. Mackey's
The Mythological Astronomy of the Ancients (1824)

"We are told by Herodotus that the Choen, or men of learning in this country [Egypt] informed him that the Pole of the Earth and the Pole of the Ecliptic had formerly coincided. I have seen in Denon's second volume of *Travels in Egypt*, two ancient Zodiacs, from a temple in Tentyra, or Dendera [see fig. E.1], where the poles have been represented in both situations; and in that which shews the Poles at right angles, there are marks which prove it was not the last time they were in that position, but the first. Capricorn is represented at the North Pole, and Cancer is divided near its middle, at the South Pole; which is a confirmation that originally they had their winter when the Sun was in Cancer. But the chief characteristics of its being a monument commemorating the first time that the Pole had been in that position are the Lion and Virgin.

"The Lion is drawn standing upon the Hydra; his tail is almost straight and pointing downward in an angle of 40 or 50 degrees; this position agrees very well with the original formation of these constellations. But in many places we see the Lion with his tail turned up over his back, ending with a serpent's head, showing that the Lion must have been inverted; which indeed must have been the case with the whole Zodiac and every other constellation, when the Pole had become inverted.

"There is also in Denon's second volume, a circular Zodiac, wherein the Lion is standing on the Serpent with his tail forming a curve downward; from which we find that, though six or seven hundred thousand years must have past [*sic*] between the two positions, yet they had made but little or no difference in the constellations of Leo and the Hydra; while Virgo is represented very differently in the two—in the circular zodiac, the Virgin is nursing her child; but it seems that they had not had that idea when the Pole was first within the plane of the Ecliptic; for in this zodiac, as given by Denon, we see three Virgins between the Lion and the Scales, the last of which holds in her hand an ear of wheat. . . ."[1]

"As the people on the Earth are insensible of the motion of the earth, they thought that the Pole of Heaven revolved around the Pole of the Earth. And if we assume a time when

From S. A.
Mackey's *The
Mythological
Astronomy of
the Ancients*
(1824)

▲

213

OUEST D'ORIGINE   SUD VRAI

NORD VRAI   AXE DU TEMPLE   EST D'ORIGINE

FIGURE E.1. THE DENDERA ZODIAC

Drawing by Lucie Lamy from Schwaller de Lubicz's *The Temple of Man*. There were two main zodiacs at Dendera, one of which (above) was circular and the other square or rectangular. These were first described by the French antiquarian Denon in his *Voyages en l'Egypte*.

From S. A. Mackey's *The Mythological Astronomy of the Ancients* (1824)

▲

214

the poles were parallel, the Pole of Heaven in eight times 25,000 [*sic*] years would seem to have described a pericyclosal figure around the Pole of the Earth like a serpent coiled eight times; and as each volve [revolution] is four degrees asunder, the figure of the serpent described by the Pole of the Heaven around the Pole of the earth in 200,000 years would sweep a circle the diameter of which would be 64 degrees i.e., 32 degrees above the Pole and 32 below it; it would be the circle of perpetual apparition in the latitude of 32 degrees. In that age, at Noon, the Ecliptic would be parallel with the Meridian and part of the Zodiac would descend from the North Pole to the north horizon, crossing the eight coils of the serpent, which would seem like an imaginary ladder with eight staves reaching from the earth up to the Pole i.e., a throne of Jove! Up this ladder then, the Gods i.e., the signs of the Zodiac ascended and descended. . . . It is more than 400,000 years since the Zodiac formed the sides of this ladder."[2]

"I cannot dismiss this article without bringing to your notice the singular monuments which other nations have erected to shew their sense of the pericyclosal motion of the Pole, which they have everywhere so blended with the respective latitudes of each country as to leave no room for suspicion.

"The two slow motions of the Pole are so proportioned to each other and produce such a complex figure in the heavens, differing everywhere in the exact proprtion of the different latitudes, that the different nations never could have agreed in their descriptions had not each nation not observed and registered for itself. Besides the eight-volved Tower of Babel in the latitude of thirty two degrees and the name of Ninophi [Nineveh] given to the chief city of Assyria, which stood in the latitude of thirty-six degrees, we find at Pekin in the latitude of forty degrees a Tower of Porcelain ten stories high, having on the top a small ornament with six rings and volves which, being multiplied by four, express the latitude of Canton at the southern extremity of the Empire. Thus this porcelain tower couples the history of heaven with that of the country in which it stands; for in the latitude of 40 degrees the North Pole is elevated so as to shew but six volves. These are facts which they never could have imagined; they must therefore have registered those circular figures from time to time as they had been observed in remote antiquity.

"Again in Egypt, we find the statue of Pluto with a serpent coiled six times around him, which represent the six volves of the Pole of the Ecliptic round the South Pole of the Earth; which shews that the statue must have been erected at about Thebes or Elephantine. Thus we see from Pekin to Elephantine and from Nineveh to the extremity of Hindoostan that the men of learning all agree in coupling the histories of their countries with that of the heavens and the ravages of the elements in those remote ages. . . ."[3]

From S. A. Mackey's *The Mythological Astronomy of the Ancients* (1824)

▲

215

APPENDIX F

PHILOLOGICAL ISSUES

The Bantu-speaking Peoples of Africa

The *Encyclopaedia of Language and Linguistics* says of the geographical origin of the proto-typal Bantu language: "One important hypothesis regarding the expansion of the Bantu languages says that they most likely originate from the border area between south-eastern Nigeria and Cameroun. From there the speakers migrated (eastward and southward) in different (unspecified) stages. . . ."[1]

There are now known to be some three hundred to four hundred Bantu languages in current existence, which would, by itself, imply a hugely ancient origin of the original root language, given the time involved in a (usually close-knit) tribal society being likely to spread and differentiate, both geographically and culturally. Philological research, however, is unable to provide any indication as to historical chronology where such antiquity is concerned. It is instead forced to rely upon reference to current anthropological orthodoxy, which, as earlier suggested, appears fundamentally ill-founded on this issue.

The Hamitic-speaking Peoples of Northwest Africa

The International Encyclopaedia of Linguistics says in relation to this subject: "For the past forty years, scholars have rejected a twofold division into 'Semitic' and 'Hamitic'; the latter was formerly conceived as comprising Berber, Cushitic, Egyptian, and part-Chadic. . . ."[2] *The Encyclopaedia of Language and Linguistics,* meanwhile, now co-classifies the Hamitic among the "Afroasiatic" or "Hamito-Semitic" group of languages.

The Berbero-Guanche Language

The International Encyclopaedia of Linguistics says of the Guanche language: ". . . extinct in the 16th century but formerly spoken in the Canary Islands. Related to the Berber language."[3]

The Basque Language

The International Encyclopaedia of Linguistics says rather curtly: "Basque is a non-Indo-European language. Its genetic affiliations are still unclear."[4]

Notwithstanding this, in his book *Dravidian Origins and the West,* Dr. N. Lahovary shows the clearly direct relationship between the Basque language and that of the Dravidians of southern India. He does so by demonstrating the existence of an ancient "Ligurian" linguistic culture that extended in ancient times from India, via Iraq and

Turkey, right across the eastern and northern Mediterranean to the Atlantic before being largely subsumed within the Indo-European cultures of the Celts in the west, the Serbs and Caucasians from the north, and the Hamito-Semitic peoples from the south. In pointing out the general differences between the African Bantu languages and those of the Hamito-Semites and Dravidians on one side and the Indo-Europeans on the other, he makes the following broad observations:

1. That the Bantu languages not only utilize a greater preponderance of vowels, they also rely upon tonal changes to provide the necessary linguistic separations that give rise to different meanings;
2. That the Hamito-Semitic family and Dravidian languages utilize a far greater preponderance of consonants (balancing them with vowels), but are fundamentally agglutinative in nature—i.e., short root idea-words are simply joined together to provide broader ideas or complexities of meaning, according to their order;
3. That the Indo-European family of languages, based upon the Sanskrit, not only utilizes a highly concentrated and complex mix of consonants (with vowels being either concealed or highly accentuated) but also permits forms of individual word modification, including variations of inflection, which produce considerable cultural elasticity by compression or extension.

When considering the cultural background of the more ancient linguistic systems, he interestingly remarks:

> We think that the remarkable stability of these archaic languages is due, at least partly, to a psychological factor, too often lost sight of. The word, the name of a being, or of an object, had in those ancient languages, as is still the case with ancient Hebrew . . . a more or less magical value. Saying a name could call forth, in the literal sense of the term, the being or the thing; for a noun was tied to the being or thing so named somewhat as its shadow. That is the reason for the numerous interdictions to give gods a name, or to call them by their name, adjectives or the names of their attributes being used instead. The same taboo applied to the names of dangerous animals, or of originally totemic ones for the same reason. There are still today many examples of this mental attitude, in the languages of the Pacific Ocean islands and even in the Berber of North Africa.
>
> Under these circumstances, we can conceive that a name had an almost ritual value. It was therefore essential not to modify it, but to preserve it as faithfully as possible and to pronounce it always correctly, failing which it would lose its "efficiency." Even at a time when these ancient notions had been more or less forgotten, the habits acquired during so many centuries still lasted and preserved the word in its ancient form, imparting to the language an age-long stability, unknown to the languages of more recent civilizations.[5]

Not only does this serve to confirm what was said in chapter 5 concerning the ancient Egyptian attitude toward ritual and sympathetic magic, it also gives a very firm indication that the much discussed possibility of a worldwide "prehistoric" civilization and culture is no mere pipe dream.

APPENDIX G

THE EGYPTIAN VERSION OF THE INNER CONSTITUTION OF MAN

Egyptian Version	Function	Indian Version
ATMU	a divine or eternal Intelligence	ATMA(N)
PUTAH	the principle of Reason	BUDDHI
SEB	the ancestral Identity	SABDA (the "Word," or "vehicle," of divine Intent)
AKH(U)[1]	the (dualistic) perceiving Intelligence	MANAS (the personal reincarnating "Ego")
KHA-BA	the (postmortem) shade	KAMA-RUPA
BA	the "astral" soul	JIV-ANU
KHA	the "presence," or "breath"	JIVA[2]
KA	the (etheric) "double"	KAYA/LINGA SARIRA

Egyptian Hieroglyphic Names

1. CHU	divine Spirit	
2. CHEYBI	spiritual soul	
3. BAI	the rational soul	
4. ABHATI	the animal soul, or feeling principle	
5. ANKH	vitality, the Life principle, *prana*	
6. KA	the protean "double"	
7. CHAT	the dense physical body form	

APPENDIX H

CONCERNING THE DUAT

The Duat, or Tuat, is commonly translated by Egyptologists as "the Underworld," but this expression is highly misleading because of its connotations with the Christian and Muslim "Hell"—a concept completely at odds with the ancient Egyptian way of thinking. The Egyptian symbol for the Duat was a valley between two mountains, with a river running along the length of it—the Nile being regarded as its terrestrial counterpart and the Milky Way as its celestial confrère. On each bank of the river there supposedly lived a vast number of daemonic and elemental entities, among whom were to be found a host of apparently malcontent spirits, hostile to any extraneous creature or being who entered the valley.[1]

FIGURE H.1. EGYPTIAN SYMBOLIC REPRESENTATION OF THE DUAT

The symbolism of the Duat has, from the outset, caused Egyptologists a great deal of puzzlement because of its clearly astronomical associations. Yet what could it possibly represent? In fact, the answer becomes rather clearer when we draw an association with the natural *vesica piscis* shape of star clusters found at the center of our own galaxy, for the great god of objective Creation in the universe was Tum (Atum-Ra). He was represented by the Egyptians as a self-emanating mound in space—hence the English word *tumulus*—the upper part of the *vesica*. But below the celestial horizon we see the valley shape of the Duat in the "reflection" of the tumulus. Within the confines of this combined duality, the solar god Ra-Tem (the lesser alter ego of Atum-Ra) was then depicted as pursuing a perpetually revolving cycle of existence. Half of this cycle was spent above the celestial horizon—hence the idea of the "day sun"—while the other half was spent below it in the "valley" of the Duat—as the "night sun." When the two movements are brought together, however, in one continuously flowing cycle, we see the full, wavelike shape of the Duat, as depicted by the Egyptians.[2]

FIGURE H.2. SECTIONAL VIEW OF THE GALAXY

The valley of the Duat itself had twelve divisions, which were associated with the twelve hours of the night by virtue of the tradition that the "dead" sun god Ra passed through

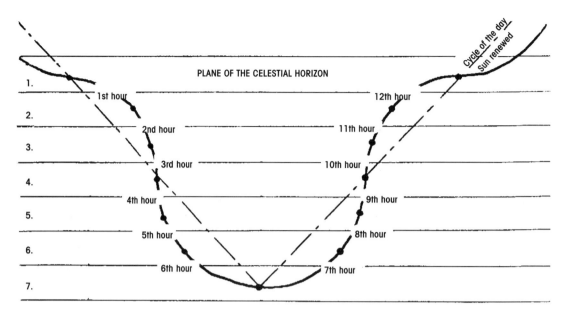

FIGURE H.3. THE CYCLE OF THE NIGHT SUN THROUGH THE DUAT

them during the night en route to that place (supposedly in the heavens) at which he rose again, renewed, at the beginning of each day. Now, the number twelve provides an immediate suggestion of there being an underlying association with the zodiac. However, we have otherwise pointed out that the Egyptian system of states of being (represented by them as circles) was in fact sevenfold. Is there then a conflict? Well, the short answer is no—provided that you begin with the understanding that the Underworld is as seen from above—i.e., from the macrocosmic, divine state—and not from the purely anthropocentric human point of view, which actually forms a part of it. The answer to the conundrum is shown in figure H.3.

Figure H.3 depicts the seven states of being that, as one composite, comprise the lowest of seven macrocosmic planes—in line with the dictum "As above, so below" of the divine Thoth–Hermes Trismegistus. Thus the progression downward and back again to the highest (divine) substate necessarily involves twelve sequential stages, as we can easily see. The downward "fall" then involved the temporary "death" of the god consciousness, which, however, was fully recovered, or renewed, at the moment of regaining the divine state. From a rather different angle, the representation of the Duat as a valley between two hills is a perfect metaphor of a cycle of incarnation, for the Duat—on a constant day-following-night basis, pursues a wavelike, serpentine (or helical) path, with crests and troughs, zeniths and nadirs.

It should always be kept very firmly in mind that the Egyptians openly regarded Osiris himself as the very personification of the Duat.[3] Consequently, the otherwise paradoxical idea of the sevenfold nature of the objective deity (Osiris) also being synonymous with the twelve hours of the night (during which Ra travels through the Underworld) makes complete sense. Predictably, the very same image (and meaning) is evident in the Greek myth of Helios ("Hel-Eos" being the luminescent light of the lower planes of existence), which Christian and Islamic theologians have so traduced in their bizarrely confused conceptions of "Hell."

APPENDIX I
CONCERNING THE GOD-NAME SEKER

The term Seker, or Sokar, as applied to Osiris in his "risen" form as Ptah-Seker-Ausar, appears to be particularly related (in symbolic terms) to the necropolis of Thebes. The Shabaka Texts confirm that Osiris was buried there within a large expanse of the surrounding area,[1] and otherwise that Seker is where Osiris "came into the Earth," assisted by Isis and Nephthys.[2] The Pyramid Texts helpfully add that Isis and Nephthys "found Osiris . . . when his name became Seker"[3]—i.e., when his phenomenal nature began to manifest, presumably as a sphere of light.

We have already mentioned in chapter 7 the direct association between Seker and the circling dance of the Sufi dervishes, the *zhikr*. We have also suggested an association between Memphis and the sacral chakra of the god; and in further verification of that, the Shabaka Texts tell us: "He (Horus) is the uniter of the Two Lands, proclaimed in the great name "Ta-tenen," "South-of-his-Wall," "Lord of Eternity" . . . in the district (nome) of the Wall (i.e., Memphis) the place where the Two Lands were united. Then sprouted the two Great Magicians (uraei, symbolic of the Souls) upon his head. . . ."[4]

The name Ta-tenen is, we suggest, yet another pun. Thus for *Ta* read *Ptah* and for *tenen* read *tenon*—the modern word (passed down by master masons from antiquity) used by carpenters to describe the projecting (male) end of a piece of wood that fits into a receiving (female) mortise section to bring about a perfect union, directly reminiscent of sexual correspondences. We would suggest that the overall implication is that the "Two Lands" represent the higher and lower consciousness of the god, which—when united—become self-creative. Thus it is that the Osiris principle is drawn into the "Wheel of Rebirth."

Seker (hence, quite certainly, the modern place-name Saqqara) otherwise appears to occupy the whole of the Fourth Division and part of the Fifth Division of the Duat, the latter being where the "capital city" of Rastau was located.[5] The latter place was depicted as protected by a double-headed, back-to-back sphinx called Aker (elsewhere described as a hierarchy of gods ancestral to Ra himself[6])—which, we suggest, is merely another alter ego of As-r (i.e., Osiris). While it would take far too long to go into great detail here, the implication is (yet again) that of the fourth and fifth planes of consciousness in the septenary system (counting downward) which we have already seen otherwise described. Thus the Fifth Division is consistent with the mental (or psychological) plane, or state, from which emerges the (Egoic) creative impulse (the *akhu*), which descends into mother-Matter. Interestingly, R. O. Faulkner (translator of the Pyramid Texts and the Coffin Texts) interprets Seker as "the term for a ramp or slide for moving the sarcophagus into a tomb."[7] However, quite apart from the other, obvious connotations, the word perhaps indicates in a generalized sense an inclined celestial axis—perhaps therefore comprising definitive "roads" to and from the stars along which gods, demigods, and other advanced souls might travel.

APPENDIX J

CONCERNING SEBEK, SET, AND HORUS

The Path to Immortality is hard and only a few find it. The rest await the Great Day when the wheels of the universe shall be stopped and the immortal "Sparks" shall escape from the sheaths of substance. Woe unto those who wait, for they must return again, unconscious and unknowing, to the seed ground of the stars, and (there) await a new beginning.

—FROM THE *DIVINE PYMANDER* OF HERMES TRISMEGISTUS

In order to understand the essential nature of the esoteric metaphor involving these various identities (and all their various subidentities in the Egyptian system of thought), it is necessary to bear in mind at all times that they symbolize characteristic aspects and faculties in Nature with which we as human beings are already familiar, through direct experience of them in our own consciousness. In brief, they symbolize the expansive (creative) and contractive (disciplinary) instincts within our nature, which is a reflective microcosm of the very same principles throughout Universal Nature.

To begin with, then, Sebek the crocodile god and Horus the Elder jointly represent the twin aspects of the objective nature of the incarnating god (Ra). Sebek is that aspect of the invocative Demiurge (the Divine Soul) that draws down the wholly noumenal divinity into the sphere of potentially objective being. Horus the Elder represents the cosmically reawakened consciousness of the Demiurge in its latent, or potential, state. Behind and above both of these, however, stands the figure of the cosmic Set, whose full name, Setekh, appears to be derived from two words—*Set* and *Akh*—denoting the beam of light that is projected from the Eye of Ra. It is this beam of light that, containing within itself the massed hierarchies of "divine sparks" (the *akhu*, or "little Eyes"), represents the greater returning consciousness of the Logos (Amen-Ra); for these are the divine progenitors of Man (Adam Kadmon) himself. It is therefore through the auspices of the macrocosmic SET that the eventually and individually Self-evolved Intelligence (Ptah-Seker-Ausar) will ultimately return "home" to his point of origin within the mind of Ra as a fully fledged *akh*, otherwise known as an Unas—a perfected god-man.

As the "Divine Sparks" fall into the field of generation, they begin to differentiate into subgroups, although ignorant of the various states into which they are falling. Some of these "divine infants"—like the humble but potent hydrocarbon in a drop of rain—instinctively set about reorganizing their newfound environment, thereby carving their own personal "kingdom" out of the local field of Nature. These ignorantly self-seeking "sparks" are then what the Egyptians typified as the lesser, or microcosmic, Set—the local "adversary" with the forked tail, peculiarly shaped head, and squared ears.

Although the Sebek principle (associated astronomically with the constellation of Draco) is clearly responsible for dragging the "sparks of light" down into the sphere of objective existence (provided by the "World Soul"), it falls to the god Khnemu to design the many and varied body-forms that the "sparks" will adopt, from the highest to the lowest; for the originally single hierarchy of "sparks" differentiates into many subhierarchies, each of which then "falls" to a different level in the various planes of being within the World Soul. Horus the Elder, on the other hand, representing the highest aspect of (universal) consciousness of the Demiurge, is concerned with the evolution and eventual liberation of the consciousness of the as yet almost blind "sparks." However, it is the Ptah principle that is depicted as animating the various body-forms created by Khnemu.[1] Thus it is these two who are described and depicted as the "Great Architect" (or "Artificer") who jointly create Man "upon a potter's wheel"—the revolving plane of the zodiacal ecliptic.

It should be obvious from this that Osiris represents that aspect of the "fallen" consciousness of Ra that can descend no further than the intermediate spiritual plane within the World Soul. Hence it is here that we find the plane of light (again, the Milky Way) that divides the ethereal upper world from the phantasmal lower world into which the angled "ladder" of the Duat is dropped. Only a fragment of the light from the spiritual plane can descend to the lower depths, and it is this that was depicted in the forms of Horus the Child (who, descending via the ecliptic path, was stung in the leg by the zodiacal Scorpion) and Horus the Younger. However, it is the latter aspect that comes into direct conflict with the lowest of the "fallen" (and by now "lost") "sparks" which originally emanated from the Eye of Ra.

These, as already suggested, are the microcosmic Set, the fount of the increasingly self-centered nature that (via evolution through the mineral, plant, and animal kingdoms) reaches its lower apotheosis in the human being. However, once these two opponents (Set and Horus) have come to terms with one another, they become the strangely composite Horus-Set figure (see fig. 6.5).

The phenomenal effect of this is to be seen in man's own everyday experience when purely personal instincts react against the naturally philanthropic spiritual impulses that well up within his consciousness. Our selfish, elemental instinct is thus itself Set, while the hovering and swooping spiritual sense is the Horus nature in action. Once these are reconciled—with the Horus nature in overall command—there begins a fresh cycle of evolutionary activity, progressively involving the influence this time of Horus the Elder. The latter, as the expression of an already extant spiritual (as opposed to merely human) consciousness, then works with Horus-Set and Anubis-Apuat to enable the Osiris nature in man to begin the heavenward climb back to its Source. However, there then follows yet another and even more titanic phase of conflict—this time between Horus the Elder and Sebek.

The ancient Egyptian depiction of the constant struggle for supremacy between these two superior protagonists derives from the idea of the by now semidivine Individuality (in man) having to fight to maintain its identity against the instinctively entropic tendencies of cosmic Nature. Thus, the spiritual figure of Horus the Elder eventually transmutes into the semidivine Horus-Behutet, the "son" of Ra-Herakhte (symbolically represented as the winged disk). His aides are the Shemsu-Heru (the "Companions/Followers of Horus")—a sacred name signifying the company of adept-heroes of the spiritual hierarchy. They are sometimes referred to in the Egyptian texts, somewhat mystifyingly, as "blacksmiths." However, this is an esoteric metaphor related to the fact that their highly evolved capacities incorporate the ability to wield pure spiritual energy (light)—i.e., "celestial metal."

Herakhte means "Horus of the Horizon"—an expression that has to be taken in a dualistic sense because the "horizon" referred to is not merely the horizontal one at the end of our line of sight over the Earth. The Egyptians—recognizing that our world and its concentrically overshadowing soul counterpart were both spherical in shape—knew that the horizon is merely part (i.e., an arc) of what the Ancients called the "crystal sphere" (of the soul-body). The circumference of the latter was then the greater "horizon" of the body of Osiris within the periphery of which was believed to lie the greater Horus consciousness in a state of divine latency, or potentiality. When this same consciousness "fell" (as Sebek and Horus) toward the center of the sphere, the process of incarnation began, for at the center of the "crystal sphere" was our physical planet. Then, as the dawning light of the sunrise began to emerge upward, seemingly through the very crust of the Earth into the outer world, so light began to flood the sky. That which had been darkly latent and had fallen had now become self-creatively active, manifesting itself as a sphere of light. The daily reappearance of the Sun thus became symbolic of the cyclic reemergence of Ra in the form of the multifold Horus-consciousness of mankind in the mass, from which the individual then emerged as a single ray of light, eventually liberating itself from the greater mass.

Interestingly, in that respect, we find *hor* or *her*—the Egyptian root of the name Horus—scattered around in other traditions, on every occasion producing the same idea of spiritual liberation through personal effort. In the Greek tradition, Herakles (our Hercules) is none other than *Hera-kleos* (*kleos* being a Greek word meaning "famous"), while our own word *hero* comes from the same source. There are many other such examples—south of Egypt, in East Africa, we find among the speakers of Swahili (a mixture of Bantu and Arabic) the word *uhuru*, meaning "freedom." Mount Sinai—from which Moses was said to have ascended from this world—was otherwise referred to in Exodus as "Mount Hor-eb."

It is as a result of the semidivinity and consequent spiritual freedom of the truly initiated pharaohs and temple hierophants that they were shown as possessing the capacity to wield spiritual force in the very literal sense of its life-giving power. Hence it is, we suggest, that so many artistic depictions show the pharaoh (as well as the gods themselves) pointing the ankh at someone else in apparent benediction. It seems as though this is probably another visual metaphor indicating the use of the breath in the same way as the Sufi sheikh does in giving the blessing of *baraka* (virtue). There are, among the Egyptian records, various traditions of nobles and even princes from other countries coming to Egypt in order to have the pharaoh breathe upon them and thereby invest their activities with his blessing.[2]

In concluding, therefore, it is clear from close study of the various metaphors and allegories that Horus is ever representative of the principle of self-conscious Intelligence in the furtherance of Divine Purpose on behalf of the "Ever Unseen God." It is because of this that the principle is represented as the hovering hawk—which closely overshadows the outer persona and invests it with the higher sense. It is here that the symbolic conflict with Sebek arises, for Sebek (in our world) represents the incessant and unquestioningly repetitive recycling principle throughout visible and invisible Nature. Set, on the other hand, fulfills a complementary function in objective Nature on behalf of the Logos. Perhaps that is why we find the presence of (the macrocosmic) Set active at the temple of Ombos?

APPENDIX K

The Circumpolar Stars and the "Mill of the Gods"

In order to understand the significance of the ring of circumpolar stars to the Ancients we must again wander into the field of metaphysics. The Ancients—as we have already seen—viewed any "field of creation" as spheroidal, or "atom-shaped," in its pregenetic nature. As we have also seen, this eternal, self-regenerating, spheroidal entity (the "soul" principle) produced out of itself, at the beginning of each cycle of self-existence, an inherent principle of polarity that gave rise to the dual "Father-Mother" principle. It was then in the organic interaction of these two polarities that the third universal principle (the Son, manifesting as light and expressing equilibrium) came to appear.

In figure K.1A, we see this same progression, with the overlapping circles of influence representing the third principle. But it is in the latter that the first phenomenal manifestation occurs—in the form of the circumpolar stars, hence the heaven world of the Kabiri-Titans (Elysium) ruled by Kronos (Saturn). Figure K.1B, then, depicts a second interaction in which the Kabiri and the cosmic "Mother" principle unite—hence the allegorical story of Oedipus, who unwittingly "married his mother"—thereby engendering the parallel story of the "fallen Elohim."

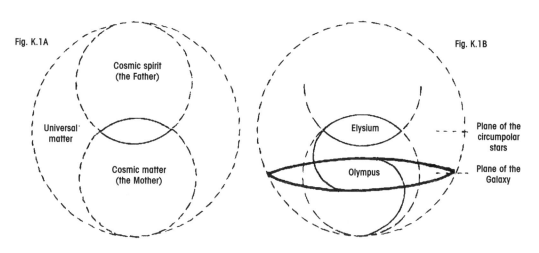

FIGURE K.1. THE COSMIC PRINCIPLES OF FATHER, MOTHER, AND SON

The product of this latter creative union was then the multiplicity of stars constituting the plane of our galaxy—the Greek "Olympus" ruled by the "fallen" Titan couple Zeus-Hera (i.e., the dual "Iao(s)-Heva," or "Jahve"). This is also the "metal plate of heaven" that we find in the Egyptian tradition. As we can see from figure K.1B, the triple universal principle has repeated itself on a lower turn of the spiral, for all phenomenal existence—whether ethereally subtle or physically objective—takes place within the field of "the Great Mother." However, it is in the movement of individual sidereal systems above and below the celestial equator (i.e., the "Duat") that the various ancient myths of "gods, heroes, and men" appear to have been derived. It is also from this that the principles of "esoteric geometry" (and its accompanying numerological significances) can be derived.

If the Titans—the Kabiri, or Kheperi—were indeed the "self-born cosmic sons" of the "eternal Father-Mother," it is here that we find the origin of the ancient teaching as to man's own essential divinity, for the twin hierarchies of (divine) Man and Angel together constituted the complementary aspects of the consciousness of a parent Titan-god. The temporary "death" of the latter (by segmentation and a "fall") was then always followed in the myth by a process of cosmic regeneration (through a gradual spiritual individualization—as a "hero"—of mankind) in which the eventually reconstituted consciousness became that of a fully fledged hierarchy of individual gods. Hence it was that the ancient Egyptians had as their primary ambition a return (as a god) to the circumpolar stars.

In *Hamlet's Mill*, Giorgio de Santillana and Hertha von Dechend mention Ludwig Ideler having confirmed that "Kotb [i.e, Kochab], the common name of the Pole, really means the axle of the movable upper millstone which goes through the lower, fixed one—what is called the 'mill-iron.' . . . The sphere of heaven was imagined as a turning millstone, and the North Pole as the axle bearing in which the mill-iron turns. . . ."[1] In the context of Egyptian cosmogonic myth, the lower mill-iron into which the "hook" of the "axle bearing" fits is Ursa Major, which rolls around the plane of the Galaxy, within which we find the recumbent Osiris, representing the hierarchies of "fallen" gods. In this manner, the *apuat* of Ursa Minor was seen not only to hold the combined celestial mechanism (the divine heaven of the circumpolar stars and the lesser celestial heaven of the Milky Way) together, it also otherwise helped to crush the "harvested wheat" (arising out of human experience) and thus also to separate the life-regenerating essence from the "dead chaff."

Referring back to chapter 9 (and fig. 9.7 in particular), it would appear that at the southern celestial solstice, the two constellations of Ursa Major and Ursa Minor actually appear to mesh (the root word *mes* or *mesk* in Egyptian was associated with birth or conception[2]). This cyclical fusion of the three aspects of the "Mill of the Gods" is then followed by their disengagement—described in the Norse myth as the supposedly disastrous falling apart that causes complete disruption in Nature, with the "wrecked" millstone subsequently falling "to the bottom of the sea, with its hole become the funnel of the whirlpool."[3] But there its remains gave rise to the fertilization of the whole ocean—just as the severed phallus of Ouranos did in the parallel Greek myth.

In relation to figure 9.4, Ursa Minor (as the circumpolar *apuat*[4]) opens the "Eye of Ra" (the "brow chakra" of the god at Abydos). This critical conjunction is symbolized by the pregnant hippopotamus goddess, Ta'Urt—which is why, in the Dendera zodiac, Ta'Urt is

The Circumpolar
Stars and the "Mill
of the Gods"

▲

228

shown holding a peculiar, wedge-shaped instrument. The latter is clearly symbolic of the star Polaris in Ursa Minor, from which position projects the Apuat hound[5] (see fig. E.1). The fact that it appears to emanate from the awakening "Eye" also clearly confirms the nature of the oddly shaped projection (again, looking like a wedge) shown under the "Eye of Ra," thereby defining it as we have previously suggested. Hence, the light emanating from the "Eye" itself is the "wedge" that fixes the vertical polar axis associated with Polaris.

**FIGURE K.2.
THE EYE OF RA**

When we turn to the central axis of the "world mill" itself, we find that the Egyptians had incorporated it also into their religious and political symbolism. In figure K.3, we see two pictures of the "Djed pillar," one upright and the other at an angle to the vertical. Now, this particular totem was of immense significance to the Egyptians because, as the very "backbone" of Osiris, it signified both power and stable strength. By association, therefore, it represented the cultural stability and political majesty of the Egyptian empire itself! Reading between the lines, however, it is clear that it also symbolized the axial stability of the universe, often referred to as the "body of (the cosmic) Osiris." The two god figures in the relief also tend to corroborate the supposition of a "World Axis" symbolism, for the female figure (representing the celestial pole?) stands upright and supports it while the darker, male figure (representing the ecliptic pole?) is actually responsible for holding it in place at an angle to the vertical.

The construction of the Djed is itself of interest because there appear to be a number of integral, visual metaphors arranged into it, in sequence. For example, the two tall, spatula-shaped (also septenary) extrusions comprising the top of the Djed are otherwise to be seen incorporated into the high crowns worn by the cosmic gods, such as Amen-Ra, the god's head being taken by the world sphere on the uppermost register. The implication is that

FIGURE K.3. THE DJED PILLAR

The Circumpolar
Stars and the "Mill
of the Gods"

▲

229

this fourteenfold section represents the fourteen aspects of consciousness in universal Nature—i.e., the very source of all manifest existence. Yet more can be inferred from the four horizontal registers, the intervening designs between them, and also the lower half of the pillar itself, for these are all seemingly representative of Tattu. Rather interestingly, the clearly related Dravidian word *tettu*,[6] meaning "to weave," when associated with the Sanskrit *tattva*, indicates that the lower half of the Djed represents the "dynamic weave" of elemental Nature that comprises the engine and chassis of the objective universe.

The Circumpolar
Stars and the "Mill
of the Gods"

▲

230

APPENDIX L

CONCERNING URSA MAJOR

The constellation of Ursa Major (Khepesh in the Egyptian language, meaning "journey") was regarded symbolically, not only by the Egyptians, but also by several other ancient (and distantly located) cultures, as a "coffin." As Santillana tells us in *Hamlet's Mill,* the Sioux Indians of the United States do so, as do the Arabs, who call it a "funeral bier."[1] The Egyptians themselves gave to the pregnant hippopotamus goddess (who held the thigh of the cosmic bull attached to a chain) the highly significant name Ta'urt, the *urt* meaning a "coffin," or "cemetery"[2] (there also being associations with flooding), while *ta* is an auxiliary word meaning "to emit/cause to be/do/become something."[3] In the ancient Indian traditon, the *asuras* (fallen angels) were themselves emanated from "Brahma's Thigh." The Egyptian word for "leg" or "thigh" was *sebeq,* while *sebekh* meant "to be master of/have power over"[4] and the name Sebek was of course that of the crocodile god. These various phonetic similarities and double meanings are certainly not mere coincidences, however. All are related to each other, the central concept and the astronomical associations as described.

Now, if the *asuras* (As-r's) that were ejected from "Brahma's Thigh" were then indeed the hierarchy of As-r/Osiris, as we have suggested, the cycle of Isis and the dual Anubis-Apuat going looking for the fourteen pieces of his "corpse" is completely self-consistent, in both a mystic and an astronomical sense. The fact that the Mayan culture of ancient Mexico saw Ursa Major as the isolated single leg of Texcatlipoca, which the great cosmic crocodile (Cipactli) had bitten off (an

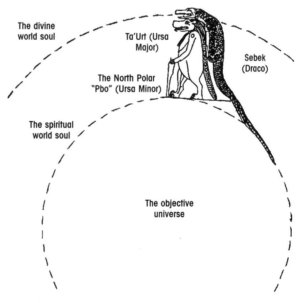

FIGURE L.1. THE GREAT TRIPLE CONJUNCTION AT THE CELESTIAL POLE

almost mirror image of Kronos cutting off the phallus of Ouranos), adds yet further corroboration (as Santillana again shows), for the zodiacal sign of Taurus is usually shown as being minus a limb or two.[5] Thus, quite logically, when Ursa Major and Taurus were seen closely reassociated in the heavens, the "Divine Bull" (temporarily) regained its potency, and this seems to have coincided (as far as the Ancients were concerned) with the appearance of a new cycle of mankind involving a new race (of souls?) appearing in our world.

Remembering how most ancient traditions had it that Creation began in the wake of a vast cosmic Flood, it seems highly probable that the latter referred to a flood of (star) light, rather than to a universal Deluge, as most interpreters would have us believe. Thus, if a swath of celestial light appeared cyclically to emerge from certain of the stars in Ursa Major and/or Ursa Minor (as meteor streams, perhaps?) by virtue of their cyclical associations in the sky relative to the celestial equator, would this not provide us with the origin of the "myth"? Alternatively, might it not be caused by the precessionary cycle drawing our solar system back through the plane of the Galaxy when the visual density of stars in the sky would be enormously increased?

The sequential story of the death and resurrection of Osiris clearly involves several major astronomical movements. In the first—which appears to involve a triple conjunction of Ursa Minor, Ursa Major, and the "head" of Draco—the implication is that the Titan god-hierarchy of As-r's associated with the constellation of Ursa Major is dragged downward (from a state of complete cosmic subjectivity) by Sebek (Draco) into a cycle of incarnate existence within the World Oversoul of our local system. This spheroidal Oversoul is the "Mill" (or "Quern") of the Gods of Norse legend, and we find Ursa Minor at its northern pole acting as the handle that the gods use to turn it on its axis. In the Egyptian tradition, this same World Oversoul is depicted as the permanently pregnant hippopotamus goddess, Ta'Urt,[6] known to the Ancients as the "World's Mother" and also the "concubine of (the cosmic) Set." As a result, these inseminated "fallen gods" become "trapped" inside her body only to emerge from there later within the "coffin" of their spiritual soul-bodies (*sahu*). Something of this is allegorically depicted in figure L.1 by the cosmic crocodile (i.e., Draco) climbing upon the back of Ta'urt. Ursa Major, breaking away from its temporary union with Ursa Minor (the latter elsewhere represented as the "heavenly axle" to the funeral carriage), now follows a downward path in the heavens (see the plinth upon which Ta'Urt stands in fig. L.1) during which it "mutates" into the leg of the cosmic bull (As'r-Hapi—the Greek "Serapis") and eventually swings into position, so it would seem, to replace the "missing leg" of Taurus.[7] This latter astronomical location is, however, also shared with that of the giant figure of Orion, with its seven stars. Consequently, we might suggest, the self-evident implication is that these two constellations—Ursa Major and Orion—also come into conjunction at some point in the overall cycle. The further implication then is that at least some of the spiritual souls (*sahu*) of the As-r's, hitherto contained by Ursa Major, are dropped off at this stage, within the constellation of Orion (also tellingly called Sah by the Egyptians) but can "fall" no further. Here they must therefore stay; but from this vantage point they can periodically influence the cycle of precession at the time of the celestial winter solstice, when the vernal equinox is in the sign of Leo. This, then, is the moment of Zep Tepi—"The Great Return"—and it would appear that it coincides with Ursa Minor being astronomically "in opposition" to Ursa Major.

Whereas at the time of the great conjunction of Ursa Minor, Ursa Major, and the head of Draco, the divine world and the spiritual world are united, when Ursa Major reaches the lowest point in its great outward cycle, it would appear temporarily to unite with and fertilize the lower world of the astral soul of Ra—represented by the precessionary cycle. Interestingly, in this respect, we find in the Indian esoteric tradition that the "Seven Brothers" of Ursa Major were regarded as being united by marriage to the "Seven Sisters" of the Pleiades—the latter having already been suggested as our own solar system's parent nebula.

As a consequence of all this, one might expect to find that the ancient esoteric tradition involved a succession of lesser "Divine Sparks" and spiritual soul hierarchies being forced to undergo experience in the lower world system. Here (again following the ancient tradition of universal self-sacrifice) they would themselves have to educate an evolving hierarchy of lesser "Divine Sparks" and soul-beings to take their place before they could themselves return "home." It is undoubtedly as a result of this lower union in the psycho-spiritual worlds that the phenomenon of mankind was believed to make its (temporary) appearance in our world system.

APPENDIX M

THE ASTROTERRESTRIAL AXES AMONG EGYPT, GREECE, AND THE LEVANT

Figure M.1 has fundamentally the same features as figure 9.7, although its range pushes much further northward into the Mediterranean and ancient Assyria. As we can see, by extending both the northeastern frontier of Egypt and the axis from Abu Simbel through Suez via Abydos, these are found to coincide on the southern coast of Cyprus. They appear to do so at a point consistent with the location of the tiny rocky island of Petra-tou-Romiou, which is where—so tradition had it—Aphrodite (Venus) was born, rising immaculately out of the foam of the ocean on a conch shell and then proceeding to Paphos on the west coast.[1]

The associated symbolism seems to point to the two main axes shown in the figure, axis A and axis C, which are parallel, representing the lower and upper peripheries of the "ocean of milk"—i.e., the plane of the Galaxy. Thus the diagonal axis between them should effectively represent the inclined (ecliptic) path that the pristine spark of divinity had to travel before emerging into objectivity as a "human (astral) soul." Bearing in mind that the Greek myth had Kronos, after castrating his father Ouranos, throwing the phallus into the ocean (where it disintegrated, so spreading his creative principle throughout Nature), the allegorical image of Aphrodite—symbolizing the attractive Love principle inherent in human experience—being born from the oceanic foam, is entirely consistent with the Egyptian myth of the missing Osirian phallus, as already described.[2]

An associated point of interest is that the northeastern frontier of Egypt (as shown) evidently symbolized the southern limit of the biblical "Promised Land" where the ancient "As-relites" eventually found themselves deposited by the cyclically returning "phallus" (or leg) of the cosmic bull (Ursa Major—see also fig. 9.4). The fact that Moses (apparently a form of "Ptah," as we have already seen) was not allowed to cross over the river Jordan (another interesting north–south axis), as the Old Testament has it, but is instead made to die of old age (although still hale and hearty) in the land of Moab[3] (just before the Israelites pass over the river border, led by Joshua), appears highly suggestive. It indicates that, its job being done, the divine principle of creativity that Ptah represents is withdrawn back into the Divine Consciousness (of Ra) to await the next great cycle of opportunity.

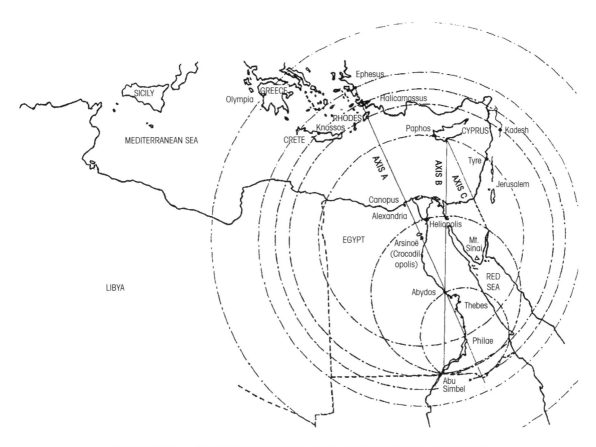

FIGURE M.1. ASTROTERRESTRIAL AXES ORIGINATING IN EGYPT

The way in which the whole biblical story is otherwise told might itself lead us to further questioning of many more accepted traditions, including the founding of Jerusalem itself by the "Khabiru-Hebrews." The same line of inquiry could well lead us to conclude that the original "crossing of the Red Sea" was only ever meant to describe a symbolic reference (probably of an astronomical nature) rather than an actual historical event—particularly when we discover that, as seen from Abydos, the distance from the Great Bitter Lake (where the crossing is believed to have occurred) to Mount Sinai covers almost exactly 40 degrees of arc, while the Israelites were supposed to have spent forty years in the Sinaitic "wilderness" before finally occupying the "Promised Land."[4]

In a different context, axis A coincides at its northern end on Rhodes with the circumference of the same circle that passes through Abu Simbel. The fact may be entirely coincidental, but the main city harbor on the island of Rhodes is where one of the Seven Wonders of the Ancient World (the Colossus) was supposedly to be found, while the Pharos of Alexandria (the first lighthouse and also one of the Seven Wonders) faced Rhodes across the Mediterranean along the very same axis. One wonders (if the axis is indicative) whether the fact that archaeologists have been unable to find the remains of either the Pharos or the Colossus (both said to have collapsed into the sea during an earthquake) is perhaps due to their so far having looked in the wrong places.

The Colossus (a huge bronze statue over one hundred feet in height) is known to have represented the Underworld solar deity Helios (derived by the Greeks from the Chaldeo-Assyrian Hel-Eos), and in this location—relative to axis A in figure M.1—one might speculate that it perhaps symbolized the furthest point of his "fall" or the perimeter of the ecliptic path as far as the territory of "Egypt" was concerned. The emphasis on the god's stance, supposedly (although improbably) astride a watery enclosure (a harbor), is itself suggestive. However, if we extend axis A yet further northward, we find that it passes quickly through Helicarnassus and then Ephesus—in each of which cities was also to be found one of the Seven Wonders of the Ancient World. At Helicarnassus stood the 140-foot-high marble "Mausoleum," supposedly built for King Mausolus by his sister-wife, Queen Artemisia, while at Ephesus stood the Temple of Artemis (Diana), a vast marble building, over 340 feet in length and 160 feet in width, and with some 127 columns over 60 feet in height. Are these ancient personalities then merely metaphors?

That these axes and circumferences passing through such symbolically important places (others are also shown in fig. M.1) could be pure coincidence strikes this author as somewhat improbable. It seems far more likely that ancient Arsinoë[5] (Crocodilopolis) was actually the main cartographic center of antiquity that Professor Hapgood was trying to find—as described in his book *Maps of the Ancient Sea Kings*—rather than Philae or Alexandria, as he originally thought probable.[6] Bearing in mind that Egyptian mystic tradition had it that it was here that "Ra rose in the First Time,"[7] the consistent carto-graphical and mystical orientation to Arsinoë (as a matter of course) of all major temples (and probably all cities generally) throughout the eastern Mediterranean seems quite logical, even over a period of possibly several millennia (or tens of millennia). That the orientation appears to have been fundamentally of an astronomical nature is also unsur-prising, given the fact that Sabean (star-oriented) religious cultures are known to have been general throughout the Middle East by the fourth millennium B.C. and must have long preceded that era.

APPENDIX N

CORRELATIONS BETWEEN THE EGYPTIAN AND GREEK MYSTERY SCHOOLS

Because so little is known of the actual rites of the Egyptian Mystery Schools, we are forced to gather much of our information on this subject by inference from a number of related sources. The Masonic ritual is one of these. The Greek Eleusynian, Orphic, and Bacchic Mysteries provide a further three,[1] the Greeks having—self-admittedly—drawn their knowledge and its associated customs from the Egyptians, very possibly via Crete, which was almost certainly at one time an Egyptian colony.

The Masonic ritual, first of all (although by now quite varied due to at least two millennia of progressive change by the French, English, Scots, and Americans), is fundamentally threefold in nature and progression—as one might expect from an Egyptian origin. The basic stages of initiation involve (1) Entered Apprentice; (2) Fellow Craft(sman); and (3) Master Builder.[2] However, it is clear that these initiatic orders, although secret in ancient days (because they involved knowledge far beyond that of mere building techniques), nowadays involve merely degenerate forms of an original ritual. Furthermore, there are grounds for surmising that, although not publicly discussed, there are higher (still deeply esoteric) orders and rituals that are still quietly pursued even today. Thus the so-called Raising of the Master would be but the prelude (if considered worthy) to a far higher series of initiations in which the exoteric Master Builder rebecomes an Entered Apprentice on a higher and wider turn of the evolutionary spiral.

The Eleusynian Mysteries are commonly believed by scholars to have commenced only about 1400 B.C., although this appears highly open to question. They were separated into the Greater and Lesser Mysteries, the latter being celebrated every year in the spring and the former in the autumn—although, so it appears, only every five years. Women and children were admitted to the Lesser Mysteries, which were clearly oriented toward a spiritually focused understanding of the cycles of Nature generally and the awakening of the "soul-sense." It also seems that the whole community was closely involved, only those who had killed another person being prohibited from taking part.

The rites of the Eleusynian Mysteries revolved around the legend of the abduction of the goddess Kore, or Persephone (the daughter of Demeter), by Hades—brother of Zeus and king of the Underworld.[3] The underlying theme involved principles of alternating

Correlations
between the
Egyptian and
Greek Mystery
Schools

▲

237

cycles of birth and death (i.e., regeneration). These graphically introduced the individual to the idea of the soul's conditional immortality, amid the immense hardships involved in reincarnation and the round of human existence. In the rites, the spiritual soul, astral soul, and the *ka* or "etheric double" of Nature in the round were symbolized by Zeus, Demeter, and her daughter Persephone, respectively, for Hades had stolen Persephone away to his Underworld kingdom. Demeter, who was responsible for the cyclical return of spring and the regeneration of Nature, refused to carry on her godly duties unless her daughter was returned.[4] Eventually, Zeus interceded and ordered that Persephone return to her mother for six months of the year, while otherwise remaining in the Underworld for the other six months as Hades' queen.

The Greek Underworld was almost a carbon copy of the Egyptian one, and it is quite clear that the original symbolism meant that the cyclical return of Persephone to her mother represented that period when the objective world underwent a period of spiritual "obscuration," prior to its regeneration by Persephone renewing her "imprisonment" in the Underworld (i.e., the outer world of human existence, akin to "captivity in Egypt"). However, the idea of the potentially individualizing divinity in man was not even incorporated into these Mysteries, but instead was found elsewhere, as we shall see.

It is suggested that the Orphic Mysteries actually provided the next, higher stage of initiatory progression—notwithstanding modern scholarship's refusal to consider such an idea. They involved the personalities of Orpheus and Eurydice, who seem, respectively, to have symbolized the spiritual Ego and the personality of the individual.[5] The story has Eurydice being stung in the heel by a venomous snake, then dying and going to Hades. Orpheus, her husband—a (spiritual) king in his own right and a follower of Dionysus since he once visited Egypt—goes after her and, descending into the Underworld, charms Pluto and Persephone with his music and singing. He then requests that she be allowed to return with him to the surface "of the earth"—symbolic of the natural heavenly state of the spiritual soul. Persephone intercedes with Pluto on his behalf, and Pluto eventually agrees on the sole condition that Orpheus not look back toward her during his return journey. Orpheus does of course look back, right at the last moment as he emerges into the "daylight," and so forfeits Eurydice, who has to remain in the Underworld forever.

Orpheus, represented as pining for his lost love, is himself torn to pieces by the Corybantes/Bacchantes (elemental followers of the god Dionysus) while sitting by the entrance to the Underworld, grieving for her.[6] This, somewhat stunningly, is represented as a "humane" act on the part of Dionysus, who feels sorry for Orpheus. However, the symbolism becomes clearer when we find that the Bacchantes, upon his orders, scatter the pieces of Orpheus's body across the land, while his head is put into the river Hebrus to float down to the sea. The head is subsequently recovered and thereafter kept "in a cave sacred to Dionysus"[7]—interestingly paralleled in the Egyptian tradition by the head of Osiris being supposedly buried at Abydos or the "secret face" of the hidden god Khem always being concealed in a sacred coffer guarded by the Apuat hound.

The esoteric meaning again stands clear, for it relates to the cycle of personal spiritual evolution. Originally, Eurydice (symbolizing Matter of a particular quality in the psycho-spiritual spectrum) is separated from the primordial heavenly state by the serpent—the

Correlations
between the
Egyptian and
Greek Mystery
Schools

▲

238

Demiurge—so signifying a new round of Creation and an associated duality of existence. Orpheus, after his first attempt, is no longer able to descend into the Underworld, but is forced to remain at its entrance for unspecified aeons, the "being torn to pieces" representing the prolonged and varied series of reincarnations of his projected nature that, quite separately, cycle through the Underworld and thereby assist in the evolution of elemental Nature through association. The severed head (which implies a continuity of postmortem existence) then seemingly represents the mind-knowledge, or Egoic memory (the *akhu*), which persists from cycle to cycle.

The third and final part of the Greek Mysteries involved the Bacchic, or Dionysian, Rite, which related directly to the cycles of experience of the "Divine Spark" (the Pythagorean Monad) itself—the highest aspect of the inner man. The story involves Dionysus, the already "twice-born" (with horns like Ptah and Moses, plus a crown of serpents[8]), after a series of adventures marrying Ariadne. She, it will be remembered, had provided Theseus with the thread to escape from the maze after he had killed the Minotaur, and she became the mother of Dionysus's six children, these plus the two parents representing a complete, esoteric octet.[9] Dionysus, however (somewhat like Orpheus), began childhood also by being torn to pieces, this time by the Titans after distracting him through fascination (like Narcissus) at his own appearance in a mirror—the latter appearing to represent the "soul-world" beneath the plane of divine existence. Having dismembered and eaten his body (an image very similar to the dismemberment of Osiris by Set), the Titans found themselves facing the wrath of Zeus (symbolizing the Divine Soul, or Demiurge), who hurled his thunderbolts at them and so burned them to cinders. The latter—inevitably containing the essence of Dionysus—then sprang to life as the human race, and, as the latter is seen gradually to become reunited (in consciousness of the higher orders), so Dionysus himself is esoterically made to become whole again.[10] In the meantime, however, so the tradition has it, the heart of Dionysus (representing the evolving spiritual Ego) was found by Pallas Athene (apparently symbolizing the evolutionary urge, or spiritual ambition in man) and, lifting it out of the elemental world, she placed it in an intermediate, heavenly world—i.e., that of the "spiritual soul," or *saha*. As we have already seen, the name Sah was that given to the constellation of Orion by the Egyptians, and its proximity to the star cluster of the Hyades produces yet another association. Hence the Greek tradition referred to them as the nymphs of Mount Nyasa, home of the Muses, who reared Dionysus as a child and who were thus rewarded by Zeus by being turned into a heavenly constellation.[11]

Again, the number of cross-correspondences with the ancient Egyptian mystical imagery appears very striking—particularly the symbolism of the god being "torn into pieces," which pieces then have to be recovered and reunited before the full cycle is complete. Interestingly, the Bacchic Mystery seems to have given rise to an ancient secret society called the Dionysian Architects. Their constitution, principles, and doctrines were very similar to those of the Freemasons, and they are known to have been responsible for the design and construction of many of the great buildings of Europe over the last two thousand years or so. It seems not unlikely that, although they themselves drew their origin and inspiration from ancient Egypt, the Arab and later European masons and cathedral builders were perhaps their direct descendants.

Correlations
between the
Egyptian and
Greek Mystery
Schools

▲

239

APPENDIX O

ON THE SIGNIFICANCE OF DOUBLE STATUARY IN EGYPT

Nowhere in the ancient world, other than in Egypt, do we appear to come across the sculpted phenomenon of differently sized but combined statues, the smaller standing on or immediately next to the feet of the greater. The essential meaning of this seems, so far, to have completely escaped both the logical and intuitive perceptions of most Egyptologists. This is despite the fact that every single artistic depiction in ancient Egypt—particularly the strangest-looking ones—always deliberately highlighted (while simultaneously concealing) deep esoteric truths. We find these particular statues at a select number of temples along the Nile. Figure O.1 is of one located at Luxor, and it has rather laughably been given an entirely literal name by scholars, who call it King Pir. Pir, however, is a Sufi name, very specifically denoting one of the stages of initiation on the Path at which the individual joins "the company of saints," or "spiritual lords"—hence the British "peers of the realm." The initiatory stage in question appears to be the first on "the higher Way," when the initiate becomes suffused with spiritual light "from above" although he has not yet achieved a fully realized spiritual self-consciousness.[1] By earthly standards, however, he is indeed a "king"—through now being in complete command of his own worldly nature.

We meet by comparison other, smaller figures elsewhere, with various associated meanings attached to them. On the west bank at Thebes we find the two seated god-figures of the "whistling Colossi" of Memnon, each with two smaller (female) figures by the side of their legs, the top of the heads of these being

FIGURE O.1. STATUE OF THE INITIATED "PIR" AT KARNAK

slightly lower than the gods' knees. At Abu Simbel, there are eight of these same-sized female figures standing on either side of the four sitting gods' legs, with four yet smaller ones in between the gods' legs. Egyptologists regard these twelve figures as the daughters of Rameses II, largely because they have not been prepared to cast their imagination any further afield. Bearing in mind the self-evidently varying height and type of headdress of each trio, however, it seems reasonable to surmise that each outer pair has spiritual/divine associations, while the smaller ones (with no headdress) between the legs of each god are correspondingly associated with the lowest and most objective sphere of existence.

Returning to the figure of "King Pir," however, it is surely noteworthy that the formal headdress of the smaller figure reaches up to the very fork of the legs of the greater figure. As the headdress appears to have represented that which is created by man to fit on top of the sevenfold organs of psychic perception in his head—thereby creating a "bridge" between the physical awareness and the psycho-spiritual state—does not this proximity automatically suggest a specific (generative) correlation between the two figures, perhaps as two aspects of one and the same intelligence? It is also interesting that only female figures actually stand on or adjacent to the gods' feet. Bearing in mind that the female nature was regarded as being instinctively and organically tied to the material world,[2] this surely reinforces our point of view. It is suggested, then, that the two figures at Luxor respectively represent the divine Self of the initiate (hence its titanic size) and the trans-figured astral soul-vehicle, the latter having "become" at one with the spiritual soul as a result of the Osiris-nature of the initiate having itself been liberated.

APPENDIX P

THE MEANING OF ETHER/AETHER ACCORDING TO THE PRINCIPLES OF HERMETIC SCIENCE

Until the mid- to late nineteenth century, the "etheric" state was a completely respectable and accepted part of orthodox scientific theory, which saw it as the invisible, underlying medium of all energy transference and atmospheric existence. That concept lost its credibility in the eyes of scientists when physicists came to the conclusion that the real substratum of Nature had to be a ubiquitous "soup" of subatomic particles that came together under certain (unspecified) conditions to form organized "atoms." This, in their eyes, disproved the age-old theory of the Greek philosopher Democritos that the atom (his *atomos* having been borrowed from the Egyptian *Atum*) was both eternal and indivisible and also moved around in a universally fluid "etheric" continuum, the constituent nature of which remained otherwise unspecified.

Regrettably, those same scientists failed to recognize that Democritos was actually describing the universal "soul" principle that, according to ancient philosophy, underlies and gives rise to all possible objective manifestation throughout macrocosmic and microcosmic Nature—from a universe to a mineral atom. They also failed to appreciate that the same ancient occult conception viewed the soul principle itself as having a concentric and hierarchical organization. Hence the greater soul entity, during its cycle of activity, emanated from itself a whole series (or ethereal spectrum) of lesser soul entities, each being a perfect, holographic microcosm of its parent. It is one such spectrum that constitutes the ethereal (i.e., "etheric") mass of the objective universe, the astrophysicist's "dark matter" being its most inertially concentrated form.

These atomic soul entities, then—comprising the fifth element in Nature, or rather the third in the unfolding sequence, according to occult science—were emanated from a sixth element-state (the second according to occult science), which appears to be the true (and altogether homogeneous) "atomic soup." The latter is readily equatable with what quantum physics calls the "chaos state" from which there puzzlingly emerges "order"— manifesting as the organized atomic (i.e., "soul") state in which the first archetypal dif-

The Meaning of
Ether/Aether
According to the
Principles of
Hermetic Science

▲

242

ferentiation occurs as the "aether." The septenary composition of the universe, commonly accepted by all ancient metaphysical systems of thought, thus seems to have arranged itself as follows:

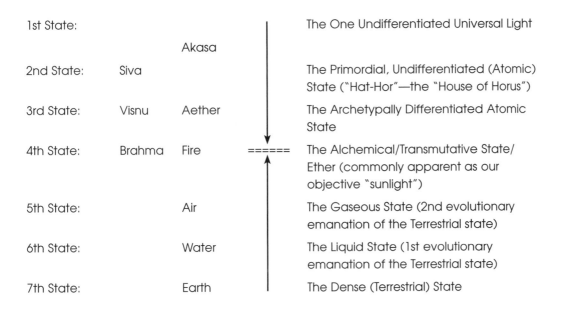

1st State:			The One Undifferentiated Universal Light
		Akasa	
2nd State:	Siva		The Primordial, Undifferentiated (Atomic) State ("Hat-Hor"—the "House of Horus")
3rd State:	Visnu	Aether	The Archetypally Differentiated Atomic State
4th State:	Brahma	Fire	The Alchemical/Transmutative State/ Ether (commonly apparent as our objective "sunlight")
5th State:		Air	The Gaseous State (2nd evolutionary emanation of the Terrestrial state)
6th State:		Water	The Liquid State (1st evolutionary emanation of the Terrestrial state)
7th State:		Earth	The Dense (Terrestrial) State

What even very few students of Hermetic philosophy seem to appreciate, however, is that this hierarchically septenary sequence was itself regarded as part of a yet greater spectrum of which it was but the seventh and lowest substate. Similarly, its own seventh state—the dense physical—contained within itself an exactly corresponding microcosmic septenary. This is the essence of the ancient idea that Creation was itself infinitely septenary—hence the ancient Hermetic axiom "As above, so below." What our modern physicist also fails to take into consideration in his researches is the possibility that the subatomic particle phenomena that he perceives in his experiments might themselves be merely evanescent ("etheric") elemental existences anchored by family ties to the octave of existence that we call the "mineral kingdom" (of which gases and liquids are but aspects), the field of which extends throughout the objective universe. Internally septenary (and inert) in their own right, the atoms can nevertheless be induced to produce a short cycle of phenomenal activity, emanating particles the path of which the physicist is able to trace in an emulsified liquid. The characteristics that the emanated particles demonstrate, however, are entirely dependent upon the quality and quantity of energetic force brought to bear upon them. Hence it is that every experimental variation in the scientist's laboratory will tend to produce another (interestingly, always triple) set of particles.

Hermetic science (in the hands of experienced alchemists) took the view that every gaseous atom contains within itself a characteristic "root essence" of the mineral kingdom, thereby providing the "signature" of its parentage and continuing relationship. Now, when each such atom is brought under compressive pressure by modern technology, the effect of releasing it is explosive—like that of a coiled spring unleashing its potential energy, so producing a phenomenal effect (i.e., particle "offspring")—akin to an electrical surge.

Alchemically, however, the gaseous atom, when sufficiently expanded (rather than compressed), reaches a critically sustained point of maximum tension and then momentarily inverts upon itself (i.e., it implodes) to produce a hugely powerful vortex. That vortex then draws into the field of the gaseous state (i.e., the atmosphere—the element of Air) the immensely potent (albeit noumenal) energies of the latent third (aether) state.[1] When occurring naturally, the air becomes electrically ionized with the literal "birth" of this hitherto latent energy, itself possessing a spectrum of creative intelligence—i.e., the "Brahma" principle. The divinely (i.e., ionospherically) impregnated matter then falls to earth and is thereby drawn into a vastly long evolutionary cycle through the mineral, plant, animal, and finally human kingdoms, through which experience it becomes immeasurably diversified in both character and faculty and also builds up a comprehensive memory of organic relationships.[2] Hence various parts of the mineral kingdom constantly exude an "etheric double," which thereby renders them chemically active.

In the ancient esoteric philosophy, Man—whether the microcosm or the macrocosm— was himself an integrated expression of all the seven states within a given spectrum (or "octave") of existence. However, only when fully aware of this fact did he become a fully fledged "god," even though already containing within his own auric field his very own soul-self-created universe.

The Meaning of
Ether/Aether
According to the
Principles of
Hermetic Science

▲

244

ON THE LEVITATION OF STONE
BY THE USE OF SOUND

While the levitation and suspension of the human body in midair has been witnessed and quite reliably attested to innumerable times throughout recorded history, the auto-levitation (and transportation) of huge stones seems to have far less evidence to support it. One well-known exception involves a large basalt rock some four feet in diameter and two feet in height at Shivapur in India. In apparent response to the mere recitation of the name of a local saint, this can be raised in the air by about six people, each using only one finger. This author personally knows someone with a doctorate in engineering science and an impeccable sense of objectivity who has himself witnessed this phenomenon twice. On each occasion, the rock remained suspended about five feet off the ground for about fifteen seconds and then fell back to earth with a huge thud.

The question of sound being able to produce autoreactive effects in materials and bodies (through sympathetic response to sonic waves) is neither new nor disputed by orthodox science. The effects vary between the reductively destructive—in which materials either slowly liquidize or otherwise shatter at a certain high frequency—and the coherently constructive—for example, in the case of a bow string drawn across the edge of a sheet of glass on which sand has been sprinkled, where the sand then organizes itself into clearly defined geometric patterns. These days, sound can even be used as a cutting tool. Actual levitation, however, remains a challenge.

In the book *Anti-Gravity and the World Grid*—comprising a selection of articles on the Earth's magnetic field as a grid that gives rise to all sorts of curious electromagnetic phenomena—there is an article by Bruce Cathie titled "The Acoustic Levitation of Stones." In it he cites "an intriguing extract from an article published in a German magazine" in which a Swedish engineer (in 1939) actually witnessed Tibetan monks levitating and projecting large stones a distance and height of some 250 meters during a local building project:

> In the middle of the meadow, about 250 meters from the cliff, was a polished slab of rock with a bowl-like cavity in the center. The bowl had a diameter of one meter and a depth of 15 centimeters. A block of stone was manoeuvred into this cavity by yak oxen. The block was one meter wide and one and one-half

meters long. Then 19 musical instruments were set in an arc of 90 degrees at a distance of 63 meters from the stone slab. The radius of 63 meters was measured out accurately. The musical instruments consisted of 13 drums and 6 trumpets.

Eight drums had a cross-section of one meter, and a length of one and one-half meters. Four drums were medium size with a cross-section of 0.7 meters and a length of one meter. The only small drum had a cross-section of 0.2 meters and a length of 0.3 meters. All the trumpets were the same size. They had a length of 3.12 meters and an opening of 0.3 meters. The big drums and all the trumpets were fixed on mounts which could be adjusted with staffs in the direction of the slab of stone. The big drums were made of 3 mm thick sheet iron and had a weight of 150 kg. They were built in five sections. All the drums were open at one end, while the other end had a bottom of metal on which the monks beat with big leather clubs. Behind each instrument was a row of monks.

When the stone was in position, the monk behind the small drum gave a signal to start the concert. The small drum had a very sharp sound and could be heard even with the other instruments making a terrible din. All the monks were singing and chanting a prayer, slowly increasing the tempo of this unbelievable noise. During the first four minutes nothing happened; then as the speed of the drumming and the noise increased, the big stone block started to rock and sway, and suddenly it took off into the air with an increasing speed in the direction of the platform in front of the cave hole 250 meters high. From time to time, a stone split and the monks moved the split stones away.[1]

Just how credible this story might be is uncertain because of the regrettably inadequate backup evidence, an associated film having apparently been "confiscated" by the firm for whom the Swedish engineer was working. The idea remains interesting, however, on the grounds of the author's associated theory as to acoustic geometry, rhythm, and pitch apparently creating a particular type of synchronistic energy "path" along which a large stone could be magnetically repelled from a starting point.

Bearing in mind that the 200-plus ton stone slabs forming part of the enclosure walls around the Sphinx could not have been moved into place by the largest and most powerful cranes in the world today[2] (the same being true of similar edifices at Tyrhens in Greece and at Machu Picchu in Peru), one is inevitably moved to wonder at an ancient engineering knowledge that we, with our much vaunted technology, are unable to replicate today. The latest orthodox hypothesis as to the ancient method of shifting large blocks of stone using human muscle power alone involves the use of sleds drawn along roads or ramps that have a surface coating of wet clay, which has a virtually zero resistance to traction. However—apart from the fact that no sign of clay has been found in relation to the surfaces of these large ancient edifices—this method will not work with very large blocks on any surface with an upward gradient of much more than 4 to 5 degrees to the horizontal. Even then, the problem of finally maneuvering and/or lifting such gigantic blocks into their ultimate resting places makes the whole process inconceivable.

If an altered surface tension—induced by a specific pattern of resonance—is indeed the key to the mystery, the problem remains an obdurate one for science. That is because the latter regards the principle of surface tension as quite different from that of magnetism, whereas ancient magical practice clearly seems to have believed that there was no fundamental difference between the two. In addition, whereas modern science has rejected the ancient belief in a universal fluid medium/agent (i.e., the ether, or world *ka*) from and to which all electromagnetic, physical, chemical, and other properties supposedly derive their genesis and final reversion, the Ancients clearly believed that they knew enough about it to draw at will upon its infinitely powerful mechanical properties, using a combination of mantric sound and creative visualization. That is unfortunately about all that can be said on the subject at present.

NOTES

Introduction

1. R. Bauval and A. Gilbert, *The Orion Mystery* (London: William Heinemann, 1994), chap. 10.

2. Bauval and Hancock have collaborated rather more recently on the highly successful *Keeper of Genesis* (London: William Heinemann Ltd., 2001), which, however, continues to focus all eyes on the Giza plateau in particular (and Heliopolis to a lesser extent) in relation to the idea of a treasure chamber of Atlantean information potentially being concealed under the Sphinx. However, as we shall see in later chapters of this book, by doing so they omit any possible mention of a vast amount of other, considerably more important "concealed" information scattered (very visibly) all over Egypt, most of it having an astronomically based nature, indicating a far, far older period of temple and pyramid building than they themselves are, as yet, willing to concede.

3. G. Hancock, *Fingerprints of the Gods* (New York: Crown Publishers, 1995), 267.

4. I. Velikhovsky, *Earth in Upheaval* (London: Abacus, 1956), chap. 1.

5. As Jeremy Naydler describes in his clear and well-argued book on Egyptian sacred culture, *Temple of the Cosmos: The Ancient Egyptian Experience of the Sacred* (Rochester, Vt.: Inner Traditions, 1996).

6. Regrettably, our contemporary theologians are so effete in the face of "rational" science that most of them hasten to avoid at all costs any attempt to rationalize the possibility of a definite, albeit supramundane, field of existence. But the materialistic turn in Egyptology occurred several decades ago. As Alexandre Piankoff (a well-known translator of Egyptian texts) says in his book *The Tomb of Rameses II:* "[T]he approach to the study of Egyptian religion has passed without transition from one extreme to another. For the early Egyptologists, this religion was highly mystical and mysterious. . . . Then came a sudden reaction; scholars lost all interest in the religion as such and viewed the religious texts merely as source material for their philological-historical research." A. Piankoff, *The Tomb of Rameses II* (Princeton: Princeton University Press, 1954), 33.

7. How, then, is it that a mechanically sophisticated astronomical computer (the "Antikythera") was found at the beginning of this century in a 2,000-plus-year-old shipwreck off the island of Rhodes? Archaeologists have made a replica model using more than thirty gears from the original. Dry cell batteries are also believed to have been in use over 2,000 years ago. But how old were these technologies already by then?

8. C. Scarre, ed., *The Times Atlas of Archaeology* (London: Times Books Ltd., 1988), 59.

9. Ibid., 120.

10. *Homo sapiens sapiens* was somewhat arbitrarily evolved out of politico-academic necessity by archaeologists as a later and supposedly more evolved form of the much earlier *Homo sapiens*.

11. However, the very latest findings in Southeast Asia (in Papua New Guinea in 1997) are now threatening to push this back to at least 200,000 years ago, while also throwing into doubt the standard orthodoxy that intelligent mankind originated in East Africa and from there spread to other parts of the world. See *The Times Atlas of Archaeology*, 62.

12. But see appendix D for further amplification and comment on these issues.

13. M. Bernal, *Black Athena: The Afroasiatic Roots of Classical Civilization* (London: Free Association Books, 1987), vol. 2, 274.

Chapter 1: Cosmic Seasons and Astronomical Cycles

1. R. A. Schwaller de Lubicz, *Sacred Science: The King of Pharaonic Theocracy*, trans. A. and G. VandenBroeck (Rochester, Vt.: Inner Traditions, 1982), chap. 7; J. Sellers, *The Death of Gods in Ancient Egypt* (London: Penguin, 1992), 193.

2. See West's *Serpent in the Sky: The High Wisdom of Ancient Egypt* (Wheaton, Ill.: Theosophical Publishing House, 1993); and, among others, Bauval and Gilbert's *The Orion Mystery;* Bauval and Hancock's *The Message of the Sphinx: A Quest for the Hidden Legacy of Mankind* (New York: Crown Pub., 1996); and Hancock's *Fingerprints of the Gods*.

3. Hancock, *Fingerprints of the Gods*, 241–64.

4. Bauval and Gilbert, *The Orion Mystery*, 196 (quoting Edgar Cayce).

5. Hancock, *Fingerprints of the Gods*, 270–71.

6. Amen-Ra clearly seems to have represented the principle of the universal Life-force, which although unseen is yet omnipresent in every microscopic fragment of the cosmos. As this principle was the very basis of all purposeful existence in universal Nature, it logically gave rise (in due cycle) to all manner of forms and hierarchies of intelligence and consciousness. Bearing in mind the widely accepted modern concept of natural evolution, in which organic forms gradually evolve out of cells, which are themselves evolved out of base atomic substance, the logical corollary of the theory is that all matter must, in fact, be fundamentally organic—that is, life-bearing. Ergo, the universe is itself organic. As atomically organized matter emerges from chaos to produce instinctive order (as confirmed by quantum mechanics) and as such an instinct can only be the product of memory (which is itself a faculty of consciousness), it logically follows that natural order and consciousness are twin aspects of one and the same universal Life principle. Thus, the universe is not only organic, it also possesses an infinite field of consciousness out of which emerges an evidently hierarchical spectrum of evolving intelligence. Hence, we might suggest, there is fundamentally little difference in the direction in which modern science is traveling and the metaphysical beliefs of the Ancients—only modern science has not quite "arrived" at the same, inevitable point of perception.

7. E. A. W. Budge, *The Gods of the Egyptians*, 2 vols. (New York: Dover, 1969), vol. 2, 69.

8. C. H. Hapgood, *Maps of the Ancient Sea Kings* (London: Turnstone Books, 1966), 175.

9. F. Press and R. Siever, *Earth* (San Francisco: Freeman, 1974), 252–56.

10. Rather curiously, our scientists seem to believe this phenomenon to be specific to Earth, due to another theoretical "wobble" in the planetary axis. We seek to show why that view may be in error in appendix A at the back of the book, where the direct mathematical and astronomical relationship between the Sothic year (involving a 1,460-year cycle of great importance to the Egyptians) and the Great Sidereal Year is also explained.

11. Schwaller de Lubicz, *Sacred Science*, 170–71.

12. Such ideas are anathema to modern astronomical orthodoxy, which regards the phenomenon of precession as purely Earth-specific and due entirely to the pushing and pulling influences exerted by the Sun and Moon on our planet's own magnetic field. The mathematics of such influences, though carefully worked out by scientists to support this idea, make no allowance for the inherent possibility that such influences might themselves be repetitive components in a mathematically self-consistent series of such influences within our galaxy—that is, a microcosmic "clone," like a wave within a greater "carrier wave."

13. S. Hawking, *A Brief History of Time* (New York: Bantam, 1990), chap. 3.

14. Rather interestingly, the four main festivals of the Celtic year—Samhain, Imbolc, Beltane, and Lugnasad—were held at times corresponding with the beginnings of our calendrical months of November, February, May, and August. Nobody has hitherto been able to explain the rationale of these timings because they do not even nearly coincide with the annual equinoxes and solstices of our

Earth year. As these festivals occur one decanate (ten degrees) into the respective zodiacal houses of Scorpio, Aquarius, Taurus, and Leo, one is forced to concede the probability that the Celtic tradition was itself based on the greater astronomical environment and was thus tied to the celestial equinoxes and solstices of the Great Year rather than to those of the ordinary solar year.

15. See Hapgood, *Maps of the Ancient Sea Kings*, 178–86. Such precipitation in the tropical and subtropical zones of our planet would undoubtedly have been paralleled by snowfall of equally heavy and prolonged magnitude in the polar and temperate zones, thereby re-creating the ice caps and also the phenomenon of glaciation extending from the caps toward the subtropics.

16. Ibid., 178.

17. Press and Siever, *Earth*, 252–56.

18. Ibid., 255.

19. J. Petterson, *Scientific American* (August 1950).

20. As our own astronauts have discovered while orbiting Earth, our planet—seen from its dark side—is fundamentally an electrically driven organism: The vitality of the lower atmosphere that provides the continuity and fertility of organic existence in nature is derived from incessant lightning storms (dozens at a time) constantly circling the globe.

21. Velikhovsky, *Earth in Upheaval*, chap. 1.

22. M. Murray, *The Splendour That Was Egypt* (London: Sidgwick and Jackson, 1962), 299.

23. During a total eclipse of the Sun, all the brightest stars and planets can be clearly seen in the daytime sky from within the area of shadow. At this time also, the air itself suddenly becomes very still and the temperature drops sharply. This could not logically arise if "sunlight," per se, existed between the sky and the observer in shadow.

24. The Ancients seem to have recognized this as well and to have accordingly incorporated the idea into their stories of the escapades of the gods and demigods. The astronomical basis of Greek and Hindu myth, for example, is particularly self-evident, although modern scholarship has inverted the true picture by suggesting that the astronomical associations only followed in the wake of such "semibarbaric" traditions, themselves the supposed product of mere superstition.

25. Press and Siever, *Earth*, 16–21.

26. Modern scientific theory is only just beginning to come around to the idea that levity might actually be a force in its own right—one, however, that is the wholly natural counterpart to gravity. Nevertheless, research into this proposition is still at an early stage and it has thus not yet become part of established scientific orthodoxy. However, another school of thought has it that gravity and levity are both merely aspects of the universal law of attraction and repulsion and are thus not separate forces at all. So much for the Grand Unified Theory!

27. Press and Siever, *Earth*, 498–522.

28. Plato, *Timaeus and Critias*, trans. D. Lee (London: Penguin Classics, 1971), 35. Also see appendix B.

29. "These two visitations [of destruction by fire and water], we are told, descend in turns after very long cycles of years. When the agent is the conflagration, a stream of heaven-sent fire pours out from above and spreads over many places and overruns great regions of the inhabited Earth." Philo, *On the Eternity of the World*, vol. 9, trans. F. H. Colson (Cambridge: Harvard University Press, 1941).

30. H. P. Blavatsky. *The Secret Doctrine* (Los Angeles: Theosophy Company, 1947), vol. 2, 785.

31. Ibid.

32. *The Pyramid Texts*, 2051.

33. Notwithstanding that meteoric iron was indeed used for certain sacred instruments.

34. As M. Riordan and D. Schramm discuss in *The Shadows of Creation* (Oxford: Oxford University Press, 1993), chap. 3, interestingly, the cutting edge of modern astrophysics has itself accepted the fact that all galaxies are surrounded and interpenetrated by vast haloes of electromagnetically

charged "dark matter" (the nature of which is not yet understood) that are themselves somehow responsible for the continuing coherence and gravitational stability of each galaxy in space. But if this is the case with galaxies, why should not the same principle hold good for individual solar and planetary systems, as well as for man himself? In addition, astrophysical research has discovered that galaxies seem to cluster socially in space, not at random, but "like filaments," in a manner that looks "foam-like or sponge-like in appearance" (pp. 138–39). But is this fundamentally any different to the way in which the auric (that is, "etheric") "double" of man the microcosm appears to the clairvoyant? We doubt it, and we might otherwise mention in addition that the cellular structure of bone as seen under the microscope also takes on a very similar appearance. Bearing these facts in mind, the mention in the Pyramid Texts of the bones of the cosmic Osiris being of "celestial metal" clearly implies that the ancient Egyptians were somehow able to see into or otherwise theorize metaphysically about the structure of deep space.

35. There is another direct correspondence between the various myths, for the Greek Aphrodite was supposed to have been "born from the foam of the ocean," rising out of it on a conch shell, like the Hindu symbolism of the god Brahma seated on a lotus, floating on the "waters" (of space).

36. The word *thesu*, which Wallis Budge (keeper of Egyptian Antiquities at the British Museum for over two decades) believed to mean "either the vertebra or some internal organ of the body which resembles a tied knot or knotted cord, . . ." in fact appears to mean the (etheric) spinal cord with its psychophysical arrangement of chakras. Budge, *The Gods of the Egyptians*, vol. 1, 42.

37. In *Theurgia—The Egyptian Mysteries*, a compilation of the very detailed replies of the Egyptian high priest Abammon to the inquiries of the Greek philosopher Porphyry on the subject of Egyptian mystic tradition and occult theory. See Iamblichus, *Theurgia, or The Egyptian Mysteries*, trans. Alexander Wilder (The Metaphysical Publishing Company, 1911), 220–21.

38. The Chaldeo-Babylonian *kabir* and the Vedic god Kubera are synonymous with the Egyptian *Kheper* (Ra), the term signifying the demiurgic, self-generated creator gods of the local universe.

39. *Asclepius III*, trans. Sir Walter Scott (London: Solos Books, 1992), 24–25.

Chapter 2: Geological, Geographical, and Climatological Issues

1. Hancock, *Fingerprints of the Gods*, 465–70, quoting Flem-Ath's *When the Sky Fell*.
2. The idea of crustal displacement was originated by the late Professor Charles Hapgood and described in his book *Maps of the Ancient Sea Kings*. See Hancock, *Fingerprints of the Gods*, 10, quoting Hapgood's book.
3. Col. J. Wilford, *Asiatic Researches*, 10 vols. (London, 1806), vol. 3.
4. Blavatsky, *The Secret Doctrine*, vol. 2, 314, 740 et seq.
5. Ibid.
6. Interestingly, we find Iamblichus (Proclus in *Timaeus* b.1) saying, "The Assyrians have not only preserved the memorials of seven and twenty myriads of years [270,000 years] as Hipparchus says they have, but likewise of the whole apocatastases and periods of the seven rulers of the world." One wonders if there is any connection between this and our later suggestions that the Atlanto-Aryans of Daitya might have been the ancestors of the Hamitic peoples of northwest Africa, distant progenitors of the much more recent Semites.
7. Hapgood, *Maps of the Ancient Sea Kings*, 36.
8. Ibid., 229.
9. Ibid., 67.
10. Ibid., 182.
11. "Strataform Initiative" in *Oceanography* 9, no. 3 (1996), sponsored by ONR.
12. Which, only a little longer ago, geologically speaking, were themselves attached to a far greater landmass incorporating all of northwest Africa, including modern Morocco and the Atlas

Mountains and probably Spain and Portugal too, thereby separating the Atlantic and western Mediterranean at, or close to, Gibraltar—the location of the fabled "Pillars of Hercules."

13. *Encyclopaedia Britannica (Macropaedia)*, vol. 17 and vol. 23.
14. *The Times of London Science Report*, 26 September 1995.
15. Which fact certainly seems to suggest that the most major geomagnetic shifts and their associated continental cataclysms take place at intervals of 800,000 years or so.
16. See the *Encyclopedia Britannica (Macropaedia)* for details, s.v. "Africa," "Europe," and "Alps."
17. *The Times Atlas of Archaeology*, 62.
18. Which implies that the land bridge between Gibraltar and Tangier still existed some 700,000 years ago. See *Encyclopaedia Britannica (Macropaedia)*, vol. 17.
19. Ibid., vol. 18, 549 et seq.
20. J. Imbrie and K. Palmer-Imbrie, *Ice Ages: Solving the Mystery* (New Jersey: Enslow Publishers, 1979).
21. *The Times of London Science Report*, 26 September 1995.
22. Plato, *Timaeus and Critias*, 38.
23. *Encyclopaedia Britannica (Macropaedia)*, vol. 18, 549 et seq.
24. Hapgood, *Maps of the Ancient Sea Kings*, 182.
25. Ibid., chap. 8. Interestingly, the *Encyclopaedia Britannica (Macropaedia)*, vol. 20, 734 tells us that "Glacier ice today stores about three-fourths of all the fresh water in the world. Glacier ice covers about 11% of the world's land area and would cause a world sea-level rise of about 90 m (300 feet) if all existing ice melted." The chronological timing of the last (extended) pluvial period—between the celestial winter solstice and the celestial spring equinox (12,500 to 6,000 years ago)—seems to suggest the probability of this being a cyclical phenomenon, occurring every 26,000 years, as the Ancients themselves indicated.
26. West, *Serpent in the Sky*, 225–32.
27. Although the highly sophisticated hydrological engineering of the early Egyptians, involving an immensely extended canal network (with locks), between Asyut and the Faiyum certainly enabled them to siphon off huge amounts of excess seasonal floodwater and store it in the Faiyum Depression, a vast man-made reservoir to the west of Memphis, even larger than the whole area of Greater London. In this way, they were able to maintain strict control over the extent of the annual inundation, via a complex system of irrigation channels, thereby ensuring water availability for crops and general use throughout the year.
28. I. Shaw and P. Nicholson, *British Museum Dictionary of Ancient Egypt* (London: Book Club Associates, 1995), 310.
29. *The Times Atlas of Archaeology*, 120.
30. Ibid.
31. Bauval and Gilbert, *The Orion Mystery*, 169–74.
32. W. Flinders Petrie, *A History of Egypt* (London: Methuen and Co., 1895), 5. This has subsequently been confirmed by geologists, who regard the whole area of modern Libya and western Egypt, plus the Mediterranean, as having once formed the bed of the giant (inland) "Tethys Sea." *The Times Atlas of Archaeology*, 53.
33. Flinders Petrie, *A History of Egypt*, 2–5.

Chapter 3: The Disappearing "Atlantes"

1. *Encyclopaedia Britannica (Macropaedia)*, vol. 18, 855 et seq.
2. Z'ev ben Shimon Halevi, *Kabbalah* (London: Thames & Hudson, 1979), 10.
3. Budge, *The Gods of the Egyptians*, vol. 1, 150.
4. Ibid., 299.

5. *The Times Atlas of Archaeology*, 66.

6. Ibid., 82.

7. See appendix E, which details a remarkable series of observations concerning ancient zodiacs and monuments as "celestial clocks" by an early-nineteenth-century antiquarian, S. A. Mackay of Norwich.

8. Herodotus, *Euterpe*, 142.

9. Blavatsky, *The Secret Doctrine*, xxvi.

10. *The Times of London Science Report*, 26 September 1995.

11. Blavatsky, *The Secret Doctrine*, vol. 2, 740.

12. An even more degenerate strain of apparently earlier humanity than the much later Neanderthals. But see appendix D.

13. *The Times Atlas of Archaeology*, 54 et seq.

14. Wilford, *Asiatic Researches*, vol. 2, ch. 7; the Egyptian mystical tradition in question was supposedly handed down by semidivine intelligences over one million years ago.

15. *The Times Atlas of Archaeology*, 52.

16. See Genesis, ch. 6.

17. Schwaller de Lubicz, *Sacred Science*, 59.

18. I. Donnelly, *Atlantis: The Antediluvian World* (London: Sidgwick and Jackson, 1960), 136, 147.

19. Ibid., 143–50.

20. Ibid., chap. 5.

21. *The Times Atlas of Archaeology*, 70–71.

22. Ibid.

23. Blavatsky, *The Secret Doctrine*, vol. 2, 314.

24. While paleomagnetic research confirms that the earth's poles periodically reverse, no sensible theory has yet been advanced as to why this phenomenon should occur. Furthermore, it seems sometimes to be assumed that the planet itself turns upside down in order to achieve the necessary magnetic switch. However, if one takes into consideration the axial angle of our solar system's path in relation to the greater sidereal system of which it forms part, and then follows the same principle in relation to the latter's relationship with the Galaxy itself, the probable reason becomes self-apparent. The electric field of the galactic plane almost certainly determines the various polarities within our solar system. Consequently, a transit across its equatorial tropics would undoubtedly cause a massive electromagnetic deflection. As our solar system's 25,920-year round implies an orbit around a parent star (or constellation) of far greater magnitude, it is the axial path of the latter that would need to drag our system through the "celestial plate" of the galactic equatorial plane, roughly every three quarters of a million years. In this we see one of the myths of Osiris that we shall take up in greater detail in a later chapter. It should then quickly become evident just how advanced the astronomical knowledge of the ancient world must have been.

25. Hapgood, *Maps of the Ancient Sea Kings*, 190.

26. Although the Levantine Phoenicians are generally regarded as the founders of Carthage, on the coast of modern Tunisia, facing Sicily, there is reason to suggest that, long before, it had been a Hamitic (that is, originally Atlantean) colonial city.

27. It may be sheer coincidence, but that part of West Africa lying directly east of the Cape Verde Islands (Senegal–Sierra Leone) is also due east of the West Indies, Caribbean Islands, and Central America generally. The latter is, of course, where the remnants of giant African-faced Olmec statuary are still to be found today, and, there being no trace of either their origin or fate, or of any prehistoric civilization in that part of western Africa, such an association directly implies that the origins of the colonists of both lands must have existed somewhere in between them. Unsurprisingly, somewhere in the mid-Atlantic (possibly including the Caribbean Islands) would still seem the likeliest bet.

28. Neither the Berber nor the Tuareg are of Semitic origin (despite some intermarriage with the Semitic Bedouin and the western African), the features of both being much more self-evidently of the Indo-Caucasian type. Both are fiercely independent with a social and political culture that bears a strong resemblance to that of the Pathans of Afghanistan. The Berbers have a copper-colored skin while many Tuareg appear fair-complexioned. Furthermore, both speak Arabic with a highly characteristic infusion of Hamitic (i.e., non-Arabic) expressions. Consequently, it is not difficult to see in these types the disparate remnants of a far more ancient, purely Hamitic-speaking people (see also appendix F) whose original center of civilization and culture had been destroyed in prehistory, by either war or cataclysm, or both. Their naturally aggressive nature and geographical location draws the immediate inference of their being the descendants of Plato's Atlanteans.

29. Fage and Oliver, eds., *Papers in African Prehistory* (Cambridge: Cambridge University Press, 1970), 139–45.

30. Murray, *The Splendour That Was Egypt*, xxi.

31. G. Rawlinson, *Ancient Monarchies* (London, 1880).

32. Archaeologists regard the last Cushitic empire as having commenced only around 1000 B.C. However, as with their ideas concerning ancient Egyptian civilization and culture, they seem to be taking into consideration only the reanimated embers of something far more ancient. The similarity of the architecture of the Cushitic empire (located between Nubia and the Red Sea, to the south of Egypt) confirms the close relationship of their culture with that of the Egyptians, itself known to have extended much further south into Nubia (present-day Sudan). The name Cush (actually Ksh) appears to have been derived from the historically recognized kingdom of Kesh in northwestern India—hence the modern state of Kashmir, close to the Hindu Kush mountains.

33. *British Museum Dictionary of Ancient Egypt*, 51.

34. Wilford, *Asiatic Researches*, vol. 3, 334.

35. Hapgood, *Maps of the Ancient Sea Kings*, 123, 202.

36. Blavatsky, *The Secret Doctrine*, xxiii et seq.

37. Ibid., vol. 2, 780, 764.

38. Interestingly, the Mayan god of light and air was called Xiutehcutli, pronounced *shu-te-khu-lhi*. The *lh* sound is phonetically the same as the *tl* in Atlas and even the modern Welsh *ll* as in Llandudno. This is highly suggestive of a common linguistic background that can only have been "late Atlantean."

39. Wilford, *Asiatic Researches*, vol. 3, 300.

40. As we shall see in later chapters, *ba* is a Hamito-Semitic (that is, ancient Egyptian) word for the lesser "soul" entity.

41. Known to the Egyptians as Mntw (hence the Indo-Tibetan *mandala* from *mntw-lha*) and to the North American Indians as Manitou, the "Great White Spirit."

42. The word *vahan* is Sanskrit and means "body" or "vehicle," the *v* being commonly pronounced as a soft *w* by Indians.

43. *Khu* signifies a "divine offering," while *kuk* (meaning "head") and *kukh* (meaning "dog") were esoteric puns mystically relating a demigod or high spiritual adept to the star Sirius.

44. In the first century A.D., Diodorus Siculus wrote of the original colonizers of Egypt: "The (ancient) Egyptians were strangers who, in remote times, settled on the banks of the Nile bringing with them the civilization of their mother country, the art of writing and a polished language. They had come from the direction of the setting sun and were the most ancient of men" (quoted in C. Berlitz, *Atlantis*, 135). In other words, they had come from the direction of the Atlantic Ocean. Interestingly, they also regarded themselves as a red-skinned race, as depicted in some of their temple paintings.

45. Plato, *Timaeus and Critias*, 37 et seq.

46. The story, as told by Plato, had the Atlantean empire extending, in the south, all the way from the Atlantic coast to Egypt's western border (thereby necessarily incorporating the strategically vital port city of Carthage) and, in the north, incorporating Spain, southern France, and Italy.

47. But see appendix F as regards this relationship and ancient linguistic issues generally.

48. The Guanche tongue spoken in the Canary Islands up to the sixteenth century (when it died out) is recognized by philologists as having extensively incorporated Hamitic expressions, used even today by the Berber people of the Atlas. Unfortunately, such expressions have, in turn, become so depleted in use among the Berbers themselves—due to the precedence of the common Arabic spoken across North Africa for the last thirteen hundred years at least—that it is no longer recognizable as once having had a distinct identity of its own. A fundamentally accepted tradition in the Canaries has it that the original Guanche people were exceptionally tall with fair complexions, blond hair, and blue eyes—which clearly indicates an Indo-Caucasian (perhaps Nordic) type. Additionally, fair-haired and blue-eyed "Libyans" are clearly to be seen in very early Egyptian art, some of them evidently living in the western Delta area—a fact remarked upon by the Roman historian Pliny, who referred to them as "white Ethiopians." This then would appear to suggest that the Guanche-Berber are indeed the scattered and disparate remnants of an ancient Poseidonian empire that once stretched all the way from the home island (Madeira-Canaria) to the western border of Egypt.

The ten statues of the Guanche kings located in Tenerife (see fig. 3.2) seem to verify the historic traditions of the islanders on these issues, for they are sculpted in a distinctively "classical" style, the individual figures having clearly Indo-Caucasian features and a physical body height considerably taller than the Iberians who rediscovered the islands in about the fifteenth century and systematically set about a classical policy of local genocide. The Guanches themselves were amazed at the Spanish incursion because they believed that the rest of mankind had all been killed in the devastating cataclysms that had destroyed their own culture millennia before—an almost certain reference to the destruction of Plato's Atlantean island. The Guanches also clearly followed a religious or mystic culture shared with the Egyptians, for they practiced mummification, and their main devotional icon was the whippet, a smaller version of the greyhound—hence the name of the islands (Canaria) being derived from *canis*, meaning "dog." The whippet (as Upuat) was central to the ancient Egyptian mystic tradition and also had a very specific astronomical association attached to it.

Chapter 4: The Appearance of Culture and Civilization

1. *British Museum Dictionary of Ancient Egypt*, 218.
2. The Egyptian pharaoh Menes looks remarkably similar to the Greek king Minos and the culturally associated, bull-oriented Minoan civilization of Crete appears to have occupied the same zodiacal period of Taurus (circa 4300 B.C.–2150 B.C.). Are the two then merely alter egos? See also Murray, *The Splendour That Was Egypt*, 12–13.
3. Ibid., 11.
4. Herodotus, *The Histories*, trans. Harry Carter (Oxford: Oxford University Press, 1962), 186.
5. Blavatsky, *The Secret Doctrine*, vol. 1, 231; vol. 2, 590.
6. Budge, *The Gods of the Egyptians*, vol. 1, 331 et seq.
7. Herodotus, *Histories*, 186.
8. Budge, *The Gods of the Egyptians*, vol. 2, 90.
9. "There had been four occasions when the Sun rose out of his wonted place—twice while there rising where he now sets and twice setting where he now rises"—a clear reference to the astronomically visual effects of the equinoctial precession. Herodotus, *Histories*, 149.
10. K. McLeish, *Children of the Gods* (London: Longmans, 1983), 213.

11. Blavatsky, *The Secret Doctrine*, vol. 2, 433 et seq.

12. Manly P. Hall, *The Secret Teachings of all Ages*, xxi et seq.

13. The expression "Children of Israel" seems originally to have been intended to signify mankind in general—but in a spiritual sense, as *As-r-El (As-r* being the Egyptian form of the name *Osiris)*—the semidivine progeny of the Demiurge—the El being the Elohim already mentioned in the Old Testament. Thus the name Israel (given to the metaphorical Jacob after he had "fought the angel" at Beth-el signified a semidivine or celestial state, "the Promised Land" to which the offspring of his twelve sons (a purely zodiacal metaphor) would return at "God's own appointed time." "Captivity in Egypt" was thus merely another zodiacal metaphor used by the Egyptians themselves, meaning an enforced round of human incarnation during the Great Sidereal Year. It seems that the Hebrews, while "in captivity" in Egypt (more probably being an expatriate merchant community from greater Indo-Persia, like the modern Parsis in India), took from the Egyptians the latters' well-known certainty of being the metaphorical "Chosen People"—yet another example of the ancient esoteric tradition having become distorted through literal interpretation. Interestingly, Norman Cantor—professor of history, sociology, and comparative literature at New York University, in his recent book *A History of the Jews* (HarperCollins) states categorically that "the biblical version of Jewish history is nothing more than a national Creation myth . . . more than a century of archaeological research in Iraq and Egypt has produced not one piece of empirical evidence that Abraham, Jacob, or Moses ever existed." Was the Old Testament then merely a series of originally esoteric teachings dressed up as popular parables for the uninitiated masses of the Egyptian population at large—including a well-integrated Hebrew community?

14. *The Times Atlas of World History*, 52 et seq.

15. Murray, *The Splendour That Was Egypt*, 1.

16. *The Times Atlas of Archaeology*, 124–26.

17. West, *Serpent in the Sky*, 187–97.

18. Murray, *The Splendour That Was Egypt*, 2, 4–6.

19. Donnelly, *Atlantis: The Antediluvian World*, 44–50.

20. Ibid., 46.

21. As nearly all western European languages are now recognized as having their roots in Sanskrit, the ancient Indo-Aryan sacerdotal language of prehistoric Aryavarta (a mighty kingdom once supposedly existing between northwest India and the Caucasus), one can only wonder at how many thousands of years it took for Sanskrit itself to have been fully evolved. As we shall see in subsequent chapters, the ancient Egyptians used a great many expressions that, both phonetically and in interpretation, closely (and often exactly) match those that we find in the Sanskrit language or its root words. This can be no mere coincidence. It clearly points to very ancient, transcontinental cultural relationships.

22. R. E. Asher, ed. *Encyclopaedia of Language and Linguistics*, vol. 1, s.v. "Afroasiatic."

23. *International Encyclopaedia of Linguistics*, appendix F.

24. This thought is echoed in the impressively scholarly *Black Athena*, by Professor Martin Bernal, who has recently challenged the "pure" Indo-European origin of classical civilization. He says: "A small but increasing number of scholars has convinced me that there is a genetic relationship between the Indo-European languages and those of the Afroasiatic language 'superfamily.' . . . I therefore believe that there must once have been a people who spoke Proto-Afroasiatic-Indo-European. Such a language and culture must have broken up a very long time ago. The latest possibility would be the Mousterian period 50–30,000 years ago, but it may have been much earlier." Bernal, *Black Athena*, vol. 1, 11.

Chapter 5: Egyptian Magic and the Law of Hierarchy

1. Budge, *The Gods of the Egyptians*, vol. 1, 117–18, 131–41.

2. Ibid., 137. The Egyptian word *neter* (*neteru* is plural) is identical with the Latin word *natura*, meaning nature. Hence it is clear that the Egyptians' consideration of the gods as "principles" confirms that they saw universal nature as an expression of an underlying or overshadowing intelligence. This is, of course, the essence of the modern Gaia hypothesis, although orthodox science would not yet commit itself thus far.

3. Ibid., 164.

4. Ibid., 283 et seq.

5. Iamblichus, *Theurgia*, chaps. 2, 3; 44.

6. Ibid., chap. 4.

7. Budge, *The Gods of the Egyptians*, vol. 1, 265–67.

8. Ibid., vol. 2, 299–300. In fact, the Egyptians regarded the gods as having seven souls—thereby, we might suggest, containing within their nature all the seven planes or states of material (including psycho-spiritual) existence within the body of Atum-Ra. Interestingly, they also held that the god had fourteen "doubles," each of these (intelligence, strength, splendor, power, and so on) representing some sort of reservoir of faculty upon which the spiritually knowledgeable could draw at will. This bears a close resemblance to the (modern) materialistic application of kabbalistic theory. The term *saha* is found in the Hebrew Kabbalah as *zohar*, with the *Sefer ha Zohar* misleadingly translated as *Book of Splendors*.

9. Donnelly, *Atlantis: The Antediluvian World*, 205.

10. *Dzhyan* is also found as *tsampo* (or *shamba*), derived from the Sanskrit *skambha*, meaning a pillar or pole—or otherwise, by inference, the central axis of a centrifugal mechanism, such as the astronomical "mill of the gods" described in the book *Hamlet's Mill*, as we shall see in chapter 9. *Dzhyan* itself is the Tibetan form of the Sanskrit *dhyan(a)* (meditation). The Assyrio-Chaldean name Kabir(i) appears to be synonymous with both the Vedic god Kubera and the Egyptian god Kheper (Ra), who represented the principle or occult faculty of self-regeneration.

11. The two hierarchies emanated by the Deity—Man and Angel—are depicted as the two "pillars of Wisdom," or "*sephirotic* trees" of Masonry and Kabbalism. The kabbalistic Crown *sefirah* (Kether) is clearly associated with the Egyptian Kheper (Ra) and is described as the "beginning and end of all existence—which equates it with the Pythagorean Monad." The two *sefirot* surmounting the Pillars of Wisdom/Mercy and Understanding/Justice have been confirmed by Kabbalists as YHVH (Jahve) and Elohim, respectively. The word *sefirah* itself appears to be derived from the root word *suf*, meaning *breath*—i.e., pure Being—hence the derivation of the Sufi tradition. Thus *sefirah* arises from the linguistically telescoped *suf-Ra*, the "breath of Ra." The Greek word *sophia* (wisdom) seems to enjoy the same origin and essential meaning, albeit with Chaldeo-Assyrian overtones. It derives from *suf-ea*, *ea* being one member of their primordial Divine Trinity. See Z'ev ben Shimon Halevi, *Kabbalah*, 9; and Budge, *The Gods of the Egyptians*, vol. 1, 143–45, 265–66.

12. Donnelly, *Atlantis: The Antediluvian World*.

13. See *Theurgia*, the reply of the priest-sage Iamblichus to various questions on occult and esoteric matters put by the Greek Porphyry.

14. Blavatsky, *The Secret Doctrine*, vol. 2, 764.

15. Budge, *The Gods of the Egyptians*, vol. 2, 299.

16. Iamblichus, *Theurgia*, 220–21.

17. Curiously, perhaps, the modern scientific approach to Darwinian evolutionary theory is fast coming around to the idea that if matter is actually able to evolve into organic entities, there can, in reality, be no such thing as truly inorganic matter. But "orthodox" science is in no rush to accept such a "radical" idea.

18. In various cultures, often oceans and continents apart, we find the serpent revered as a symbol of knowledge and wisdom. Sometimes (as with the Masai of East Africa) there is also an unwillingness to kill snakes due to an anciently held belief that the souls of the dead reincarnate in serpent form— yet another example of how an ancient (metaphorical) mystical tradition has fallen into degenerate literalism and so transformed itself into merely ignorant local superstition.

19. R. Panikkar, *The Vedic Experience* (London: Darton Longmans and Todd, 1977), 350–53.

20. Ibid., 351.

21. The fact that material substance is crystallized light is now confirmed by relativity and quantum theory, as well as being the ultimate expression of the holographic principle. However, the Ancients believed that there existed varying qualities of light in the cosmos, each giving rise to its own dimension of being and perception. That comprising the ethereal substratum of Earth's own lower atmosphere—called the "astral light" by nineteenth-century Hermeticists—was itself regarded as the merely inverted counterpart, or "reflection," of the "heavenly light" (emanating from the stars) in which the spiritual soul participated and of which it was itself constituted. The astral light was thus not only the lesser realm of the many and varied elemental hierarchies in nature, but also that from which the material of man's own etheric "double" (the Egyptian *ka*) was borrowed by the *ba* to act as the foundation and localized agent for each physical incarnation. At death, when the *ba* finally withdrew, the *ka* became an empty, ghostly "shade" or doppelgänger, the material of which gradually dissolved back into the astral light.

22. The same principle was believed to apply to the human being inasmuch as an increasingly spiritualized consciousness caused an equivalently progressive transmutation and literal transfiguration of the body form from inside outward. As Wallis Budge put it in *The Gods of the Egyptians:* "The priests of Ra declared that the blessed fed upon light, were arrayed in light and became beings of light" (vol. 2, 119). This is generally assumed to refer entirely to the postmortem state, but the original texts clearly indicate otherwise.

23. Iamblichus, *Theurgia,* 79–80.

24. Budge, *The Gods of the Egyptians,* vol. 1, chap. 5.

25. Perhaps the most obvious of these relates to the practice of mummification, which has generally been regarded as having always been a purely funerary custom of the Egyptians. However, upon looking more deeply into the associated symbolism, a very different picture emerges, which suggests (among other things) that it may not originally have been the general custom after all. To explain: The goddess Net/Neith, wife and mother of Amen-Ra, was regarded as the deity of mummification, and the priests of her temple at Sais in the Delta held an annual "festival of lights" dedicated to her. Her personal emblem was a pair of crossed arrows in front of what looks like a shield, or cartouche, and for this reason scholars have associated her with the Greek goddess Artemis, the huntress. However, she is also somewhat inexplicably the patroness of weaving, which hardly sits comfortably alongside hunting! Esoterically, however, the symbolism of the arrow refers to the shaft of light that, when "woven" with others, produces the form of the "light body," or *ka*—the double, of which Net is the cosmic counterpart. Hence the mummified Osiris, Ptah, and Khonsu all symbolize the temporarily arrested, or quiescent (objective), state in which a divine principle is being held.

26. J. Sellers, *The Death of Gods in Ancient Egypt,* 255.

Chapter 6: Two Egyptian Mystery Traditions Reconsidered

1. Budge, *The Gods of the Egyptians,* vol. 2, 142–47.

2. Ibid., vol. 2, 123 et seq., and 186 et seq.

3. E. A. W. Budge, *Legends of the Egyptian Gods* (New York: Dover, 1994), 247.

4. The divine Man, per se, remains eternally invisible. He is only ever able to manifest a portion of

himself through the agency of a soul body provided by the demiurgic hierarchy of archangels—that is, by the *neteru,* divine offspring of the cosmic mother goddess Net. This then becomes his "tomb," or "coffin."

5. Budge, *The Gods of the Egyptians,* vol. 1, 361–63, vol. 2, 214.

6. Sometimes (mistakenly) thought to be sixteen, an error derived from the associated fact that the priests used sixteen instruments to ceremonially reconstitute the "body of Osiris."

7. Directly related to the twenty-eight-day lunar cycle by virtue of the Moon's (reflective) effect on man's psychic nature.

8. This is perhaps more readily understood if we draw a scientific analogy involving two electromagnetic fields, one considerably more powerful than the other. As the two fields attain a certain proximity, a spark of (hitherto latent) electricity suddenly appears within the periphery of the powerful field and "jumps" across to the other one, which (given certain circumstances) becomes momentarily luminous, due to its own mechanical inertia responding to the greater electrical charge.

9. The name Nephthys (as Nebkhet—meaning "lady of the body of the gods") was also used by the Egyptians to mean the end, or outer limit, of anything (Budge, *The Gods of the Egyptians,* vol. 2, 256). Thus its ultimate phenomenal expression became the *ka* or ethereal double that relied entirely upon the astral *ba* for its own organization, stimulation, and direction. The *ka* is essentially an unorganized substratum of universal substance (referred to in some cultures as the Black Virgin), but its organization into a luminous "spider's web" of localized energies produces, in turn, a localized electromagnetic framework around which the molecular matter of the dense body-form then gathers to produce the human shape with which we are so familiar.

   Anubis—traditionally the messenger and "Opener of the Ways," as well as being the "god of the dead"—always accompanied the psycho-spiritual nature of man both into incarnation and also back through the "veil of death," into the "chamber of judgment." But he could himself proceed no further into the spiritual world. Nevertheless, as we shall see later on, this limited, cyclo-interlocutory function of Anubis (and other Egyptian traditions) relates him in a microcosmic sense to the star Sirius. The true Egyptian name of the latter, however, was *sbd*—sometimes misleadingly anglicized by Egyptologists as *sept.* In fact, the pronunciation should be more akin to *sabda* (the vowels being shortened in spoken Hamito-Semitic). That, however, renders it very similar to the Sanskrit *shabda* (also pronounced with shortened vowels), meaning "word." Were both Anubis (the son of Set) and Sirius then "the Word made flesh" (that is, made objective) in a higher and lower, but still esoteric, sense, as man and heavenly home of the god-man, respectively?

10. Budge, *The Gods of the Egyptians,* vol. 2, 125.

11. Hathor has always been regarded by Egyptologists as somehow closely related to Isis, and also by the fact that the very name *hat-Hor* related her to Horus. Quite what that relationship was, however, was never made explicit. However, she was also the wife of the high god Atum-Ra—hence the symbol of the cow's horns (usually taken as a representation of the Moon) actually seems to indicate a partial association with a higher sphere of consciousness. Thus the crescent of the horns is perhaps more accurately to be considered as signifying a limited arc of that higher sphere of being.

12. J. Tyberg, *Sanskrit Keys to the Wisdom Religion* (n.p.: Theosophical University Press, 1940), 68.

13. M. P. Hall, *The Secret Teachings of All Ages,* 77.

14. A late Hermetic term meaning the halo of "dark matter" closely surrounding and interpenetrating the surface of our planet.

15. Budge, *The Gods of the Egyptians,* vol. 2, 263–64. The name Apuat has itself been spelled in a variety of different ways, such as Upuaut or Upuat. It has even come down to us in the English language as *whippet,* the smaller version of the greyhound. But the root of the name is also to be found in the Sanskrit—for example, in the verb *upa-ut-kram,* meaning "to ascend by degrees,"

highly significant in the context of initiation in the Mysteries. The symbolism of two jackals is of considerable relevance from an astronomical point of view, as well as a magical one, as we shall see in chapter 9. Anubis was often referred to as the "permanent companion" of Isis, and there is thus good reason to associate Anubis (rather than Isis herself) with the star Sirius (known as Sothis by the Greeks and Sbd by the Egyptians), the "Dog Star." As described in *The Sirius Mystery*, the Dogon people of West Africa—seemingly drawing upon ancient Egyptian knowledge—understood the concept of a "second companion," for they knew of Sirius being a binary star. Even more interestingly, they were of the opinion that it was the smaller and almost hidden "companion" (Sirius B) that was the more powerful of the two, responsible for the cyclical flowering of all aspects of nature on our planet.

When related to the idea of a second Apuat associated with the spiritual counterpart to the merely psycho-terrestrial Anubis (thereby relating the spiritual to the divine state), this becomes of really crucial significance. As we shall see in chapters 9 and 12, Isis appears to be more directly associated with the orbital path of Sirius than with the star itself, while it is the jackal Apuat (and not Anubis) depicted as lying on and guarding a "box of treasure," as shown in fig. 6.9. The latter represents the Sekhem—the vehicle of Khem, the "god of the secret face" (that is, of man's hidden divinity), for Apuat itself bore the title Sekhem Taui, ". . . which came forth from the tree Asert" (see R. K. G. Temple, *The Sirius Mystery* [Rochester, Vt.: Destiny Books, 1998], 2). Wallis Budge otherwise tells us that "Anubis was the opener of the roads of the North and Apuat the opener of the roads to the South; in fact, Anubis was the personification of the Summer Solstice and Apuat of the Winter Solstice" (see Budge, *The Gods of the Egyptians*, vol. 2, 145; also the *British Museum Dictionary of Ancient Egypt*, 140–41). However, for reasons to be explained later on, it is clear that the original association lay with the celestial solstices.

16. Budge, *The Gods of the Egyptians*, vol. 1, xii et seq.
17. Here we find a clear association between Egyptian and Hindu myth, for Visnu (the Universal Soul) is—like Osiris—depicted as having a blue- (or blue-green) colored body. He is also shown as lying asleep at the bottom of the cosmic ocean (like the cosmic Osiris lying prone amid the stars of the Milky Way, the celestial river) with a lotus emanating from his navel and floating up to the surface, with the god Brahma sitting upon it. Ra is likewise often shown seated upon a lotus, as are the four "sons of Horus"—Imsety, Duamutef, Qebesenuef, and Hapi. These four, shown emerging from the waters of Chaos upon which Osiris's throne is placed, might themselves be regarded as representing the incessant reincarnation of universal principles in cosmic nature. Thus if Osiris were to be regarded as symbolizing the spiritual, fifth element (Aether), these four would take the part of the other, objective elements—Fire, Air, Water, and Earth.
18. Murray, *The Splendour That Was Egypt*, 210–11. Egyptologists usually present ancient Egyptian views on this subject as showing interest only in the "afterlife," as though there was but one incarnation as far as they were concerned. This, however, does not square up with the whole ancient ethos associated with cyclical repetition in Creation. Nor does it coincide with the Egyptian idea of spiritual evolution being positively achievable via the Mysteries until the divine state is regained in full self-consciousness, as opposed to the original state of "divine ignorance" in which the "fall from Grace" was depicted as having occurred. Some of their magical invocations also seem specifically to confirm the fact.

Chapter 7: Gods of the Abyss and Underworld

1. Budge, *The Gods of the Egyptians*, vol. 1, preface and 4 et seq.
2. Ibid., vol. 1, 283–89. See also vol. 1, 113–14: "Throughout Egypt generally, the company of gods of a town or city were three in number and they were formed by the local deity and two gods who were associated with him and who shared with him, but in very much less degree, the honor and

reverence which were paid to him. Speaking generally, two members of such a triad were gods, one old and one young, and the third was a goddess who was, naturally, the wife or female counterpart of the older god. . . . The conception of the triad or trinity is, in Egypt, probably as old as the belief in the gods."

3. Ibid., vol. 1, 291–95, 306.

4. Herodotus, *Histories*, 149–50.

5. R. Graves, *The Greek Myths* (London: Book Club Associates, 1985), 10–11.

6. As Budge describes it, "Amen" or "Amon," alone or as a prefix, means "THAT which remains eternally hidden" (i.e., objectively unmanifest) because it is the essential emanation of the cosmic Mind of the Unseen Logos. The god Amen himself was usually depicted as either ram-headed or falcon-headed. *The Gods of the Egyptians*, vol. 2, 2.

7. Ibid., vol. 2, 33.

8. Ibid., vol. 2, 93.

9. Ibid., vol. 1, 302.

10. See appendix H.

11. Budge, *The Gods of the Egyptians*, vol. 1, 353.

12. Hence the much misunderstood allegory of Tum creating the objective universe from an act of masturbation.

13. A. Besant and B. Das, trans., *The Bhagavad Gita*, 123.

14. As Wallis Budge tells us, "Ptah and Khnemu were jointly responsible for creating and populating the universe." *The Gods of the Egyptians*, vol. 2, 354.

15. Ibid., vol. 2, 355.

16. The name Amen-Ra signifies the objective self-projection of the extracosmic Logos—the unmanifest but ever-present One-ness of the initiating life principle of our local universe. He is thus the true representative of the immanent *and* transcendent solar Logos. Although itself perennially unseen during the cycle of its own activity, this Logos still manages to project a sufficient proportion of its life into its vehicle (the universe of our galaxy) to infuse it in such a manner that all the gods, demigods, and hierarchies of daemons and souls that it emanates respond and act together to give progressive and coordinated expression to Divine Purpose. The first cosmic objectivity is represented as the substratum of light itself—that of the Milky Way—symbolized as the primeval self-generation of the goddess Net/Neith. Atum-Ra then represents the seventh and lowest aspect of the sevenfold cosmic universe, the partially manifested microcosm of the unmanifest macrocosm; but because it is only a partial representation, it is also the source of all distortion and error in the (local) universe—hence the fact that the Egyptian tradition has Atum-Ra suffering all sorts of problems with his local "world management."

   As suggested in a previous chapter, the name Adam (as Adam Kadmon) is synonymous with Atum. Kadmon appears to be derived from the compounding of *khat* (the physical body principle) and *man* (the mind principle). Thus the compound divine man is the *fons et origo*, as well as the evolutionary aim, of all objective Creation—i.e., within our "local universe."

17. See Iamblichus, *Theurgia*, 64–70, 176–77.

18. Graves, *Greek Myths*, 1–2.

19. Budge, *The Gods of the Egyptians*, vol. 1, 297–98, and vol. 2, 87 et seq.

20. Thus Ra-Tem is the evolutionary, organically vital aspect of Atum-Ra, as Eros is in relation to Ouranos-Gaea.

21. Budge, *The Gods of the Egyptians*, vol. 1, preface.

22. Ibid., vol. 2, 50.

23. Ibid.

24. The septenary principle is found extensively throughout the Egyptian metaphysical system—the

goddess Seshat (a female counterpart of Thoth-Tehuti) had as her emblem the seven-petaled flower. It essentially symbolizes two triplicities (i.e., polar complements) connected by a mediating principle of equilibrium—hence the maternal "*ka.*" The sevenfold principle is otherwise common throughout nature anyway, there being seven stages involved in all organic growth and development. There are also seven tones in the octave of the harmonic scale, which, as the Pythagorean philosophy made clear, was how the principle of Divine Order came into being to create the manifest universe out of Chaos. The sevenfold Khnemu, however—supposedly being a ram-headed god (there is a suggestion of his being associated with the zodiacal sign of Capricorn, which would render him "goat-headed")—is quite clearly of the *deva*-daemonic hierarchy in nature; that is, that which unfolds the seven planes of existence into which the divine man will fall, whereas Ptah (as Ptah-Seker-Ausar) represented the comprehensively "redeemed" divinity in man, as the thoroughly "rounded-out" expression of Divine Purpose, in terms of an evolving individuality of consciousness. Notably, Seker (sometimes pronounced *sokar*) appears to be a philological alter ego of the Sufi "*zhikr,*" meaning an anchored, rhythmic, spinning "dance," as practiced by the whirling dervishes.

25. Budge, *The Gods of the Egyptians,* vol. 2, 54–55.

26. M. P. Hall, *The Secret Teachings of All Ages,* 37.

27. The name Osiris is the Greek form of the Egyptian *As-r,* which we anglicize as AUSAR. It appears to coincide rather interestingly with the verbal root of the Sanskrit word *as* (meaning "to be") and is otherwise to be found as *asher* in the Hebrew kabbalistic expression Ehyeh Asher Ehyeh ("I am That I am"). Thus the original meaning of the name Osiris seems to have been "THAT"—the imponderable, self-created (i.e., immaculately conceived) divinity in man—by virtue of man's origin as the emanation and offspring of the great god Ra. In that respect, we can also see clear associations with the Nordic gods, the Aesir, the Sanskrit Asura (a "fallen" and thus imperfect god), the Persian Ahura (Mazda), the later Zoroastrian Asa, and even the Indo-Nepali expression *hajur,* which simply means "lord." *As-t* (the Egyptian form of Isis) then appears to be related to the Sanskrit *asat,* meaning the "sphere of illusion"—the objective world, or universe.

28. Both Ptah and Khnemu were depicted by the Egyptians as creating man "upon a potter's wheel." The wheel itself represents the principle of cyclic progression—the "wheel of necessity" (i.e., the ecliptic path of the zodiac)—involving constant reincarnation. Ptah represents the highest divine principle in man, the coordinated expression of Divine Purpose (on behalf of Amen-Ra). Thus it is that both Thoth and Ma'at are often regarded as being subsumed within his nature. The name Ptah itself appears to be synonymous with the Indo-Aryan (Sanskrit) *pitar,* meaning (divine) "father" or "ancestor." There is also a suggestion that the name Buddha is an Oriental version of it. Interestingly, Ptah is (like Osiris) depicted as being swathed in funerary bandaging.

29. Budge, *The Gods of the Egyptians,* vol. 2, 355.

30. Interestingly, the all-seeing Eye of Ra can be depicted with the curling line under it to either right or left, these usually being taken to represent the Sun and Moon, respectively, the latter also being regarded as the "Eye of Thoth." However, with the alternative of a single, central divine eye, the downward (almost straight) line might be taken to describe not only the nose of the god, but also, apparently, the same shape as the "anchor post" of the Cosmic Bull (i.e., Ursa Minor). It thus suggests itself as representing the "divine breaths"—i.e., the emanated gods—while the curling lines might thus symbolize the objectively manifesting consciousness of the daemons and souls, according to under which side of the eye they are located.

31. Budge, *The Gods of the Egyptians,* vol. 1, 3.

32. Ibid., vol. 2, 148 and 153.

33. Ibid., vol. 1, 104, and vol. 2, 148. As Budge says: "[I]nasmuch as the titles 'Lord of Abydos' and 'Lord of Tattw' (almost certainly corresponding with the Hindu *tattva*) occur in connection with others which have reference to Osiris in his capacity as governor of the Underworld, the Abydos

and Tattu mentioned here are mythological cities and not cities upon Earth. But even if this be so, it matters little, for we know that the Egyptians fashioned their mythological cities after the manner of their earthly cities and that their conceptions of things spiritual were based upon things material." Unfortunately, Budge has made an assumption here that is completely back-to-front. The Egyptians' spiritual concepts gave rise to material expression, not the other way around. Indeed, it would be difficult to conceive of any intelligent human being, in any age, deciding to "lock the spiritual door" after the architectural follies of commercial or other necessity had already been allowed full license.

34. Ibid., vol. 2, 155.

35. Interestingly, the Egyptian name for the Underworld (Duat or Tuat) is the reverse of *taut*, the phonetic stem of the god names Tehuti and Ta'Urt. This is no coincidence either. It clearly expresses the principle of reflection—"As above, so below"—although back-to-front, as in a mirror—which reminds us of the allegorical story of Narcissus, who, trying to find the "water nymph" Echo, mistakenly "fell in love" (i.e., became entranced) with his own reflection in a "pool of water."

36. M. Murray, *Egyptian Temples* (London: Sampson, Low, Marston, 1939), 175.

37. Ibid., 171.

38. However, the location of Coptos (just north of Thebes) was also originally of great spiritually symbolic significance, particularly in relation to the ithyphallic god Min, the main deity there.

Chapter 8: The Ancient Esoteric Division of Egypt

1. Murray, *The Splendour That Was Egypt*, 173.

2. Budge, *Gods of the Egyptians*, 120.

3. The ancient Semitic system of numerological significances (clearly adopted by the Hebrews from either the Egyptians or the Babylonians) had twenty-two alphabetical consonants, while vowels per se—being regarded as sacred—were treated as possessing a double potency. As we shall see in chapter 9, they appear to have been esoterically linked to the Apuat of Isis.

4. There were 42 Assessors, or "Judges of the Dead," in the Osirian "Chamber of Judgment." A coincidence? Hardly.

5. A. A. Bailey, *A Treatise on Cosmic Fire* (New York: Lucis Press, 1925), 344. The system in question is generally regarded as *theosophical* because, based upon the cosmological and metaphysical concepts described by H. P. Blavatsky (in 1888) in her book *The Secret Doctrine*, which she described as a review of the one eternal source of all religions and theogonies, both ancient and modern. Blavatsky was herself a cofounder (in 1875) of the Theosophical Society (see also the glossary). Later thinkers and writers in the same field have adjusted Blavatsky's system of "universal principles" to produce a corresponding scheme of "planes of consciousness."

6. Blavatsky, *The Secret Doctrine*, xxiii.

7. Murray, *Egyptian Temples*, 180.

8. Budge, *The Gods of the Egyptians*, vol. 2, 44 and 50.

9. Ibid., vol. 2, 50. "The spot on the island (of Elephantine—regarded as 'the first city that ever existed') out of which the river rose, was the 'double cavern', Qerti, which was likened to two breasts from which all good things poured forth . . . and from it the Nile God (Hapi) watched until the season of inundation drew nigh and then he rushed forth like a vigorous young man and filled the whole country" (vol. 2, 57). The symbolic double cavern between two hills can (as well as the two islands of Elephantine and Philae) otherwise be seen as a clear reference to the symbol for the god Tum/Atum-Ra, who, as the seventh and lowest cosmic aspect of Ra, formed the Underworld out of the lower half of his own nature (as a river valley—representative of the Duat of spirit and matter) from the diffused Chaos of space. Around this cosmic duality, we might further infer, flowed the Milky Way. But see also appendix H.

10. Ibid., vol. 2, 55.

11. Ibid., vol. 2, 53.

12. Murray, *Egyptian Temples,* 171.

13. The fact that Sebek and Horus the Elder are shown in the temple as taking responsibility for the east and west banks of the Nile, respectively, seems to confirm beyond any doubt these associations of the two sides of the river with form and consciousness. That is because (from the sun god's viewpoint, in his counterclockwise ecliptic cycle) the east side down to Heliopolis represented the "dying" solar cycle, whereas the west side (from Giza southward) is where the sun god's powers of self-regeneration are felt, thereby promoting centrifugal growth and a consequent sense of liberation (in man).

14. Budge, *The Gods of the Egyptians,* vol. 2, 241.

15. Which again indicates the sympathetic influence of the extracosmic mind of the solar Logos (although obviously at a lower turn of the spiral) over the initiate at this point in his spiritual evolution. At this stage, the latter was regarded as having achieved full command over his own compound temporal nature—the physical senses, the "astral" desires, and the hitherto arrogant and incontinent mind. He had thus become one of the Piru. Not for nothing was Karnak the largest temple complex in Egypt—and the only one with a simultaneously dual north–south, east–west orientation.

16. Khonsu (Eros)—like Ptah and Osiris—is depicted here swathed in mummification bandages (representing "death" by imprisonment in the Underworld), but with a hawk's head on which is perched the solar disk of Ra within a crescent, the latter itself symbolizing cyclic outgoings and returns, i.e., periodicity—hence an orientation still toward man's lower nature.

17. Schwaller de Lubicz discusses this in greater detail in his book *Sacred Science,* 126–37.

18. In front of the Ramesseum were three huge statues, one of a seated king, upon which was inscribed the words: "I am Simandius, the King of Kings. If anyone desires to know who I am or where I lie, let him outdo what I have done." According to Diodorus Siculus, the tomb, or sanctuary, of the (almost certainly allegorical) pharaoh-king Simandius "was surrounded with a golden circle, 365 cubits in circumference and a foot and a half thick. In it were described from cubit to cubit the 365 days of the year, the course of the stars and what they signified to Egyptian astrology." Murray, *Egyptian Temples,* 132. Egyptologists regard Rameses II as the historical alter ego of Simandius (a curious Greek corruption of User-Ma'at-Ra), but this is quite clearly absurd merely from considering the enigmatic suggestion contained in the inscription.

19. Ibid., 160–61.

20. The system of progressive initiation in ancient Egypt (of which we see but a pale shadow in the modern Masonic ritual) involved elevation within the priesthood via a graded sequence of "expansions of awareness" that enabled the astral *ba* of the candidate to become increasingly sensitive to (and thus conscious of) the light emanated by the individualized spiritual *saha*—the Sekhem in which the divine consciousness of man was believed to rest. If the approach of the Indian guru or the Japanese Zen master to their disciples is anything to go by, various preliminary periods of application, probation, and actually apprenticed discipleship would have had to be undergone before actually being initiated into the Mysteries proper. The same approach that we see today in the Far East has been consistently followed for well over two thousand years, and the severity of discipline adopted over 2,500 years ago is clearly evident in the methods of Pythagoras, who had his neophytes keep absolute silence for two years before being accepted even as probationary disciples. As Pythagoras seems to have absorbed most of his philosophical and theurgical system from the Egyptians (in whose temples he is believed to have spent over twenty years), we can be fairly sure that his methods closely followed those that he himself had to undergo during his own training. It also seems very likely that those same systems of occult

and spiritual training had been evolved and used by the Egyptians themselves for many thousands of years before even that time.

In relation to the sequence of initiations, the first involved total domination of the physical senses and appetites; the second, similar control over the emotions—in order to free the intellect. The third then required total dominion over the intellect and the coordinated personality as a whole. This then made possible the higher (spiritual) initiations.

21. Murray, *Egyptian Temples*, 163.

22. As Margaret Murray tells us: "The temple is not orientated by the Sun; but in accordance with inscriptions in the temple itself, the orientation lay from Orion (the Egyptian *Sah*) in the south to the Great Bear (Ursa Major) in the north. The legend of Horus of Edfu shows clearly that he and the Sun-god were two distinct deities." *Egyptian Temples*, 163.

23. Budge, *The Gods of the Egyptians*, vol. 1, 84–85.

24. Ibid., vol. 2, 54.

25. Ibid., vol. 1, 501.

26. Ibid., vol. 2, 355.

27. Bearing in mind that Khnemu was as clearly associated with the process of creation as Sebek was with the principle of "divine death" by embodiment within the world, it seems highly likely that both these god aspects of Ra are simultaneously implicit in the temple at Abu Simbel. In answer to the criticism that the wall engravings here (in the name of Rameses II) were original, one might query whether (as at Giza) there actually were any original engravings needed at all to satisfy the requirements of cosmic invocation by sympathetic magic.

28. As Wallis Budge and others have pointed out, there are extensive and very obvious similarities between the story of Jesus and that of Osiris, which quite clearly show the extent of Egyptian influence in providing a "working theology" for the infant Christian Church as a counter to the powerfully resurgent Neoplatonism and Mithraism of the time. By the time of the later pharaonic dynasties, the myth of the death and resurrection of Osiris had changed more than somewhat from the original version. By then, priestly theology had "evolved" sufficiently to allow Osiris to bring about his own (uncorrupted) bodily resurrection, completely unaided. It seems likely, therefore, that the story surrounding Jesus may have been "adjusted" to show him as the actual divine manifestation of Osiris; and as the mythic Osiris was depicted as the very incarnation of Ra, it is not difficult to see how the curious concept of Jesus being both man and God Almighty actually came about. Murray, *Egyptian Temples*, 60.

29. Ibid., 50.

30. Ibid., 56.

31. The very name Hor-Samtaui is clearly indicative of this because while Horus represents the principle of consciousness, *sam* means "to be consumed by burning" and *taui* means the "Two Lands" (figuratively, of Upper and Lower Egypt). The metaphor would then seem to involve the human sense of objective duality being superseded by (and absorbed in) the first "fiery" perception of all existence as a spiritual unity, or continuum.

32. Murray, *The Splendour That Was Egypt*, 210.

33. G. de Santillana and H. von Dechend, *Hamlet's Mill* (Boston: Macmillan, 1977), 242.

34. In fact, the Nile originally had seven mouths in the Delta, of which these two were geographically the outermost.

35. Bearing in mind our previous contention that the serpent was itself symbolic of the (demiurgic) soul principle and its associated range of knowledge, "death" here clearly involves the soul entity renouncing its own independence and accepting the "higher purpose" projected upon it by a yet more highly evolved intelligence—thereby becoming the willing slave and dedicated agent of the latter.

36. Budge, *The Gods of the Egyptians*, vol. 2, 96–97. The original name Anu (or Annu) given by the

Egyptians to the city of Heliopolis is synonymous with the On of the Hebrews. Budge indicates that both names meant "house of the sun," while it was also here that "souls were joined unto bodies in thousands" (E. A. W. Budge, *The Egyptian Book of the Dead* [1898; reprint, New York: Dover, 1967], cxxxiv). Now, "house of the sun" (or sun god) is another way of saying "soul-body"—hence the association between Anu—also used by the Brahmans of India, as in the Sanskrit expression *anu-padaka,* meaning a "self-born" or "parentless" soul (something also symbolically represented by the supposedly "phallic" lingam)—and the Atomos of the Greeks. Hence also the view by the philosopher Democritos as to the "atom" (clearly derived from *Atum*) being an "eternal and indivisible" principle throughout Nature—an idea completely misunderstood by the materialistic science of the nineteenth century, which thereby ended up with the now discarded "billiard ball theory" of atomic physics. The phoenix was itself, of course, entirely self-regenerative, returning cyclically to Anu to lay its egg, described by Herodotus as "a ball of myrrh"—a substance esoterically associated with suffering (through forced renunciation) and thus connected with the path of initiation. Interestingly, otherwise (as we shall see in chapter 9) Heliopolis would seem to have had a probable association with the brightest of the Pole Stars—Vega, in the constellation of Lyra (the Harp). One ancient Greek tradition had Vega as the swooping vulture (Ma'at) snatching up the harp of Orpheus (a Greek metaphor for the astral soul, perhaps?), while the Hindu Brahmans associated Vega with the vanquishing of the evil *asuras* by the gods; see R. Hinckley-Allen, *Star Names* (1899; [reprint, New York: Dover, 1963] 285–86). Either and both of these fit our Egyptian scenario very adequately indeed.

37. Budge, *The Gods of the Egyptians,* vol. 2, 107.

38. Ibid., 96–97.

39. In unconscious confirmation of the same underlying principles, Budge cites the Book of the Dead, in which the deceased is made to say: "I am the Bennu, the soul of Ra and the guide of the gods in the Tuat; let it be done unto me that I may enter like a hawk and that I may come forth like Bennu 'the Morning Star'" (*The Gods of the Egyptians,* vol. 2, 97). Is this not otherwise a clear indication of the intention to reincarnate? It also implies that the image of the hawk (which has already stooped from "on high" amid the fiery stream of life) perched on the phallus of the mummified Osiris is not symbolic of Isis (as is commonly believed to be the case) but, rather, of the emergent Horus-seed itself.

40. It is interesting to note in connection with this very matter that the symbol of the twenty-second nome of Upper Egypt—of which the capital city is Memphis—is the chopping knife.

Chapter 9: Completing the "Jigsaw Puzzle"

1. Bauval and Gilbert, *The Orion Mystery,* 195, 279–80.

2. The name Ra-Tem is derived from the root *tem,* meaning "to make an end of." The god of that name was that aspect of the sun god that ended the day as the "night sun." Ra-Tem was also closely associated with Atmu (the Egyptian equivalent of the Hindu *atma*), meaning the pure spiritual essence radiated forth by the incarnating divinity. See also Budge, *The Gods of the Egyptians,* vol. 2, 87.

3. In Egyptian mystical theology, the serpent—clearly also resembling the Indian *kundalini*—was forced to "vomit up" that which it had swallowed whole at the end of the last cycle of manifestation. This otherwise confirms that it is the Elohim-serpent-soul that, as the Demiurge, is also esoterically the maternal "bosom (or womb) of Creation." The imagery is synonymous with one of the personas of the Hindu god Krishna (see the *Bhagavad Gita*).

4. As Herodotus himself tells us: "It is at Heliopolis that the most learned of the Egyptians are said to be found" (*Histories,* 130). Another tradition has it that Solon, Thales, and virtually all of the most well-known Greek philosophers visited the great college at Heliopolis, while both Pythagoras and Plato actually studied there for extended periods of time (Budge, *The Gods of the Egyptians,*

vol. 1, 332). Democritus, the Greek philosopher associated with the supposedly crude theory of the *atom* (the word itself having been derived from the Atum principle), also studied there.

5. Bauval and Gilbert, *The Orion Mystery*, 172–74, 237–41.

6. Budge, *The Gods of the Egyptians*, vol. 2, 361.

7. West, *Serpent in the Sky*, 225 et seq.

8. The reason for the fundamental importance of the circumpolar stars is discussed in appendix K.

9. Graves, *Greek Myths*, 14–15.

10. Dynastic tradition had it that the head of Osiris was buried at Abydos. See Budge, *The Gods of the Egyptians*, vol. 2, 117–18.

11. This same star (Eta Draconis) is (most agreeably) a binary, thereby confirming the Osiris-Isis context here. Polaris is also a binary star, which explains the proximity of Elephantine and Philae and the associated symbolism of the Cataract.

12. It is, perhaps curiously, the starless equinoctial pole that acts as the northern part of the "spindle" around which our little local universe rotates. However, there appears to be some deep esoteric significance in the fact that Draco, the Dragon or Cosmic Crocodile, is protectively curled around this "hole"—almost certainly because it was seen as the primordial point of access into our system of those "gods" whose destiny it was to "fall" into it.

13. "It was supposedly in Lake Moeris, in the Faiyum, that Ra rose in the 'very First Time' when the Heavens and Earth were created; and it was this rising which formed the first great act of Creation, because as soon as Ra rose, he (evidently as Shu) separated the Earth from the sky. Here also was supposed to live the Great Bennu (phoenix) Bird." Budge, *The Gods of the Egyptians*, vol. 2, 58–59.

14. Ibid., vol. 2, 249.

15. In the Pyramid Texts of Unas, we find that "Unas is the Bull of Heaven. . . . He taketh his seat and his back is toward Seb [at Heliopolis?] . . . the power which has been given to him as the Great Sekhem makes him to become as the great Sahu (Orion) with the gods. . . ." (Budge, *The Gods of the Egyptians*, vol. 1, 34, 39). This enigmatic statement now becomes pregnant with self-evident meaning. As regards verification of the actual movement of Ursa Major in the heavens, we find in one of the appendices to the Hindu *Matsya Purana:* "Muniswara in his commentary on the Siromani . . . observes that the Seven Rishis (the seven stars of Ursa Major) are not, like other stars, attached by spikes to the solid ring of the Ecliptic, but revolve in small circles around the northern pole of the Ecliptic, moving by their own power in the ethereal sphere above Saturn, but below the sphere of the stars." *Matsya Purana*, appendix 8, xci.

16. Notably, both Kochab and Dubhe (the first star in the head of Ursa Major) appear to pass through this same location. This perhaps serves to explain why, at Abu Simbel, we find the two major temples of Ra and Hathor side by side, as described at the end of chapter 8. It would also seem from this that the stellar orientation of the four "ventilation shafts" in the Great Pyramid indicates opposite extremes of the path of the ecliptic during the Annus Magnus.

17. As Santillana and von Dechend observe in their book *Hamlet's Mill* (p. 73): "The Arabs preserved a name for Canopus . . . : *Suhail el-wezn* (Canopus Ponderosus) the heavy-weighing Canopus, a name promptly declared meaningless by the experts, but which could well have belonged to an archaic system in which Canopus was the weight at the end of the plumb line, as befitted its important position as a heavy star at the South Pole of the 'waters below.'"

18. As outlined in appendix L in relation to Ursa Major and "the Mill of the Gods."

19. Budge, *The Gods of the Egyptians*, vol. 2, 131 et seq.

20. The reader's attention is again drawn to the appendices in relation to Mackay's *Mythological Astronomy of the Ancients*—see his description of the ecliptic path forming an angled spiral "with 22 or 23 volves."

21. Bauval and Gilbert, *The Orion Mystery,* 191–93.

22. Einstein's theory of relativity has shown us not only that light has mass, but also that at the speed (i.e., in the state) of light, time ceases to exist. Does this not perfectly equate with the idea of an ethereal body form in which the mystical consciousness has no sense of time (but rather of universality) although nevertheless is aware of cycles of activity involving a perceived Divine Purpose and its incessant movement toward self-fulfillment? Why therefore should it not be that the consciousness of the hero-adept finds itself capable (at will) of moving around the solar system, among "the gods," in the *saha,* or spiritual light-body, while that of the astral soul remains "earthbound" by the ionospheric sheath of our planet? By way of cross-correlation, Professor Raimundo Pannikar, in his anthology of the Hindu Vedas, *The Vedic Experience* (pp. 315, 324), says: "Reality . . . is wholly composed of light and this statement should not be taken merely figuratively. Light shines everywhere because everything that is, is made of light. Light is being. Furthermore, to make a distinction between light and things that are composed of light is an abstraction of the mind." Does this not merely echo the ancient Egyptian attitude?

23. H. Falk-Ytter, *Aurora* (London: Floris Books, 1985), chaps. 3 and 4.

24. Ibid., 35.

25. The associated concept bears an apparently striking resemblance to the principles involved in the "morphogenetic field" theory of the well-known biologist Dr. Rupert Sheldrake as propounded in his book, *A New Science of Life* (Rochester, Vt.: Inner Traditions, 1995), 240 et seq.

26. Wilford, *Asiatic Researches,* vol. 8, chap. 7 (the Mahabharata section of the Adipurva).

27. In the Greek myth, after his earthly mother, Semele, had been destroyed by seeing Zeus face-to-face, the still fetal Dionysus (also the archetypal divine Man) was carried up to Olympus by Hermes (i.e., Tehuti) and was there contained within the thigh of Zeus. From here he was then subsequently reemanated (i.e., "twice-born") (McLeish, *Children of the Gods,* 38). Does not this allegory suggest that the astral soul-body was at some evolutionary stage contained concentrically within the spiritual soul-body? Yet another Greek legend had it that after finding that one of her nymphs (Kallisto) had become pregnant by Zeus, the goddess Artemis changed her into a bear and sent hunting dogs after her. However, Zeus rescued her just in time, and, once her child was born, he set her permanently in the heavens as the constellation Ursa Major. The child was her son Arcas—ancestor of the people of the fabled Arcadia—and upon his death, he too was fixed close by in the heavens, as the constellation Boötes (the Herdsman), of which the main star is Arcturus (ibid., 214–15). One cannot help but wonder, in the face of this, if these astrogeographic associations somehow subsequently became so mixed up that the "herdsmen of Arcadia" evolved into the Khabiru-Hebrew-Hyksos "shepherds" of the Old Testament. The expression *shepherds* is also, of course, easily equated with *guardians* and, as the *asura*-daemons and "guardian spirits" were one and the same, the implication is suggestive. Other general traditions from around the world concerning Ursa Major are mentioned in appendix L.

28. We find these associations even in the Celtic myth, for Uther Pendragon (the illicit father of King Arthur) is very clearly none other than User-ben-Draco, while Arthur is himself a Europeanized version of As-r.

29. Besant, *Bhagavad Gita,* 108.

30. Santillana and von Dechend, *Hamlet's Mill,* 81.

31. A. Reville, *Apollonius of Tyana* (Whitefish, Mont.: Kessinger, 1866, 2003), 36 and 41. It is noteworthy that even in the New Testament, Jesus is, within the space of a few verses (in John 20:17), shown as appearing suddenly in person, on two different occasions among his own disciples, even when the room in which they were hiding was locked.

Chapter 10: Sacred Geometry and the "Living" Architecture of Egypt

1. This approach was initiated by Schwaller de Lubicz in the 1950s and, although this author has not read much of his work, salient points in it are described in John Anthony West's informative and amusingly pungent book *Serpent in the Sky*.

2. Murray, *Egyptian Temples*, 160.

3. Which has also institutionalized current Egyptological belief that none of the original temple structures could be older than about 5,000 years.

4. See *Histories*, 143.

5. Budge, *The Gods of the Egyptians*, vol. 1, 339–41.

6. Schwaller de Lubicz, *Sacred Science*, 26 et seq., 281 et seq. Bearing in mind their undoubted astronomical, architectural, and engineering genius, plus their passion for exactitude, we can safely assume that the Egyptians had to be capable of "fine-tuning" the degree of arc in a manner similar to our own modern geometrical techniques.

7. The sexagesimal system was (supposedly) first devised by the Babylonians, but the Egyptians would also have known of it; otherwise, how could they have achieved such amazing accuracy in their engineering and astronomical alignments?

8. Budge, *The Gods of the Egyptians*, vol. 1, 340.

9. As Peter Tompkins otherwise reminds us in his *Secrets of the Great Pyramid* (London: Allen Lane, 1973), 159–67, the astronomer Sir Norman Lockyer (at the beginning of this century) pointed out that all Egyptian temples were oriented toward both the Sun and a particular star in its helical rising. In connection with the former, the orientation was such that, exactly at the summer solstice, the focused radiance of the rising sun passed through all the pylons and inner colonnades of the temple, eventually coming to rest in the central sanctuary—the "holy of holies." The solar light clearly represented the phenomenon of divine illumination, as well as enabling the priest-astronomers to determine the exact length of the solar year.

10. This is the principle involved in "cymatics," which involves the study of wave-forms. It shows how a specific vibration in a given material will always produce very specific ethereal forms. Consequently, any such given form can be made to manifest only through an act of invocation involving the precise use of that specific wave frequency.

11. It is worth recalling that the great Gnostic work "Pistis Sophia" was actually written by the early Coptic Christians. It involved the division of the world into twelve parts bounded by a gigantic serpent—an image obviously adopted from ancient Egyptian mystical symbolism. Hermeticism, Gnosticism, Masonry, Kabbalism, and Rosicrucianism all clearly owe their genesis to the philosophy of Egypt and its apparent "alma mater" among the semidivine Adept Teachers of the land of Pun(t). See Budge, *The Gods of the Egyptians*, vol. 1, 266–68.

12. Bauval and Gilbert, *The Orion Mystery*, 115–16.

13. The subject of other chambers is dealt with in greater detail in chapter 12, where we spend some time looking at the whole question of astronomical issues related to the various chambers, passageways, and vent shafts.

14. The entrance to the pyramid (quite remarkably when considered alongside the other, geometrical relationships we have seen) appears to be located at a point precisely akin to that of the tear duct in the human eye. As the evolving hierarchy of human souls seems to have been regarded as the "tears of Ra" (welling up *ab nihilo* from within the outer Eye), the metaphorical association seems to be rather more than merely coincidental. The orientation of the Descending Passage toward the circumpolar stars (Alpha Draconis in particular) is also doubtless connected with this.

15. The rites of Mithras, for example, had seven initiatory grades, which correspond very interestingly to those in both the Egyptian and the Greek Mysteries—and also with the "Opening of the Seven Seals" in the Book of Revelation (perhaps unsurprisingly, given its Gnostic origins). As with the

others, the Mithraic system's second initiation (that of "Occult[ist]") confirmed the initiate's first true contact with spiritual awareness per se. The fourth initiation (the Lion grade) then had a distinctively astronomical association with the constellation of Leo, the god Kronos, and the beginning and end of time—at least as far as the human incarnational cycle was concerned.

As Stuart Gordon tells us in his *Encyclopaedia of Myths and Legends* (London: Headline Books, 1993), 243: "In the Mysteries of the Ancient World, up to ten stages of initiation were common. The first three involved teachings alone—a discipline the Greeks called *catharsis* (cleansing). The fourth degree required direct participation in the deeper Mysteries. In higher degrees, the powers of the candidates evolved to a point at which they were considered 'reborn.' In India, such men were called *Dwijas,* a Sanskrit word meaning 'twice-born.'"

16. P. Lemesurier, *The Great Pyramid* (Shaftesbury, Dorset, U.K.: Element Books, 1987), 207.

Chapter 11: The Esoteric Significance of the Sphinx and Pyramids

1. The Egyptian name for Giza was Ra-stau (sometimes written as Restau or Rostau)—the suffix *sta* appearing to be (yet again) Sanskrit in origin and meaning "staying (or abiding) place." The Egyptian *sta* correspondingly means "to drag" or "to tow." Hence we might translate Ra-stau as "the anchorages of Ra." The *u* attached to *sta* merely indicates a plurality.

2. Bauval and Gilbert, *The Orion Mystery,* 103, 238.

3. For example (quite apart from the various Sanskrit words already mentioned), Herodotus refers to the most senior Egyptian priest-teachers as "the Choen"—which as *chokhan* is an Indo-Tibetan word meaning "adept teacher-in-chief." However, it is also found as Cohen, the name of the Hebrew teacher caste, which indicates the degree of the Hebrews' integration.

4. Budge, *The Gods of the Egyptians,* vol. 2, 42–47.

5. Sirius "B" travels in an elliptical orbit with Sirius "A" as one of the foci of the ellipse. That Sirius is the one star in the heavens apparently unchanged in its path (over recorded millennia) by the precession of the equinoxes implies that it is almost certainly the focal point around which our own constellation (and our own solar system within it) revolves. However, that is not to suggest that Sirius is itself the star around which our solar system directly orbits. That star would appear to be one of those in our own nebula—the Pleiades, even though modern astronomical orthodoxy would (as yet) deny the possibility of our being part of this same star group.

6. Bauval and Gilbert, *The Orion Mystery,* 171–74, 192–93.

7. Ibid.

8. Budge, *The Gods of the Egyptians,* vol. 1, 3.

9. Bauval and Hancock, *Keeper of Genesis,* 255.

10. Bauval and Gilbert, *The Orion Mystery,* 216 et seq.

11. See appendix N for a more detailed examination of the initiatory process by way of correlation with the Greek Mysteries, which were supposed to have been derived from Egyptian counterparts. Interestingly, Margaret Murray mentions that Diodorus Siculus—a visitor to Dendera in the first century B.C.—confirmed that the temple rites there were a carbon copy of those enacted in the Eleusynian Mysteries (with which he was personally familiar) only excepting the names of the deities (Murray, *Egyptian Temples,* 54). If that is so, one would expect the Orphic and Dionysian Mysteries also to have been represented in one or other of the Egyptian temples upstream from Dendera, if not elsewhere as well.

12. Here again we find a stream of direct correspondences with the Greek Mysteries. One of the best-known Greek legends had Zeus disguised as a pure white bull, carrying off the maiden Europa (the youngest and fairest of seven sisters, or female companions), and then, after changing into an eagle (or hawk perhaps?), ravishing her. Europa subsequently gave birth to three sons—Minos (clearly Min), Rhadamanthys (Rd-Mntw in Egyptian), and Sarpedon (Serap-Adon perhaps?).

Zeus then marries Europa off to one Asterius (clearly a star-king), the son of Cometes(!), who happily adopts her children but has no others by her. Zeus subsequently appointed the three sons "Judges of the Dead." Quite apart from the fact that the Egyptian hieroglyph for Min was the "winding wall"—symbolizing the maze, or labyrinth, in which we otherwise find the Cretan Minotaur—a symbol, like the Sphinx, of the "thinking animal" that is the human being, the whole legend leads one rather unavoidably to the conclusion that the Ancients seem to have regarded our solar system as the missing "seventh sister" of the Pleiades—hence, perhaps, the emphasis on the sacred bull and the universal septenary system found in so many ancient religions. See Graves, *Greek Myths,* 67, 96–97.

13. Bauval and Gilbert, *The Orion Mystery,* 109–10.

14. The word *kau,* in this particular context, appears to mean "a substance offered to the gods"— spiritual dedication perhaps?

15. One might surmise that the very name Khepren (otherwise Khafre) is derived from Kheper (spiritual self-awareness) and Ren (the *name,* or emergent spiritual individuality)—the combination thereby symbolizing the dominance of a focused spiritual self-will in the initiation associated with this pyramid. Similarly, Menkaure (Men/Min-Kau-Ra) seems to imply the meaning "the ('ero-ic' or generative) mind yielded in self-sacrifice to Ra." *Khufu,* similarly broken down into its constituent linguistic parts as Khu-Fu, implies the presence of the divine spirit *(khu)* plus the "divine serpent"— *fu* (the same as the Sino-Tibetan *fo)*—thereby also suggesting the meaning "dragon's breath." (The Chinese dragon and the Egyptian "flying serpent-soul" were synonymous.) Interestingly, ancient Chinese tradition has it that a great stranger king, Tai-Ko-Fo-Ki, came and lived in China in ancient times. He introduced picture writing plus arts and sciences, including calendrical astronomy. Now *tai* is oddly like the Egyptian *taui* (meaning "the two kingdoms" of Heaven and Earth) and *ki* (or *chi*) is a Chinese word denoting psycho-spiritual power and/or knowledge. The fact that Ko-Fo-Ki is otherwise depicted as having short bull's horns on his head (as is also the Hebrew Moses) indicates that Ko-Fo (i.e., Khufu) was none other than Buddha—an Oriental version of Ptah, whose alter ego (Hermes Trismegistus—the divine Thoth-Tehuti), according to tradition, was said to have introduced the very same knowledge to Egypt in the most ancient times.

16. The Sphinx itself was dedicated to Ra-Temu-Khepera-Heru-Khuti (Budge, *The Gods of the Egyptians,* vol. 2, 361). Bearing in mind that Ra-Tem was the chief god of Heliopolis, we suggest that his immediate offspring (Tefnut and Shu, the self-generated "lion-gods") should also be found represented in the vicinity. One might therefore speculate that the objective one (Shu) is symbolized by the Sphinx, while its noumenal counterpart (Tefnut) is represented by the cyclically returning constellation of Leo. The two would then face each other, east–west, across the Nile at that cyclical time in the Annus Magnus when the "light" of the Great Return once more began to promise its renaissance. At that same time, the constellation of Orion would have had a particular angular visibility in the southern night sky. (But see Bauval and Hancock's latest book, *Keeper of Genesis,* for details.)

17. Budge, *The Gods of the Egyptians,* vol. 1, 167.

18. Lemesurier, *The Great Pyramid;* P. Tompkins, *Secrets of the Great Pyramid* (London: Allen Lane, 1973).

19. It is suggested that the first two initiations "of the threshold" (to the Inner Mysteries) would have been accorded in the Menkaure and Khepren pyramids, each of these having only one chamber, whereas the Great Pyramid has three. This progression (like all the others we have come across) is not the result of mere chance or coincidence. See also appendix N concerning the comparative triple sequence inherent in the Greek Mysteries.

20. As both vent shafts are foreshortened, the related symbolism has to be that the candidate now stood on a "threshold" and had to move on a little further before he could directly face the influences provided by Sirius (Anubis) and Kochab (Apuat).

21. Chronologically akin to the reported transfiguration of Jesus, which preceded his capture, trial, and crucifixion.

22. The underlying idea was that the psychic atmosphere of the objective universe was filled with entities so intent upon maintaining the status quo (evidently the celestial world has its own "Establishment") that they would seek by all means possible, through fear and/or glamour, to subvert the onward and upward progress of the divinity in man. They presumably realized that, once returned to unity with the "Mind of God," such an event would trigger a fresh round of celestial change, which they themselves feared by virtue of their own nature representing the principle of (rhythmic) cosmic inertia.

23. The fourth initiation in the series—judging by the correspondence *(virag)* in the Hindu esoteric system—involved indifference to the reactions of one's own (human) sensory organism while still not as yet fully aware in the spiritual world—hence the idea of "crucifixion" of the initiate's consciousness, suspended as between Heaven and Earth. Following this extreme crisis, the faculty of individualized self-consciousness was said to pass "through the veil" separating the two worlds, hence involving "death" to the material world while awakening and being "raised up" in the spiritual state. Once this had been achieved by the power of the will, the "risen" master soul could apparently choose of his own volition whether he would return to the outer world of human existence or continue his work "from the inner side." The safe return to physical consciousness then seems to have constituted the denouement of the (external) "fifth degree."

24. Such ideas—although perhaps extraordinary to the Western mind—are found extensively throughout the various Oriental traditions. Budge himself confirms (referring to the Book of the Dead): "We have in this latter passage a proof that the Egyptians conceived it possible for a man to attain to all the attributes of a divine being or, let us say, an angel, and at the same time to enjoy an existence upon Earth as well as in heaven" (*The Gods of the Egyptians*, vol. 1, 163). Was this not the essence of the pharaoh's divine capacities in any case? Quite apart from the reported capacities of Jesus in this same direction, others such as Apollonius of Tyana were reputedly able to appear in two places simultaneously, though at great distances apart. See Reville, *Apollonius of Tyana*, 36 and 61.

25. Bauval and Gilbert, *The Orion Mystery*, 135–36.

26. Figure 11.1 clearly shows that the geometric capstone had to be a symbolic microcosm of the pyramid in toto—hence a "god-seed" in its own right.

    As the Pyramid Texts confirmed, the pyramid was symbolic of Osiris himself. Consequently—as Ptah-Seker-Ausar—Osiris would have been expected to appear ultimately in his spiritually complete, or semidivine, form. As the candidate for initiation was himself Osiris, such an event had to be the denouement of the whole evolutionary process on Earth. However, an even greater stage of development was clearly regarded as being also achievable—as allegorized in the god-figure of Unas, whose own pyramid (with its own astronomical significance) is to be found at Saqqara. The potential of man attaining a complete divinity is specifically alluded to in the texts, whereby the self-evolved Unas, having absorbed all the powers and faculties of the various creator and other gods in his own nature, through personal effort and experience becomes even greater than the great god Tem, said to have been the original initiator of the whole Creation process—at least, in relation to our world system (Budge, *The Gods of the Egyptians*, vol. 1, 39). The fact that Unas was himself regarded as the "Son of Sirius" (*Pyramid Texts*, 458) clearly implies that Sirius was itself the "guardian" of the cosmic "divine spark." By simple deduction, then, this would associate Sirius with the very heart center in the manifest body of the Logos (Ra)—hence the esoteric relationship between Anubis and Sirius.

Chapter 12: The Internal Geometry of the Great Pyramid

1. Tompkins, *Secrets of the Great Pyramid*, 287 et seq. (appendix by L. Stecchini).
2. Bauval and Gilbert, *The Orion Mystery*, chap. 10.
3. Ibid.
4. Bauval and Hancock, *Keeper of Genesis*.
5. Ibid.
6. Ibid., 135–36.
7. Bauval and Hancock, *Keeper of Genesis*, 70–72. As Jane Sellers tells us in her book *Death of Gods in Ancient Egypt* (pp. 41–42): "Orion first appeared heliacally on the horizon at the Spring Equinox. . . . In the skies of the 8th millennium, as autumn advanced, Orion appeared at nightfall further and further west. When darkness arrived, the constellation would be seen close to where the Sun had set. Finally, it would follow the Sun so closely that it would be lost in the west in the evening twilight. Thus began Orion's seasonal absence from the heavens (of 70 days below the horizon). Then, in the spring, just before dawn on the date when light and darkness were in balance, a specific star of Orion would appear once again. It would appear, but now would be on the other side of the Sun, rising in the east, just before sunrise in the pre-dawn sky."
8. The correlation between the two *vesicas* produces a mathematical sequence of 8:13:21, this proportion being otherwise that of phi (the "golden mean" or "golden section"), although found here in a rather unusual configuration. Extraordinarily, given the context here of the "Eye of Ra," phi, or $(1 + \sqrt{5})/2$, involves the "vanishing point" in a visual field of perspective—symbolic of infinity. The numerical correlations are also worthy of note because 13 multiplied by phi = 21, and 13 divided by phi = 8 (phi itself = 1.618). The ensuing sequence 8:13:21, then, involves a progression of 5:8—i.e., a double octave that overlaps on the equivalent of the musical major third. Curiously also, the overall shape of the overlapping *vesicas* bears a rather striking resemblance to the human brain.
9. Bauval and Gilbert, *The Orion Mystery*, 222–23.

Chapter 13: Reflections

1. Hancock, *Fingerprints of the Gods*, 144; Santillana and von Dechend, *Hamlet's Mill*, chap. 4.
2. Budge, *The Gods of the Egyptians*, vol. 1, ix.
3. West, *Serpent in the Sky*, 215.

Appendix A: The Relationship between the Sothic Year and the Annus Magnus

1. "From several passages (e.g. Unas 251) we learn that one company of nine gods was called 'the Great' and that another company was called 'the Little' . . . and in Pepi I line 273, where we read that the two lips of Meri-Ra are the eighteen gods; and again in line 407 where Pepi I is said to be 'with the eighteen gods in Qebhu' and to be 'the fashioner of the eighteen gods.'" Budge, *The Gods of the Egyptians*, vol. 1, 86.

Appendix B: From Plato's *Timaeus*

1. Plato, *Timaeus and Critias*, trans. Desmond Lee (London: Penguin Classics, 1971).
2. The Egyptians confirmed as much to Diodorus Siculus, Herodotus, Strabo, and Pliny. Although nineteenth-century British civil engineers in Egypt were highly doubtful of such a stupendous feat and merely believed the Faiyum to flood periodically as an "act of God," the balance of probabilities seems still to lie with the Egyptians having told the truth, even though being historically inaccurate as to the actual period of the work having originally been carried out. Wallis Budge outlines the issues in greater detail in his book *The Nile: Notes for Travellers in Egypt* (11th ed., 530–35).

Appendix D: From Schwaller de Lubicz's *Sacred Science*

1. *Sacred Science,* 52–53.
2. Ibid., 57.
3. Ibid., 58.
4. Ibid., 59

Appendix E: From S. A. Mackey's *The Mythological Astronomy of the Ancients* (1824)

1. *The Mythological Astronomy of the Ancients,* 30–31.
2. Ibid., 65–66.
3. Ibid., 86.

Appendix F: Philological Issues

1. *Encyclopaedia of Language and Linguistics,* vol. 1, 302 et seq.
2. *International Encyclopaedia of Linguistics,* vol. 2, 36.
3. Ibid., vol. 1, 174.
4. Ibid., vol. 1, 162.
5. *Dravidian Origins and the West* (London: Orient Longmans, 1963), 78–79.

Appendix G: The Egyptian Version of the Inner Constitution of Man

1. It seems quite probable—given the fact that the phonetic pronunciation is so similar and the meaning exactly the same—that the Egyptian group word *akhu* is the linguistic ancestor (via the Greeks and Romans) of our modern word *ego*. The close cultural associations between ancient Egyptian and Indian metaphysical thought are clearly visible throughout the above, although aspects of the Indian system appear, by comparison, to have been rather more intellectual in presentation.
2. In the Sanskrit, *jivo-asur* rather interestingly means "breath of life." So here also we find *as-r* as a mutually shared metaphysical expression describing the same, commonly perceived universal principle.

Appendix H: Concerning the Duat

1. The fact that the daemonic and elemental beings organic to the Duat supposedly reacted against divine interlopers (i.e., man) was therefore due to the fact that the latter represented the principle of change, in connection with the attempt to fulfill a higher, divine purpose.
2. It is not difficult to understand, in retrospect, why it was therefore that the Ancients equated the cyclical movement thus described as the uncoiling of a great cosmic serpent and why the periphery of the spherical aura was itself regarded as the body of that same serpent. Thus the "serpent" was regarded as universally symbolic of the enfolding soul principle itself.
3. Budge, *Gods of the Ancient Egyptians,* vol. 1, 172.

Appendix I: Concerning the God-Name Seker

1. E. A. W. Budge, *The Egyptian Heaven and Hell* (London: Kegan, Paul, Trench, Trübner & Co., 1905), vol. 3, 131.
2. M. Lichtheim, *Ancient Egyptian Literature,* 3 vols. (Berkeley: University of California Press, 1973), vol. 1, 53.
3. R. O. Faulkner, *The Ancient Egyptian Pyramid Texts,* 2 vols. (Oxford: Oxford University Press, 1998), lines 1256–57, 200.
4. Lichtheim, *Ancient Egyptian Literature.*

5. S. Hassan, *Excavations at Giza,* (Oxford: Oxford University Press, 1932), 265.
6. E. A. W. Budge, *An Egyptian Hieroglyphic Dictionary* (London: John Murray, 1920), vol. 1, 11b.
7. R. O. Faulkner, *The Egyptian Coffin Texts,* 3 vols. (London: Warminster, 1973–78), vol. 3, 134.

Appendix J: Concerning Sebek, Set, and Horus

1. Hence the completely misunderstood and very ancient rite of the Knights Templar, who put the sacred goat Khnemu (subsequently renamed Baphomet) at the center of their ceremonies of worship of the "Great Architect of the Universe" (G.A.O.T.U.), and, being sworn to absolute secrecy as to the true and sacred meaning, had to suffer the ignominious and deadly consequences of being branded by ignorantly prejudiced Christian theologians as "devil worshipers."
2. See Bernal, *Black Athena,* vol. 2, 426, for one example. Jesus does the same with his own disciples (see John 20).

Appendix K: The Circumpolar Stars and the "Mill of the Gods"

1. *Hamlet's Mill,* 138.
2. E. A. W. Budge, *Hieroglyphic Vocabulary to the Book of the Dead* (London: Kegan Paul, 1911), 186–87.
3. Santillana and von Dechend, *Hamlet's Mill,* 146.
4. In the Greek legend, Oedipus—upon discovering to his horror and shame that he has married his own mother—blinds himself with a "pin" taken from her clothing. In other words, human self-consciousness begets spiritual blindness. The *apuat* is clearly double-edged!
5. Which explains why Apuat was regarded as having emanated from the tree Asert—this being simultaneously the "Tree of Life" and the top of the "World Pole," the trunk of which extended downward through the Pleiades.
6. Lahovary, *Dravidian Origins and the West,* 219.

Appendix L: Concerning Ursa Major

1. Santillana and von Dechend, *Hamlet's Mill,* 384.
2. Budge, *Hieroglyphic Vocabulary to the Book of the Dead,* 111, 438–39.
3. Ibid., 438–39.
4. Ibid., 340.
5. Santillana and von Dechend, *Hamlet's Mill,* 247–48.
6. As already indicated, Ta'Urt is in fact symbolic of the demiurgic Oversoul of our local universe. Interestingly, the Hamitic Berber of the Sahara still use the word *ta-hort* or *ta-wrt* to mean a gate, or door. See Lahovary, *Dravidian Origins and the West,* 218.
7. We should also bear in mind that the Egyptians referred to Ursa Major as "the thigh of Set" (i.e., the macrocosmic Set).

Appendix M: The Astro-Terrestrial Axes among Egypt, Greece, and the Levant

1. The name Petra-tou-Romiou is translated literally as "stone of Romiou," with Romiou being regarded as some unknown ancient name. However, to the suspicious eye of this author, it looks remarkably akin to Ra-Miou—"the Great Cat Ra" of the Egyptians. One other Greek tradition, however, has Aphrodite first appearing on the shores of the small island of Cythera, just south of the Peloponnesian peninsula of the Greek mainland. See Graves, *Greek Myths,* 15.
2. McLeish, *Children of the Gods,* 3–4.
3. Deut. 34:4–7.
4. In Exod. 12:37 the Israelite contingent consisted of some 600,000 men alone, before even

considering women and children. The idea of such an army of refugees actually being able to survive in Sinai for even a year stretches the imagination well past breaking point. The clear implication is thus that the whole story is entirely symbolic and was in fact drawn from the ancient myth of the "divine sparks," or Asuras (As-r's), which "fell" en masse as a complete hierarchy.

5. Interestingly, the "Seven Sisters" of the Pleiades (sometimes depicted as the "magic girdle of Aphrodite") were occasionally shown surrounding their father, Atlas, in grief at his enforced labor of having to support the heavens on his shoulders. Even more interestingly, the original name of the brightest star in the group (Alcyone) seems to have been Alcinoë—which subsequently evolved into Arsinoë. Here then is yet another suggestion that (taken in conjunction with fig. M.1) our own solar system is itself a member of the Pleiades group—i.e., the missing "seventh sister." On Arsinoë, see Hinckley-Allen, *Star Names*, 391 et seq.

6. Hapgood, *Maps of the Ancient Sea Kings*, chap. 2.

7. Budge, *The Gods of the Egyptians*, vol. 2, 58.

Appendix N: Correlations between the Egyptian and Greek Mystery Schools

1. Which, one might surmise, were practiced (usually underground) in a sequence of temples equivalent to the three pyramids at Giza, even though of distinctively Greek architectural design.

2. *The Encyclopaedia of Myths and Legends*, 173–74.

3. Ibid., 123, 150.

4. Both Demeter and Persephone were specifically associated by the Ancients with the zodiacal constellation of Virgo, which is found close to the northern celestial solstice. Thus, yet again we see the mystical logic of the 25,920-year cycle of precession around the ecliptic path being allegorically represented by a descent to and return from the "Underworld." It might be added that Demeter and Persephone were the Greek equivalents of Isis and Nephthys.

5. McLeish, *Children of the Gods*, 54 et seq.

6. The (anglicized) name Corybantes originally being derived from Kore (Persephone), the mother of the divine Iachos (the infant Dionysus, although represented as a different individuality).

7. *The Encyclopaedia of Myths and Legends*, 352.

8. Ibid., 127.

9. Graves, *Greek Myths*, 47.

10. Another tradition has the body of Dionysus being reconstituted by his grandmother Rhea, Zeus's mother, and a Titan, or cosmic god, in her own right. The interpretation here then is that of the Divine Man being reborn (i.e., thrice-born by now) within the divine state and no longer subject to the depredations of the Underworld—as the god Unas perhaps? The fact that the main emblems of Dionysus were the grapevine and the phallus clearly indicates a universal association with the Tree of Life and the regeneration attributed to the cyclical return of Ursa Major—hence also the myth of Osiris. A rose by any other name . . . !

11. McLeish, *Children of the Gods*, 217.

Appendix O: On the Significance of Double Statuary in Egypt

1. From the word *pir* (as *piru*) there is apparently derived the title *pharaoh*, suggesting that a certain stage of spirituality had been attained by (all) bearers of this title in very ancient times. *Pyr* is also a Greek word meaning the "spark in the flame," there being definite spiritual associations with this imagery, for the "divine spark" that "fell from Grace" is simultaneously the highest and lowest aspect of the divine Man. We see the same idea expressed in the Turkish name *peri-khan*, which means "angel-prince"—the significance there in fact being the "angel that came down to Earth." *Peri* has subsequently come down to us as the Anglo-Celtic *fairy*.

2. As the male and female natures are to be found simultaneously side by side in both man and woman, the intended distinction is clearly not intended as a purely biological one, but is, rather, metaphysical in nature. However, it is only the astral soul that reproduces from the substance of its own material nature (as woman does)—hence, the nature of the visual metaphor.

Appendix P: The Meaning of Ether/Aether According to the Principles of Hermetic Science

1. When taking place within the gaseous state in the higher atmosphere and evoking the energies of the ionosphere, this process is implosive and thereby maintains the cycle of electrical regeneration in nature on the surface of the planet. When such force is brought to bear on the atom within the dense state of the mineral kingdom, however, this (alchemical) phenomenon is known to modern science as nuclear fission, involving the supposed splitting of the atom. However, that expression is a complete misnomer—at least, from the alchemical viewpoint.
2. Hence the ancient Hermetic axiom of evolution: "In the stone, God sleeps; in the plant He dreams; in the beast He stirs; and in man He awakes." However, this refers merely to the lower half of the "octave" of Creation. It does not in any way serve to support the Darwinian theory of evolution as far as the spiritual man is concerned.

Appendix Q: On the Levitation of Stone by the Use of Sound

1. B. Cathie, "The Acoustic Levitation of Stones," in *Anti-Gravity and the World Grid*, ed. D. H. Childress (Kempton, Ill.: Adventures Unlimited Press, 1987), 69.
2. As confirmed by Bauval and Hancock in *Keeper of Genesis*, 28.

GLOSSARY

Adept: A spiritually advanced (human) intelligence, capable of self-conscious function within the spiritual state itself. Generally regarded as pertaining to those initiates of the fourth and fifth degree, the latter being that of the "raised Master."

Aether: The third substate (of seven, counting downward) in the unfolding cosmos. The very first atomically differentiated state. The homogeneous state or element of primary substance out of which the lesser four elements of Fire, Air, Water, and Earth are generated.

Alchemy: Named after the "dark" god Khem, whose intelligence was regarded as the divine factor behind the incessant process of mutation and transmutation in Nature. Egypt itself was known as "the land of Khem" (or Chemmia, from which we derive our word *chemistry*).

Annus Magnus: The 25,920-year cycle of the precession of the equinoxes. Otherwise commonly known as the Platonic Year, or Great Sidereal Year.

Astral Light: The "etheric" continuum that substands our planet and its biosphere and extends out into the atmosphere as far as (but not including) the ionosphere.

Astral soul: The lesser, complementary counterpart of the spiritual soul, an emanation of our own (planetary) World Soul and thus bound to the earth's biosphere.

Chakra: A localized vortex of psychomagnetic force (located in the "etheric double" of each person) that acts as a transformer of energies between the psychic state and the attached physical organism.

Chaos: The primordial, pre-objective state in which an archetypal hierarchy of divine intelligences first appears, thus initiating the systematically ordered unfoldment of the cosmos.

Daemon: A member of the divine hierarchy responsible for giving phenomenal effect to the evolutionary Will of a god. This (dual) hierarchy comprised "Planetary Spirits" (fully liberated "buddhas") in its senior echelons and merely human "sparks" (*akhu*, or "Egos") in its junior echelons.

Demigod: An adept (of at least the sixth degree) whose consciousness has transcended even the spiritual state and recognized in some measure his own divine nature. Thus the Ptah or buddha nature (of the seventh-degree initiate) is at the very threshold of godhood.

Divine: Pertaining to the eternal, nonmanifest state that preexists even the spiritual state, the latter involving objectivity in the form of some or other quality of light.

Divine Spark: The as yet undifferentiated "god-seed" that, as the polarized lower aspect of the Divine Man, "falls to Earth" and eventually gives rise to the god-orientated human intelligence.

Ego: The independently self-conscious sense of "I-ness" engendered in the lower nature of that dualistic sense of awareness enjoyed by man. The word appears to have metamorphosed from the Egyptian *akhu*.

Esoteric: That which describes the underlying (archetypal) stream of seamless universal wisdom and knowledge that invests all Creation with itself. It has to do with the "essence" of Nature in all its various aspects.

Ether: The state of apparently invisible matter that exists between the gaseous state and that of the aether and that is itself the (personalized) substance of the "etheric double." It expresses the element of Fire, or Light.

Etheric Double: That temporarily appropriated portion of the Astral Light that the astral soul uses to evolve an objective physical body-form out of itself.

Gaea: Commonly found today as Gaia, the Greek name for the Earth Mother goddess, wife of Ouranos and mother of the Titans.

God(s): The hierarchy of intelligent divine Principles that, although themselves no longer cognizable as discrete entities, pervade and animate the cosmos with the omnipresent radiance of their vital presence. Known generically by the Egyptans as *neteru,* from which we derive our word *nature.*

Hamitic: An expression coined by philologists to identify an ancient pan–North African language that, although later subsumed within it, undoubtedly preceded the Semitic family of languages. *See also* appendix F.

Hermetic: Named after Hermes the godly (Greek) alter ego of the Egyptian Tehuti, pertains to an occult philosophy that regards each septenary state of existence as a microcosmic mirror image of the one "above" it—hence, the occult axiom "As above, so below."

Indo-Aryan: Pertaining to the Caucasian racial type that, from a prehistoric cultural base on the Indus River, spread westward several hundred thousand years ago to colonize the whole of Europe and parts of North Africa.

Initiation: The progressive process of spiritual reorientation, education, and testing in which the consciousness of man (the lesser "Divine Spark") is gradually expanded until assimilated into the spiritual state and finally (later) reunited with its own macrocosmic counterpart as "the Divine Man." In the occult tradition of the ancient Mysteries, there were seven sequential initiations.

Ionosphere: The electrified atmospheric "belt" comprising the outermost auric field of our planetary biosphere.

Kha: The Egyptian term for the psycho-spiritual "presence" of human soul-consciousness, which suffuses the human bodily organism during wakefulness.

Kundalini: The hugely powerful energy of the divine "Will-to-Be" which is responsible, as agent of the soul, for the energizing of all bodily existence and also maintaining it in a constant state of coherence and dynamic functionality.

Mystery School: An occult organization dedicated to the spiritual advancement of humanity through a well-defined process of initiation involving "sympathetic experience" in sacred rituals that described divine activities in an allegorical format.

Occult: A (much abused) word that basically means "concealed" and which itself has ancient associations with the mechanism and operation of the eye. It is usually regarded as pertaining particularly to "magical" powers associated with controlling the very forces of Nature by the use of the will.

Poseidonis: The very last of the original Atlantean islands that, according to Plato, existed in the Atlantic Ocean somewhere to the west of Gibraltar and which, with its population, was submerged in a great cataclysm about 9500 B.C. Believed to be the origin of the current island group of Madeira and the Canary Islands.

Psychic: Although derived from the Greek *psyche* meaning "soul," used to denote a particular quality of supraphysical sensitivity or faculty of an occult nature that, however, is not "spiritual" per se, by virtue of being of a lower order of force.

Reincarnation: The cyclical process of "rebirth" caused by the spiritual soul alternately projecting and withdrawing its influence to and from the astral soul, the latter being the actual demiurgic agent of human bodily creation. Commonly misunderstood to involve the reappearance of the same human personality in a new body, such, however, being impossible as the latter is itself but a temporary compound of vehicular matter.

Soul: The spheroidal or ovoid ethereal body-form of the angel/*deva* kingdom in nature. Sometimes known as the "Father-Mother" principle or the "Eternal Virgin." It is psychically hermaphroditic, or of dual polarity.

Spirit: The divine *kha,* or Presence—sometimes referred to as "the Divine Breath" of the overshadowing god-consciousness.

Spiritual soul: The ethereal body-form of an advanced angel/*deva* hierarch. Composed purely of sidereal substance, it becomes the vehicle of the "Divine Man," just as the astral soul becomes the vehicle of the "lesser divine spark," the Divine Man's junior (polar) counterpart.

Theosophical: A Greek expression coined by the Neoplatonists from *theos* ("divine," or "god-given") and *sophia* (wisdom). Subsequently adopted in 1875 by the modern Theosophical Society.

Universal Life Principle: The One Life inherent in all Matter, thereby confirming the cosmos itself as an organism. Homogeneously omnipresent (as the divine Will of the god "Amen-Ra"), it was nevertheless regarded as triple in an actual cycle of objective manifestation—hence the later concept of "Father, Son, and Holy Spirit."

BIBLIOGRAPHY

Asher, R. A., ed. *Encyclopaedia of Language and Linguistics*. Oxford: Pergamon, 1994.

Bailey, A. A. *A Treatise on Cosmic Fire*. New York: Lucis Press, 1925.

Barraclough, G., ed. *The Times Atlas of World History*. London: BCA and Times Books, Ltd., 1978.

Bauval, R. and A. Gilbert. *The Orion Mystery*. London: William Heinemann Ltd., 1994.

Bauval, R. and G. Hancock. *Keeper of Genesis*. London: William Heinemann Ltd., 2001.

Berlitz, C. *Atlantis: The Eighth Continent*. New York: Putnam, 1984.

Bernal, M. *Black Athena: The Afroasiatic Roots of Classical Civilization*. 2 vols. London: Free Association Books, 1987.

Besant, A., and B. Das, trans. *The Bhagavad Gita*. Adyar, India: Theosophical Publishing House, 1973.

Blavatsky, H. P. *The Secret Doctrine*. Los Angeles: The Theosophy Company, 1947.

Bright, W., ed. *International Encyclopaedia of Linguistics*. Oxford: Oxford University Press, 1992.

Budge, E. A. W. *The Egyptian Book of the Dead*. 1898. Reprint, New York: Dover, 1967.

———. *The Egyptian Heaven and Hell*. London: Kegan, Paul, Trench, Trübner & Co., 1905.

———. *An Egyptian Hieroglyphic Dictionary*. London: John Murray, 1920.

———. *The Gods of the Egyptians*. 2 vols. 1904. Reprint, New York: Dover, 1969.

———. *Hieroglyphic Vocabulary to the Book of the Dead*. London: Kegan Paul, 1911.

———. *Legends of the Egyptian Gods*. 1912. Reprint, New York: Dover, 1994.

———. *The Nile: Notes for Travellers in Egypt*. London: Thos. Cook and Son, 1910.

Childress, D. H., ed. *Anti-Gravity and the World Grid*. Kempton, Ill.: Adventures Unlimited Press, 1987.

Davis, H., trans. *The Works of Plato*. London: George Bell & Sons, 1894.

Donnelly, I. *Atlantis: The Antediluvian World*. London: Sidgwick and Jackson, 1960.

Fage, J. D., and R. A. Oliver, eds. *Papers in African Prehistory*. Cambridge: Cambridge University Press, 1970.

Fairbridge, R. W. "The Changing Level of the Sea." *Scientific American* 202, no. 5 (May 1960).

Falk-Ytter, H. *Aurora*. London: Floris Books, 1985.

Faulkner, R. O. *The Ancient Egyptian Pyramid Texts*. Oxford: Oxford University Press, 1998.

———. *The Egyptian Coffin Texts*. 3 vols. London: Warminster, 1973–78.

Flinders Petrie, W. M. *A History of Egypt*. London: Methuen and Co., 1895.

Gordon, S. *The Encyclopaedia of Myths and Legends*. London: Headline Books, 1993.

Gorman, P. *Pythagoras*. London: Routledge and Kegan Paul, 1979.

Graves, R. *The Greek Myths*. London: Book Club Associates, 1985.

Halevi, Z'ev ben Shimon. *Kabbalah*. London: Thames & Hudson, 1979.

Hall, Manly P. *The Secret Teachings of All Ages*. Los Angeles: Philosophical Research Society Inc., 1975.

Hancock, G. *Fingerprints of the Gods*. New York: Crown Publishers, 1995.

Hapgood, C. H. *Maps of the Ancient Sea Kings*. London: Turnstone Books, 1966.

Hawking, S. *A Brief History of Time*. New York: Bantam, 1990.

Herodotus. *The Histories*. Trans. Harry Carter. Oxford: Oxford University Press, 1962.

Hinckley-Allen, R. *Star Names*. 1899. Reprint, New York: Dover, 1963.

Iamblichus. *Theurgia, or the Egyptian Mysteries*. Trans. Alexander Wilder. New York: The Metaphysical Publishing Co., 1911.

Imbrie, J., and K. Palmer-Imbrie. *Ice Ages: Solving the Great Mystery*. N. J.: Enslow Publishers, 1979.

Jacq, C. *Egyptian Magic*. Wiltshire, U.K.: Aris and Phillips Ltd., 1985.

Kenton, W. *Kabbalah*. London: Thames & Hudson, 1979.

Lahovary, N. *Dravidian Origins and the West*. London: Orient Longmans, 1963.

Lemesurier, P. *The Great Pyramid*. Shaftesbury, Dorset, U.K.: Element Books, 1987.

Lichtheim, M. *Ancient Egyptian Literature*. 3 vols. Berkeley: University of California Press, 1973.

Mackey, S. A. *The Mythological Astronomy of the Ancients*. Norwich, U.K., 1824.

McLeish, K. *Children of the Gods*. London: Longmans, 1983.

Mead, G.R.S. *Apollonius of Tyana*. London: Theosophical Publishing Society, 1901.

Murray, M. *Egyptian Temples*. London: Sampson, Low, Marston, 1939.

———. *The Splendour That Was Egypt*. London: Sidgwick and Jackson, 1962.

Naydler, J. *Temple of the Cosmos: The Ancient Egyptian Experience of the Sacred*. Rochester, Vt.: Inner Traditions, 1996.

Oldfather, C. H., trans. *Diodorus Siculus*. Cambridge: Harvard University Press, Loeb Classical Library, 1969.

Panikkar, R. *The Vedic Experience*. London: Darton Longmans and Todd, 1977.

Plato. *Timaeus and Critias*. Trans. Desmond Lee. London: Penguin Classics, 1971.

Press, F., and R. Siever. *Earth*. San Francisco: Freeman, 1974.

Rawlinson, G. *Ancient Monarchies*. London, 1880.

Reville, A. *Apollonius of Tyana*. 1866. Reprint, Whitefish, Mont.: Kessinger, 2003.

Riordan, M., and D. Schramm. *The Shadows of Creation*. Oxford: Oxford University Press, 1993.

Santillana, G. de, and H. von Dechend. *Hamlet's Mill*. Boston: Macmillan, 1977.

Scarre, C., ed. *The Times Atlas of Archaeology*. London: Times Books Ltd., 1988.

Schwaller de Lubicz, R. A. *Sacred Science: The King of Pharaonic Theocracy*. Trans. André and Goldian VandenBroeck. Rochester, Vt.: Inner Traditions, 1988.

Scott, Sir Walter, trans. *Asclepius III*. London: Solos Books, 1992.

Sellers, J. *The Death of Gods in Ancient Egypt*. London: Penguin Books, 1992.

Shaw, I., and P. Nicholson. *British Museum Dictionary of Ancient Egypt*. London: Book Club Associates, 1995.

Sheldrake, R. *A New Science of Life*. Rochester, Vt.: Inner Traditions, 1995.

Temple, R. K. G. *The Sirius Mystery*. Rochester, Vt.: Destiny Books, 1998.

Tompkins, P. *Secrets of the Great Pyramid*. London: Allen Lane, 1973.

Tyberg, J. *Sanskrit Keys to the Wisdom-Religion*. N.p.: Theosophical University Press, 1940.

Velikhovsky, I. *Earth in Upheaval*. London: Abacus, 1956.

West, J. A. *Serpent in the Sky: The High Wisdom of Ancient Egypt*. Wheaton, Ill.: Quest Books, 1993.

Wilford, Col. J. *Asiatic Researches*. 10 vols. London: Royal Asiatic Society, 1806.

INDEX